PATTERN MAKING TEMPLATES

FOR

Skirts & dresses

First edition for the United States published in 2017 by
Barron's Educational Series, Inc.

All inquiries should be addressed to:
Barron's Educational Series, Inc.
250 Wireless Boulevard
Hauppauge, NY 11788
www.barronseduc.com

Publisher: Mark Searle
Editorial Director: Isheeta Mustafi
Commissioning Editor: Alison Morris
Editors: Sophie Kersey and Stephen Haynes
Junior Editor: Abbie Sharman
Art Director: Michelle Rowlandson
Page layout: Tony Seddon
Photography: Neal Grundy

Library of Congress Control Number: 2016958533

ISBN: 978-1-4380-1001-4

Printed in China

9 8 7 6 5 4 3 2 1

PATTERN MAKING TEMPLATES

FOR

Skirts & dresses

All you need to design, adapt
& customize your clothes

ALICE PRIER

Contents

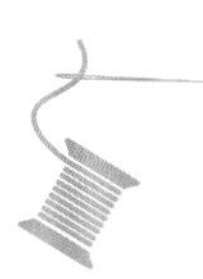

1. Getting Started

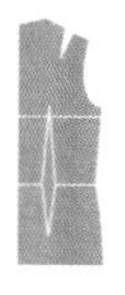

2. Your Body, Your Sloper

3. Skirts

4. Finishes for Skirts

5. Dresses

6. Finishes for Dresses

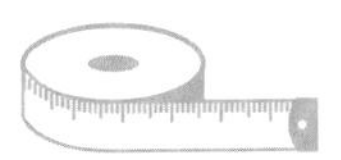

7. Fit Solutions

Introduction

This book has been written to pass on the skills and pleasures of pattern making that make it possible to create your own clothes from scratch. In our house, clothes are made, not bought, and the odd pin in the foot is a rite of passage on your way to an enviable closetful of unique designs.

A pattern is the map that guides you from an initial design to a finished garment. It can be worthy of framing and hanging on the wall, or cobbled together in the height of a creative moment from yesterday's newspaper and some sticky tape.

The starting point of good pattern making is a thorough grasp of how to manipulate two-dimensional fabric to make it fit around your three-dimensional body.

The first step is the production of a well-fitting sloper. Luckily for you, the downloadable slopers provided with this book give you the head start you need to begin drafting your own patterns right away.

Each chapter provides clear step-by-step instructions that show you how to adapt these slopers to produce the patterns for the specific designs illustrated in this book. By working through these instructions, you should gain an understanding of the fundamental techniques of pattern making that will enable you to move on to your own designs.

Don't be afraid to make mistakes—it's only fabric, and the best way to learn is to sew!

Happy pattern making!

Chapter 1

Getting Started

Tools and Equipment

You don't need much to draft a pattern. Here is a list of a few essentials plus some luxury items. Don't forget a full-length mirror so you can admire your creations!

Essentials

Something to measure with

▸ A tape measure to measure the body for which you are making the pattern

▸ A long plastic or metal ruler

▸ A set square for right angles (or use anything that is reliably square)

▸ A set of French curves: large for side seams, armholes, and necks; small for collars and pocket details (a suitably sized plate will do in a pinch)

Something to draw on

▸ You can use classic spot-and-cross paper as used in the fashion industry, which has the benefit of replicating the grain of the fabric, helping to ensure your pattern is on the right grain. It is also durable and semitransparent, which helps when you want to trace sections such as facings.

▸ You can also use tracing paper, brown paper, newsprint paper, or even old newspapers, but be careful, as the ink can rub off onto your fabric.

Something to draw with

▸ A sharp pencil—a mechanical one will give you a nice consistent line

▸ Highlighter pens in various colors for marking up different sections of the pattern

▸ An eraser, just in case you make a mistake

Something to cut with

▸ Paper scissors—never use your fabric scissors for paper as they will quickly go blunt. This must be explained to every single member of your household—different-colored handles and a big label can be useful to drive the message home!

▸ Fabric scissors—make sure they are the right size and weight for your hands. Buy the best quality you can afford. Keep them in a case under police-level protection.

▸ Rotary cutter—some people prefer a rotary cutter to scissors as it can be kinder to hands. As with scissors, do not use your fabric-cutting rotary blades for cutting paper.

Something to stick with

▸ Sticky tape—the opaque type with a matte finish is ideal because you can draw over it and it is repositionable. Keep it on a heavy holder so it only takes one hand to operate.

▸ Glass-headed pins—these are useful to pin the paper pattern pieces together as you go so you can check the fit.

Weights

▸ There are lots of weights on sale in all different shapes and sizes, but you can also use pebbles from the beach, tin cans, or a sticky-tape holder.

Storage

▸ Pattern card for creating sturdy slopers once you have adjusted them for the perfect fit. You can buy specialist card stock or find something in your local art store.

▸ Pattern hooks—for hanging your slopers (or bend a wire coat hanger)

▸ Large envelopes for storing your patterns

For your wish list

- A notcher—don't be tempted to buy a cheap one as they tear the paper instead of clipping it
- A pattern drill—this is a single-hole punch that you use to mark dart points and the positions of pockets, buttons, and so on
- A tracing wheel—for tracing sections of paper patterns or tracing existing clothes to turn them into pattern pieces
- A dress form—useful for testing your designs

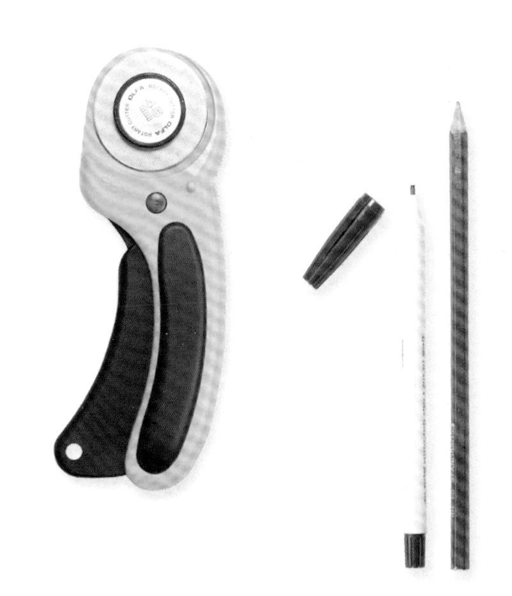

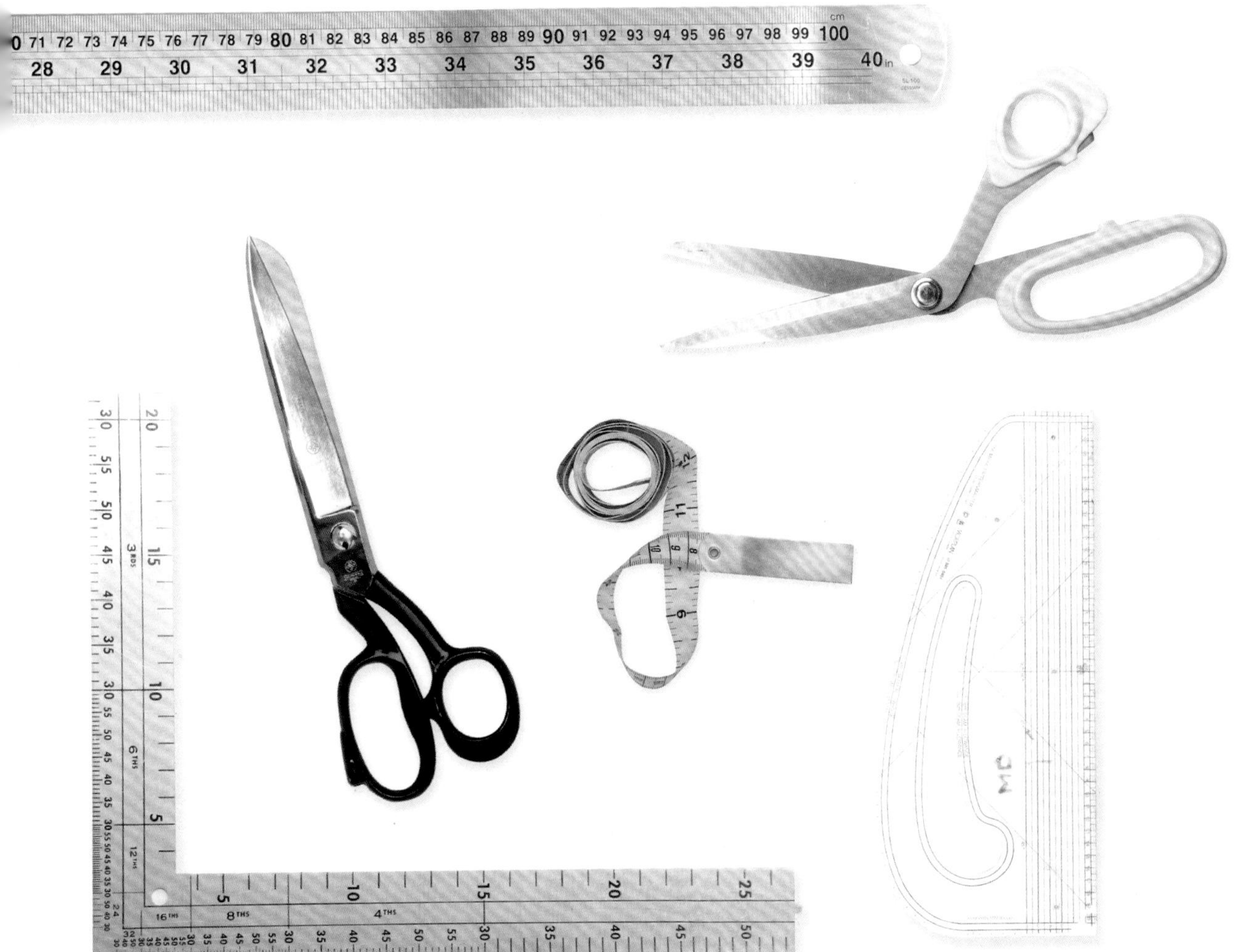

Choosing Fabric

There are two approaches to choosing fabric: One is to seek out a fabric for a style you have in mind, and the other is to start with a fabric and choose a style to suit it.

Many people find that the latter option leads to the most inspired designs and satisfying results. There are a number of factors to consider when choosing fabric:

- Is it right for the design? Fabric should always suit the style of item you intend to make—if it is soft and flowing, pick a design such as the One-Shoulder Dress on page 100. If it is crisp and sharp, the Kilt on page 68 may be a better choice.
- Do you love the color and texture? No matter how beautifully you draft the pattern and finish the garment, if you don't like the fabric or it doesn't suit you, you will never be completely satisfied.
- Is it practical? Consider whether your fabric is "dry-clean only" or can go in the washer and dryer.
- Is it good quality? As it takes time and effort to produce a lovely garment, make sure your fabric will stand the test of time.

TIP

> Keep a scrapbook of designs to inspire you next time you go through your fabric stash.

A–Z of fabrics

One of the joys of making your own clothes is that you can be creative with the wealth of colors, textures, and prints available. Don't be scared to experiment with mixing and matching.

Here's a list to get you going:

A—Aertex®, Angora

B—Bamboo, Bark cloth, Batiste, Beaded, Boiled wool, Bouclé, Brocade, Broderie anglaise

C—Cashmere, Challis, Chambray, Chiffon, Corduroy, Cotton, Crepe, Crepe de Chine

D—Damask, Denim, Double jersey, Drill, Dupioni

E—Egyptian cotton, Elephant corduroy

F—Faille, Felt, Flannel, Fleece, Fur (faux or real)

G—Gabardine, Gauze, Georgette, Gingham, Grosgrain

H—Habutai, Herringbone

I—Interfacing

J—Jacquard, Jersey

K—Knit

L—Lace, Lamé, Lawn, Leather, Leatherette, Linen, Lycra® (spandex)

M—Melton, Microfiber, Mohair, Moleskin, Muslin

N—Neoprene, Net, Nylon

O—Organdie, Organza, Ottoman

P—Plastics, Polyester, Poplin

Q—Qiviut, Quilted

R—Raw silk, Rayon, Rib, Ribbon

S—Satin, Scuba, Seersucker, Sequinned, Serge, Shantung, Silk, Spandex, Stretch, Suede

T—Taffeta, Tartan, Tulle, Tweed, Twill

U—Ultrasuede®

V—Velour, Velvet, Vinyl, Viscose

W—Wool, Woven

X—X-ray (see-through)

Y—Yarn, if you want to start from scratch!

Z—Zebra print, Zibeline

One of the chief delights of making your own clothes is the amazing variety of fabrics available. Thanks to online shopping you can now choose fabrics from across the world. As well as all the traditional wools, silks, linens, and cottons there are lots of new eco fabrics that are worth investigating, such as bamboo and hemp. Don't be afraid to experiment by making up a pattern in an unlikely fabric—try a georgette coat or a tweed camisole.

Patterns and prints

There are some great prints out there, from small-scale abstract designs to giant oversized florals and everything in between. Thanks to recent advances in digital printing, you can even make your own!

The most important thing to consider when using a printed fabric is the placement of the pattern on the fabric:

- Do the checks or stripes match? This is a sign of a couture garment and will make your clothes stand out from those in the stores.
- Are there flowers growing upside down or animals falling out of the sky? It's worth taking extra time when cutting a representational print to make sure the pattern is placed in the correct direction and centered on your pattern piece.
- Have you noticed a nap? Fabrics such as velvet, corduroy, and fur all have a directional texture.
- Would it be more interesting if cut on the bias? For example, striped fabric can be joined at the seams in order to create a chevron design.
- Does your fabric have a border print or an interesting selvage? Save yourself time by using it for your hem.

Understanding quality

With fabric it should be all about the touch. Always ask yourself: Will it feel nice to wear?

One of the best ways to test a fabric for quality is the crumple test: Take it in your hand and scrunch it up. The creases will drop out of a good-quality fabric easily, but an inferior fabric will remain crumpled. Buy the best fabric that you can afford.

Make sure you check for any defects in the piece before you buy. Defects might include a crooked weave, misplaced pattern, dye variations, dirty marks, or pulled threads. Natural fabrics like silk, wool, and linen have inherent irregularities, so try not to place them where they will draw attention to themselves.

TIP

Don't forget to look in the remnant box of the more expensive fabric stores—there may not be enough for a whole garment, but a luxurious trim could lift it to the next level.

Lining and interfacing

A bold choice of lining will make your design special. Don't spoil all your hard work with a cheap lining. Remember, you don't have to use a traditional lining fabric—cotton and silk also give a luxurious finish.

Using good-quality interfacing of the right weight will help your garment keep its shape and look good longer.

Estimating how much you need

When you're in a fabric store estimating how much fabric you need for a design, the best way to think of it is in lengths—how much fabric do you need from top to bottom?

Remember to add a length for sleeves, or extra for a style with lots of fullness. To be really sure, you can lay your pattern pieces out on a piece of fabric before you go to the store and see how much you need—or even take them with you.

TIP

It's a good idea to steam wool fabrics or wash cottons before you cut them to anticipate any shrinkage. Some silks prefer a dry iron—test a corner first.

Having said all of that, one final piece of advice is: Never be afraid to break the rules! The worst you can do is waste a piece of fabric—and even then, you can always use it to make something smaller such as a tote bag or to start work on a patchwork quilt.

Basic Terminology

Like all specialisms, pattern making has its own terminology. Here are a few terms that you will come across as you work through this book.

Apex The pointed end of a triangular dart, or the "apex of the bust," the fullest part of the bust.

Back dart A seam that narrows the back from the shoulder blades into the waist.
Bag out Flipping your fabric right-side out once you're done sewing right sides together.
Bias binding Narrow tape cut on the bias, used for finishing edges or encasing seams. Buy off the roll or make your own.
Bias cut The technique of cutting pattern pieces at 45 degrees to the selvage to create stretch and drape.
Box pleat A pair of parallel pleats forming a raised panel at the front.
Bust dart A dart to give 3-D shaping to the bust. It can have a number of locations on the bodice.
Bust point This marks the apex of the bust (see above). Pivot your darts from here.
Button stand A reinforced strip of fabric used to place buttons and buttonholes.

Casing A channel for threading with elastic or ribbon to create gathers or ruching.
CB Center back.
CF Center front.
Cowl A triangular wedge of fabric added to a design to create drape, usually at the front or back of the neck.

Dart A triangular seam used to create a 3-D shape—the foundation of all pattern making!
Dart legs The two sides of the triangular dart—they need to be of equal length.
Design lines The lines (seams) on a pattern that define a style. These can stand alone or be combined with fit lines, for example, panels or yokes.
Dolman sleeve A sleeve grown on to (made in one piece with) the bodice, which creates underarm folds.
Draft To draw a pattern.
Dress form A molded torso shape used for the fitting, draping, and display of garments.
Drill A tool for making holes, used to add markings to pattern pieces to indicate the apex of darts, pocket placement, and buttonholes.

Ease The amount of room a garment allows beyond the measurements of the body.

Facing A mirror-image copy of part of the edge of a garment, placed on the inside and joined with a seam to form a tidy finish. Often strengthened with interfacing.
Fit lines Lines on a pattern that are necessary to create fit, for example, darts and panels. Can be combined with design lines.
French curve A wooden or plastic template for drawing curves, such as armholes, necklines, hip lines, or fancy shaping.
French dart A long, diagonal dart from the waist to the bust point, sometimes curved.
French seam A neat double seam for fine fabrics. Often associated with couture garments.

Grain line The line on a pattern that indicates the correct angle at which to place a pattern piece on the fabric. This is vital to making your garment hang straight—ignore at your peril!

Hem The seam along the bottom edge of a garment.

Interfacing Often a non-woven fabric that can be ironed on or sewn in to give strength and structure where needed, for instance, on button stands, facings, or collars.

Kick pleat A small overlap at the back of a skirt to allow room for walking.
Knife pleat A single-sided pleat.

Leaf edge The outer edge of a collar.
Lining An inner shell for a garment that gives a tidy finish and a luxurious feel.

Muslin A trial garment made in muslin fabric or some other inexpensive substitute. You can make a muslin of a section of a garment rather than the whole thing to test the design or fit.

Notcher A handy tool for cutting notches.
Notches Marks around the edge of a pattern that are used to line up pattern pieces and mark the positions of darts. Think of them as friendly signposts, which are very important for the accurate construction of patterns.

Panel A section of a garment. It can be purely for style or can incorporate shaping.
Pattern The 2-D rendering of a 3-D garment. This is the conduit between a design and a finished garment.
Pin hem A very narrow hem, good for curved hems and fine fabrics such as chiffon.
Pivot To move a pattern piece or reposition a dart from a fixed point.
Pocket bag The part of a pocket hidden inside a garment. Often made from lining fabric.
Princess seam A seam that curves from the armhole or shoulder through the bust to the waist. Great for curvy figures.

Raglan An armhole shape that incorporates a section of the shoulder into the sleeve.
Rouleaux Thin tubes of fabric cut on the bias and turned right-side out, either with a large needle and strong thread or with a specialist turning hook. Used for straps and ties.
Ruched Gathered on one or more sides of a seam.

Seam allowance Extra fabric around the edge of a pattern piece to allow the seams to be sewn.
Self-facing A facing that is cut as part of the main pattern piece and folded back on itself without a seam.
Selvage The long, finished edge of fabric when it comes off the roll.
Serge stitch An industrial seam finish produced by a specialized machine. Makes a good, stretchy seam for knit fabrics.
Set square A template for marking straight lines and angles.
Shoulder dart A major fitting dart, running from the shoulder seam to the bust point.
Slash and spread A technique to create fullness, achieved by cutting into a pattern piece and spreading and/or pivoting it. One of the chief concepts of pattern drafting.
Sleeve head The top part of a sleeve that fits into the armhole.
Sloper A close-fitting shell that forms the starting point for a pattern.
Spot-and-cross Specialist pattern-cutting paper marked with spots and crosses to aid drafting.
Stay tape A flat tape, usually made from cotton, used to stop edges from stretching, for instance, on pocket openings.

Waistband A folded-over length of fabric placed at the waist of a garment. Usually strengthened with interfacing.
Waist dart A vertical dart that shapes either the bodice from bust point to waist or the skirt from waist to hip.

Yoke A horizontal, shaped panel that can incorporate darts, usually placed at the shoulder or between the waist and hip.

Chapter 2

Your Body, Your Sloper

Introduction to Using Slopers

A sloper is a close-fitting shell that fits neatly around the body, following its contours. All patterns are derived from slopers. In this book, the slopers have already been drafted for you and are available to download (see page 24).

It's a good idea to start by downloading the Darted Dress Sloper with Set-in Sleeve, as the majority of styles in this book (and beyond) spring from this. Alternatively, if you already have a sloper you like, you can go straight on to drafting the patterns.

How to download the slopers

Step 1: Identify your size

Take your tape measure and turn to pages 32–33 for detailed measurement instructions. To be sure of accurate measurements, enlist a measuring buddy!

Step 2: Identify your sloper

Compare your measurements to the size chart opposite to identify which sloper to download. The slopers are provided with two bust options for each size, as the bust area is the most difficult to fit. If you are not sure which to choose, download both options and make up the front sections in muslin to see which gives the best fit (see page 34). If you find your top and bottom measurements relate to different-sized slopers on the size chart, you can mix and match—see Fit Solutions on pages 136–141.

Step 3: Download your sloper

To download the slopers, either scan the QR code on the sloper pages or visit tinyurl.com/j3c8p6z, where you will find links to download each of the slopers in all sizes as PDFs.

The slopers are shown on the following pages:
Page 24: Darted Dress Sloper with Set-in Sleeve (dress and skirt, front, back, sleeve)
Page 25: Darted Dress Full Bust Sloper with Set-in Sleeve (dress and skirt, front, back, sleeve)
Page 26: Dartless Dress Stretch Sloper with Set-in Sleeve (dress and skirt, front, back, sleeve)
Pages 27–28: Sleeve slopers (Set-in Sleeve in three lengths, Dolman Sleeve, Raglan Sleeve)
Pages 29–30: Collar slopers (Shirt, Peter Pan, Soft and Fluid, Standing)
Page 31: Pocket slopers (In-seam, Patches 1 and 2)

Each size is listed as a link to a single PDF document, which is ready for you to download and print.

Step 4: Print your sloper

The sloper PDFs are formatted to print at US letter size or A4. You should use US letter size if you are based in the US and A4 if you are based anywhere else. It is important to ensure your slopers are printed at full scale, or the sizing will not be correct. Your print settings should be set to "full scale," "100%," "actual size," or equivalent, according to your printer software. There is a test square on the first page of every sloper—print this page only and check that the test square measures 2 x 2 in. (5 x 5 cm).

Step 5: Stick your sloper together

Once your test page is printing at full scale, print the whole document and assemble your sloper. Each page is labeled with registration circles plus lettered rows and numbered columns. Use the circles to align the pages at the corner points and then tape together.

Step 6: Cut out your sloper

Cut out your sloper carefully and sew as a muslin for a test fit. Remember that it does not have seam allowances, so you will need to add your preferred amount. See Checking the Fit on page 34 for instructions on how to sew your muslin and check the fit of your sloper.

Once you are happy with the fit, you're ready to start creating the styles of your dreams.

NOTE

The slopers in this book range from US sizes 2 to 16 (UK 6 to 20) with plenty of instructions on how to adapt these for your figure.

Size Chart

Size charts vary, as you have probably discovered when shopping for clothes. Use this simple one to identify which sloper to download.

US SIZE	2	4	6	8	10	12	14	16
UK SIZE	6	8	10	12	14	16	18	20
Bust	30 in. (76 cm)	32 in. (81.5 cm)	34 in. (86.5 cm)	36 in. (91.5 cm)	38 in. (97 cm)	40 in. (101.5 cm)	43 in. (109 cm)	46 in. (117 cm)
Waist	25 in. (63.5 cm)	27 in. (68.5 cm)	28 in. (71 cm)	30 in. (76 cm)	32 in. (81.5 cm)	34 in. (86.5 cm)	36 in. (91.5 cm)	38 in. (97 cm)
Hip	34 in. (86.5 cm)	36 in. (91.5 cm)	38 in. (97 cm)	40 in. (101.5 cm)	42 in. (107 cm)	44 in. (112 cm)	47 in. (119.5 cm)	50 in. (127 cm)

Get to know your sloper

It is a good idea to take a look at the sloper to familiarize yourself with it and all the information it contains.

The slopers

The Darted Dress sloper is made up of half a back, half a front, and a whole sleeve. When cutting it out, you should fold the fabric and cut double. The center front (CF) should be placed on the fold, while the center back (CB) should be cut with seam allowance to allow for an opening.

Seam allowance

These slopers don't have any seam or hem allowances. This is because once you start using them to make different styles, it gets confusing if there are seam allowances along some lines and not others. Additionally, you may want different-width seam allowances in different areas of your pattern. Remember, you are in charge!

Grain lines

The slopers are marked with grain lines (a) that show how they should be placed in relation to the grain of the fabric. It is important to stick to these and to transfer them onto any patterns that derive from the sloper.

Notches

The slopers are marked with notches (b) that guide you in accurately aligning the pieces together. These should also be transferred onto any patterns that derive from the sloper.

Fit lines

These slopers are marked with fit lines in gray: bustline, waistline, and hip line. These are useful when you draft patterns from the sloper and help you to orientate the design onto the body.

DESIGN DARTS AND SEWING DARTS

> On the front bodice there is a difference between a design dart, which pivots from the bust point, and a stitching dart, which should end 1½–2 in. (4–5 cm) away from the bust point. This distance is marked on the sloper as a dotted line circle surrounding the bust point (bp). Always pivot from the bust point when drafting patterns, or the bust point may end up in the wrong place. After pivoting, remember to shorten the dart, or your darts will come to a nasty point at the bust. Shift any seams so that they skim past the bust point, rather than running across it.

> You don't need to shorten the back waist dart unless you want to for pattern design reasons.

Fitting darts

Fitting darts are also marked in gray: front shoulder dart, front waist dart, and back waist dart. These provide the essential shape that helps the sloper mold around the contours of the body. The positioning of these darts is the fundamental tenet of pattern design: You can move them wherever you like, as long as the overall volume of the bodice remains the same.

Design lines and dart positions

The slopers are also marked with some common design lines and dart positions in red. These will aid you when you come to draft the patterns in this book. The design lines marked are front yoke and back yoke.

The design darts marked are:

1. Princess seam to armhole (p–w)—runs from the middle of the armhole, through the bust point (bp) to the waist

2. Shoulder dart (sh–bp)—this is one of the fundamental fitting darts, but if continued to the waist, it also forms a princess seam to the shoulder (sh–w)
3. Neck dart (n–bp)
4. Center dart (c–bp)
5. Waist dart (w–bp)
6. French dart (f–bp)
7. Side dart (s–bp)

Sleeve sloper

The sleeve sloper (see below right) is marked with a vertical center line and a horizontal line between the underarm points (up). It is important to ensure when drafting sleeve patterns that your underarm points are aligned or you will end up with a twisted sleeve.

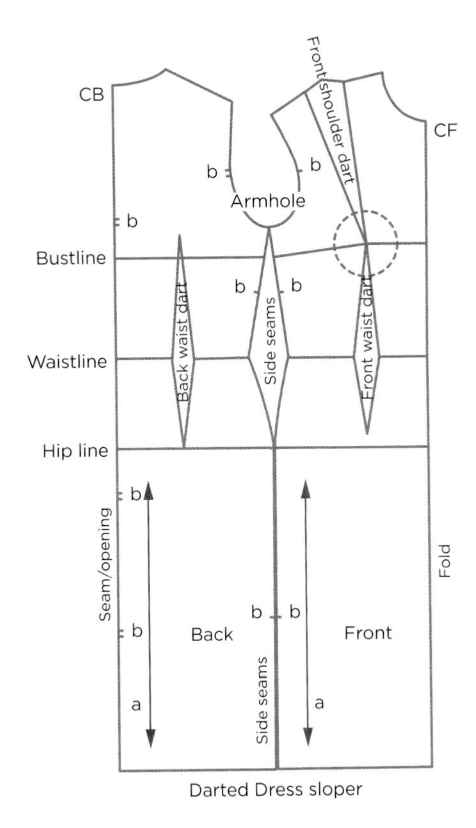

Darted Dress sloper

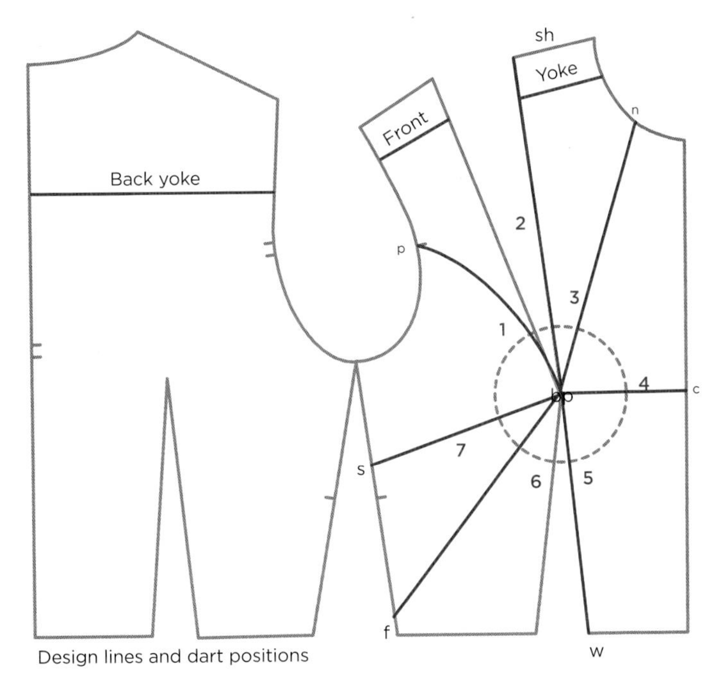

Design lines and dart positions

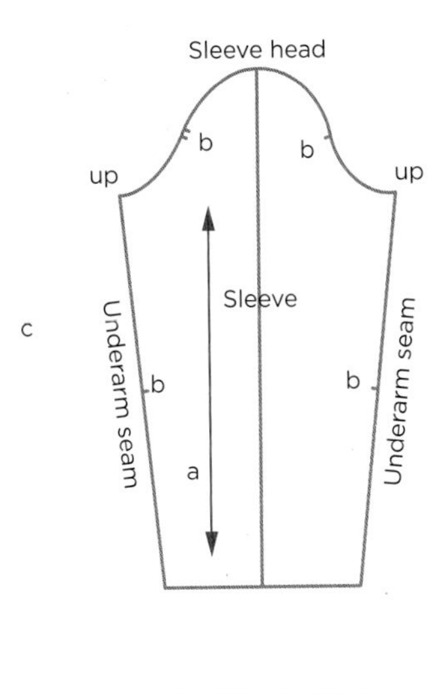

Set-in Sleeve sloper

The Slopers

These are the slopers you can download at tinyurl.com/j3c8p6z (see page 20).

Darted Dress Sloper with Set-in Sleeve

You will come to know this sloper well, as it forms the foundation for the vast majority of the skirt and dress patterns in this book.

For skirts, trace the skirt section of the sloper at the desired waistline for the pattern, which for some styles may be above or below the waistline marked on the sloper.

The set-in sleeve is designed to fit into the armhole with some ease.

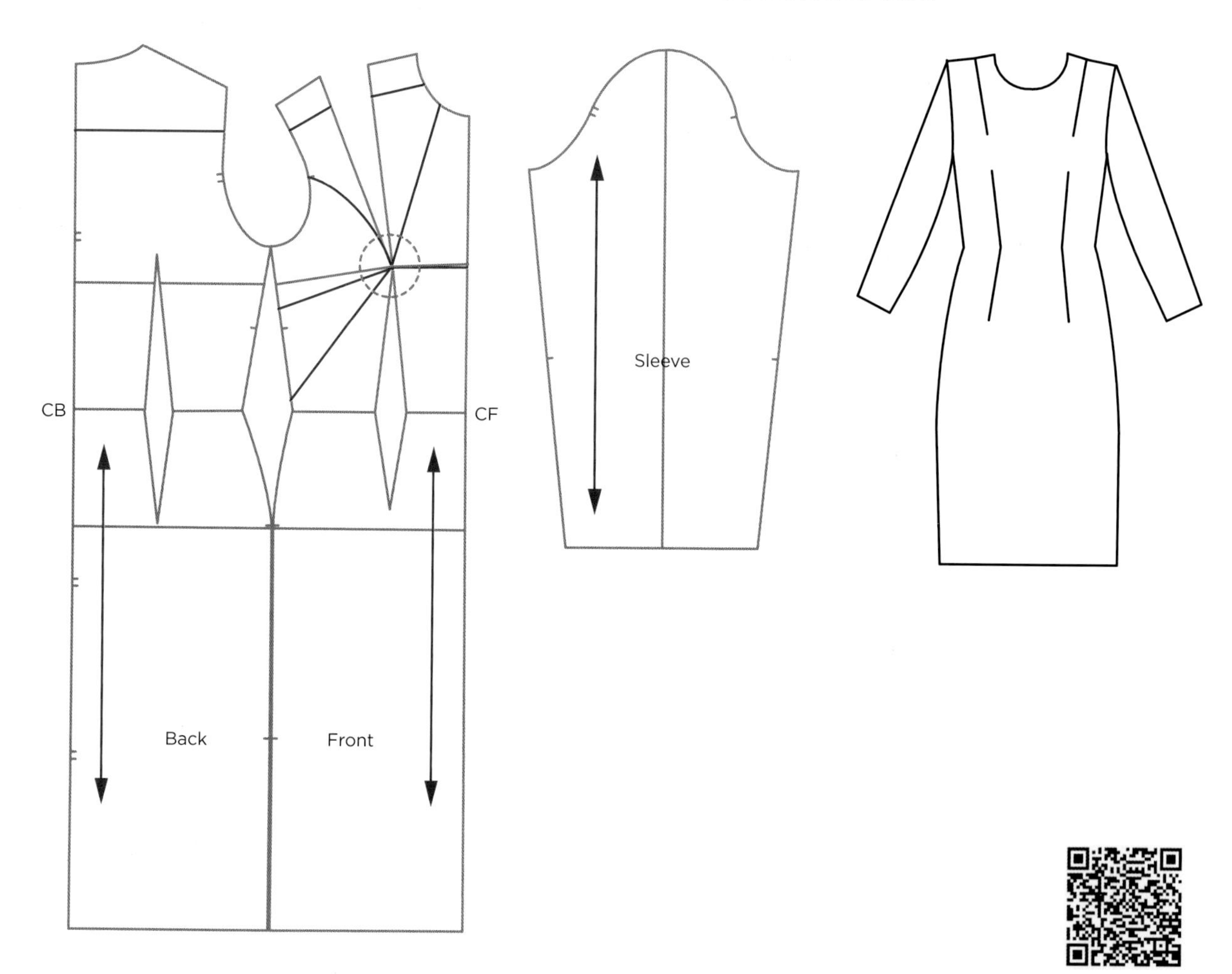

tinyurl.com/
j3c8p6z

Darted Dress Full Bust Sloper with Set-in Sleeve

This sloper is identical to the regular Darted Dress Sloper, but is drafted to fit a fuller bust.

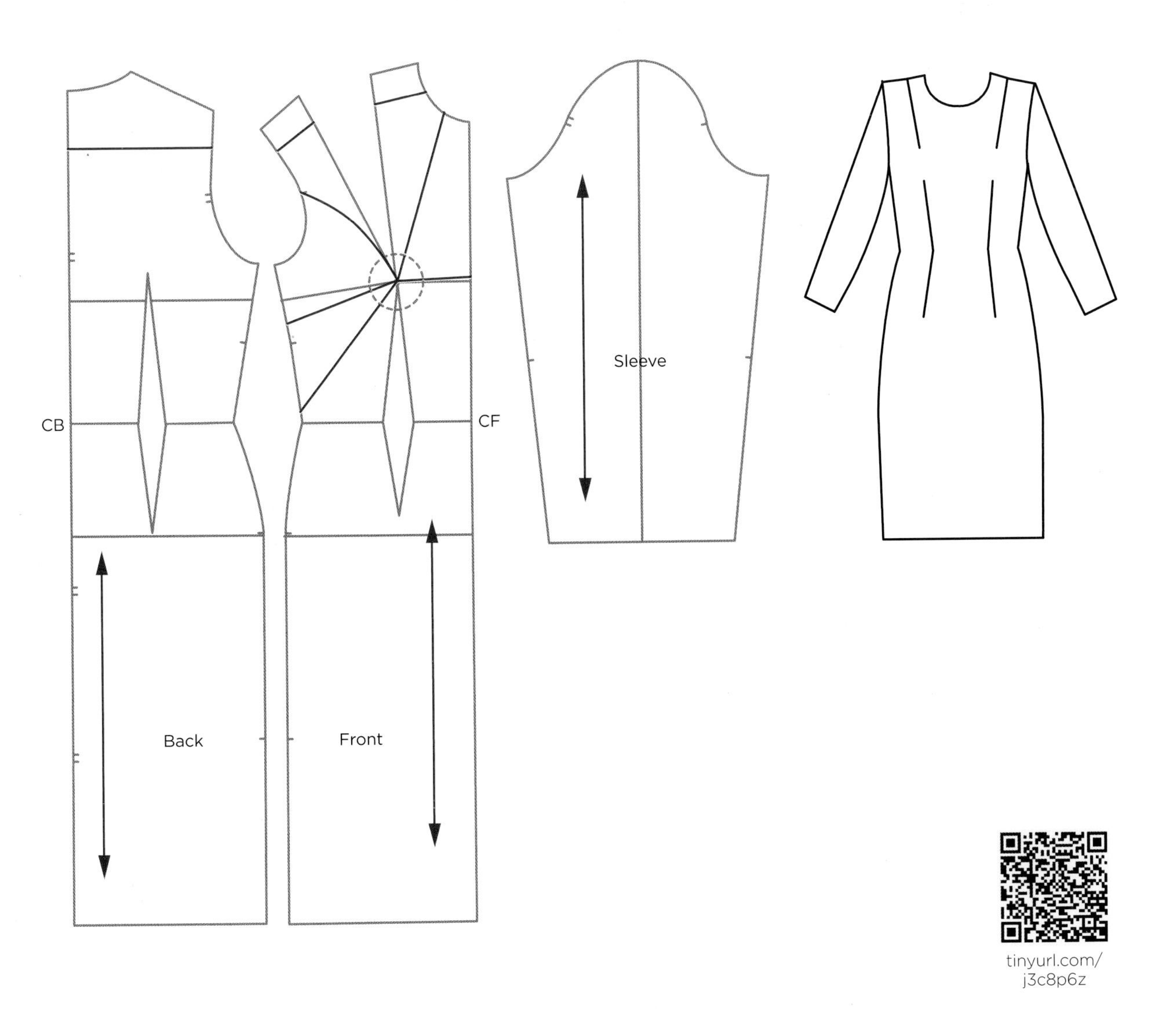

tinyurl.com/j3c8p6z

Dartless Dress Stretch Sloper with Set-in Sleeve

This sloper is for use with stretch fabrics and was used to make the Tube Skirt (page 58), Negligee (page 104), and Maxi Dress (page 114). It's good for quick, simple sews. The sleeve is a tighter fit with this sloper. Often fabrics such as wool, cotton, viscose, or silk jersey are knitted with spandex, which helps them to hold their shape and makes them ideal for this sloper.

You'll see that the sloper does not include any bust shaping, which is why there is no full-bust version. Shaping is provided by the stretch in the fabric. Every stretch fabric is different—you can make a smaller size if it is extra stretchy.

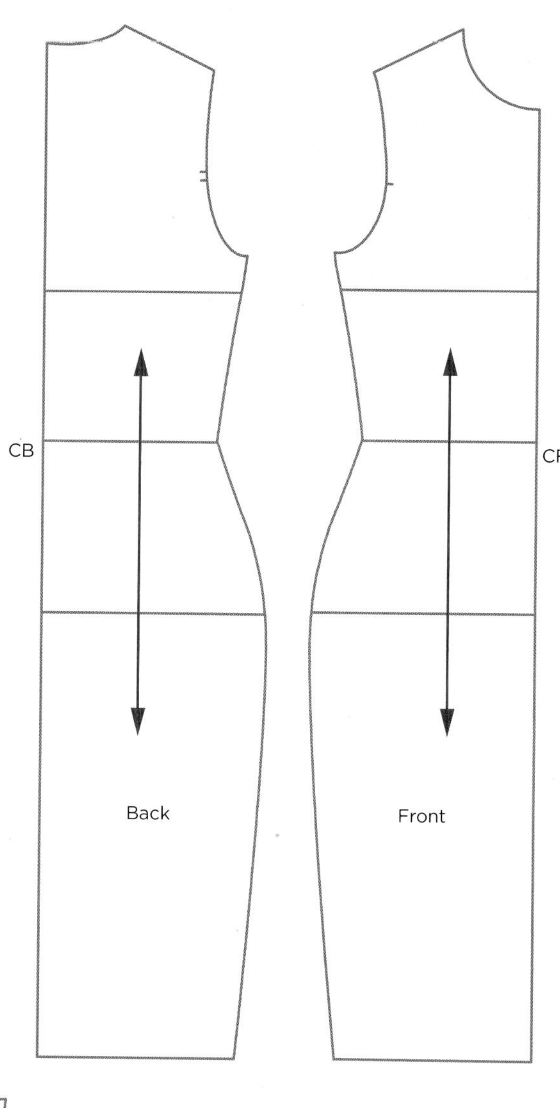

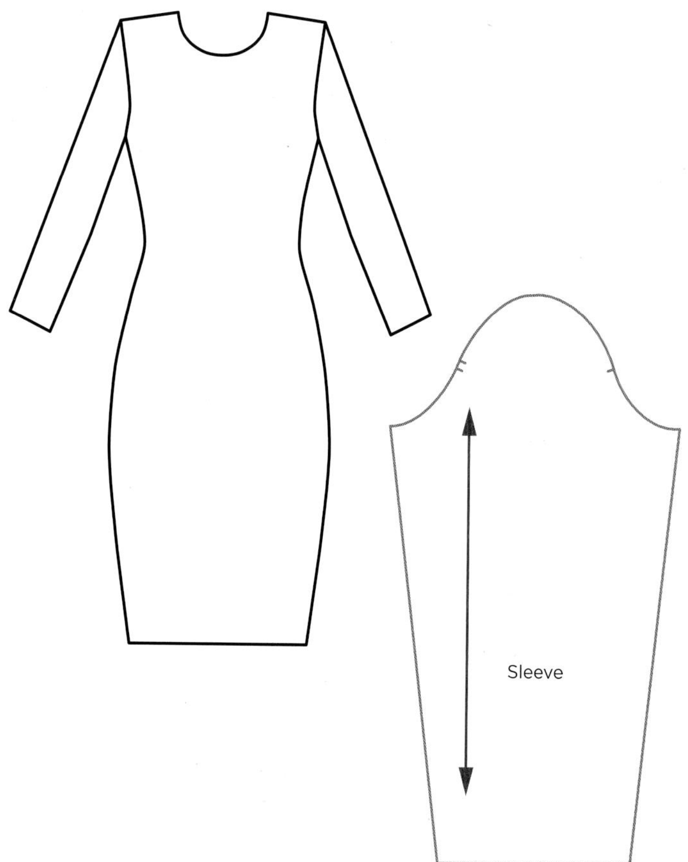

tinyurl.com/
j3c8p6z

Sleeve slopers

Set-in Sleeve sloper in three lengths. This sleeve is designed to fit both of the Darted Dress slopers.

The sloper has a little bit of ease at the sleeve head and fits reasonably snugly, with room to move at the elbow. It is marked with three lengths: short, three-quarter, and full. Of course, you can choose to cut it off wherever you want!

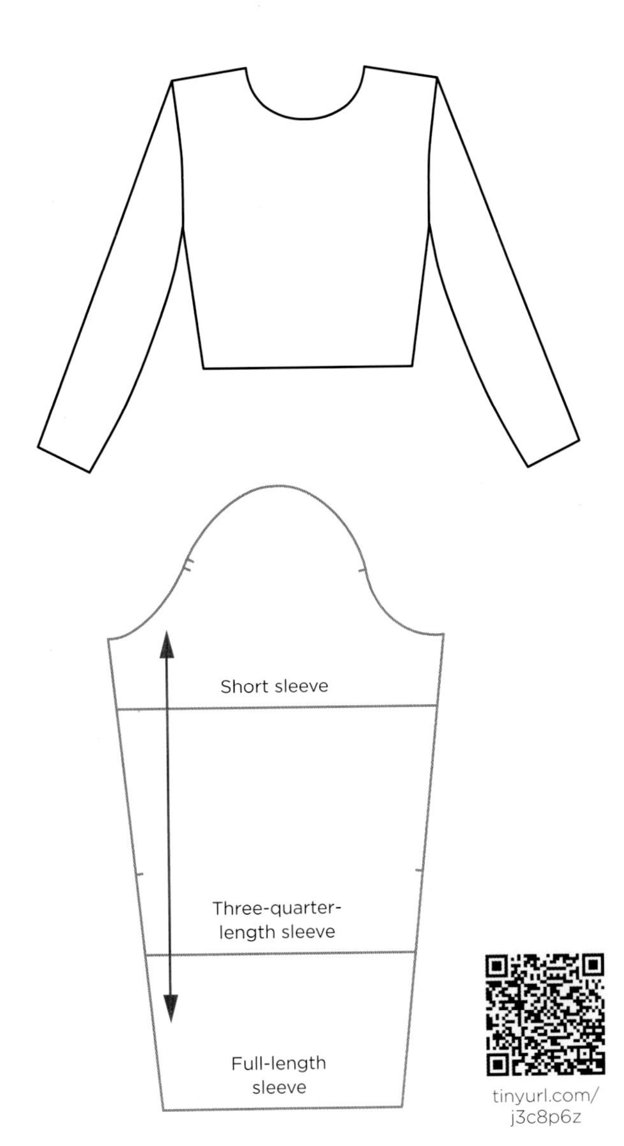

tinyurl.com/j3c8p6z

Dolman Sleeve sloper

This sloper includes the bodice as there are no seams at the armhole. Combine with the skirt pattern of your choice to make a whole dress. It is used to make the Gown pattern (page 116) and the Batwing Sleeve variation (page 126). It's quick and simple to sew because there is no sleeve to set in. Adjust the length of the sleeve parallel to the sleeve hem.

Raglan Sleeve sloper

For this sloper, part of the neck seam and all of the shoulder seam are transferred from the bodice into the sleeve. This is used to make the Sweater Dress pattern (page 94) and the Ruched Sleeve variation (page 127). It is a good choice for sporty styles in stretchy fabric as it has plenty of room in the armhole.

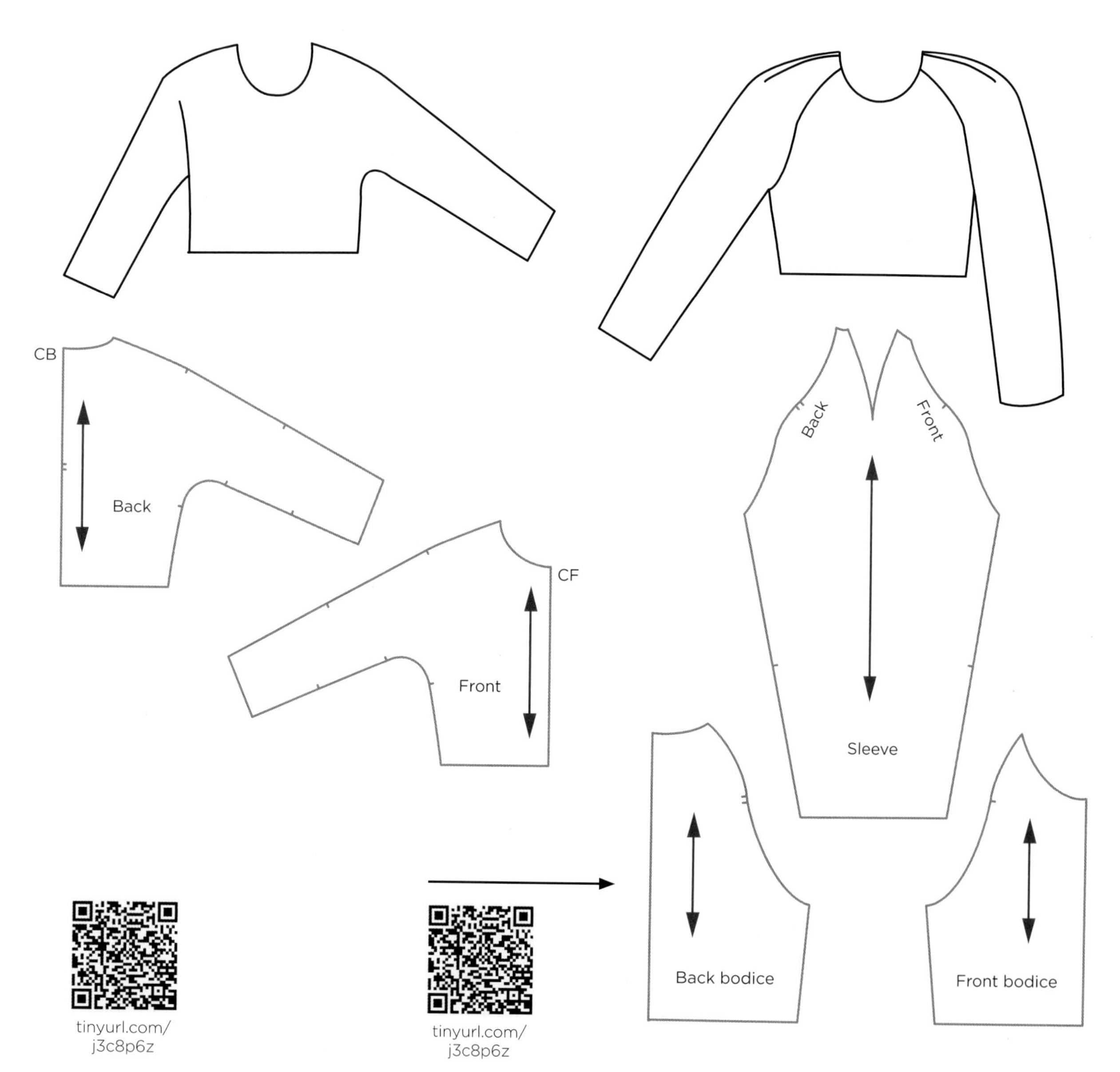

Collar slopers

Cut the sloper along the dotted lines and spread to fit your neckline.

Collars are almost always cut double and bagged out.

Shirt Collar

The Shirt Collar is designed to sit up around the neck. Check that the neckband on the collar matches the button stand on the bodice. Some firm interfacing will give your collar a crisp edge. A variation is the Scalloped-Edge Collar—see page 123.

> TIP
>
> Trim ¼ in. (6 mm) from the leaf edge of the under-collar piece to make the seam roll to the underside of the collar.

Peter Pan Collar

The Peter Pan Collar is designed to sit flat on the shoulders and around the back. Experiment with a contrast fabric for different looks—how about lace, leather, or organza?

A variation is the Sailor Collar—see page 125.

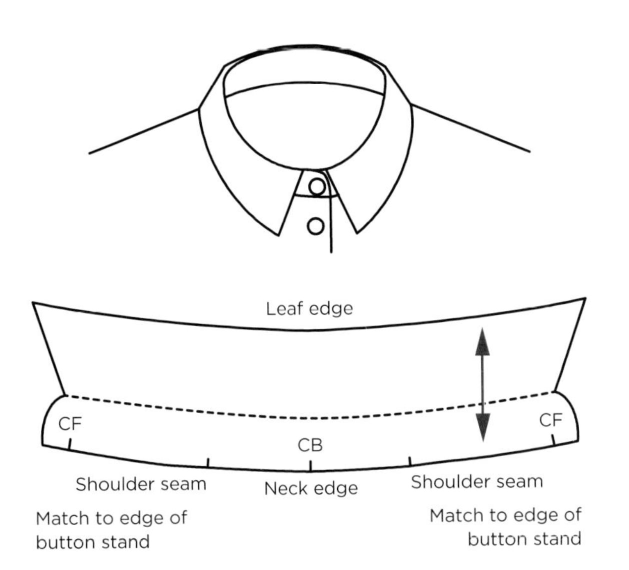

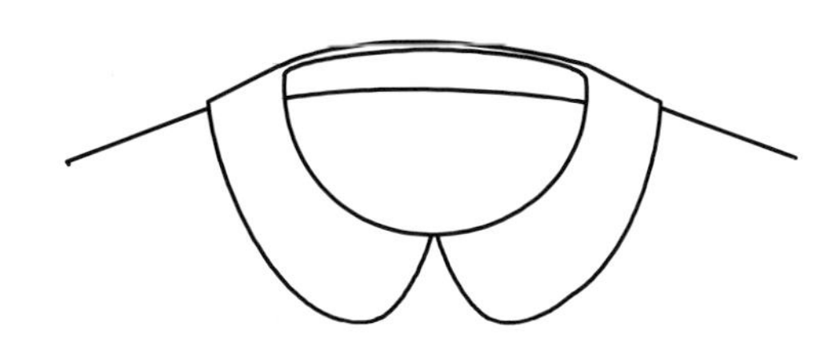

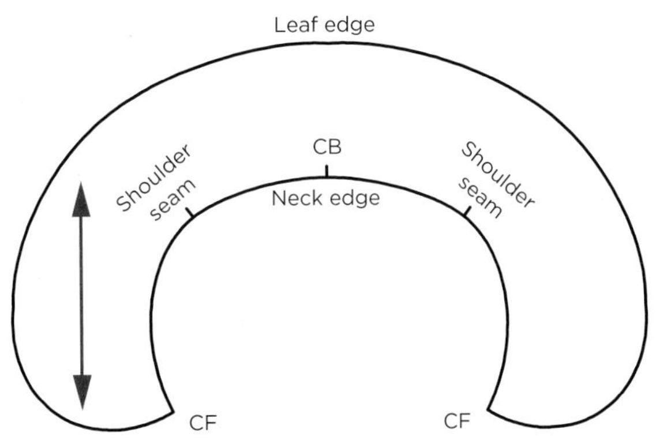

tinyurl.com/j3c8p6z

tinyurl.com/j3c8p6z

Soft and Fluid Collar

For this collar, you first need to alter the neckline of the bodice into a soft V (see Necklines, page 120) and match it to the neck edge of your collar. It looks like an odd shape, but it works. A variation is the Off-the-Shoulder Collar—see page 124.

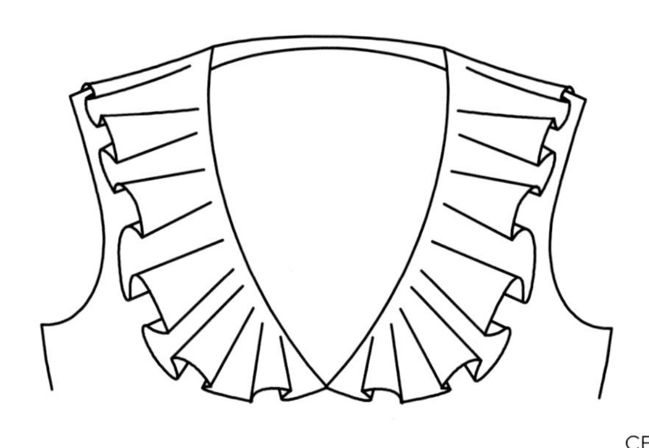

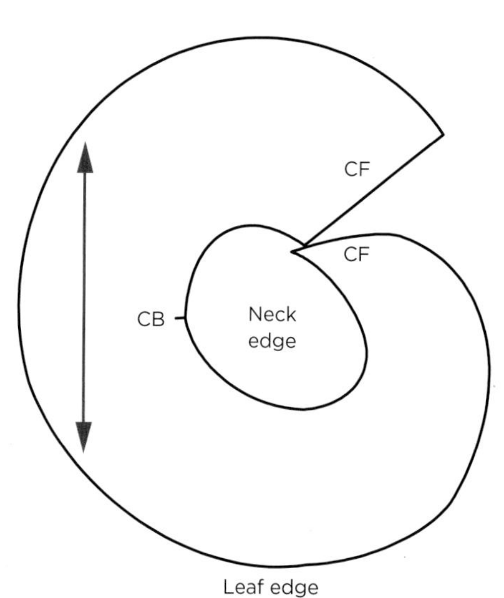

tinyurl.com/
j3c8p6z

Standing Collar

The Standing Collar sloper is drafted to finish edge to edge at the CB/CF—add an overlap for closure if necessary. Curve corners to make a Mandarin Collar. A variation is the Soft Roll Collar—see page 122.

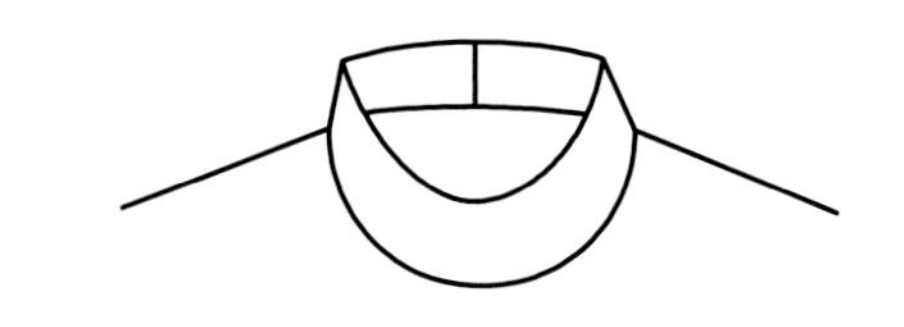

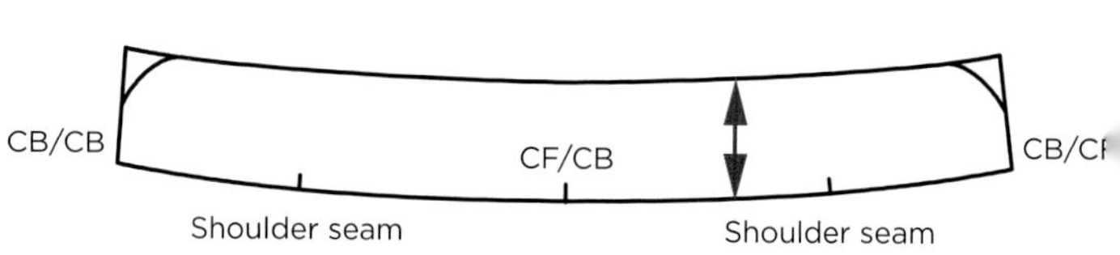

tinyurl.com/
j3c8p6z

Pocket slopers

Pockets come in many shapes and sizes—here are a few to get you started. See Pockets in the Finishes for Skirts chapter on pages 76–77 for more ideas and information.

In-Seam Pocket

In-seam pockets need a back and a front, so cut two pairs. Use lining fabric if your garment fabric is delicate or bulky.

Patch Pocket 1

This is a classic patch pocket shape. Add seam allowances. Bag out with a lining or add a self-facing.

Patch Pocket 2

An alternative patch pocket shape—the point at the top folds to the outside.

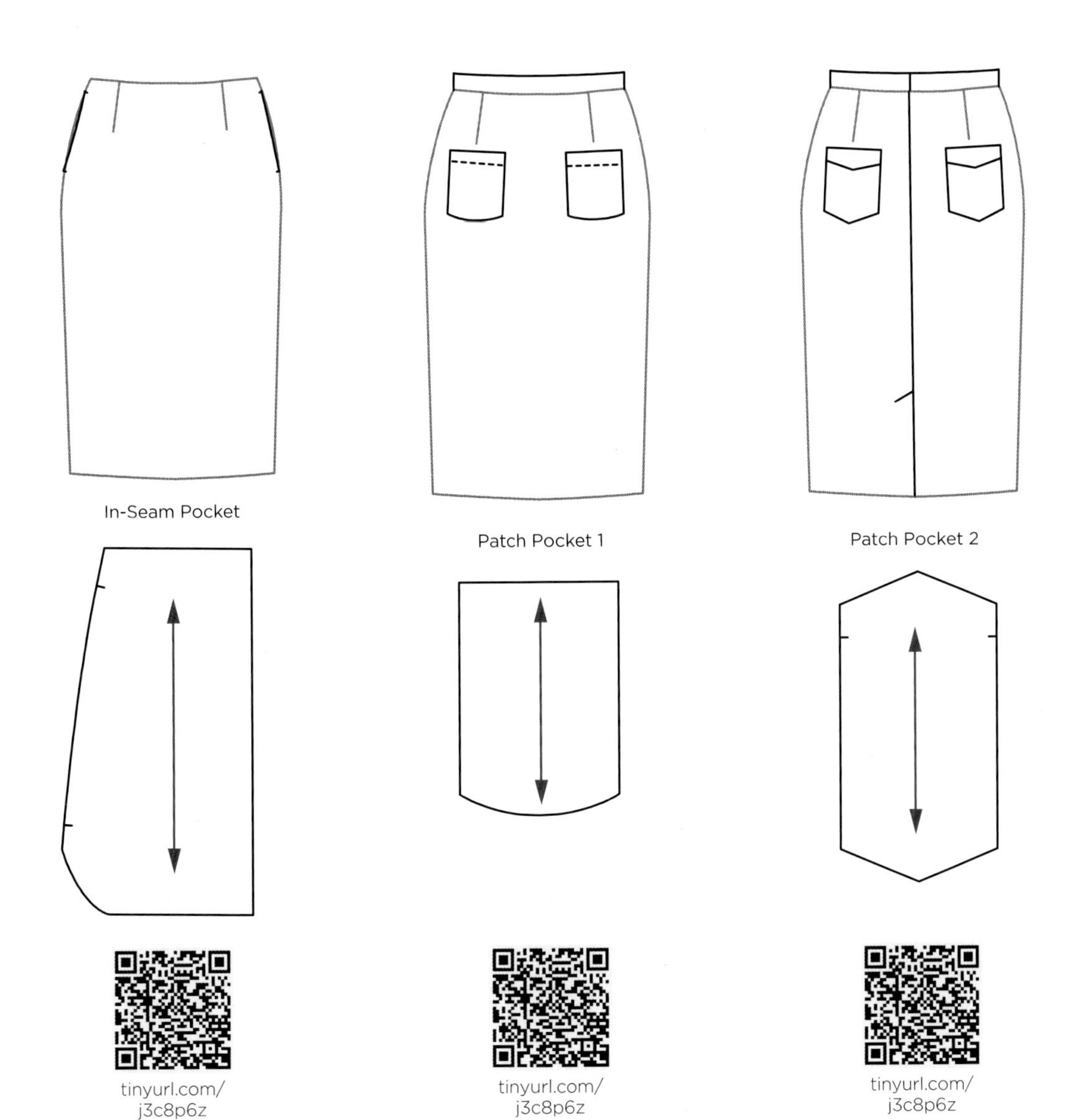

tinyurl.com/j3c8p6z

tinyurl.com/j3c8p6z

tinyurl.com/j3c8p6z

Measurements

These are the key measurements that you need to take when drafting patterns. To identify which of the downloadable slopers is going to be the best fit for your body, you simply need accurate bust, waist, and hip measurements (see the Size Chart, page 21). Many teachers and books ask you to take dozens of measurements of every contour of your body, but it is often better to keep things simple as you are more likely to be accurate this way. You will have a chance to make adjustments once you have sewn your sloper muslin.

MEASURING TIPS

> Find a friend—it is much easier to measure someone else than it is to measure yourself.

> Stand naturally in a relaxed stance with your feet together.

> Don't pull the tape measure too tight or too loose—remember the correct ease is already built into the sloper.

> Take every measurement twice: You'll be amazed how much they can differ!

1. **Shoulder length** From the corner of the neck to the tip of the shoulder.
2. **Bust length** From the top of the shoulder, where the bra strap sits, to the apex of the bust, known as the bust point (bp).
3. **Bust circumference** Around the fullest part of the bust and straight across the back.
4. **Waist circumference** Around the waist, in between the bottom of the rib cage and the start of your hip bones—not necessarily where your pants sit.
5. **Hip circumference** Around the fullest part of the hips. This can vary from person to person and may include the rear end or the tops of the thighs. Look sideways in the mirror and measure in a few places to find the widest point.
6. **Length from nape to waist** From the bottom of the neck to the waist, along the back.
7. **Arm length** From the tip of the shoulder to the wrist, running the tape measure past the elbow with a slightly bent arm.
8. **Length from waist to knee** Along the side of the body from the waist to the middle of the knee.
9. **Length from waist to ankle** Along the side of the body from the waist to the ankle bone.

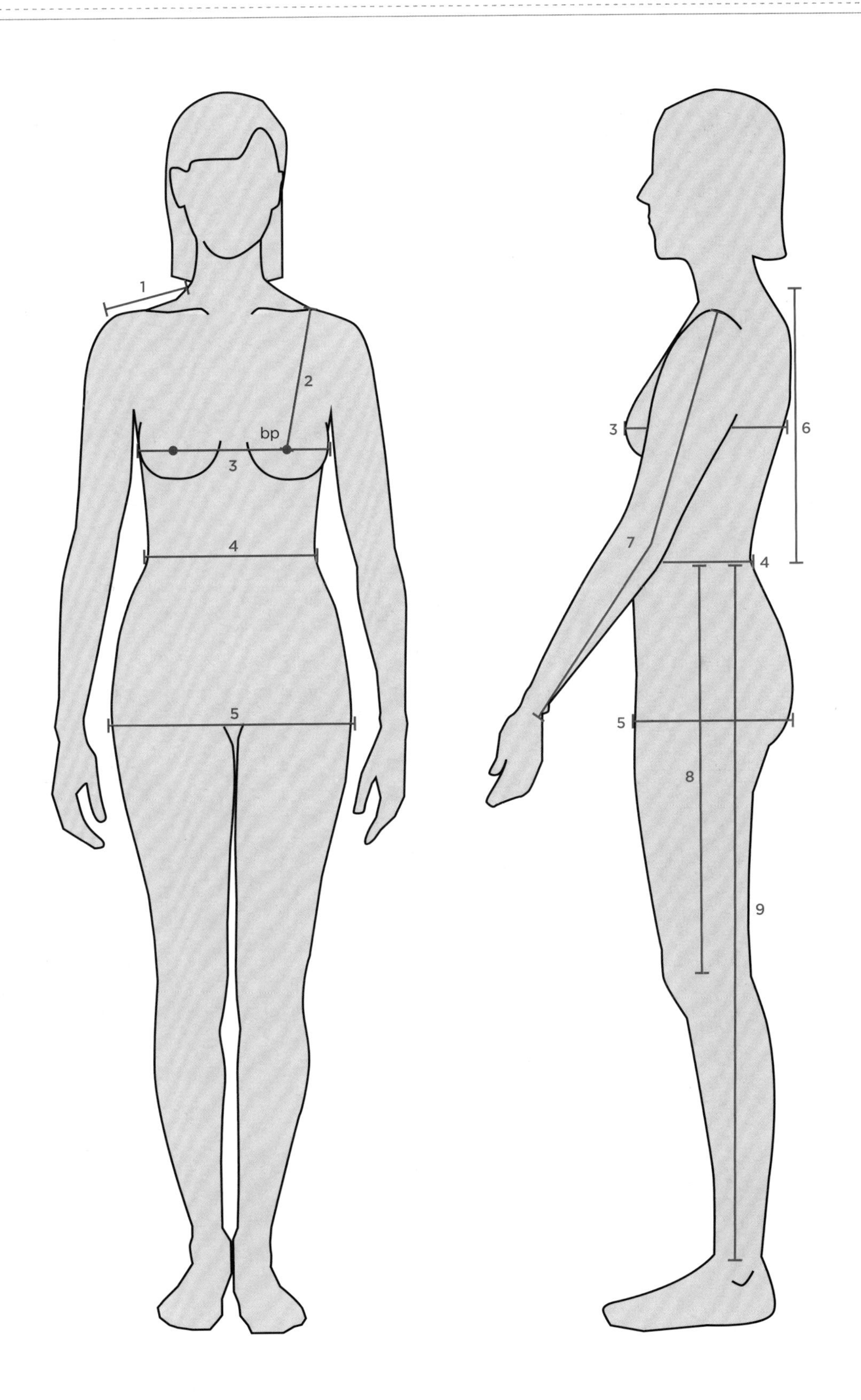
1
2
bp
3
4
5
3
6
7
4
5
8
9

Checking the Fit

The slopers are designed to have a snug fit so that any patterns that are derived from them are as accurate as possible. Even on a loose-fitting style, starting from a close-fitting sloper will ensure a well-proportioned pattern.

One of the joys of drafting your own patterns is in achieving a personal fit according to how you like your clothes to look and feel. To be satisfied with the garments you make from your slopers, it is imperative that you take the time at this stage to get the muslins fitting just how you like. It's all in the preparation!

These instructions show you how to adjust the fit of the Darted Dress Sloper with Set-in Sleeve. A perfectly fitting sloper will skim the contours of the body and feel like a second skin. It should feel comfortable walking around, sitting down, and jumping in the air. Remember, muslin is not the most alluring fabric, so if it looks OK in the muslin, imagine how fabulous it will look in a gorgeous fabric!

Sewing a muslin

Sew your sloper in muslin to try out the fit.

Dress

- Fold the muslin in half lengthwise and iron in a crease. This will form a useful center line when you open it.
- Place the front sloper onto the muslin with the center front (CF) along the fold.
- Place the back sloper on the muslin with the center back (CB) toward the selvage, leaving enough space for a seam allowance along the CB, as the finished muslin will have a back opening.
- Trace around all the edges of the slopers and mark in the darts. Note that for the muslin, you should sew in the entire dart, without shortening, as for fitting purposes you want to see if the bust point of the sloper matches that of your body! It also allows you to see how much you might need to shorten the darts so that they sit well around the apex of the bust.
- Mark the bustline, waistline, and hip lines onto the muslin—this will help you to see if they are sitting in the right position when you try it on.
- Mark the notches.
- Add a seam allowance to the shoulder, armhole, and side seams. Do not add a seam allowance to the neckline, as this will make the neck hole smaller and will affect how it sits on the shoulders. There is no need to add a seam allowance on the hem, as the fit is not affected by length.
- Cut out the muslin slopers.
- Using a contrast-color thread and a long stitch, stitch in the darts, followed by the seams, making sure to sew along the lines carefully. Remember to leave an opening on the CB seam from the hip line to the neck so you can get into the muslin.

Sleeve

- With the muslin folded lengthwise, place the sloper onto the fabric with the grain line parallel to the fold.
- Trace around the whole sleeve, mark in the notches, and add a seam allowance. As with the dress, it is not necessary to add a seam allowance to the sleeve hem.

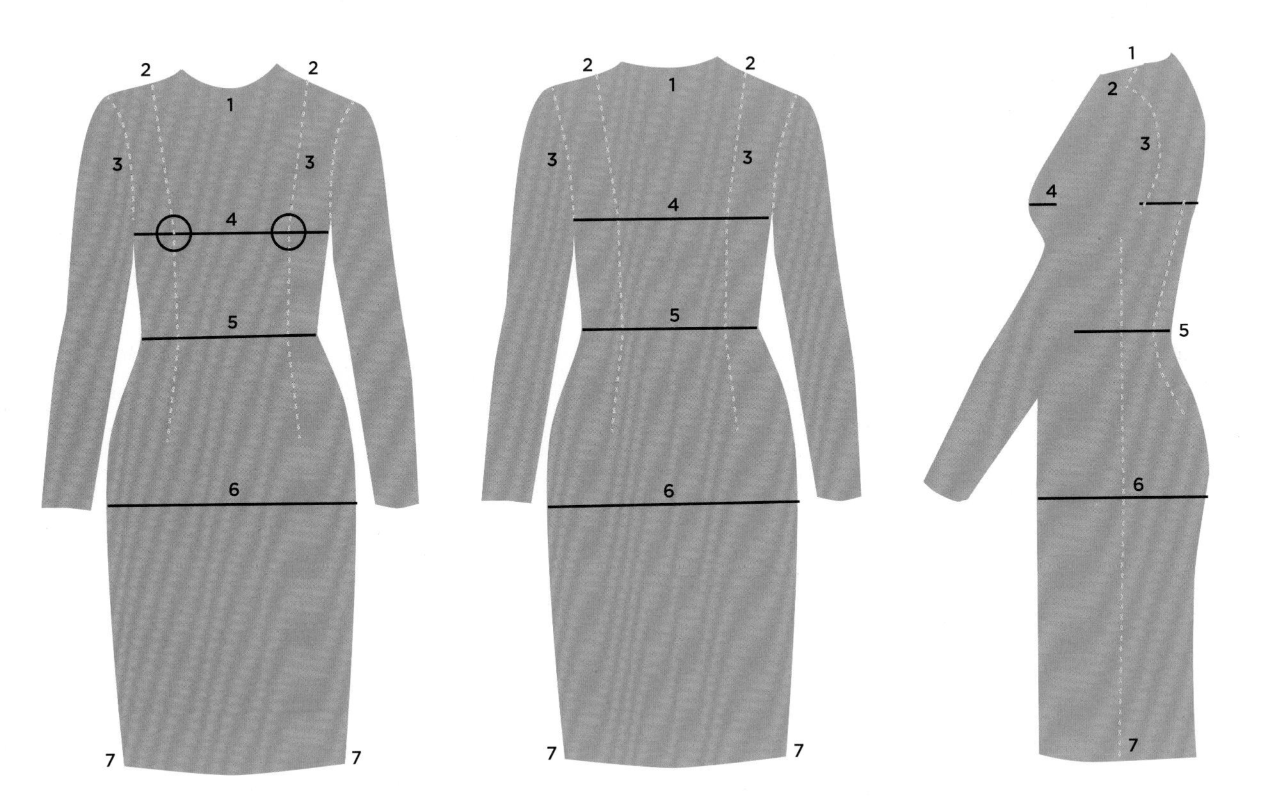

- Cut out through both layers of fabric to create a pair of sleeves.
- Stitch the long underarm seam and fit the sleeve head into the armhole.

What to check

Here are the things to look out for, shown from top to bottom in the diagram opposite:

1. Does the neckline fit smoothly and snugly around the neck?
2. Do the shoulder seams match the length of your shoulders and sit flat to the body?
3. Are the armholes comfortable, not too tight or too loose, and are you able to move your arms easily?
4. Is the bustline flattering, with the bust point at the apex of the bust? Does it sit well across the back?
5. Is the waistline comfortable, and does it sit in the right place at the front and back?
6. Do the side seams skim the hips at the widest point without pulling or gaping?
7. Are the side seams hanging straight at the hem?

If the answer to any of these questions is "no," please turn to the Fit Solutions chapter (pages 134–141) for details on how to make adjustments in order to achieve the perfect fit.

Marking Up Slopers

Once you are happy that you have a perfectly fitting sloper, it is a good idea to use some strong card stock so that it can be traced out again and again. The diagram (right) shows how your final marked-up Darted Dress sloper should look. Use the original printed download as a guide for the placement of dart positions.

1. Notches for the ends of the shoulder dart, legs, armholes, sleeve head, and seams
2. Punched holes at the dart points (use a pattern drill or stab and snip with scissors)
3. Grain lines
4. Labels for the Center Front and Center Back
5. Fit lines: waist and hip
6. Front and back yoke lines
7. The different dart positions and bp (red dot)
8. Sleeve lines (centerline and between the underarm points)

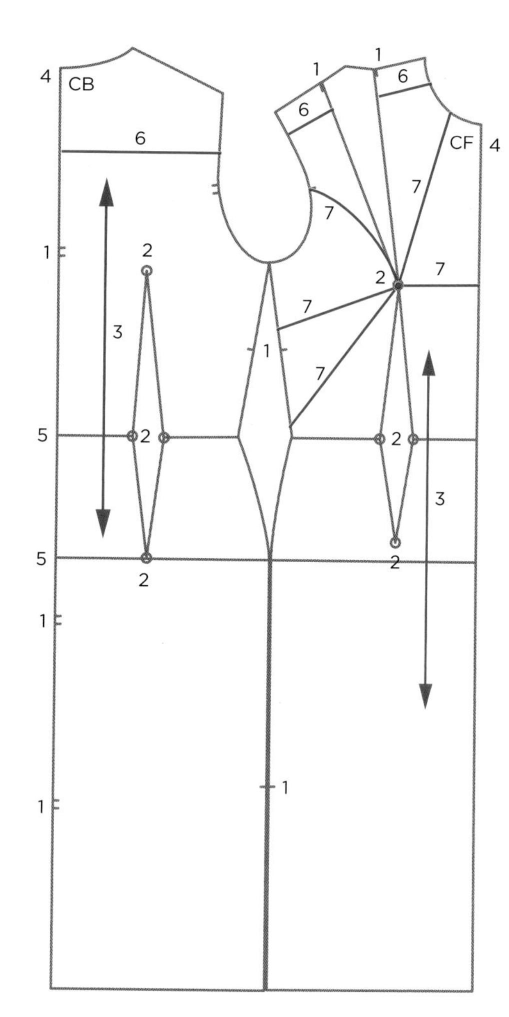

Transforming slopers into patterns

When you start to make a pattern, the first step is always to transfer your sloper onto another piece of paper, including all the markings relevant to the pattern you want to create. Your original card sloper should be treated carefully but the paper version can be cut, ripped, and pinned!

The projects in this book explain how to convert the slopers into patterns for the skirts and dresses shown. The garments in the photographs have been drafted exactly as illustrated in the diagrams. Ideas for adapting these designs are provided in the Finishes for Skirts and Finishes for Dresses chapters (pages 70 and 118).

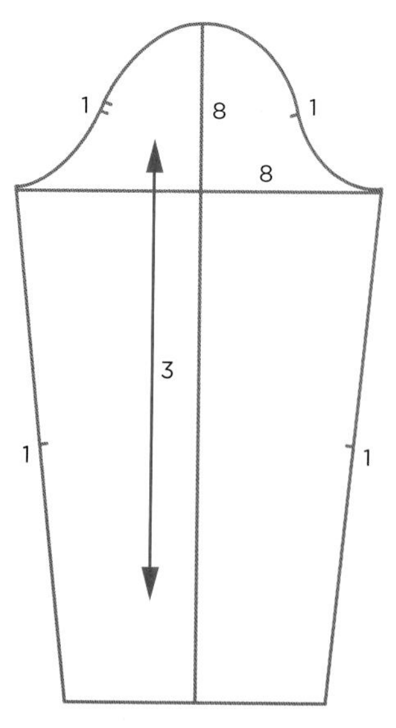

Where measurements are provided, they are intended to serve as guides only—the exact measurements and placing is up to you.

You will see that the instructional steps correspond with the numbers shown in red on the patterns. However, not all steps are marked on the pattern.

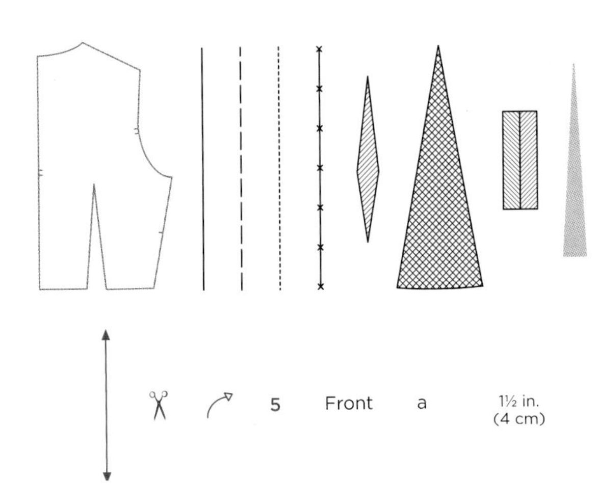

Key to diagrams

The key shown on the right explains how to read the diagrams in this book, from left to right:

Gray lines The lines of the original sloper—these are shown in gray where they remain in the new pattern so you can see how the final pattern is related to the sloper.

Black lines The new pattern lines—these may be the final cutting lines for the pattern or drafting lines that are cut and then further manipulated (see red scissors).

Wide dashed lines Fold lines, for example, waistbands or self-facings.

Small dashed lines Tracing lines for details such as facings and pockets.

Black line with crosses The crosses mark the positions of buttons.

Dart filled with diagonal lines This indicates an instruction to ignore the dart. On your paper pattern you could simply erase it, or not copy it from the sloper; however, you may still want to use it to make measurements or guide you in the positioning of other details.

Cross-hatched shape This indicates where you need to add sections to a pattern. If there is space around your copied sloper, you may just draw in a new line and cut it out in one piece. If not, use any method of collage you prefer. One way is to cut out your traced sloper, place the whole thing on top of another piece of paper, and draw from there. Often, however, you will just cut and tape new sections as required—for instance, to fill in between pivot sections or to make extra strips for A-line side seams.

Shape filled with directional diagonal lines These indicate pleats. When folded, the directional diagonal lines should match up.

Gray-filled shape Indicates where a section of the copied sloper has been overlapped, for instance, to tighten a dart.

Red double-headed arrow Grain lines—these indicate which way a pattern piece should be placed on the fabric and in most cases can be copied from the original sloper.

Red scissors These indicate where pattern drafting lines should be cut to allow for further manipulation. Often you will be asked to cut down a line to within ⅛ in. (3 mm) in order to be able to pivot a pattern to add fullness. This technique is often referred to by pattern cutters as "slash and spread."

Red arrow Indicates the direction in which to pivot a pattern piece.

Red number Refers to the numbered instructions in the text.

Black text Basic labels for the pattern pieces.

Black numbers Suggested measurements.

Marking Up Patterns

A fundamental principle of pattern making is the transformation of a sloper into a pattern. This can be seen in the different markings they each have.

A pattern is like a map that guides you from the inspiration to the finished article. It can be as meticulous and detailed or as rough and ready as you like; everyone has their own style. It is worth being disciplined, however, and making sure you mark up your patterns with the necessary information so that you can reuse them again and again.

Your first pattern could simply be the Darted Dress sloper with added seam allowances and cutting and finishing instructions.

Here's what you need to mark on your patterns:

1. **Seam allowance** A standard seam allowance is ⅜ in. (1 cm) or ⅝ in. (1.5 cm), but now that you're making your own patterns, you can refine as you please. Bear in mind the type of fabric (a fine fabric will need less than a bulky fabric), what kind of seams you are making (serged, flat, French, etc.), and whether you want to allow room for fitting and alterations. You don't need to have the same allowance on all edges of the pattern, but note what they are when you are sewing them up. For example, you might have a small seam allowance around the neckline, a standard ⅜ in. (1 cm) for the shoulders, armholes, and sleeves, and a generous 1 in. (2.5 cm) on the side seams to allow them to be taken out.
2. **Hem allowance** This also depends on your fabric—a regular seam allowance will suffice for pin-hemming a fine chiffon skirt, but you will need something more substantial on a winter wool dress. A generous hem gives a couture feel, and allows for future alterations. An extra-deep hem can be a design feature. Remember that tapered edges need to have correspondingly tapered hems so that they sit flush when folded back—as in the sleeve hem in the diagram opposite.
3. **Grain lines** These mark the direction of the pattern on the fabric and will ensure the garment hangs straight. Generally, it is best to cut the pieces up and down the grain (parallel with the selvage). This follows the warp of the fabric and is the fabric's most stable direction. You might cut across the fabric if it has a decorative edge that you want to use as part of your design, such as scalloped lace or an embroidered or printed panel. The other option is to cut on the bias to create stretch, which involves placing the grain line of your pattern at 45 degrees to the selvage. See pages 104–109 for bias-cut styles.
4. **Notches** These are like signposts that mark style and fit points and allow you to match pieces together with precision as you sew. Place notches at the ends of dart legs, at regular intervals along long seams, on sleeve heads and armholes, and at any other points where pattern pieces relate to each other. For armholes it is usual to mark a single notch on the front side of the armhole to match the front of the sleeve, and a double one on the back. It is better to have too many notches rather than not enough—if in doubt, notch!

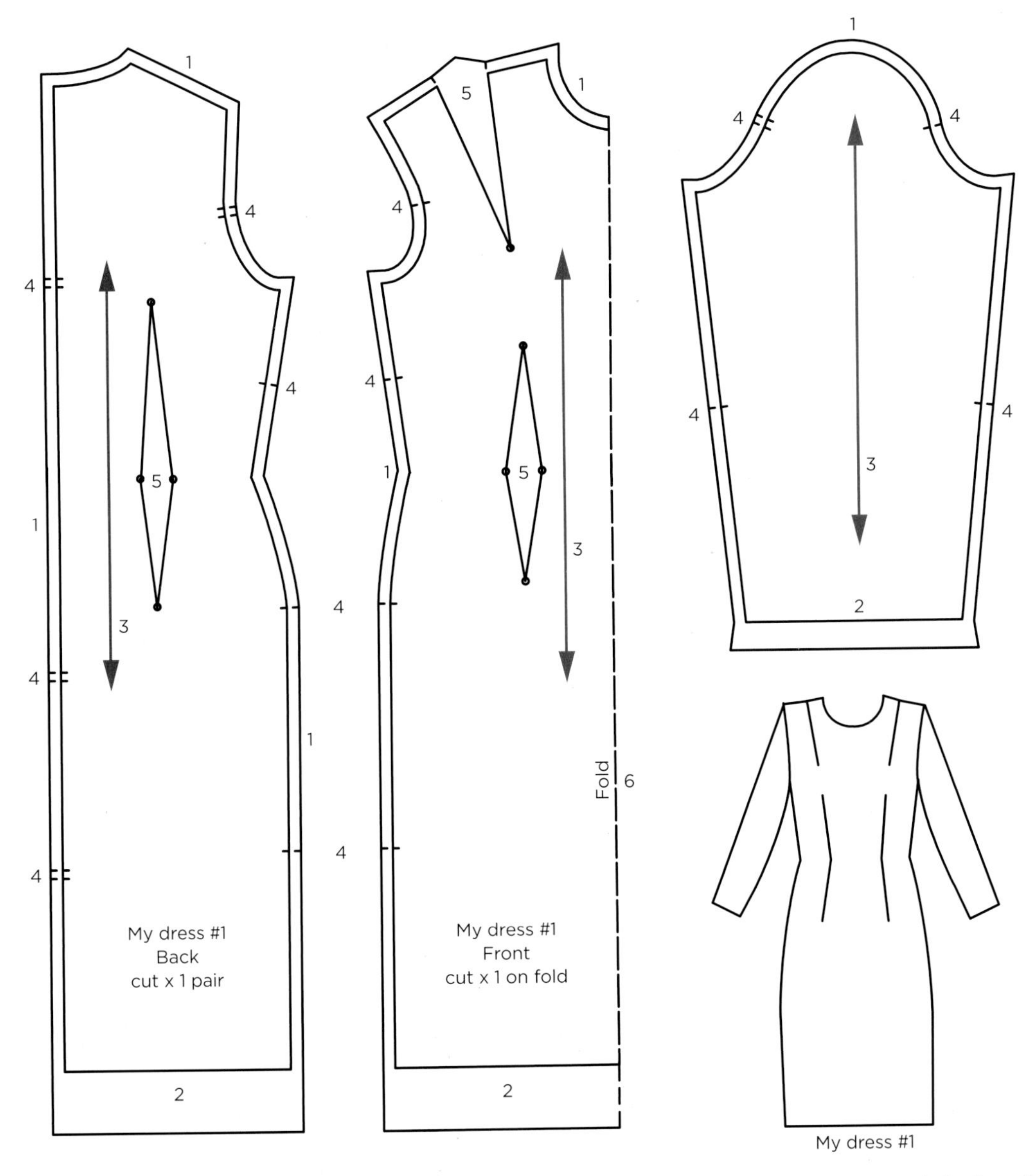

5. **Darts** For darts with legs that finish on external seams, the best way to mark each one is to fold it into the paper in the direction you want it to sit on the fabric, cut along the seam allowance, and fold back out again. This will give you a triangular shape extending from the pattern, which you could think of as a dart "hat." This means the right amount of fabric will be folded into the seam when you sew. You should also draw in the dart legs and mark notches on the seam allowance. For internal darts, use a pattern drill after this, or stab through the paper with a pin. Finish by drawing in the dart legs.

6. **Folds** Mark with a dotted line and label. This indicates that the pattern piece (most often the CF) should be placed on the fold of the fabric. It can also show where to fold an individual pattern piece, such as a self-facing on the top of a pocket, or the center of a waist tie.

Extra pattern markings

- **Gathers, pleats, and tucks** For gathers, mark a notch at each end of a section to be gathered and draw a wiggly line to indicate gathering; make sure there are corresponding notches where the gathered section joins another pattern piece. You can also add a measurement, such as "Gather to 6 in. (15 cm)." For pleats, mark each end and the center of each pleat, as well as an arrow to indicate the direction. For a pleated skirt (such as the Kilt on page 68, shown right), mark the pleats at the top and bottom to keep them parallel. For tucks, mark each end of the tuck and the direction.
- **Placement of details** Mark the corners of pockets, the positions of buttons and buttonholes, and anything else you think will be useful.

Pattern labels

- **Name of the piece** Front, back, sleeve, collar, yoke, etc.
- **How many of a piece to cut** For instance: a pair of sleeves, x 1 CF on the fold, x 4 for a cuff (2 backs, 2 fronts).
- **Center front and center back** CF and CB
- **Right Side Up (RSU)** Mark if the pattern is asymmetrical.
- **Interfacing** Mark where the piece needs interfacing, such as on collars, cuffs, facings, button stands, and tops of pockets.
- **Extra instructions** Mark any unusual instructions you might forget.

If you are making a lot of patterns, give each one a style name or number in case any of the pieces go missing. Draw a quick sketch or take a photograph of the finished piece and attach it to the envelope. A date can also be useful in case your weight fluctuates. You can also add a sheet of sewing notes.

Sewing Garments

This book is about how to draft and cut patterns, rather than how to sew garments. The following are just a few suggestions of how to give your garments a neat finish.

Order of sewing

1. Sew in any darts, pleats, tucks, and gathers.
2. Sew the main seams: shoulders, side seams, back seam, and sleeve seams.
3. Insert the sleeves.
4. Add facings, bindings, and other finishes.
5. Add closures such as zippers, buttons, and buttonholes.
6. Turn the hems, unless it is a pleated garment, in which case sew the hems as the very first step.
7. Fix any buttons.
8. Add any hand-sewn details.

Finishings

- **Facings** A facing is a section of a pattern that is traced and mirrored on the inside of a garment and joined with a seam. It gives a neat finish to armholes, necklines, front edges, and curved hems. It is usually reinforced with interfacing. If you are making a lining, you can hang it from the facing.
- **Self-facings** These are joined to the garment by a fold, rather than by a seam. They can only be drafted for straight edges, such as shirt fronts and hems (see the Shirt Dress on page 88).

LOOK OUT FOR TIPS!

There are lots of tips and ideas for constructing and finishing garments in the tip boxes throughout the Skirts and Dresses sections.

- **Bindings** Binding is another way to finish garment edges such as necklines and armholes. You can buy ready-made bias binding, or make your own from strips of fabric cut on the bias. Bias binding can enclose an edge and be visible on the outside of a garment. Alternatively, you can use narrower binding turned completely to the inside and hand- or machine-stitch so that it is invisible from the front. You can even bind the edges of your facings. If you make your own, use a fine fabric such as silk or cotton.
- **Fancy stitching** Take a look at what your sewing machine has to offer—there may be some interesting stitches in the instruction manual, such as a scalloped or picot edge. On thick fabrics, use embroidery threads to do blanket stitching.
- **Raw edges** A raw edge can be an "edgy" finish! A single line of flat, straight stitching or a tiny zigzag will prevent fraying.
- **Linings** A lining can make all the difference to the weight and feel of a garment. Use the pattern pieces to draft the lining, either up to the edge of the garment or up to the facing. Remember to add seam allowances to both the facing and the lining.
- **Closures** Garments made on domestic sewing machines are often spoiled by amateur buttonholes—there are many more interesting closures such as buttons and loops, buttonholes concealed in seams, bound buttonholes, covered snaps, hooks and eyes, zippers, pins, and kilt pins.

Chapter 3

Skirts

Pencil Skirt

This classic silhouette flatters most figures. Spend time getting the fit just right, as this pattern creates the basis for many others in this book. Try making it in smart, wintry tweed, elegant lace for evening, or casual linen for summer. You can also experiment with the length: Chop it off above the knee for a miniskirt or extend it to mid-calf for a more demure look.

Creating the pattern

Starting with the skirt section of the Darted Dress sloper:

Front

1. Lower front waist by ½ in. (13 mm) at CF (a). Draw in a new curved waistline from CF to side seam (ab).
2. Decide on the desired length of your skirt and measure down from the new waistline (ac).
3. Create the classic pencil shape by tapering in the hem: measure 1 in. (2.5 cm) toward the CF on the side-seam hem (d) and draw in a new side seam, starting two-thirds of the way down from the waistline (de). Be careful not to start too high, or you won't leave enough space for your bottom!

A PERFECT FIT

> Don't be tempted to make the pencil skirt too tight-fitting at the hips. Aim for a smooth line; otherwise, you might find that the fabric stretches with wear and creates creases.

> For this and all other pages in this chapter, the red numbers in the illustration relate to the steps in the text.

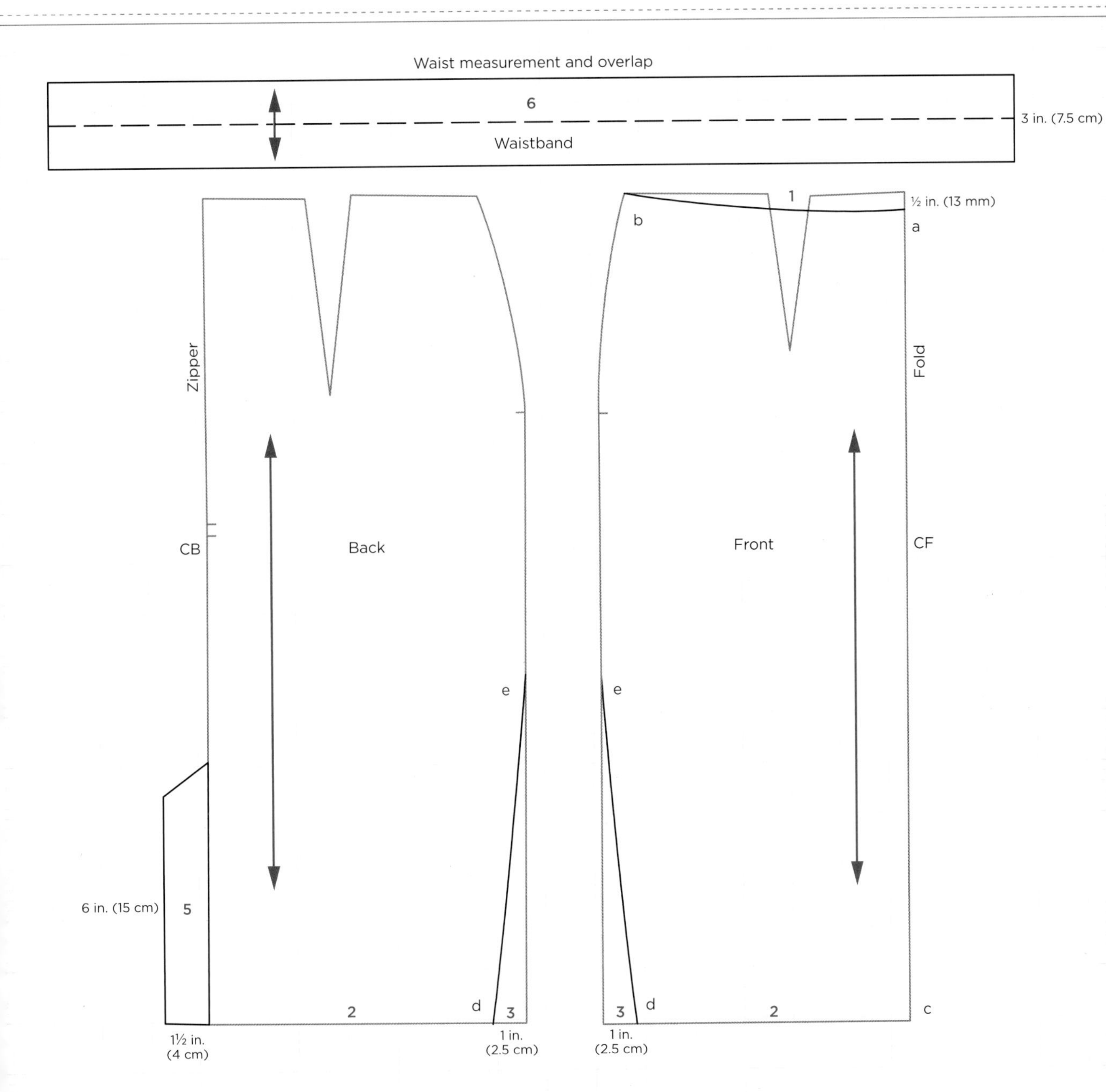

Back

4. Leaving the waistline straight, follow steps 2–3 as on the front.

5. Decide on the length of your slit: 6–7 in. (15–18 cm) is standard. Add a rectangle 1½ in. (4 cm) wide to the CB seam. Slice it off on the diagonal at the top. This is your kick pleat.

Waistband

6. Draw a rectangle to the following dimensions: Your waist measurement + 1¼ in. (3 cm) underlap for a closure x double the desired height of your waistband—1½ in. (4 cm) is standard.

A-Line Skirt

Casual and practical, with room for striding and riding a bike, the A-line skirt is a versatile shape that forms the foundation for many styles. Play with pleats and pockets to develop it further. This sharp shape is best when cut in a firm fabric such as denim, cotton twill, or wool gabardine.

MORE IDEAS

> Cut the yoke double and bag out to create a neat finish.

> You can either place the CF on the fold of the fabric or add a seam allowance to your pattern and top-stitch for extra detail.

> You can pivot farther from the yoke line (points i and j) to create more fullness in the skirt.

Creating the pattern

Starting with the skirt section of the Darted Dress sloper and working on the front and back at the same time:

Yoke

1. Line up the back and front slopers side by side and decide on the length of your skirt.

2. Make the yoke:
   ▸ Starting at the CF, mark a point 3–4 in. (7.5–10 cm) down from the waist (a).
   ▸ On the front side seam, mark a point 2½ in. (6.5 cm) down from the waist (b).
   ▸ On the back side seam, mark a point 2½ in. (6.5 cm) down from the waist (c).
   ▸ At the CB, mark a point 2½ in. (6.5 cm) down from the waist (d).
   ▸ Join the dots (ab, cd), cut, and separate from the rest of the skirt sloper. You will now have a yoke in four parts.

3. Keeping the CF and CB straight, pivot the side pieces to close the darts. You will now have a front yoke and a back yoke. Curve off waist and yoke seams on the new pattern pieces.

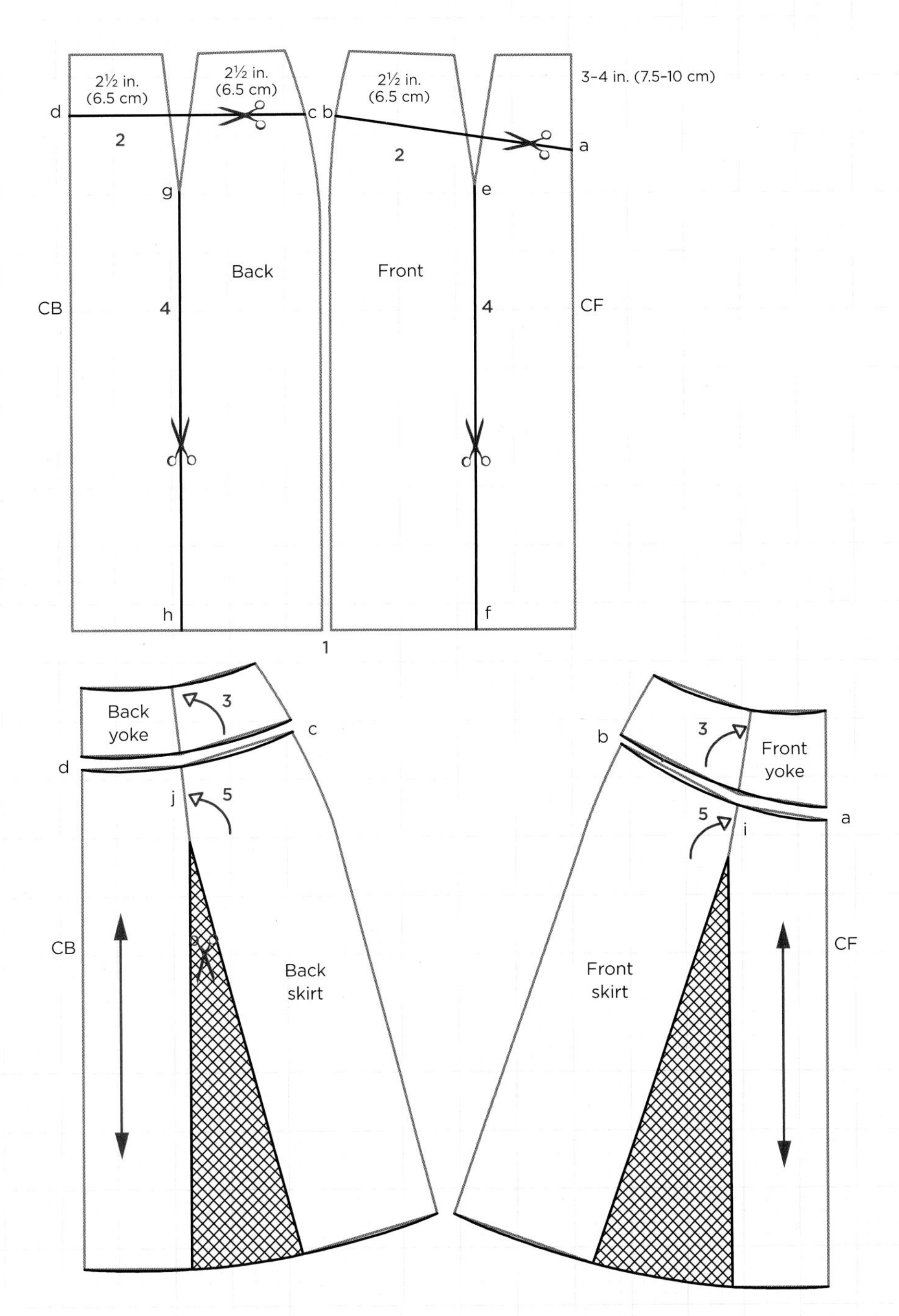

Skirt

4. Draw a line through the center of the front and back darts to the hem (ef, gh), cut, and separate.

5. Keeping the CF and CB straight, pivot the side pieces to close the darts. This creates a triangular gap in the middle of each skirt section, which will evenly distribute the extra fullness and create the A-line shape. Curve and smooth the hems and hip seams.

Godet Skirt

The term *godet* refers to the triangular inserts that add a flourish and a swish to the classic pencil-shaped skirt. Godets are a great way to use up fabric scraps and can be cut as minimal or as full as you like. This is a style you can really have fun with—try it short and flirty or ankle-length and elegant—and don't forget to twirl!

TIPS

> There are two ways to construct a godet skirt: You can create inserts as in this example, or create panels (see page 50) and insert them in between the seams.

> Iron on a square of interfacing at the tip of the godet to strengthen the join.

Creating the pattern

Starting with the skirt section of the Darted Dress sloper:

Working on front and back

1. Decide on the length of your skirt—you are going to cut into the hem, so you cannot change this later. Waist to hem on this US size 6/UK size 10 example is 22 in. (56 cm).
2. Follow the steps on page 44 to make a Pencil Skirt, omitting the kick pleat.

Front

3. Mark the placement of your godets: there should be six in total, equally placed along the hemline. To do this, divide the total width of the front skirt by three and measure this distance from the side seam (a). Remember your sloper is only working on half a skirt, so the distance from this point to the CF should be half the distance between your mark (a) and the side seam.
4. Draw a perpendicular line from point (a) to the length you would like your godet (ab). This should be roughly in line with where the pencil skirt starts to taper in at the side seam.
5. Mark 1 in. (2.5 cm) on either side of line (ab) on the hem and make a triangle (cbd).

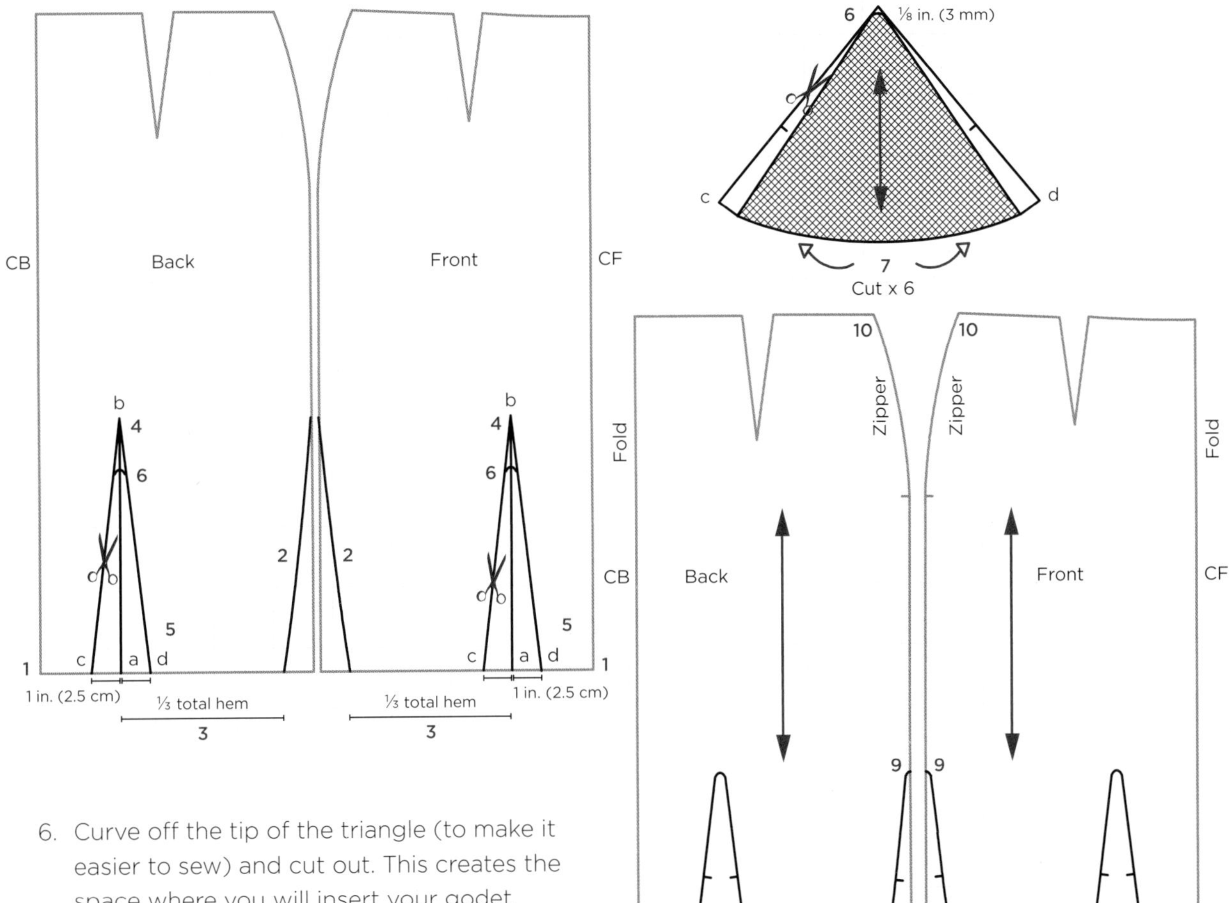

6. Curve off the tip of the triangle (to make it easier to sew) and cut out. This creates the space where you will insert your godet.

7. Take the triangle you have cut out of your skirt and cut down the centerline to within ⅛ in. (3 mm) of the tip. Pivot each section away from the center to form the fullness of your godet. The wider you make it, the fuller the effect. Curve off the space between the two sections to look like a slice of pie. Cut six godets.

8. As you have cut sections out from your hemline, you need to allow for this in the shape of your hem. Treat it like a facing: Trace and mirror along the hemline as shown in the diagram. Note that the godets should be finished with a pin hem.

Back

Repeat steps 3–7 as on the front skirt.

Side seams

9. The space for the godets in the side seam has already been made by tapering in the sloper to the pencil shape. Curve off the line where the top of the godet will be sewn in to match the front and back godets.

10. This design works best with a side zipper, so you should place both CB and CF on a fold.

To finish

Finish at the waist with a waistband or facing (see page 41).

Panel Skirt

This skirt adapts the classic pencil silhouette by raising the waistline and adding ruched front panels. The effect is a sexy, figure-hugging style that flatters existing curves or adds shape to straight hips. The skirt works beautifully in a fabric with a bit of stretch, or try combining two different fabrics for contrasting panels. A woven wool or cotton with spandex would work well for this type of skirt. The example shown uses stretch cotton sateene.

Creating the pattern

Starting with the Darted Dress sloper:

Front

1. Draw a line 2 in. (5 cm) above the waistline of your sloper and trace the skirt from here. This creates the extended waistline for the skirt.
2. Draw a line from the center of the dart to the hem (ab), cut, and separate to create two panels.
3. On the side front panel, draw six equally spaced parallel lines from the top of the skirt to the bottom of the dart.
4. Cut along each line from the dart to within ⅛ in. (3 mm) of the side seam.

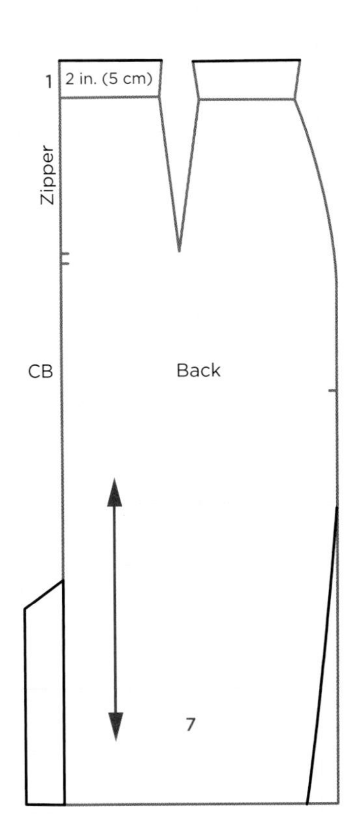

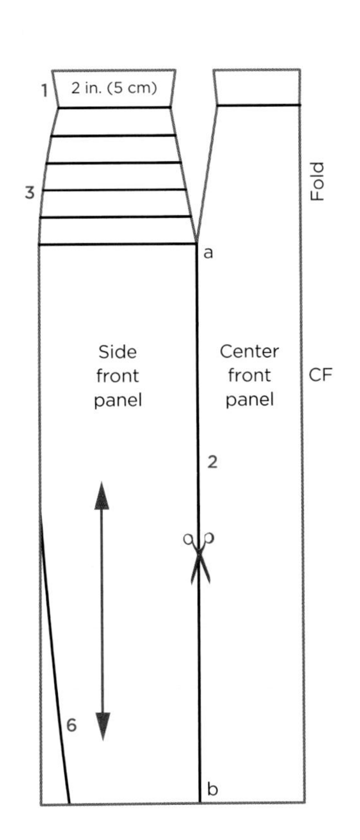

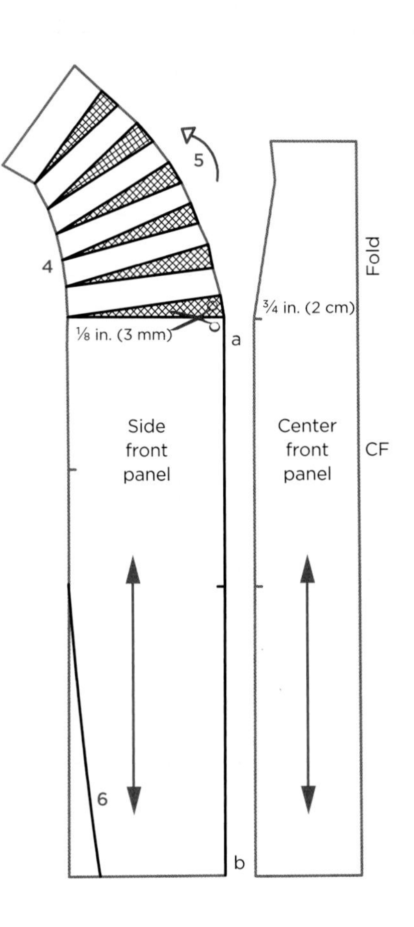

5. Open out each cut line to create $\frac{3}{4}$ in. (2 cm) gaps. It should look like an armadillo emerging from the top of your skirt sloper! This creates the extra fabric that will be gathered back into the center front panel to give the ruched effect.
6. Follow steps 2–3 as on the Pencil Skirt (page 44) to taper the hem.

Back

7. Follow step 4 and steps 2–3 as on the Pencil Skirt (page 44).

TIP

To finish the skirt at the waist, you can either use bias binding or trace a facing from the waistline.

Tulip Skirt

This is another variation on the classic pencil skirt. The pleats give a sculptural effect that adds depth to both plain and printed fabrics. Depending on your fabric, the pleats at the waist can be subtle and elegant or fun and flamboyant: The world is your tulip!

TIP

Fold pleats toward the center (the opposite way to that by which you pivoted them).

Creating the pattern

Starting with the skirt section of the Darted Dress sloper:

Front and back

1. Follow the instructions on pages 44–45 to draft a pencil skirt. On this example the width of the waistband has been increased.

Front

2. Mark your pleats:
   ▸ Pleat 1—on a new piece of pattern paper, draw a vertical line the length of your skirt at the CF fold (ab), and place your pencil skirt pattern on this line.
   ▸ Pleat 2—on the pencil skirt pattern, draw a straight line from the bottom of the dart to the hem (cd).
   ▸ Pleat 3—on the pencil skirt pattern, draw a straight line from the middle point of the side waist (e) to two-thirds of the way down the side seam (f).

3. Pivot your pattern—remember, the more you pivot, the wider your pleat. These are the measurements used on the US size 6/ UK size 10 skirt in the photograph.
   ▸ Pivot pleat 1—pivot the whole skirt from the CF hem away from your vertical line (ab) by 4 in. (10 cm). This forms your center pleat.
   ▸ Pivot pleat 2—cut through the dart and down line (cd) to within ⅛ in. (3 mm) of the hem. Pivot this section away from the CF by 6 in. (15 cm). This forms your second pleat.

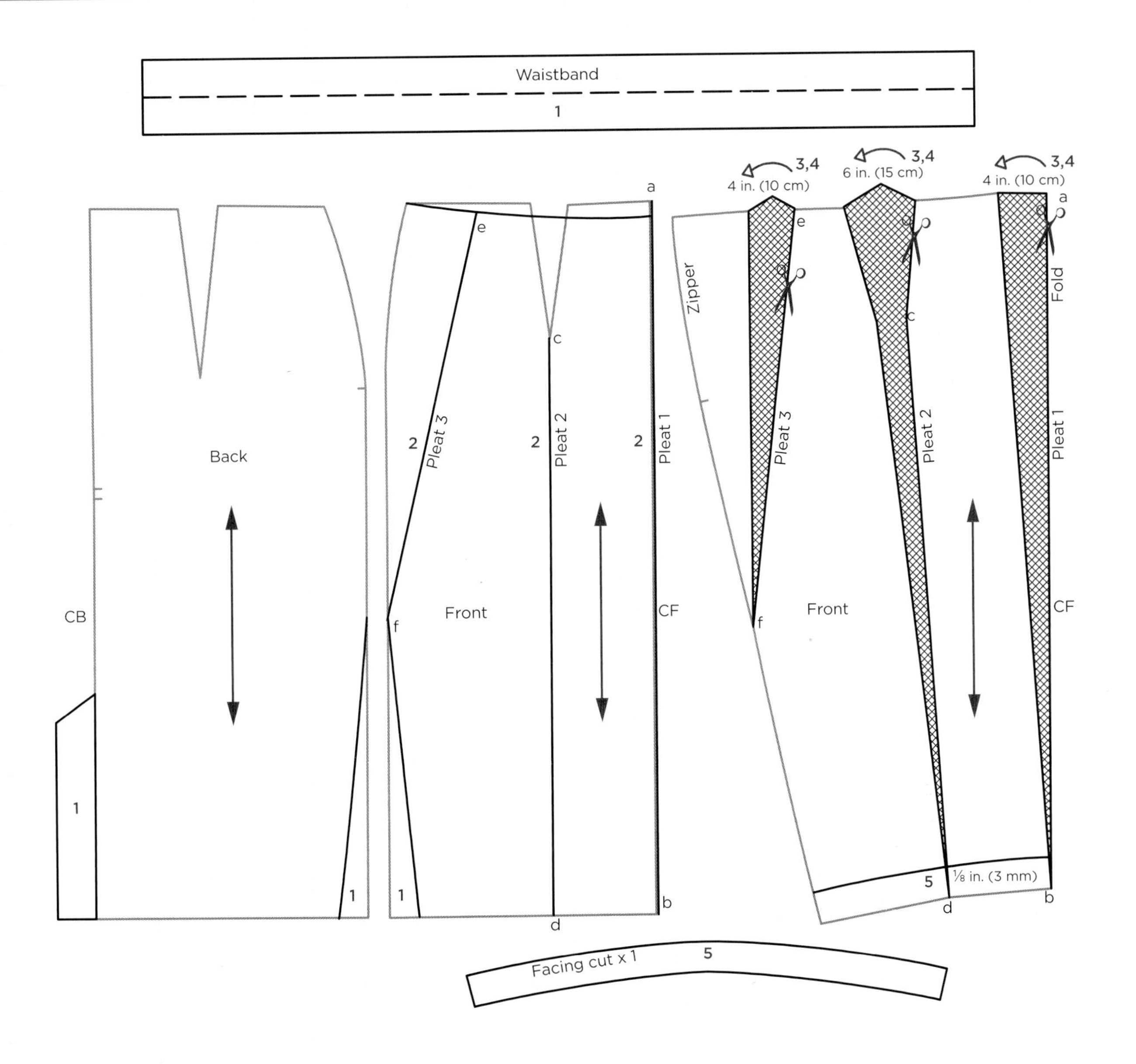

▸ Pivot pleat 3—cut down line (ef) to within ⅛ in. (3 mm) of the side seam. Pivot this section 4 in. (10 cm) away from the CF to form your third pleat. You have now created your Tulip Skirt pattern.

4. Draw around the adaptations you made to create the tulip shape onto the new piece of paper below. The easiest way to shape the tops of the pleats is to cut out your pattern with extra paper at the waist, fold the pleats in place toward the CF, and draw a smooth waistline, then add your seam allowance and cut again. When you unfold the pattern, your pleats will have perfect hats!

5. Smooth the hem and trace a facing (see page 41).

Semicircle Skirt

This skirt works best in a fabric with a nice heavy drape, for example, viscose. It is a flattering style because the yoke makes it skim over the stomach and hips (unlike the Full Circle Skirt overleaf, which juts straight out from the waist). You can adjust the fullness by altering the angle of the pivot. The button stand down the side seam is a good excuse to raid your button box.

BUTTON STAND

> Add some interfacing to your button stand to support the buttons and buttonholes.

> If you choose contrasting-colored buttons, a nice extra touch is to match your buttonhole thread to the buttons instead of the skirt fabric.

Creating the pattern

The front and back of this skirt pattern are identical. Starting with the skirt section of the Darted Dress sloper, front only:

Separating the yoke

1. Draw a horizontal line across the sloper at the bottom of the dart (ab), cut, and separate from the rest of the skirt.
2. Keeping the CF straight, pivot the side piece toward the CF to close the dart: this creates the yoke.

Adding fullness to the skirt

3. Draw a vertical line from the bottom of the waist dart to the hem (cd) and cut along this line from the hem to within ⅛ in. (3 mm) of the waist dart.
4. Keeping the CF straight, pivot the side skirt piece away from the CF to approximately a 45-degree angle. The more you pivot, the more swish you will get, but it is a good idea to check the width of your fabric at this point.
5. To make sure you have an even spread of fullness throughout the skirt, add a triangle to the side seam of your skirt section. To do this, trace half the triangle created by the space between the pivoted sections in step 4 and add this to the side seam.

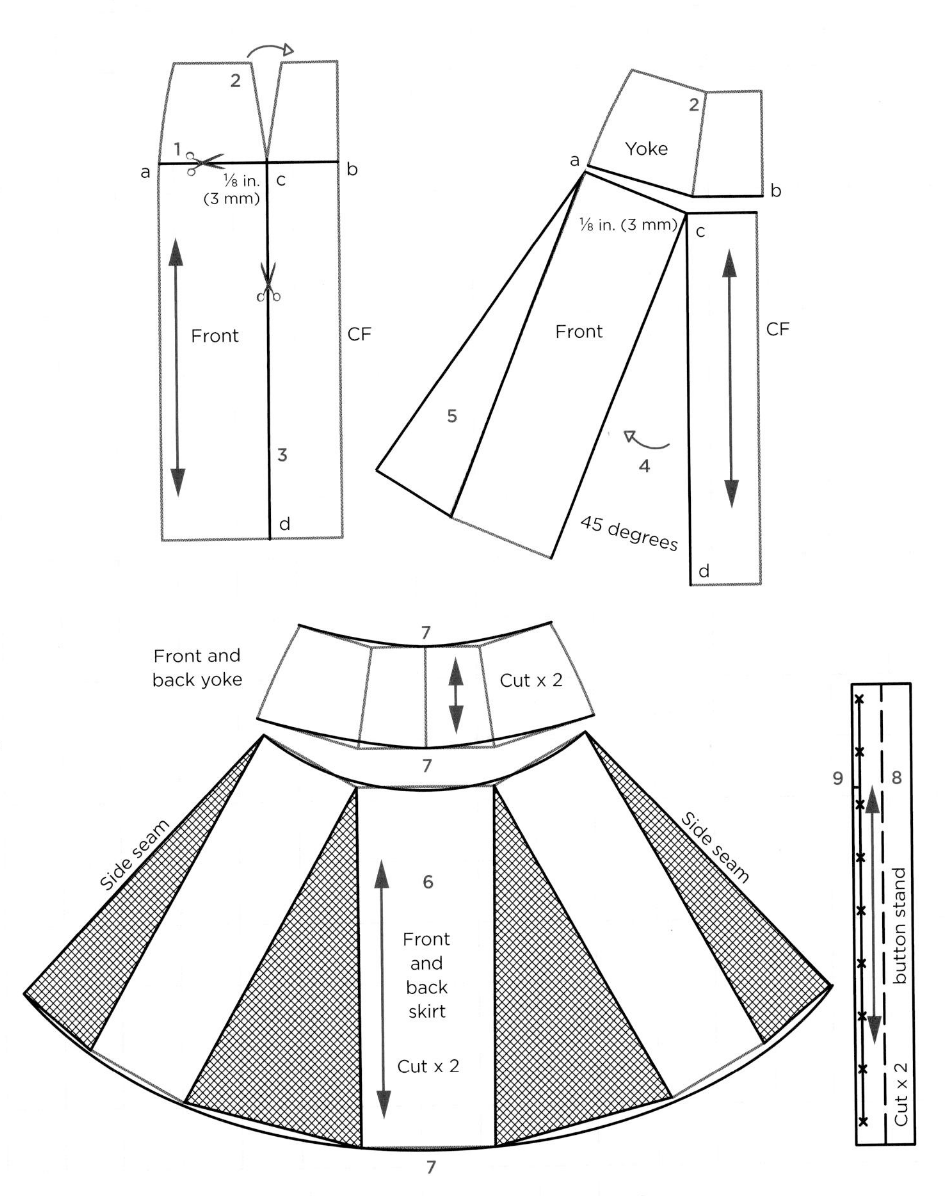

6. At this point you can convert your quarter-skirt pattern into a half-skirt pattern, as the front and back are the same. To do this, draw around the quarter-skirt pattern, flip on the CF, and then draw around it again.
7. Curve off all the edges of the pattern except the side seams.

Button stand

8. Draft a rectangle for your button stand:
   - length = length of the yoke side seam + length of the skirt side seam
   - width = 3 in. (7.5 cm)

   Mark a fold line down the center of the rectangle and distribute buttons evenly.
9. Remember to mark a notch on the button stand where the yoke side seam meets the skirt side seam.

Full Circle Skirt

This classic fifties silhouette will look great made up in a cotton print for summer. For something a little different, you could add this skirt to the bodice of the Strapless Dress on page 102 or try making it with several layers of chiffon for a decadent evening skirt. If you cut one layer of lining fabric and several layers of net, this makes a great petticoat to go under your prom dress, too.

Creating the pattern

Starting with the skirt section of the Darted Dress sloper, front only:

To create a quarter-skirt pattern

1. Decide on the length of your skirt.
2. Draw a line from the bottom of the waist dart to the hem and separate into two pieces.
3. Close the waist dart. Note: If you stop at this step, you will have a skirt with a nicely balanced flare.
4. Continue to pivot the side panel from the dart point (c) until it reaches 90 degrees from the CF.
5. Square off the side seam dart (which will now be a horizontal line) so you have a 90-degree angle at the waistline.

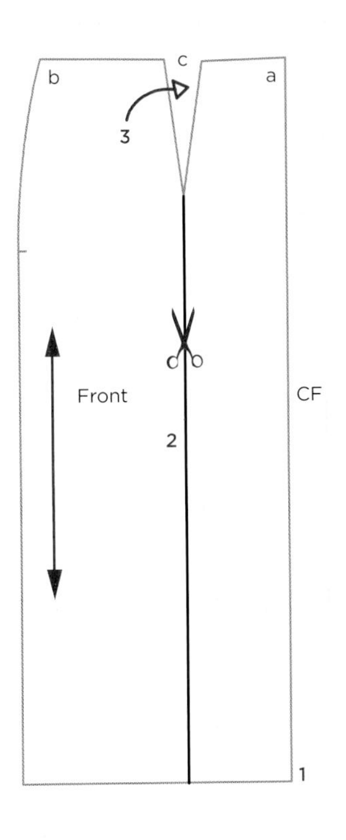

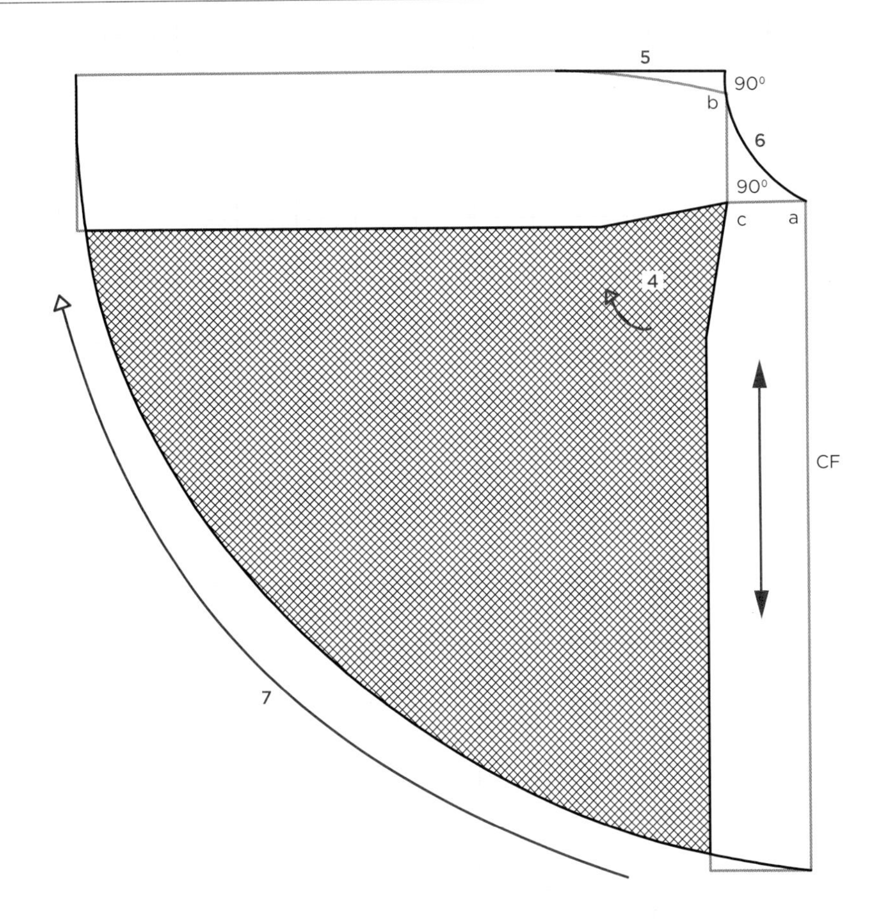

6. Turn this angle into a curve. Measure to check that it equals a quarter of your waist measurement (ac+bc).
7. Curve off the hem between the two pieces.
8. Hang from a skirt hanger or dress stand for a couple of days to allow the bias sections of the fabric to drop before you hem. You will be surprised how much it drops! To even out the hem, either enlist a volunteer to measure up from the floor with a long ruler and mark with pins, or lay the original pattern on top of your fabric and trim.

CUTTING OUT

This pattern creates a quarter of a circle skirt. How you cut it out will depend on the length of your skirt and the width of your fabric. For a knee-length skirt in wide fabric, you may be able to cut it out as a complete circle and add to an elastic waistband (you may need to lower the waist slightly). Otherwise, cut as two halves or four quarters and put a closure into one of the seams.

Tube Skirt

This is a quick, easy skirt—great for a beginner or anyone in a hurry! The pattern uses the Dartless Dress Stretch sloper (page 26), so the fabric needs to be stretchy—stretch jersey with a touch of spandex is ideal as it will hold its shape well. Look out for a bold or unusual print. Remember, you're only using the skirt section of this sloper.

Creating the pattern

Front and back are the same. Starting with the Dartless Dress Stretch sloper, back only:

Waistband

1. Decide on the width of your waistband—4 in. (10 cm) is a good starting point for a wide fold-over waistband. Measure this distance up from the waistline of the sloper and draw a horizontal line across the bodice (ab).
2. Trace and mirror the waistband on the CB/CF (bc) to create a whole pattern piece.
3. Mirror again along the top line of the waistband and mark as a fold line (abd).

FOLD-OVER WAISTBAND

Fold the waistband in half along the fold line (wrong sides together) and insert upside-down into the top of the skirt so the waistband is inside the skirt with all raw edges together. Sew (or serge) the waistband so the seam is on the outside of the skirt—the seam will be hidden when you fold the waistband down.

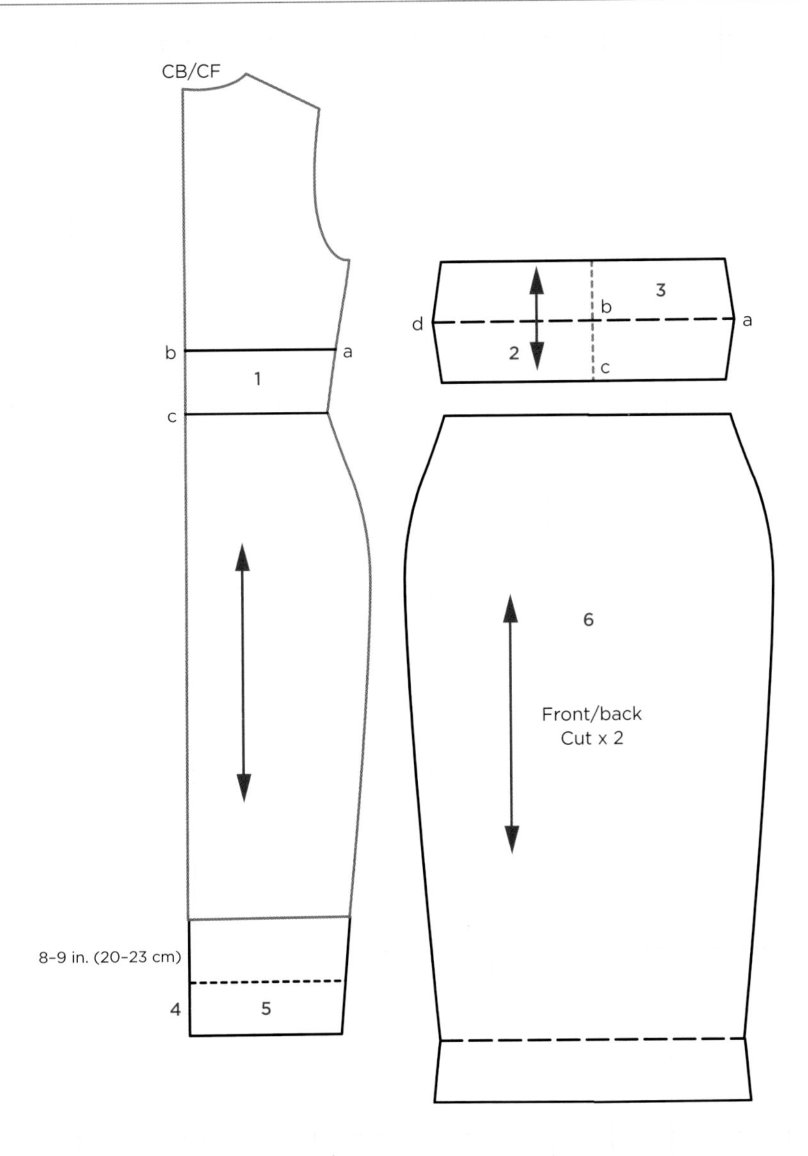

Skirt

4. For a calf-length skirt like the one in the photograph, extend the length of the skirt by 8–9 in. (20–23 cm) on the centerline, draw across at 90 degrees, and taper the side seam to meet at the hem.

5. The wide-shaped hem needs to mirror the taper of the skirt. The easiest way to achieve this is to trace and mirror along the hem like a self-facing (see page 41).

6. Trace the skirt from waist to hem and mirror on the CF/CB to create a whole pattern piece.

Bubble Skirt

The bubble skirt is a young, fun shape that works best short and makes a great statement at a party. For the pattern, you create two skirts: an inner fitted tube and the outer bubble shape that puffs out from it. The outer skirt needs fabric that will hold the shape of the bubble—try organza or taffeta. Use something soft and stretchy on the inside.

SEWING THE SKIRT

Gather the hem of the outer skirt to fit the hem of the inner skirt and seam together. Gather the waists of both the outer and inner skirts to fit the length of the waistband.

Creating the pattern

Starting with the skirt section of the Darted Dress sloper and working on the front and back at the same time:

Inner skirt

1. Bring front and back slopers together on the side seam and measure two-thirds of the way down from the waist to mark the length of the inner skirt. Draw a line across front and back slopers at this point (ab).
2. Trace front and back in one piece, ignoring the waist darts and the gap between the front and back side seams.

Outer skirt (bubble)

3. Returning to the full-length original sloper, trace front and back as separate pieces and draw lines from the bottom of the waist darts to the hem (cd, ef).
4. Cut down these lines and separate by 4 in. (10 cm), keeping waist and hems aligned.
5. Pivot the side seam skirt sections away from the CB/CF at the waist until the gap at the hem measures 8 in. (20 cm). This will add extra fullness that will be gathered onto the inner skirt to create the bubble shape.
6. Curve off the hem and waistline.

Waistband

7. Draft a straight waistband 2–3 in. (5–7.5 cm) wide. The length should be your waist + 1¼ in. (3 cm) overlap for closure.

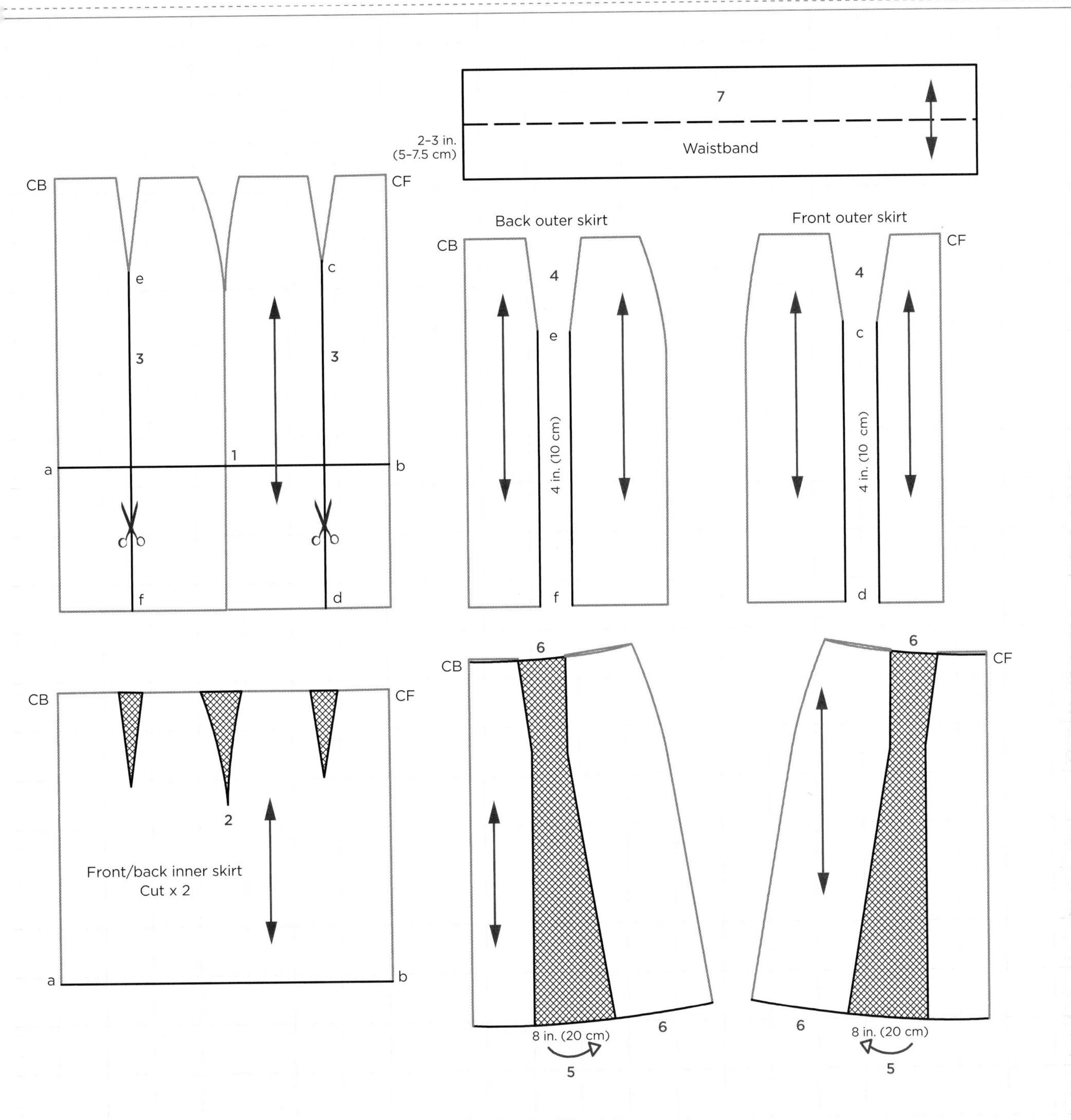

7
2–3 in.
(5–7.5 cm)
Waistband
CB
CF
e
c
3
3
a
1
b
f
d
Back outer skirt
Front outer skirt
CB
CF
4
4
e
c
4 in. (10 cm)
4 in. (10 cm)
f
d
CB
CF
2
Front/back inner skirt
Cut x 2
a
b
6
CB
6
CF
8 in. (20 cm)
6
5
6
8 in. (20 cm)
5

Dirndl

You probably made a skirt like this in sewing class at school. It is a very simple pattern—a long rectangle gathered onto a waistband—but if you draft it from your sloper, you will be sure of a good fit and well-proportioned finish. This skirt is great for showing off a nice print or as a simple base that you can embellish before sewing in the gathers. Why not try adding trimmings or rows of fancy machine stitches on the hem, or replacing the tie waist with wide elastic?

Creating the pattern

Starting with the skirt section of the Darted Dress sloper:

Front and back

1. Draw a straight line from the bottom of the waist dart to the hem (ab), cut, and separate into two sections.
2. Pull the two sections apart as wide as you like: wider for fine fabric, less for bulky fabric.
3. Reshape the side seam: Draw a straight line from the side seam waist to the hem (cd).

Waistband

4. Draft a straight waistband 2–3 in. (5–7.5 cm) wide. The length should be your waist + 1¼ in. (3 cm) overlap for closure. The ties for the bow should be made separately and be added on top of the waistband (see Tie Waistband, opposite).

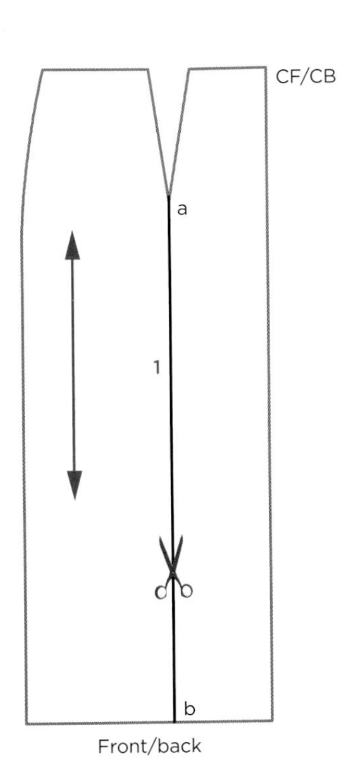

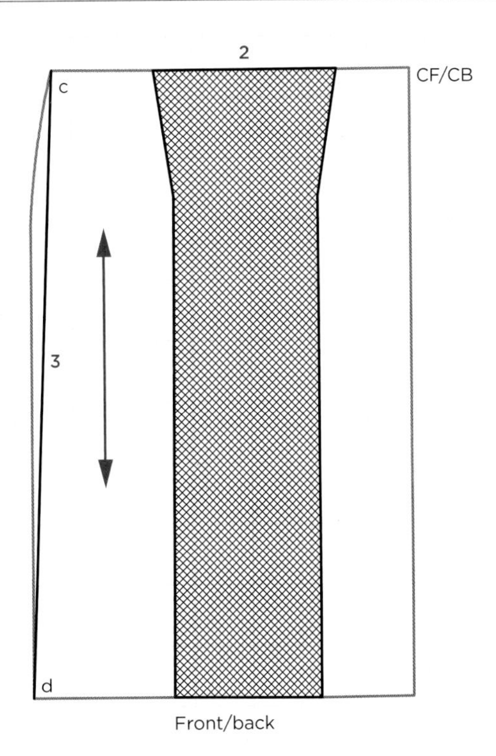

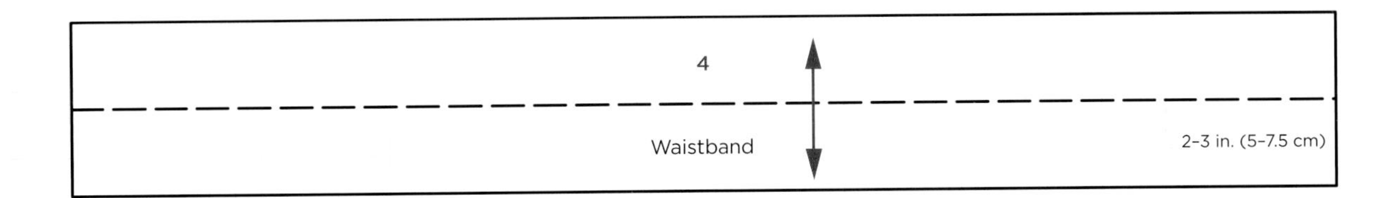

TIE WAISTBAND

The waistband will sit best if you add the ribbons on top of your waistband 1 in. (2.5 cm) to either side of the closure to leave room for the knot of the bow.

POCKETS

How about adding some pockets? Download the In-Seam or Patch Pocket slopers seen on page 31. You'll find instructions and tips for sewing them in the Finishes for Skirts chapter, pages 76–77.

Tiered Skirt

The tiered skirt is a hippie favorite with a great laid-back appearance, and all you need is some simple math to figure it out! The fabric should be something soft that will gather well—try a light cotton or jersey, or how about broderie anglaise for peasant chic? Play with patterns or use alternating stripes as shown here.

GATHERING

Gather by hand or by machine. Your machine may have a special gathering foot. If not, set your machine to the longest straight stitch and sew two parallel lines without backstitching at the ends, but rather doing a backstitch or two as you pass the center point. Push the fabric along the threads from both ends toward the center to space your gathers evenly.

Creating the pattern

Length

Decide on the total length you want your tiered skirt to be and divide this by three (or the number of tiers you want—the example shown here has three).

Example:
If you want your skirt to be 36 in. (90 cm) long:

36 ÷ 3 = 12

- Length of Tier 1 = 12 in. (30 cm) + waistband + seam allowance
- Length of Tier 2 = 12 in. (30 cm) + seam allowance
- Length of Tier 3 = 12 in. (30 cm) + seam allowance

Width

Figure out the width of each tier:

- Width of Tier 1 = 1½ x hip measurement + seam allowance
- Width of Tier 2 = 1½ x Tier 1 measurement + seam allowance
- Width of Tier 3 = 1½ x Tier 2 measurement + seam allowance

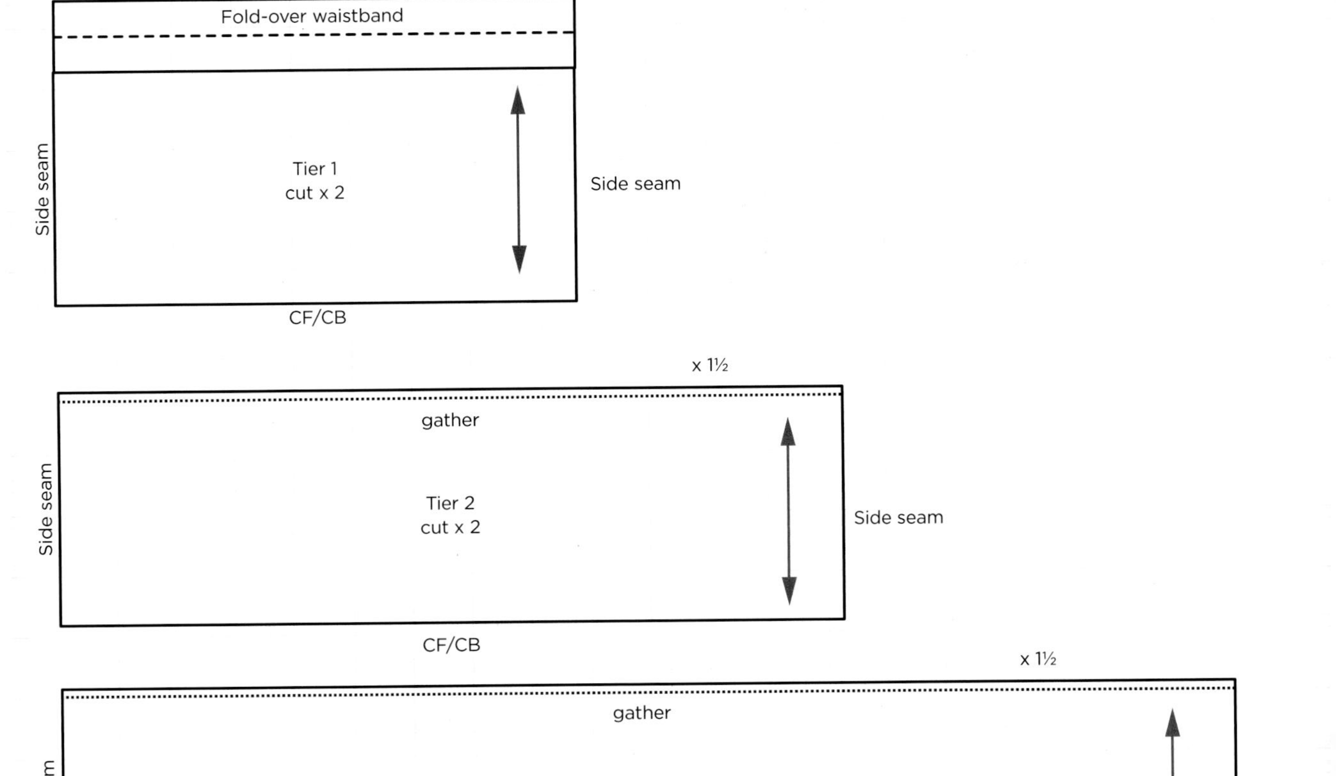

Example:
If your hip = 40 in. (100 cm)

- Tier 1 = 60 in. (150 cm) + seam allowance
- Tier 2 = 90 in. (225 cm) + seam allowance
- Tier 3 = 135 in. (337.5 cm) + seam allowance

Depending on the width of your fabric, you may have to join some widths with seams.

Elastic waistband

Choose a fairly wide and firm elastic to hold up a long skirt. Cut the elastic slightly smaller than your waist and the weight of the fabric will stretch it a little. Turn the top and then thread through the elastic.

Box-Pleat Skirt

This skirt has the neat classic fit of the Pencil Skirt, but with the swish of pleats at the hem. You can vary the proportions once you have established the basic style. Any fabric that will hold a pleat will work well, or you could try different fabrics for the top part and the pleats.

TIPS

> It's much easier to press in the pleats if you have already stitched the hem.

> A braid or cord between the two sections of the skirt adds a fancy touch.

Creating the pattern

This skirt is essentially the skirt section of the Darted Dress sloper plus a very long rectangle.

Front and back

1. Bring together the front and back side seams of the skirt section of the Darted Dress sloper and trace them on one piece of paper, flipping on the CF/CB so that you have the whole skirt (rather than just half).
2. Decide the level at which you want your pleats to start (two-thirds from the waist works well) and draw a line across the front and back (ab). Cut and separate so you have one long rectangle that runs the width of the whole skirt (abcd).
3. Insert your pleats (here comes the math!):

   To make a 1 in. (2.5 cm) box pleat, you need to add 4 in. (10 cm) of fabric at each pleat. There are a number of ways to do this.

Method 1—Collage

Divide your rectangle into eight equal sections and draw vertical lines to mark (P1, P2, P3, P4, P5, P6, P7, P8). Cut along each line and insert 4 in. (10 cm) of extra pattern paper at each pleat.

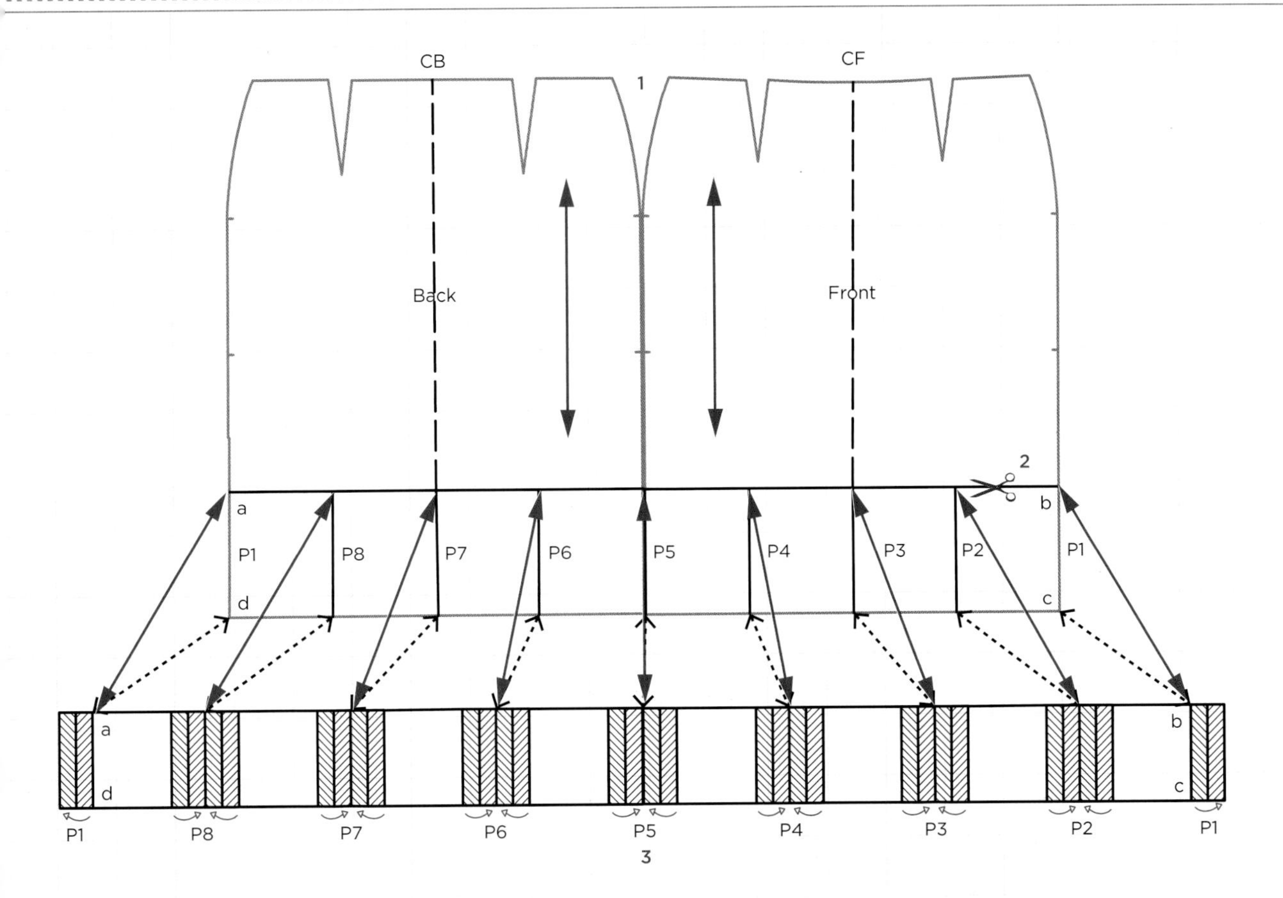

Method 2—Math

▸ Calculate the width of your rectangle. Decide the number of pleats you want (in this case, 8), multiply this by the fabric needed for each pleat (4 in. /10 cm) and add to the total length of your hem (ab x 2).

▸ Calculate the gap between pleats. Divide the total length of your hem (back and front) by the number of pleats you want (8): total length of hem ÷ number of pleats.

▸ Finally, mark the pleats and gaps on your extended rectangle.

NOTE

To make a box pleat, fold the outer edges of the pleat equally into the center point. Pleat 1 (P1) is spread equally across both ends of the rectangle.

Kilt

Plaid is the obvious choice for a kilt, and the checks provide useful guidelines when marking up the pleats. The fabric needs to be something firm that presses well—try wool or silk taffeta. Cut on the cross grain to avoid adding seams. Use a ruler, calculator, and iron when sewing, and don't forget to hem the kilt before pressing in the pleats. If you measure the length from the selvage, you only need to turn the hem once.

Creating the pattern

Start with the Darted Dress sloper and work on the front and back at the same time:

Skirt

1. Bring front and back skirt slopers together on the side seam. Ignore the darts and the gap at the side seam between the two pieces so that you have a rectangle.
2. Draw a line from waist to hem down the middle of the front waist dart (ab). Trace and mirror along the CF to create the overlap for the front of the kilt.
3. Decide on the length of your skirt, measure down from the waist, and cut across.

Pleats

4. The kilt pleats are formed using knife pleats, each needing two folds, so three extra widths of fabric. For 1½ in. (4 cm) wide pleats, this means that each pleat requires 4½ in. (12 cm) of fabric (1½ x 3 = 4½; 4 x 3 = 12).

   To calculate the pleated section of the kilt:
   ▸ Measure the distance from the front dart line (ab) to the CB.
   ▸ Divide this measurement by the desired width of each pleat 1½ in. (4 cm)—this will give you the number of pleats required.
   ▸ Multiply this number by the amount of fabric required for each pleat.

   For example, if the distance from ab to CB = 12 in. (30 cm) and desired pleat width = 1½ in. (4 cm), then number of pleats = 8 (12 divided by 1½). Multiply number of pleats by amount of fabric required (8 x 4½ in.) = 36 in. (91 cm).

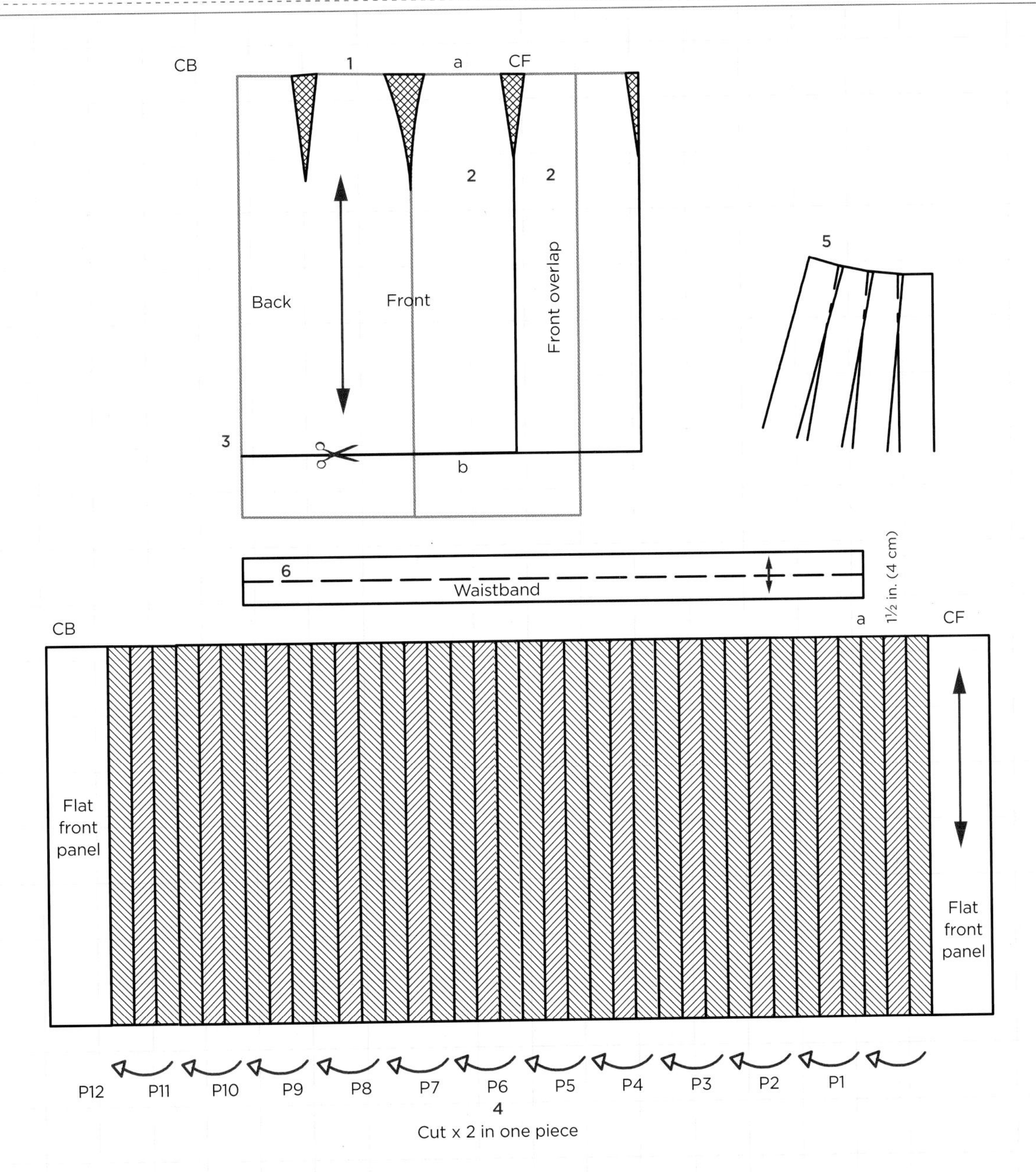

Extend the pleated section of the skirt between the front waist dart (ab) and the CB to this measurement. Cut double, mirroring on the CB so you have one long piece with a flat panel at either end of the pleated section.

5. Press in all the pleats and pin or tack in place from hem to hip level. Once you have pressed all the pleats across the whole skirt, repeat the process, slightly overlapping each pleat from hip to waistline until it fits onto the waistband. When you pull out all the tacks/pins, you'll see your rectangle transformed into a curve at the hem.

Waistband

6. Draft a straight waistband 1½ in. (4 cm) wide. The length should match the waistline of the whole kilt (your waist measurement + the flat front panel overlap).

Chapter 4

Finishes for Skirts

Back Details

Fan back

The fan back detail can be added to the Pencil Skirt on page 44 instead of a kick pleat. This version is knee-length, but it would look equally great on a midi or ankle-length skirt. A knee-to-ankle fan back would add a very fancy swish to an evening or wedding dress.

Instructions

Starting with the skirt section of the Darted Dress sloper, extended to the length you want:

1. Taper in the hem.
2. Decide where you want the panel for the fan back detail to start and how wide you want it to be at the top (ab).
3. Join the bottom of the waist dart to the start of the fan back panel (bc). A slight curve is flattering.
4. Join the top of the fan back to the hem (bd).
5. Cut along the lines and divide into three panels.
6. Add the fullness to the fan back: Draw a line down the center of the fan back panel, cut and pivot to add the required fullness at the hem.
7. For additional fullness, add further triangles to the outer edges of the panel.

FAN BACK TIPS

> Mark notches on the skirt panels before you separate them.

> Add cord, ribbon, or embellishment across the top of the fan back panel (ab).

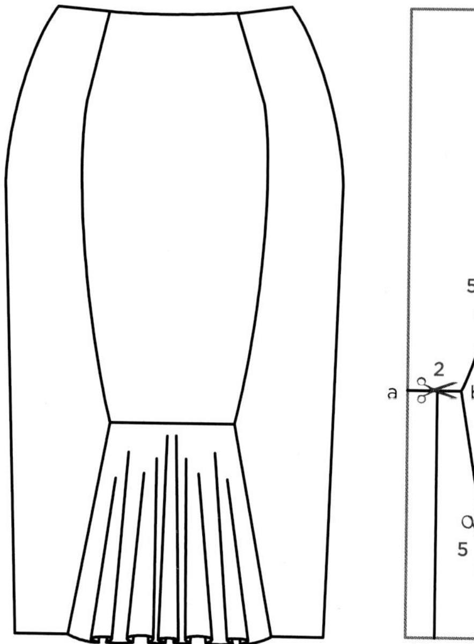

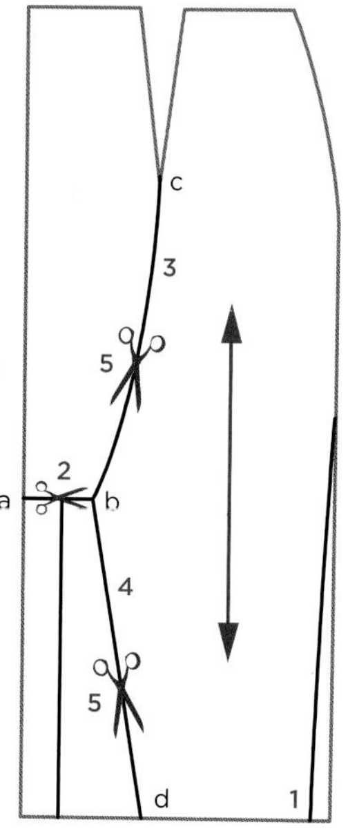

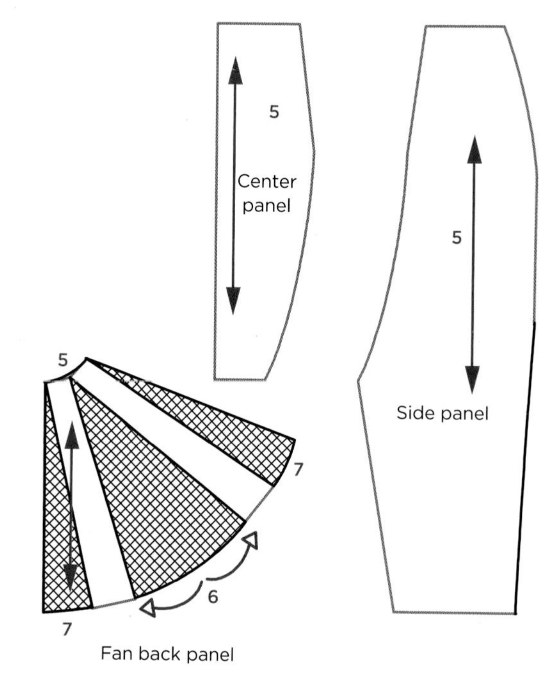

Fishtail

Another variation for the Pencil Skirt on page 44, the fishtail back detail also adds elegance and flare to long skirts. It will work on all but the bulkiest fabrics. Vary the angles to make more or less of a fishtail.

Instructions

1. Taper the hem.
2. Draw in the fishtail shape: Extend the CB back seam with a curve flaring out and down beyond the hemline, joining the tip of the curve back to the side seam at the hem. See the diagram to get a sense of the shape you want to create.

FISHTAIL TIPS

> As you now have a curved hem, you need to finish with a pin hem, curved facing, or raw edge.

> Use a French curve to create a smooth line.

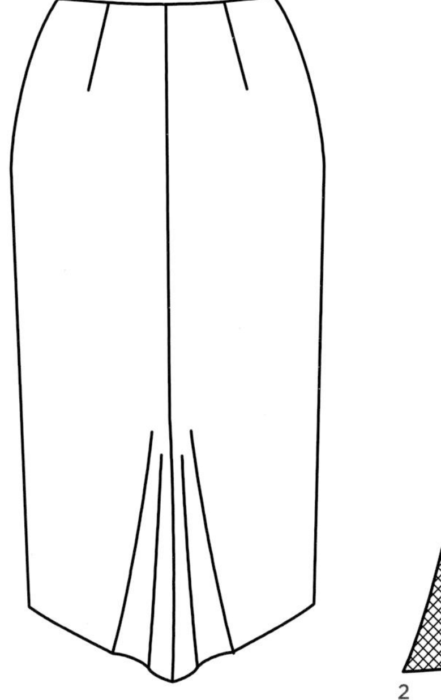

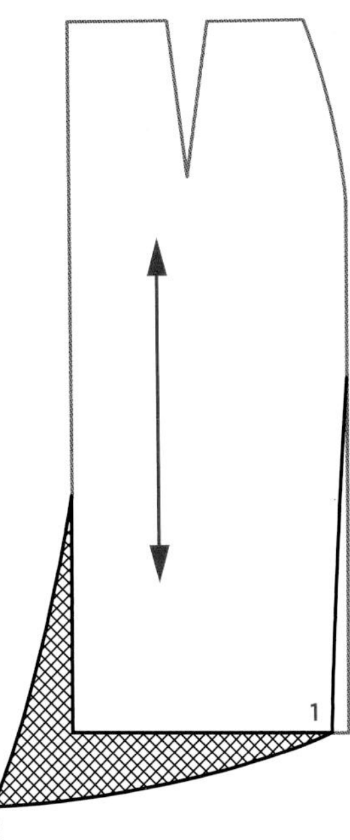

Front Details

Ruffle

You can insert a ruffle into any seam of a skirt—or indeed, create a new seam where you want to insert a ruffle. In this example it is inserted into a side panel on the Pencil Skirt (see page 44). Experiment with making the ruffle a different color or texture than the main skirt.

RUFFLE TIPS

> Finish with raw edges or a pin hem, or cut double and bag out if using fine fabric.

> Add more than one ruffle if you're inspired!

> The ruffle technique need not be confined to skirt panels—how about inserting one down the length of a sleeve, around a hem, or even along the edge of a collar?

Instructions

1. Start with the whole skirt front and split into two panels where you want the ruffle to sit (ab). In this example it is in line with the left waist dart, but it could be placed down the CF, on a side seam, or even diagonally across.
2. Draft a strip the length of the seam you will insert the ruffle into and the width you want it to be—approximately 3 in. (7.5 cm) is a good starting point.
3. Divide the strip into ten equal sections and cut across to within ⅛ in. (3 mm) of one edge.
4. Pivot each section until you have a doughnut shape with roughly equal distances between sections. When you come to sew, the inside edge of the doughnut should match the length of the seam, while the outer edge will flutter out to produce a perfect ruffle.
5. Shape the end for an elegant finish.

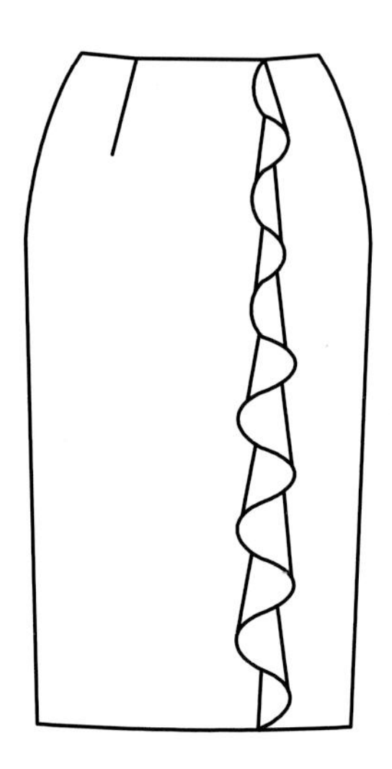

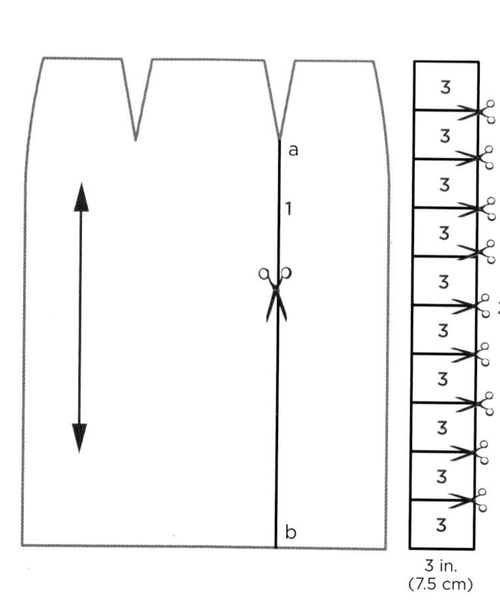

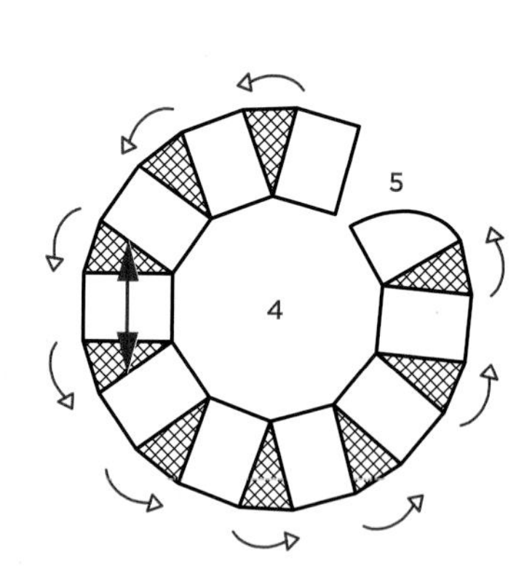

Wrap

This is a faux wrap detail because it is inserted into the side seam—so there is no chance of it becoming unwrapped! It works particularly well on the A-line Skirt (see page 46) and is a good way to show off a nice button. If you don't want to make a buttonhole, you could use a pin instead to hold the wrap in place.

Instructions

1. Trace the whole front of your skirt pattern (abcd).
2. On a new layer of paper, draft the desired shape of the wrap (aefd). This example is asymmetrical at the waist and hem.
3. Add a wide seam allowance on all edges of the wrap piece except on the side seam, mitering the corners.
4. Mark the position of the buttonhole (if using).

WRAP TIPS

> Instead of a wide hem you could draft a matching pattern piece as a lining and bag out.

> Add a square of interfacing or an extra piece of fabric on the inside of the skirt so the button doesn't tear through.

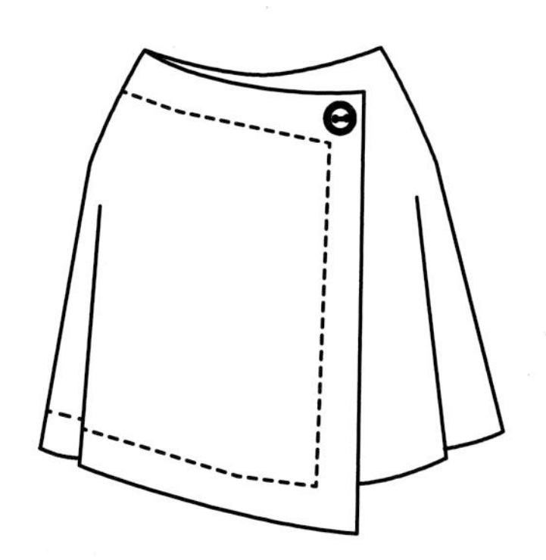

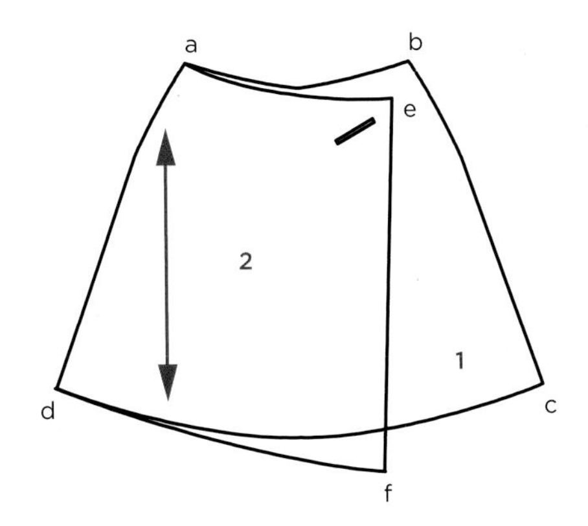

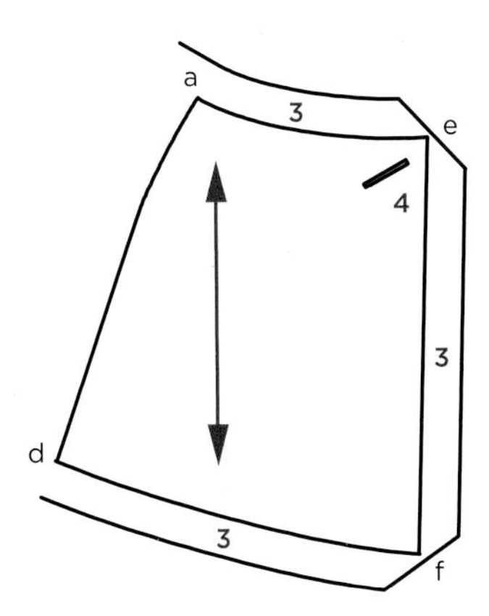

Pockets

Back pockets

Back pockets are easy to make and add a touch of fun to any skirt shape. The classic would be denim or corduroy with contrast stitching. It really is all up to you, so experiment with shape, size, fabrics, and closures—leather pocket on herringbone tweed, anyone?

Instructions

1. Draw the size and position of the pocket onto your skirt pattern and trace off (the diagram shows three example shapes).
2. You can add a self-facing at the top edge if it is straight.

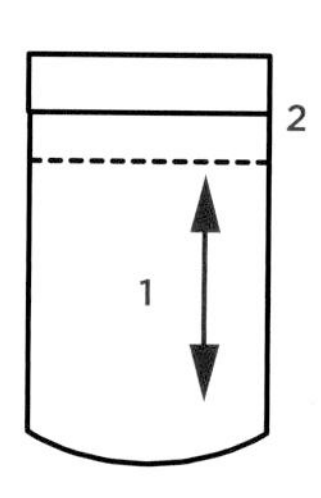

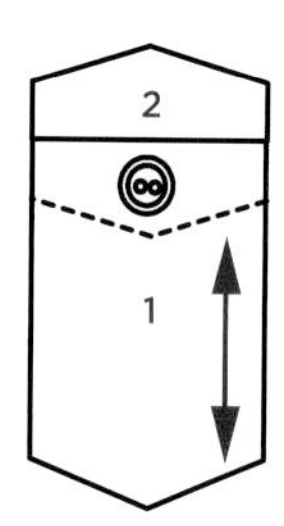

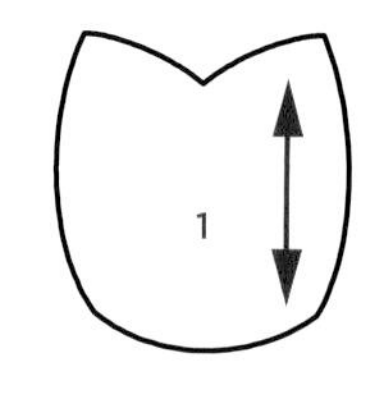

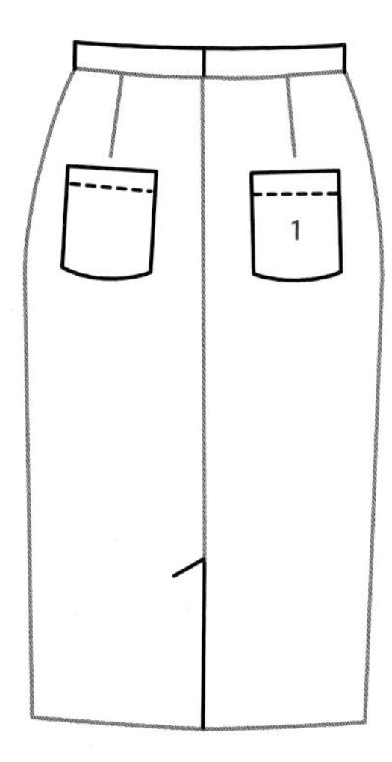

BACK POCKET TIPS

> Add interfacing to the self-facing so it does not stretch.

> Try out different shapes as shown in the diagram. Remember, curved edges cannot have self-facings, so bag out or finish with a binding.

Front pockets

If you like to put your hands in your pockets, this is the type for you! Whatever shape the opening, the principle is the same.

Instructions

You need three layers to form the pocket: the skirt front, the side pocket piece, and the pocket bag. On the skirt front pattern piece, trace off the section required for the pocket and follow the diagram shown opposite, top:

1. Skirt front: Draw a curve from the waistline to the side seam to form the shape of the pocket opening (ab). Cut and save for the side pocket piece.
2. Pocket bag: Draw another curve from the waistline to the side seam to form the depth of the pocket (cd) and trace off.
3. Side pocket piece: Trace off the pocket bag and join to the side pocket piece saved in step 1.

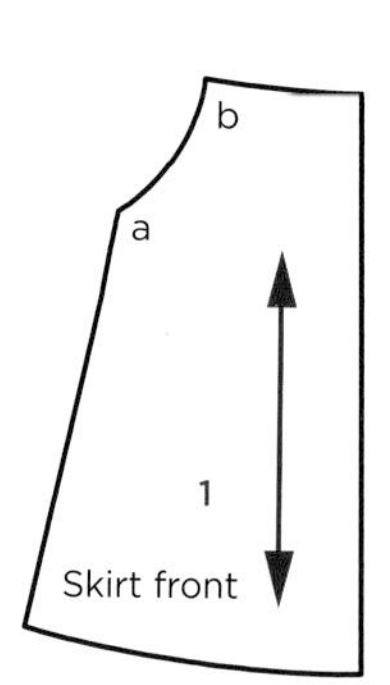

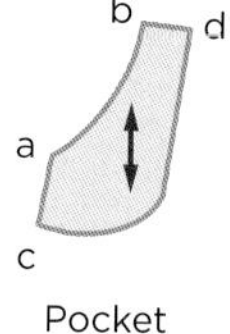

Pocket bag

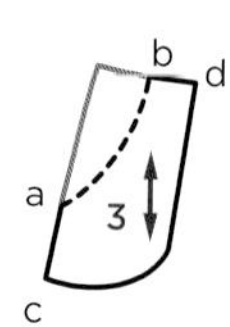

Side pocket piece

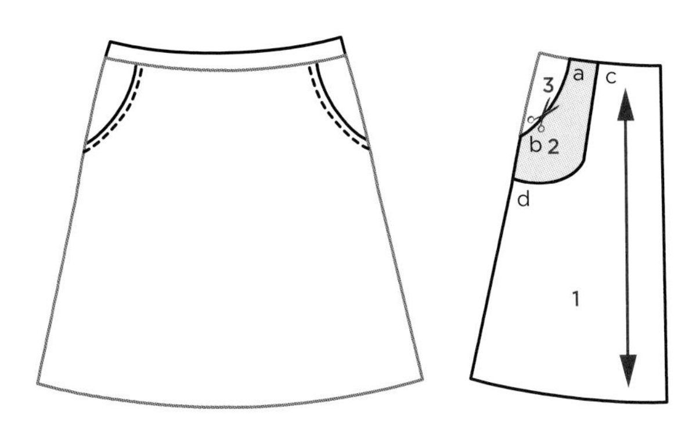

FRONT POCKET TIPS

> Add a strip of stay tape along the curved edge so it doesn't stretch if you put something bulky in it! Adding a decorative binding will have the same effect.

> If your fabric is thick or precious, make the pocket bag in plain cotton or lining fabric.

> Show off your pocket drafting skills by using a contrasting color for the side pocket piece.

In-seam pockets

If you want the practicality of pockets but don't want to make a feature of them, in-seam pockets are discreet and easy to make. Make them as deep as you need. Unlike the other pockets, these are grown on to the main pattern piece, so make sure you remember to match the front and back.

IN-SEAM POCKET TIPS

> When sewing the skirt, stitch the pocket down on the side seam by 1 in. (2.5 cm) at the top to make a neat opening (otherwise it would reach right up to the waist).

> You can trim down to a facing and complete the pocket with lining fabric if you prefer.

Instructions

1. Trace the shape of the pocket onto the skirt pattern, starting at the waistline and choosing your width and depth. The size of your hand is a good indication of how big the pockets should be!
2. Trace off and flip on the side seam to open like a book. The pocket should extend at an angle from the waist. When you fold it back, it will be sewn into the waistline, which will support the weight of the pocket.
3. Repeat on the back.

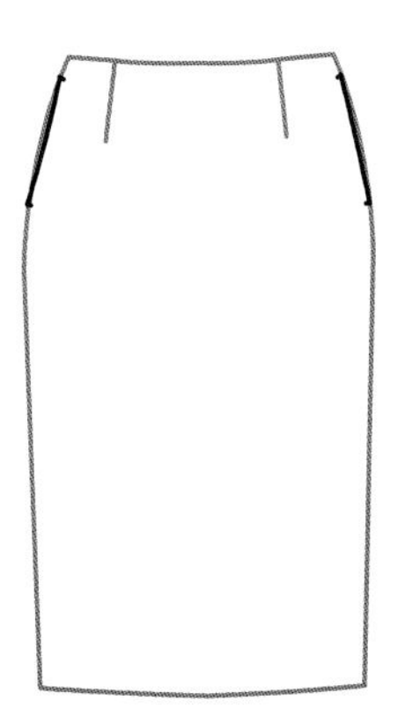

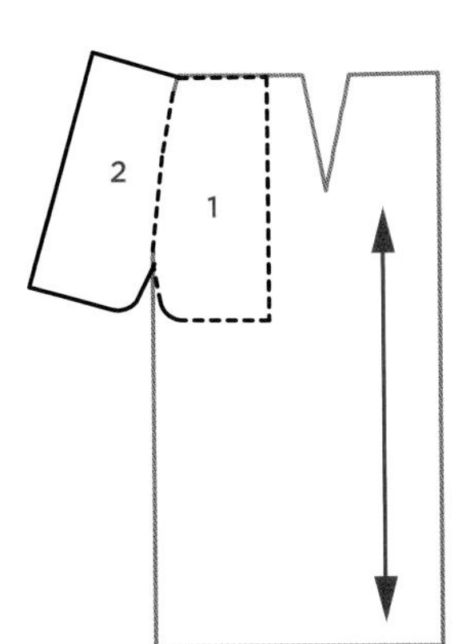

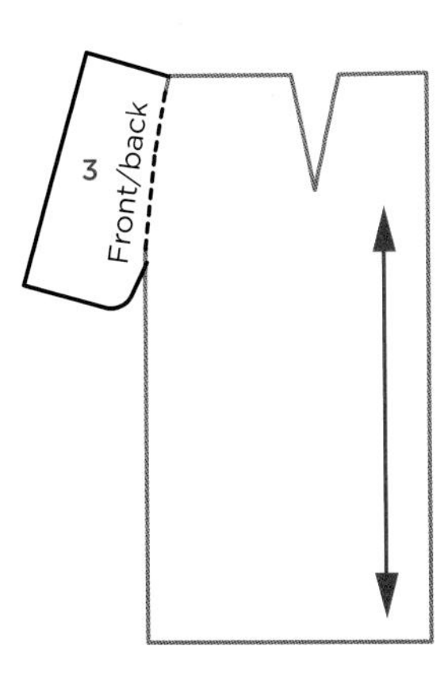

Chapter 5

Dresses

A NEW SURVEY OF SCIENCE
WALTER SHEPHERD
HARRAP

Pin-Tuck Shift Dress

The pin tucks radiating from the waist dart of this classic shift dress transform a simple shape into an elegant style, flattering both curvy and straight body types. The dress works well in a variety of fabrics: crisp silk shantung for evening, wool crepe for a smart day dress, or soft linen for a relaxed summer look. The pin tucks require some precision sewing, but the rest is straightforward. You could add a lining, or use one of the sleeve slopers to add sleeves.

Creating the pattern

Starting with the Darted Dress sloper (page 24) extended to knee length:

Front

1. Close the shoulder dart to create a side bust dart.
2. Shorten the bust dart by 1¼ in. (3 cm) from the bust point.
3. Draw in a boat neckline (see page 120).
4. Slide the waist dart toward the side seam by the width of the dart. The new dart should sit directly adjacent to the original. This makes room for the pin tucks. Shorten the waist dart by 1 in. (2.5 cm) at the bust point.
5. Trace off and mirror the pattern, joining at the CF to make a complete front. As this pattern is an asymmetric design, you will now work on the whole front rather than just half.
6. Draw eight lines radiating from the center of the left waist dart. Start at the waistline and work out, measuring equal distances above and below. These will be your pin tucks. When you sew in the dart, all the pin tuck ends will be neatly hidden inside the dart.

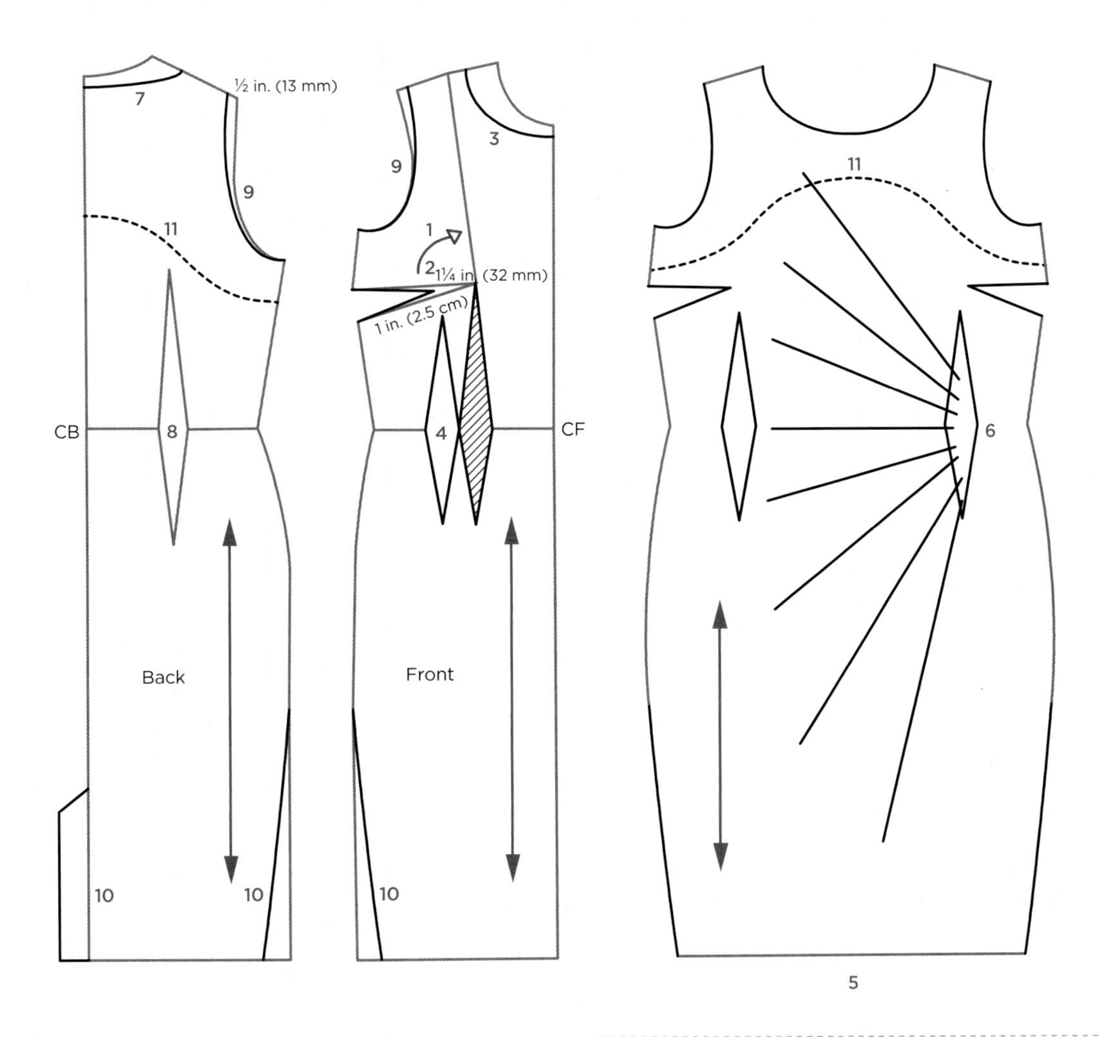

Back

7. Alter the neckline to match the front, making sure shoulder seams are of equal length.

8. Keep the dart as in the basic sloper.

Front and back

9. Narrow the armhole by ½ in. (13 mm) at the shoulder.

10. Follow instructions on page 44 for the Pencil Skirt to taper the hem and make a kick pleat for the back of the skirt.

To finish

11. Trace off a facing for the neck (see page 16).

PIN TUCKS

> Draw the lines for the pin tucks onto the right side of your fabric with a long ruler and a sharp piece of tailor's chalk. Press into sharp creases and baste into place before you machine-stitch.

> Make your pin tucks stand out with contrast stitching. If you don't have topstitching thread, thread two spools of the same color through your machine needle for a hand-stitched effect.

> For this and all other pages in this chapter, the red numbers in the illustration relate to the steps in the text.

Sheath Dress

This simple sheath dress is a great way to show off printed fabric, and it works well in many guises—try a light cotton or linen fabric for summer, a statement silk for evening, or a heavy knit for winter workwear. Experiment with details like an exposed zipper or add trimmings to the neckline or hem.

SELF-FACINGS

The side slits are formed with a self-facing—a facing that is part of the garment, rather than a separate one to be sewn on. When sewing, stitch each side seam together until you reach the top of the facing, then press the seam and facings open. Stitch a miter at the bottom corners of the hem facing, then finish around the hem and facing by hand or machine.

Creating the pattern

Starting with the Darted Dress sloper, extended to the desired length:

Front

1. Close the shoulder dart to create a side bust dart.
2. Shorten the bust dart by 1¼ in. (3 cm) from the bust point.
3. Draw in a V neckline (see page 120). A slight curve is more flattering than a straight line.

Back

4. Alter the neck to match the length of the front shoulder.

Front and back

5. Erase the waist dart.
6. Draw a straight line from the bottom of the side bust dart to the hem.

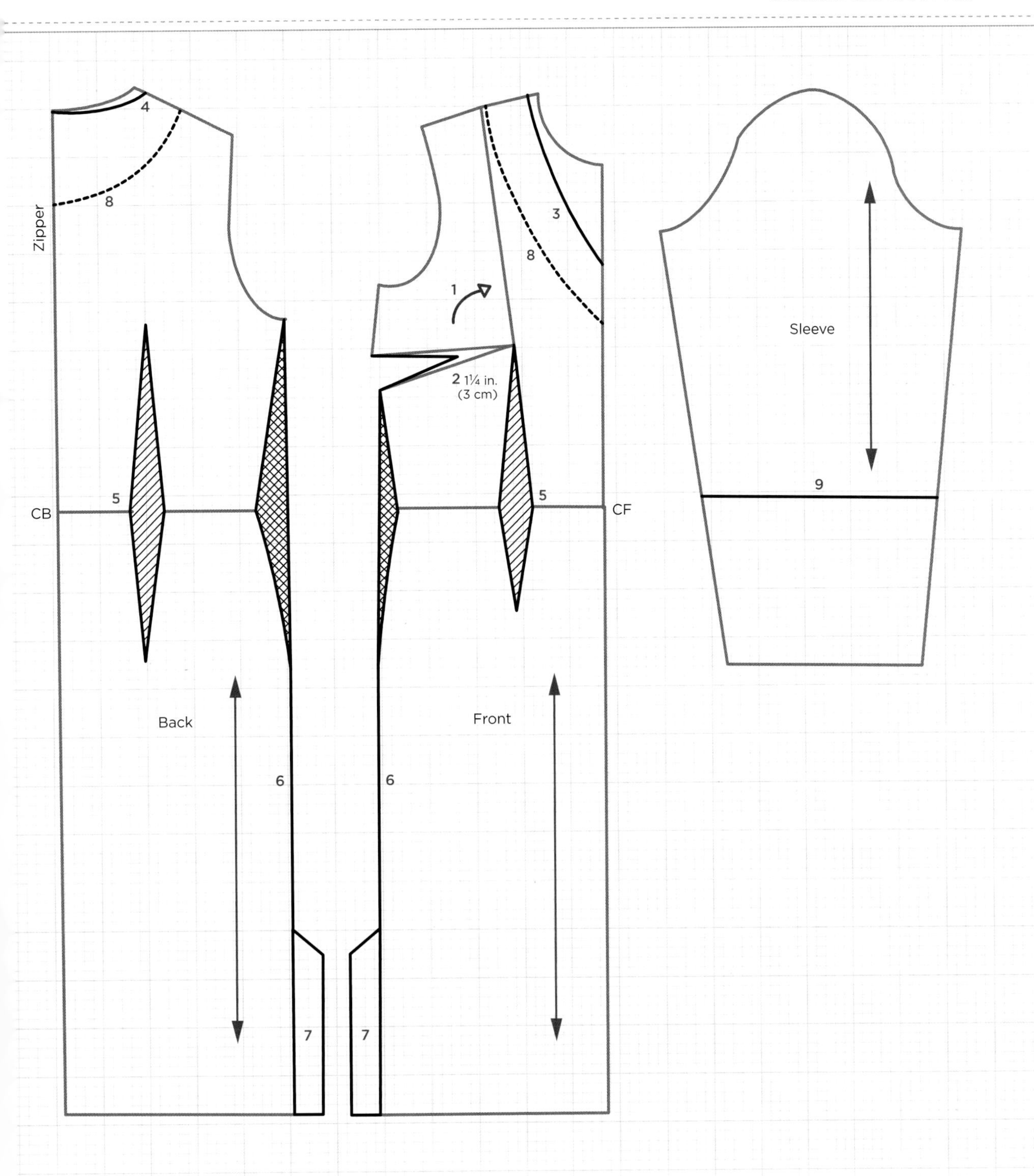

7. Add a self-facing to the side seam for the slit—as high as you dare!

8. Trace off facings for the neck as in the diagram.

Sleeve

9. Trace off the Three-Quarter-Length Sleeve sloper.

A-Line Dress

The yoke-to-hem panels on this dress emphasize its neat A-line silhouette. The pockets and short sleeves make it practical, chic, and easy to wear. It works best in a fabric that gives a crisp outline—a wool gabardine or double jersey, for example.

YOKES

Remember to cut the yoke double and bag out to make a neat finish inside.

Creating the pattern

Starting with the Darted Dress sloper:

Front

1. Close the shoulder dart and open at the waist.
2. Lower the neck by ¾ in. (2 cm) and widen by ¼ in. (6 mm).
3. Draw a line across the top of the bodice about 2 in. (5 cm) down from the CF. Cut and separate from the rest of the sloper and mirror on the CF to create one piece—this is the front yoke.
4. Pivot the dart back to its original position and draw a line through the center of the skirt dart to the hem. Cut from yoke to hem and separate into two panels.
5. On the side front panel, extend the hem from the hip line by 1¼ in. (3 cm) on the side seam and ¾ in. (2 cm) on the center panel seam. Curve off the hem.
6. On the center front panel, extend the hem from the hip line by ¾ in. (2 cm) on the side panel seam. You have now created your A-line.

Back

7. Widen the neckline by ¼ in. (6 mm) to match the front.
8. Use your front yoke pattern piece to measure the height of the back yoke. Draw a line across the top of the back bodice at this point, then cut and separate.

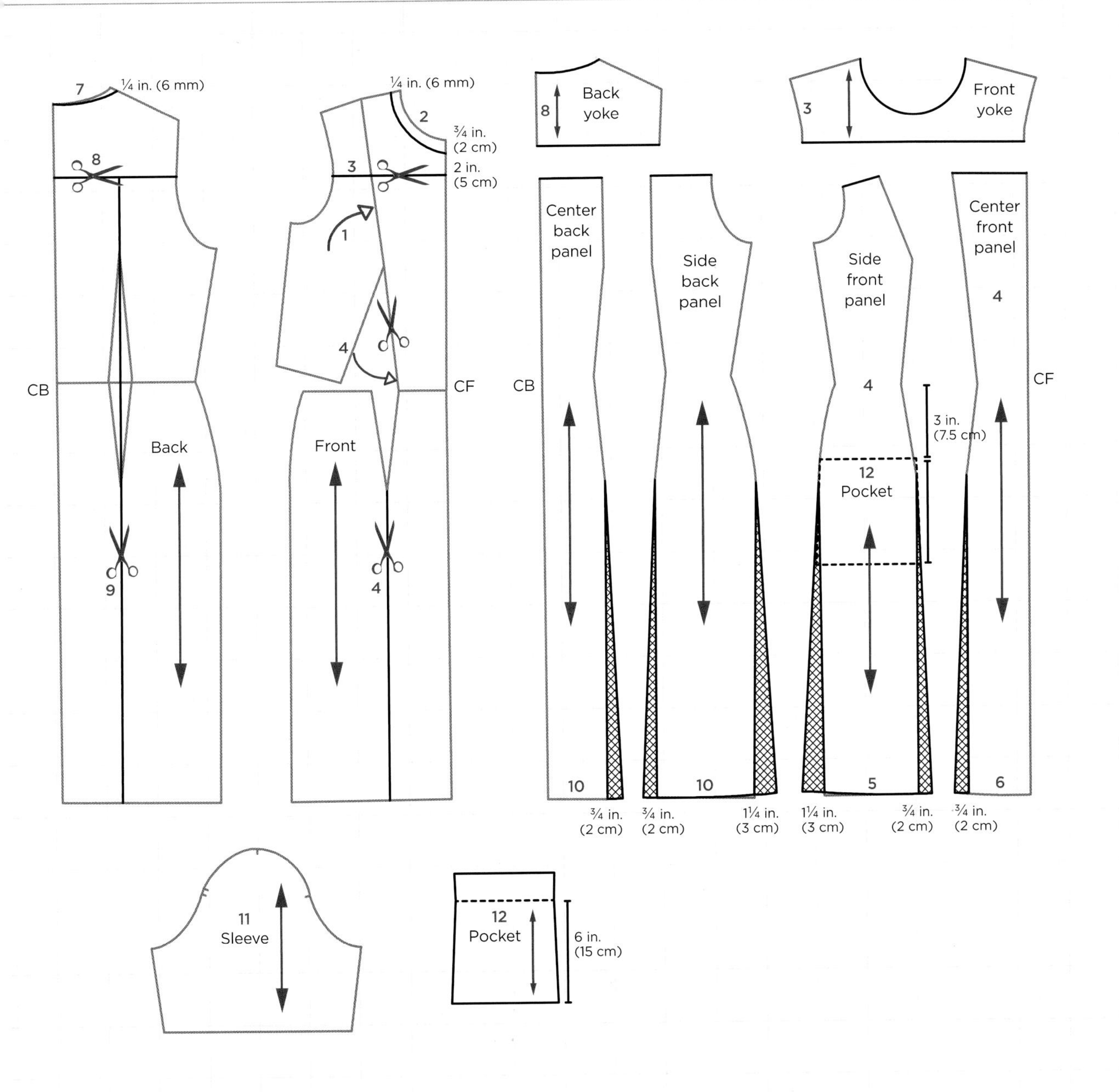

9. Draw a line from the yoke, through the center of the back waist dart, to the hem. Cut and separate into two panels.

10. Extend the hem from the hip line on both panels to match the front. Curve off the hem.

Sleeve

11. Trace off the Short Sleeve sloper (page 27).

Pocket

12. Draft from the side front panel: measure 3 in. (7.5 cm) down from the waistline and mark as the top of your pocket. Measure another 6 in. (15 cm) down from here to mark the bottom of your pocket. Trace off and add a facing at the top of the pocket.

Body-Con Dress

This is a modern classic, with panels that flatter the silhouette and give you the chance to use contrasting colors. To achieve the full body-con effect, use a double-knit woven fabric or one with a bit of stretch. As this dress is drafted from the Darted Dress sloper, you can be sure to be shaped by it, not squeezed into it! You may need to take in the side seams for a close fit. Make sure the panels still match.

Creating the pattern

Starting with the Darted Dress sloper:

Front

1. Close the shoulder dart and open at the princess seam to armhole position (see page 17).
2. Curve to create a princess seam.
3. Lower and widen the neckline by ¾ in. (2 cm) at the shoulder and CF (ab).
4. Narrow the shoulder by 2 in. (5 cm) from the shoulder point. Draw in a slight curve to meet the top of the princess seam (cd).
5. Draw a curve from the bottom of the waist dart to the hip, about 7–8 in. (18–20 cm) below the waistline (ef). The curve should mirror the princess seam on the bust dart.
6. Cut and separate to form the front side panel.

Back

7. Draw a line across the top of the waist dart (gh).
8. Draft the back shoulder straps:
   ▶ Adjust the neck and shoulder to match the front shoulder seam (ij).
   ▶ Mark the midpoint of the back neckline (k). Draw a line from this point to the top of the back waist dart (kl).
   ▶ Measure about 2 in. (5 cm) in from the armhole on the top line of the back bodice (m). Draw a line from this point to the outer edge of the shoulder strap (mj). The strap should be slightly wider at the top of the bodice and narrower at the shoulder. When sewing, cut the strap double and bag out.

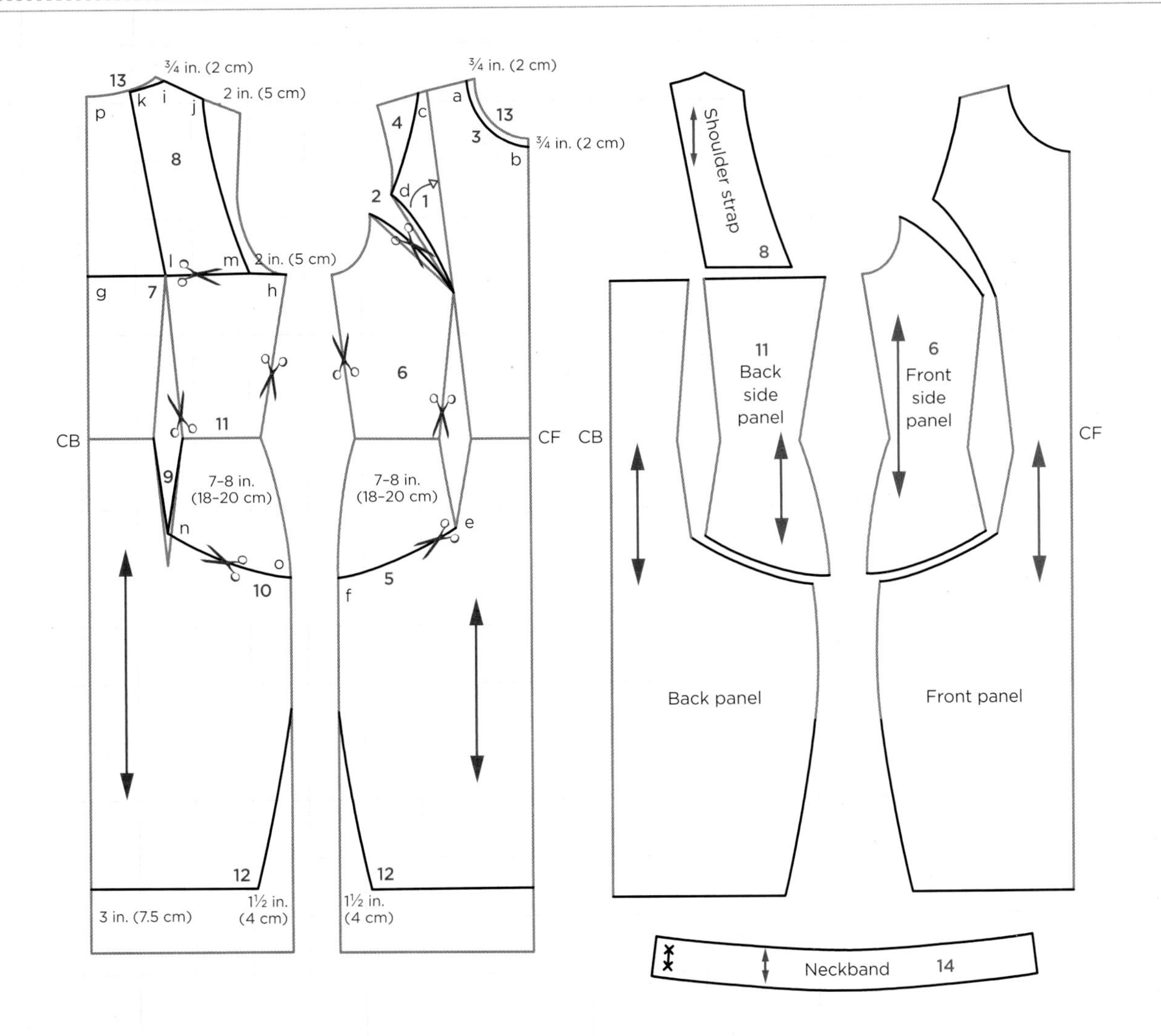

9. Shorten the back waist dart so that it matches the front waist dart.

10. Draw a curved line from the bottom of the back waist dart to the hip so that it matches the front side panel on the hip (no).

11. Cut and separate to form the back side panel.

Front and back

12. Shorten the skirt by 3 in. (7.5 cm) and taper the hem by 1½ in. (4 cm). If you are not shortening the skirt for this dress, you may need to add a kick pleat at the back so that you can walk (see Pencil Skirt, page 44).

Neckband

13. Calculate the total length of the neckband: on the front this is the length of the neckline (ab) x 2. On the back, you need to measure the distance from the CB neck (p) to the top of the shoulder seam (i).

14. Trace off the Standing Collar sloper (page 30) and adjust to this measurement. Add a button stand to fasten (see Shirt Dress, page 89).

To finish

Finish across the back and on the armhole with a facing (see page 16) or binding.

Shirt Dress

This dress gives the illusion of being a straight shape, but it is in fact drafted from the Darted Dress sloper, with the bust shaping concealed in gathers at the yoke. It works best in a fine woven fabric and will need some precision sewing to get the collar looking crisp.

Creating the pattern

Starting with the Darted Dress sloper:

Yoke

1. Close the shoulder dart.
2. Measure 2 in. (5 cm) down from the shoulder seam and draw a line from the armhole to the neck parallel to the shoulder (ab).
3. Cut and separate—this is the front section of the yoke.
4. Measure 3½ in. (9 cm) down from the neck at the CB and draw a horizontal line across the top of the bodice (cd).
5. Cut and separate—this is the back section of the yoke.
6. Join the front and back yoke sections at the shoulder seam and mirror on the CB to make one piece.

Dress front

7. Pivot the shoulder dart back to its original position so the side seams are realigned.
8. Convert the shoulder dart into tucks or gathers so it will fit onto the front shoulder seam of the yoke when sewn together (ab).
9. Lower the neck at the CF by ½ in. (13 mm).
10. Add 2 in. (5 cm) to the CF. Make a fold line ¾ in. (2 cm) from the CF to form a button stand. Remember to mirror the curve of the neck at the top.

Dress front and back

11. Omit the waist darts.
12. Lower the armhole by 1 in. (2.5 cm) and extend by ¾ in. (2 cm).
13. Draw a straight line from the bottom of the new armhole to the hem, curving off the corner to give straight, shirt-like side seams.

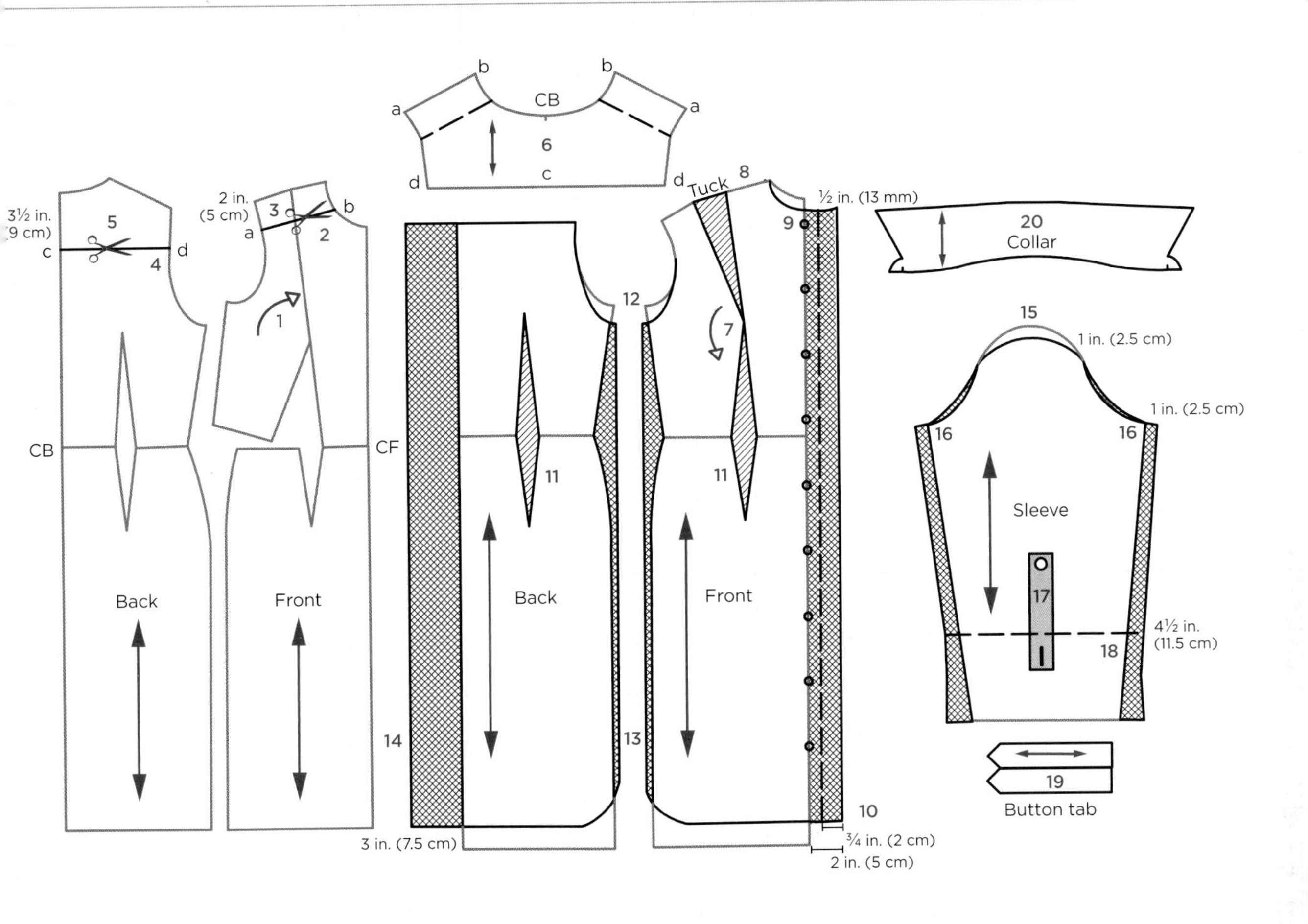

Dress back

14. Add 3 in. (7.5 cm) to the CB seam to form the back pleat.

Sleeve

Starting with the Full-Length Sleeve sloper:

15. Lower the sleeve head by 1 in. (2.5 cm). This makes a flatter sleeve with less ease.

16. Extend the underarm points by 1 in. (2.5 cm). This accommodates the lowering and extending of the armhole.

17. Mark the position of the button tab. The button should sit on the outside of the sleeve, while the tab is sewn inside and loops around the sleeve hem.

18. Create the turn-ups: Measure 4½ in. (11.5 cm) up from the bottom of the sleeve and fold the pattern paper back along this line. Because the sleeve narrows toward the wrist, you will see that there are two triangles missing on either side. Fill these sections so that the hem will line up with the sleeve when you turn it up. When you fold the pattern paper back down, the sleeve shape should flare out from the fold line.

19. Draft the button tab. Decide on the length of the tab depending on whether you want it to sit flat against the sleeve, slightly gather in the sleeve hem, or make a full turn-up.

Collar

20. Draft a Shirt Collar sloper (see page 29).

Jumper Dress

This is a style that lends itself to smart or casual depending on the fabric. Try a crisp cotton drill, a fine corduroy for a relaxed look, or how about pin-stripe wool suiting for an office dress with a twist?

BOX PLEATS

Fold and press your hem up before you press in your box pleats so that all the folds are going in the right direction.

Creating the pattern

Starting with the Darted Dress sloper and working on the front and back at the same time:

Bodice

1. With the sloper open at the shoulder dart position, shorten the shoulder seam and lower the armhole by 1 in. (2.5 cm). Draw in a new armhole joining these points, parallel to the sloper (ab).
2. Close the shoulder dart and open at the princess seam to armhole position (see page 17).
3. Mirror the princess seam on the back sloper by drawing a curve from the armhole (in line with the front armhole dart) to the top of the back waist dart.
4. Measure 1½ in. (4 cm) in from the front neck and 3 in. (7.5 cm) down from the CF and draw in a square neckline (see page 121).
5. Measure 1½ in. (4 cm) in from the back neck and ½ in. (13 mm) down from the CB and draw in a curve between these two points to lower the neckline slightly. Check that the shoulder seams match.
6. This dress is designed to be worn over a top, so add ease for a looser fit: narrow the darts by ¼ in. (6 mm) each side, and let out by ½ in. (13 mm) on each side seam.

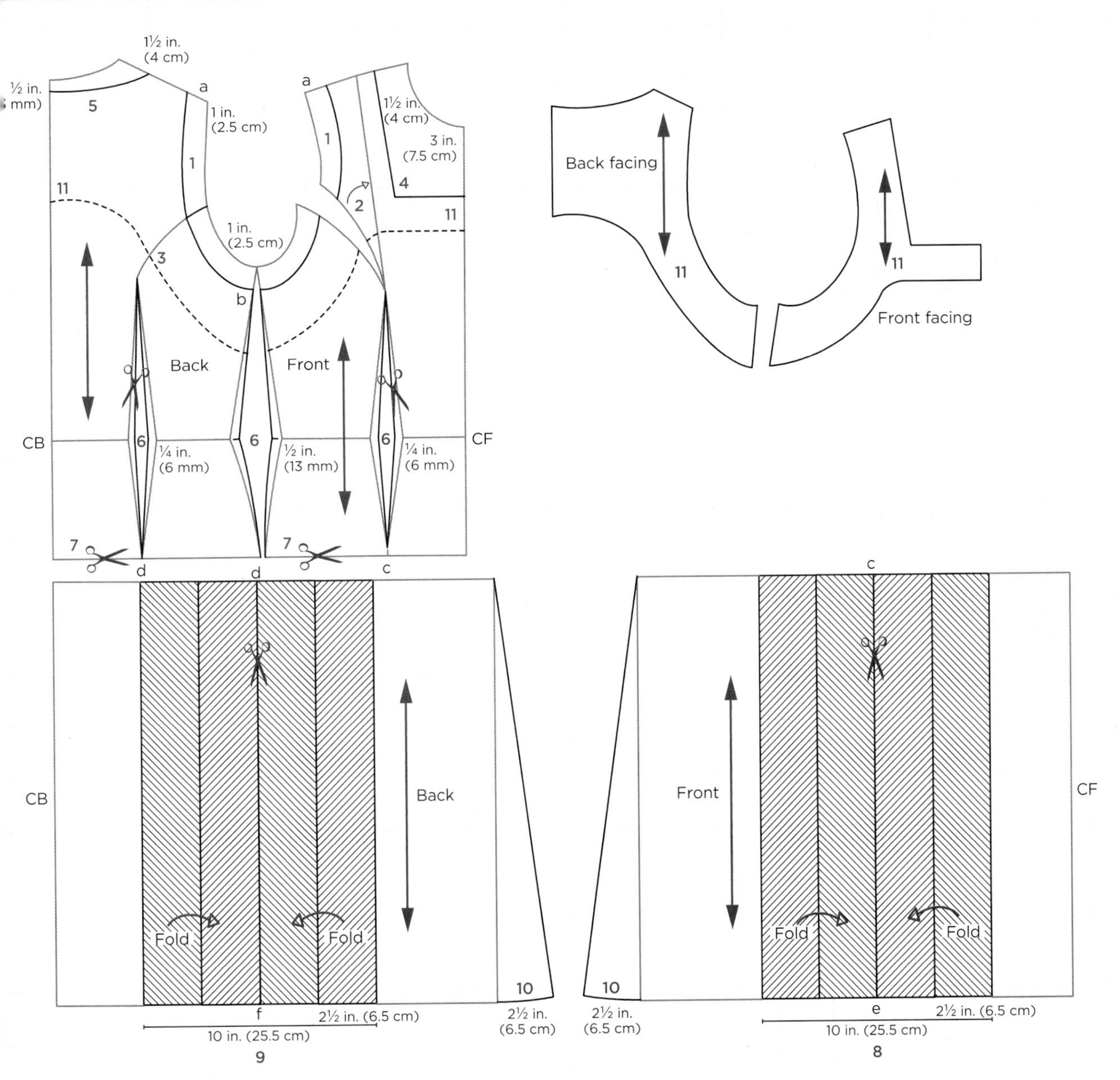

7. Draw a horizontal line across the front and back, level with the back skirt dart, and cut to separate into bodice and skirt pieces. Cut and separate the bodice into four panels along the princess seams.

Skirt

8. On the front, draw a vertical line from the bottom of the waist dart (c) to the hem (e). Cut down this line and add 10 in. (24 cm) to form the double box pleats, 2½ in. (6 cm) deep.

9. Repeat on the back skirt. Note that you will now cut the CB seam on the fold.

10. Add 2½ in. (6 cm) to the hem on front and back side seams to create a slight A-line (see page 84).

Facing

11. Follow the dotted line on the diagram to trace off a front and back facing. Join the two front sections together on the princess seam.

Apron Dress

This comfortable dress has real utility chic. With its big, practical pockets, it's great to wear for gardening or crafts. It is drafted from the back of the Darted Dress sloper, but you leave out all the darts. This shows how you can map out a pattern using a sloper, making sure you get a good fit, even on a casual style.

TIPS

> If you just want to make an apron, cut off the dress at point (f) leave out the waist tie slit, and make a neck strap instead of shoulder straps.

> If you are curvy on top or want a closer-fitting look, you may want to pinch out a small dart at the armhole as shown on the diagram (g). You may have to reshape the armhole curve a little to keep the line smooth. If you are worried about the dress covering your rear, you can extend it further toward the left back side seam.

Creating the pattern

Starting with the Darted Dress sloper, back only:

Front and back

1. You could say this dress has three backs, as the first step is to trace off the whole back sloper plus an extra back to form the front. Line them up at the armhole point—they will probably overlap slightly, depending on your size.
2. Ignore all the waist darts.
3. Fill in the gap at the waist formed by bringing the back and back-as-front pieces together.
4. Make the bodice apron shape:
   ▸ Starting on the CF, measure down 4–5 in. (10–13 cm) from the neck (a).
   ▸ The inner point of the strap (b) should be in line with the bust point (bp).
   ▸ Extend by 1½ in. (4 cm) to get the outer point of the strap and the edge of your apron front (c).
   ▸ Draw a straight line between these points (abc).

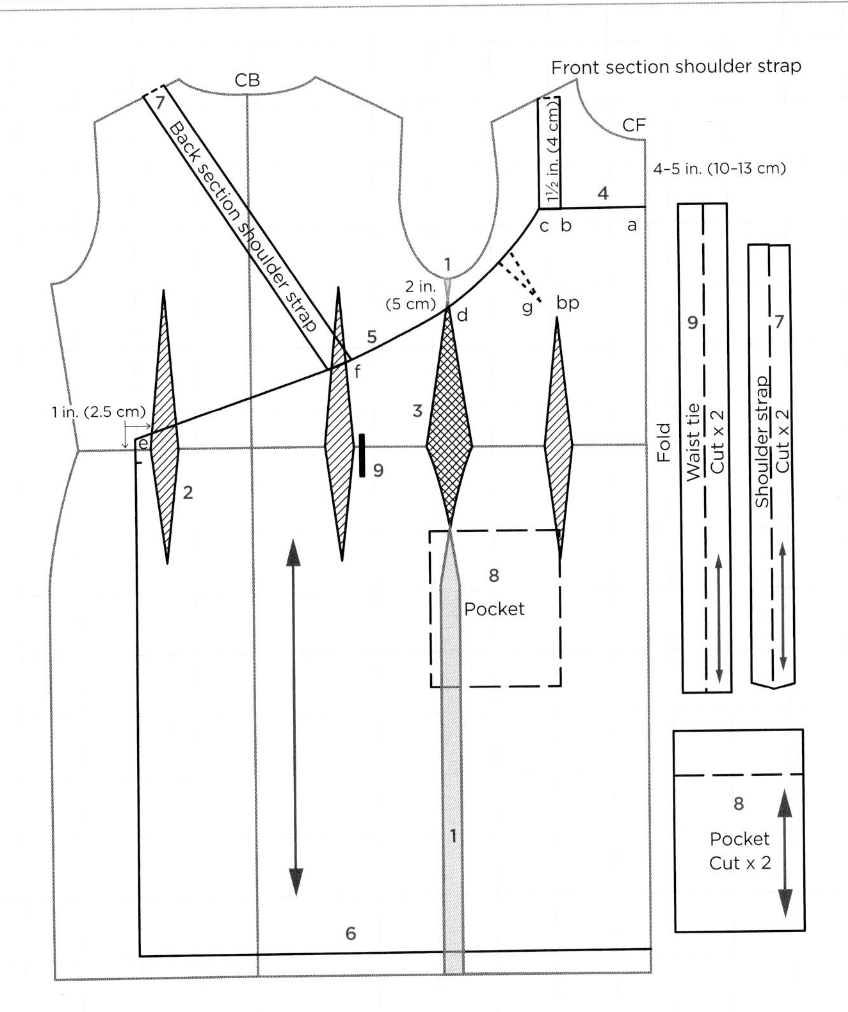

5. Make the side of the apron shape:
   ▸ Mark a point (d) 2 in. (5 cm) below the armhole.
   ▸ Mark a point 1 in. (2.5 cm) beyond the outer point of the left back waist dart and 1 in. (2.5 cm) above the waistline (e).
   ▸ Join these points in a long, sweeping curve (cde).

6. Decide on the length of your dress and complete the apron shape.

Straps

7. The crossover straps should sit at the point where the back curve passes through the back waist dart (f). Figure out the length of the straps by drafting their position on the sloper, measuring and adding together front and back lengths.

Pockets

8. Add deep patch pockets (sloper page 31, instructions page 76). Mark the position as shown on the diagram.

Waist tie

9. Mark a slit for the waist tie adjacent to the right back waist dart. Remember, this should only be on one side of the dress. Finish as you would a big buttonhole by hand or machine. A bound buttonhole is nice. Draw out a waist tie about double your waist measurement.

Sweater Dress

This dress is easy to make and even easier to wear. It uses the Raglan Sleeve sloper with a few simple modifications and is finished off with a soft, warm collar. Use a knit fabric such as a wide rib or a cable knit, and make yourself a great winter day dress to wear with leggings and boots.

Creating the pattern

Starting with the Raglan Sleeve sloper, extended to dress length, fold the sleeves along the center and line them up with the bodice as shown in the diagram.

Front

1. Lower and widen the neckline. Measure 1 in. (2.5 cm) from the neck on the shoulder line and 2 in. (5 cm) down from the neck on the CF. Draw in a new curve for the neckline.

Back

2. Widen the neckline by 1 in. (2.5 cm) at the shoulder point to match the front.

Front and back

3. Starting at the underarm point (a), make a long, smooth arc, finishing at the hemline (c). Make the widest point fall at the hip line (b), about 1½ in. (4 cm) from the original sloper.
4. Decide on the length of your dress and add a deep 3 in. (7.5 cm) hem, making sure to mirror the shape of the side seam arc (cd).

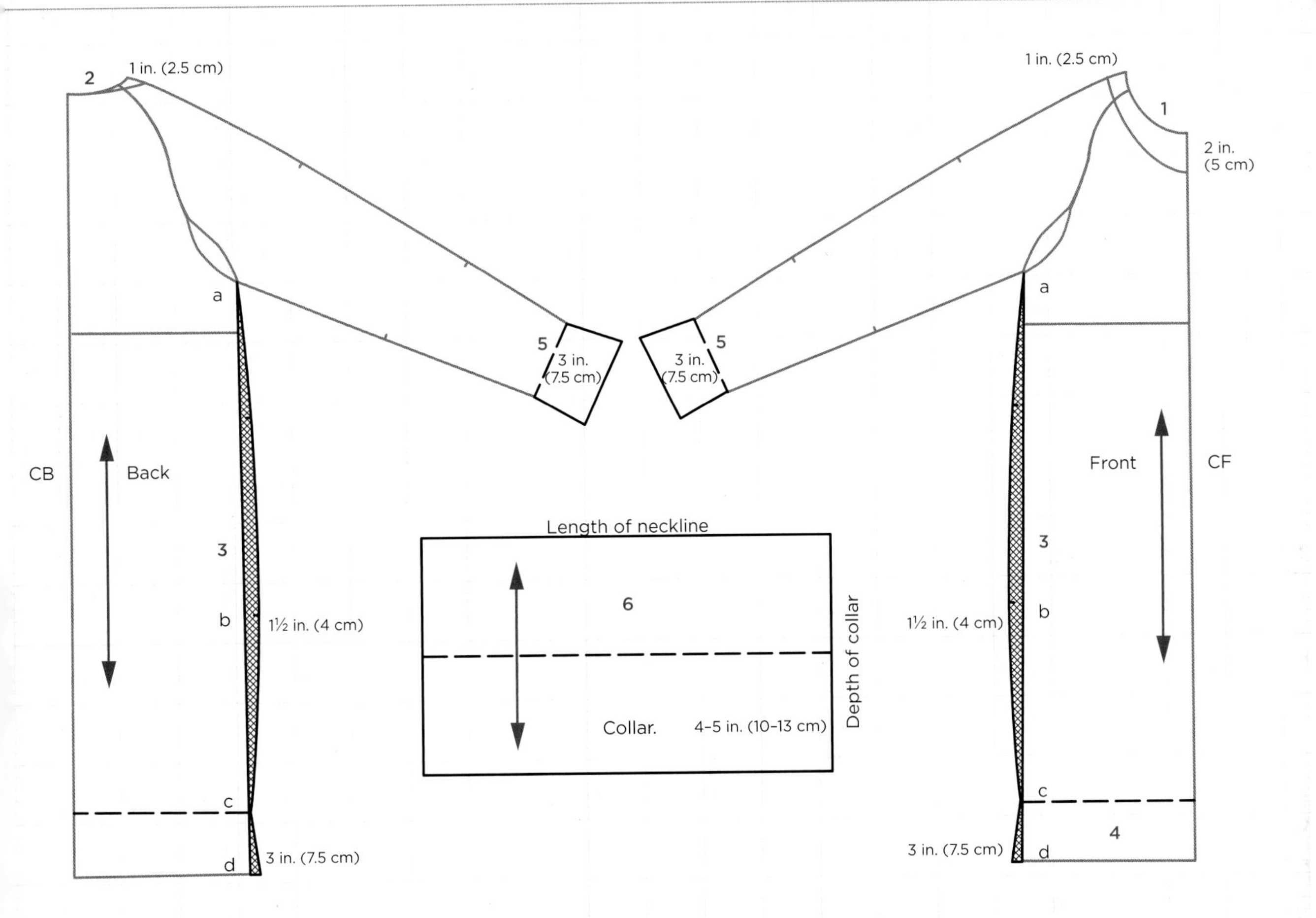

Sleeve

5. Decide on the length of your sleeve and add a deep 3 in. (7.5 cm) hem, mirroring the shape of the sleeve as you did on the hem of the dress.

Collar

6. Draft a rectangle the length of the neckline and double the desired depth of your collar.
   ▸ For the collar length, measure around the lowered neckline (front and back). If you haven't got a bendy ruler, stand the tape measure on its edge to get an accurate measurement.
   ▸ For the collar depth, 4–5 in. (10–13 cm) should be suitable.

SEWING OPTIONS

> Sew up the dress on your serger if you have one.

> Use a two-step or three-step zigzag stitch setting on your machine to make decorative stretchy hems.

Strappy Sun Dress

This dress is drafted straight from the Darted Dress sloper with only a couple of easy adjustments, making it great for speedy summer sewing. It's all about the straps, so experiment with their placement and with different widths and crossovers. Make them out of your dress fabric or choose braids, ribbons, or funky elastic.

TIPS

> Iron interfacing onto the wrong side of your fabric before cutting out the straps. Fold each strap in half lengthwise and iron to mark the centerline. Fold both edges into the center, then refold on the centerline to give you a ½ in. (13 mm) strap. Top-stitch firmly into place.

> When you come to do your fitting, you may find you need to tighten the top of the bodice at the side seam.

Creating the pattern

Starting with the Darted Dress sloper:

Front

1. Close the shoulder dart and open at the side dart position.
2. Shorten the dart by 2½ in. (6.5 cm) from the bust point.
3. Shape the front: Decide how low you would like the neckline and measure down from the neck on the CF (5 in./13 cm is a good starting point). Draw a straight horizontal line from this point until you hit the shoulder dart position just above the bust point. From here, curve the line down slightly to measure 1 in. (2.5 cm) below the armhole on the side seam. Cut and separate, discarding the top of the bodice.
4. Lower the front waist dart by 1½ in. (4 cm) so it doesn't come to an ugly point.

Back

5. Measure 1 in. (2.5 cm) below the armhole and draw a straight horizontal line from this point to the CB. Cut and separate, discarding the top of the bodice.

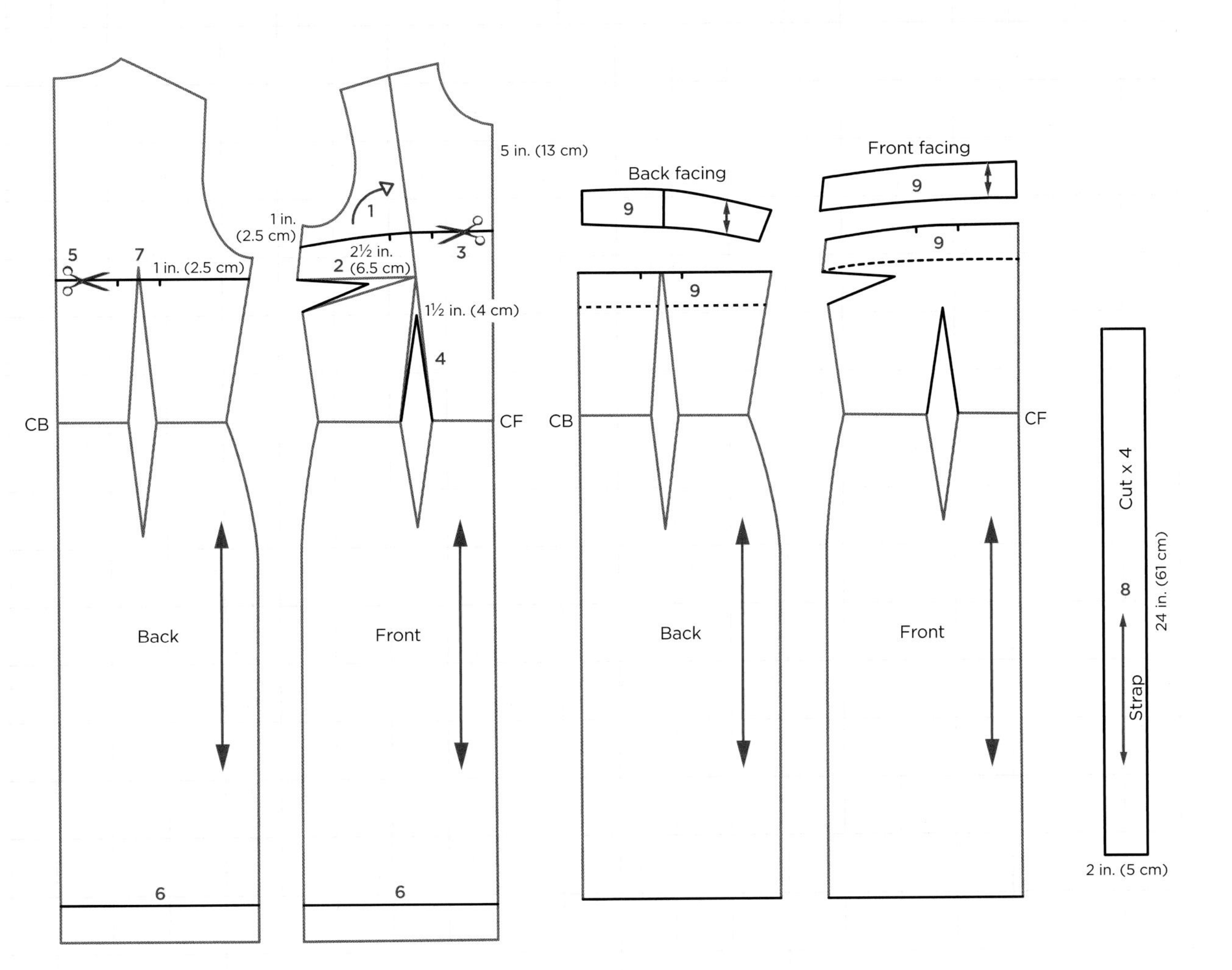

Skirt front and back

6. Decide on the length and cut or lengthen from the sloper accordingly.

Straps

7. Mark the points on the top line of the bodice where your straps will come: They should sit evenly above the bust point on the front (note that this is the bust point on your original sloper, not the new darts you have drawn, which have been shortened) and above the waist dart on the back.

8. To make the straps, cut four rectangles approximately 24 in. (61 cm) long by 2 in. (5 cm) wide. Interlace as shown right.

Facing

9. Follow the dotted lines on the diagram to trace off a front and a back facing. Join the two back sections together and make a smooth curve, then join the front sections.

Wrap Dress

Made famous by designer Diane von Furstenberg, the wrap dress has become a classic. It suits most figures and lots of fabrics, especially prints. Using the Darted Dress sloper gives a better fit than most store-bought wrap dresses, as there's a clever "slash and overlap" adjustment to avoid leaving a gaping neckline. And that's a wrap!

PRACTICE MAKES PERFECT

It's worth making a muslin and playing around to get the crossover as you like it, as once you've got this pattern right, you'll want to make it again and again!

Creating the pattern

Starting with the Darted Dress sloper:

Front

1. Close the shoulder dart and open at the French dart position.
2. Widen the neckline by 1 in. (2.5 cm) on the shoulder seam.
3. Draw a line from the bust point to the CF, continuing the top line of the French dart (ab). Cut down this line to the bust point and rotate the top part of the bodice so that it overlaps the lower part by ½ in. (13 mm). This will stop the dress from gaping at the front.

Wrap

4. Mark the point at which the dress will cross over at the front—this might be about 5 in. (13 cm) below the neckline, which is about the point where you made the neckline adjustment in step 3 (b).
5. Draw a line from the neck point (c) to the crossover point (b) and continue to a point 1 in. (2.5 cm) above the waistline and around 6–7 in. (15–18 cm) beyond the CF (cbd). Check that this distance is equal to the distance from the CF to the middle of the waist dart—you can make adjustments depending on how far you want the dress to wrap over.
6. Draw a long, sweeping curve back down from the waist point of the wrap to the CF hemline

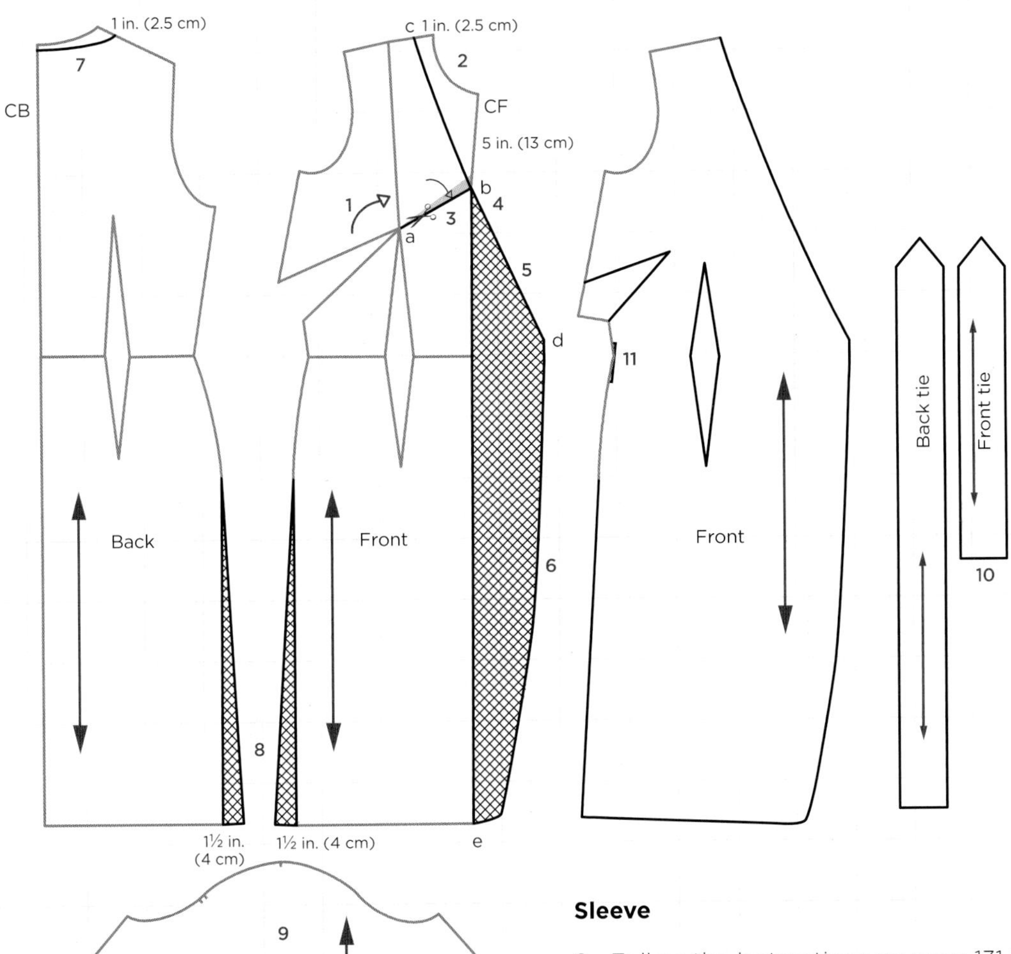

(de). For more modest wrapping, continue the line straight down from the waist (d) to the hemline, parallel to the CF.

Back

7. Adjust the neckline to match the front.

Skirt front and back

8. Extend the skirt on the hem at the side seams by 1½ in. (4 cm) to make an A-line (see page 84).

Sleeve

9. Follow the instructions on page 131 to make a cape sleeve, or swap for one of the other sleeves in the Finishes for Dresses chapter.

Ties

10. Draft two ties. The back tie will thread through the side seam and around the waist and needs to be approximately double the length of the front waist tie.

11. Mark on your pattern the point on the side seam waist where the tie will thread through. Leave this open as a slit when you sew up.

To finish

Depending on your fabric, you might want to draft a facing for the long wrap edge. Alternatively, use a binding.

One-Shoulder Dress

This dress looks spectacular but it is actually very easy to make, as the front and back are the same. You will need to make it in two layers, which has the added advantage of giving a neat finish to the neck edge and armhole. Fine fabric like georgette is ideal.

CHANNELS/CASING

Bag out at the armhole and neck edge, leaving a gap at the shoulder for the channels. Sink-stitch along the shoulder seam to hold the layers together, then stitch a seam ¾ in. (2 cm) on either side of the shoulder seam to make two channels (see diagram opposite, top right).

Creating the pattern

Starting with the Darted Dress sloper, back only (front and back are the same):

Front and back

1. Trace off the sloper and mirror on the CB. Because the design is asymmetrical, you need to create a whole pattern for this dress.
2. Lower the right armhole by ½ in. (13 mm) and extend by ½ in. (13 mm) (a).
3. Join this point to the neck point with a straight diagonal line (ab).
4. Raise the left shoulder by 1 in. (2.5 cm) at the top of the armhole (c) and draw a line from the neck (b) to this point, extending the line from here to make the shoulder 9 in. (23 cm) long (bcd).
5. Lower the left armhole by 1½ in. (4.5 cm) and extend by ½ in. (2 cm) (e).
6. Complete the left armhole by joining points (d and e) with a diagonal line.

Skirt

7. Decide on the length and measure down from the waist. Measure 5 in. (13 cm) out from the side seams on the hem. Join the armholes to the new hem (ef/ag).

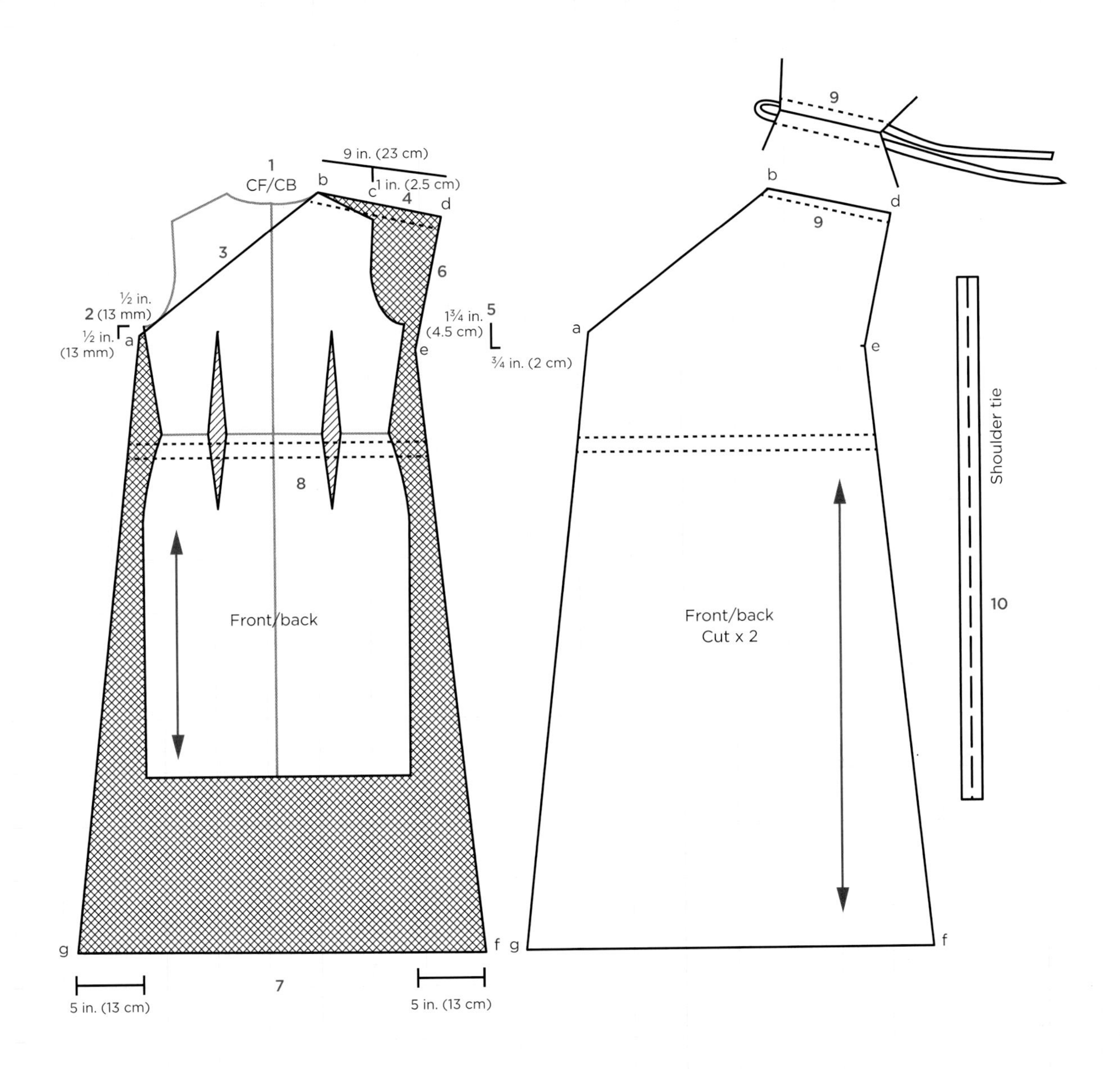

Casing

8. Mark the casing on the waist for the elastic waistband 1 in. (2.5 cm) below the waistline to allow it to blouse over at the waist. The casing should be 1½ in. (4 cm) wide for 1 in. (2.5 cm) elastic.

9. Mark the casing at the shoulder for the shoulder ties, ¾ in. (2 cm) down from the shoulder seam. Remember front and back are the same, so you will end up with two channels at the shoulder seam for the tie to loop through (see diagram).

Ties

10. Make a rouleau tie long enough to thread through the shoulder casing and tie in a pretty bow.

Strapless Dress

This vintage silhouette makes a beautiful summer dress in a bright cotton or shirting with a contrasting bodice trim. Wear it with a petticoat for full fifties flare. In a luxury fabric, this also makes a great prom dress. The versatile shape works in a number of lengths, and you could mix and match with one of the other skirt designs—the Pencil or Godet styles would look really elegant.

KEEPING IT UP

> Strapless dresses need boning to stay up. Cut a lining the same as the bodice and sew polyester boning down all the seams except the CB, where the zipper will have a similar effect. Remember to add plastic caps to each end of the bones so they don't dig into you!

> For a couture touch, your dress will stay up much better with an internal belt made from a 1 in. (2.5 cm) grosgrain ribbon sewn in at the waist (like a waist strap on a backpack). Catch the ribbon by hand at each of the seams and fasten separately at the back with a hook, making it a little tighter than the zipper.

Creating the pattern

Starting with Darted Dress sloper, bodice only:

Bodice

Working on the front and back at the same time:

1. On the front bodice, close and overlap the shoulder dart by ¾ in. (2 cm) and open the waist dart. This will keep the dress close-fitting above the bust.
2. Now, bring the back and front bodice side seams together.
3. Trace off your bodice trim:
   ▸ Measure from the neck to the center of the cleavage where you would like the center point of the dress to sit. Mark on your pattern point (a).
   ▸ Measure from the top of the shoulder along the line of your bra strap where you would like the top of the dress to sit. Mark on your pattern (b).

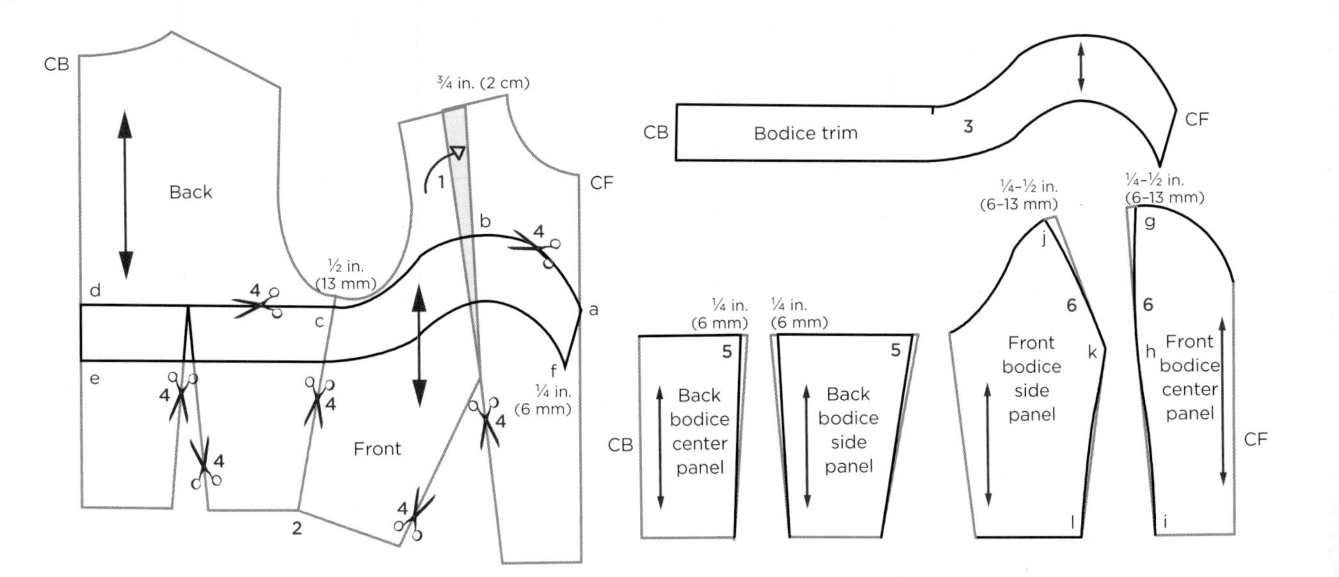

- With a French curve, the edge of a plate, or a steady hand, draw a curve from (a to b).
- Measure ½ in. (13 mm) down under the armhole (c). Continue the line from point (b), under the armhole, and across the back to the CB, skimming the top of the back waist dart (abcd).
- Draw a parallel line 2 in. (5 cm) below the top of the bodice (ef), following the curve you have just drawn. End the line ¼ in. (6 mm) from the CF and complete the shape with a small diagonal line (fa). Trace off as one piece.

4. Cut and separate the bodice into four panels along the waist darts. The top line of the panels should be the same as the top of the bodice trim (abcd).

5. On the back panels, trim down the waist darts by ¼ in. (6 mm) at the top on both sides of the dart. This will help the dress fit closely and stay up.

6. On the front panels, curve the lines of the panel seam (ghi, jkl) into a princess seam: On the front bodice center panel, trim down the top of the bust dart by ¼–½ in. (1–1.5 cm) and curve out like an opening parenthesis "(" (gh). Curve the waist dart section in like a closing parenthesis ")" (hi). On the front bodice side panel, do the same but invert the curves: The bust dart section of the seam (jk) should curve out like a closing parenthesis and the waist dart section (kl) should curve in like an opening parenthesis. Measure along the curves to check they are the same length and will fit together. This all helps to give a good shape to the bodice.

Skirt

Follow the instructions on page 56 to make a Full Circle Skirt. Make sure the waist measurements of the bodice and skirt match.

Negligee

The pattern for this body-skimming negligee is cut all in one piece from the Dartless Dress Stretch sloper, but here the stretch comes from cutting on the bias, not from the fabric. For full-on glamour, choose a fabric like double georgette or crepe silk. This would also make a great evening jacket.

CUTTING ON THE BIAS

> To ensure symmetry, you could draft this pattern as a half and then mirror and trace off down the CB. Make sure you have a whole pattern piece to place on the fabric, however, as it is not ideal to fold fabric on the bias for cutting. See the diagram for how to arrange the fabric on the bias.

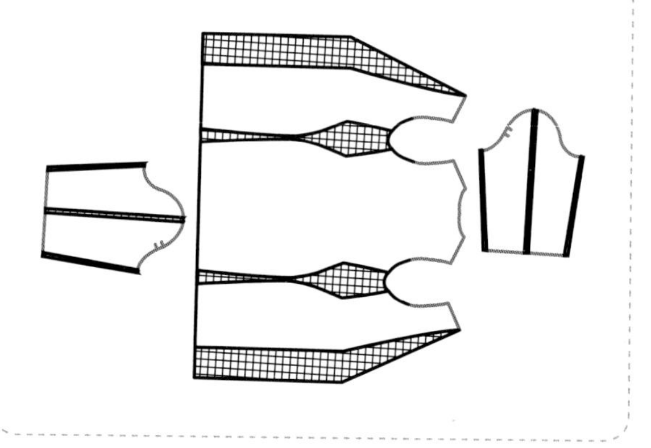

Creating the pattern

Starting with the Dartless Dress Stretch sloper, back only:

Front and back

1. Trace off the back sloper twice. Cut one of the traced-off slopers in half down the CB and arrange either side of the intact sloper along the side seams, aligned at the hem. These pieces become the open wrap front.
2. Spread the two front side pieces away from the back piece until there is a gap of 1½ in. (4 cm) at the widest point of the hip on the side seams. Keep straight at the hem.
3. Lower the armholes by 2 in. (5 cm).
4. Extend the front pieces to create the wrapover: Decide how much overlap you want and extend on the waistline and hem—5-7 in. (12-18 cm) is a good starting point.

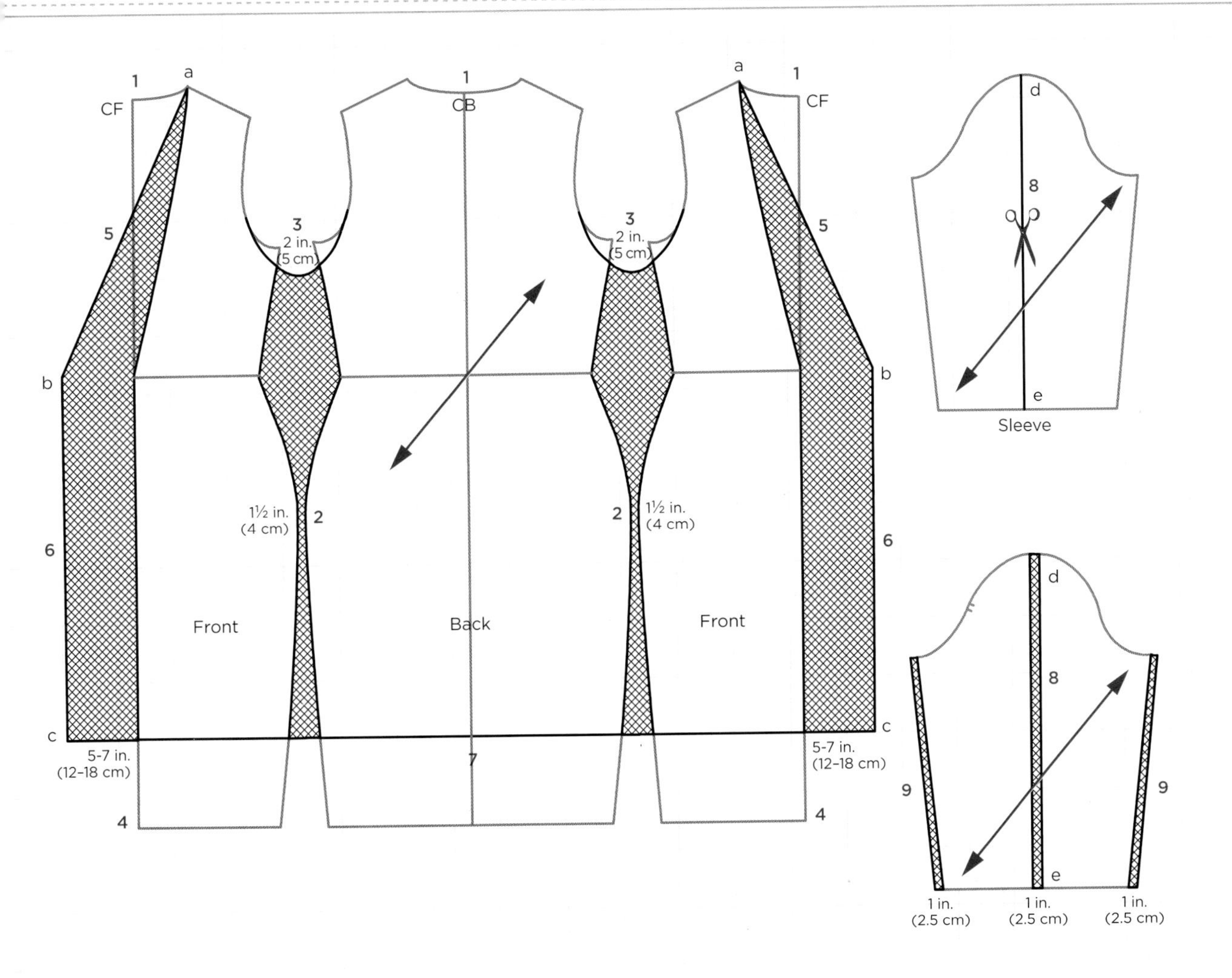

5. Draw a straight diagonal line from the neck point to the new waist point (ab).
6. Complete the line from the waist point down to the hem, parallel to the CF (bc).
7. Shorten at the hem to the desired length—remember to check the width of your fabric!

Sleeve

Using the Three-Quarter-Length Sleeve sloper:

8. Widen the sleeve to match the lowered armholes on the dress: Draw a line down the center of the sleeve from the sleeve head to the sleeve hem (de). Cut and separate by 1 in. (2.5 cm).
9. Add 1 in. (2.5 cm) to the sleeve seams on both sides. Check that the sleeve head measurement matches that of the armholes, with a little ease.

To finish

Use a contrast strip as a binding on the front edges and as a waist tie. You might want to add some belt loops on the waist side seams.

As well as making a great dress, this slip could be worn under skirts and dresses to create a smooth line, or as a nightdress. The bias cut creates a shape that will skim the figure as the fabric becomes more stretchy. You don't need much fabric, so go crazy with luxurious silk satin. Test your skills from the Godet Skirt on page 48 and add a lace godet to the side seam!

> LACE TRIM
>
> You may be tempted to sew the lace as a band around the top of the bodice, but it will make fitting easier if you cut your front and back lace pieces separately and make one long side seam with the rest of the dress.

Creating the pattern

Starting with the Darted Dress sloper:

Front and back

1. Shorten the sloper to the desired length.

Front

2. Close the shoulder dart and open at the side dart position.
3. Draw a line (ab) from the bust point (bp) to the CF, in line with the bottom point of the side dart (c).
4. Cut and separate, discarding the top of the bodice. The dart will become incorporated into the lace.

Front and back

5. Move the waist shaping into the side seams: Measure and quarter the width of the waist darts at their widest point. At the waistline, measure this distance in from the side seam (d).
6. From this point on, ignore the waist darts.
7. Draw a line parallel to the side seam from the new waist point up to the top of the bodice (dc).
8. Draw in a slight A-line from the new waist point to the hem of the skirt (de), skimming the widest point of the hips and extending by 1 in. (2.5 cm) at the hem (see page 84 on creating an A-line).

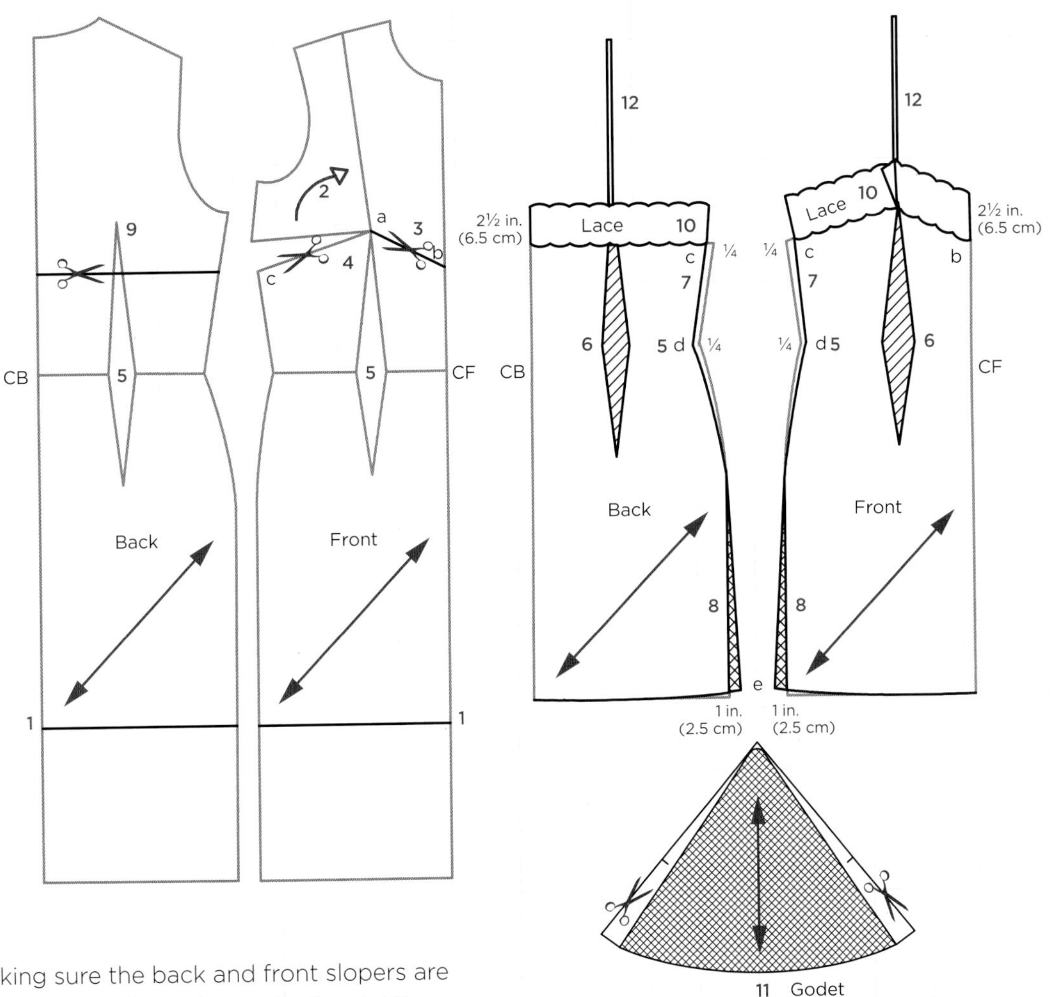

Back

9. Making sure the back and front slopers are aligned at the hem, draw a horizontal line across the back bodice in line with the bottom point of the front side dart (c). Cut and separate, discarding the top of the bodice.

Lace trim

Working on the front and back:

10. You will need a lace trim 2–2½ in. (4–6 cm) wide. Shape the lace at the bust point with a miter (see diagram, below right). This completes the dart shaping that you previously discarded. On the back, insert the lace straight across the top of the bodice.

11. For the lace godet, follow the steps on page 48 to create a godet and insert it into the left side seam. You should cut the godet from the new A-line slip pattern, not from the original straight-seamed sloper.

Straps

12. Either make rouleau straps from your fabric or buy some ribbon. Position the straps in line with the front and back dart points.

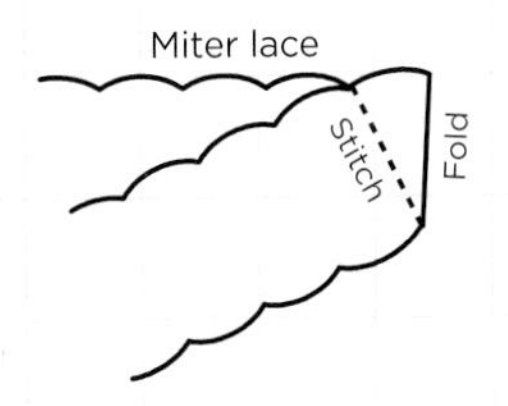

Halter Dress

Show off your shoulders in this bias-cut halter dress. The central seam gives a simple elegance when cut in a fabric like crepe, which drapes well. It's a style that makes the most of a small bust and can be casual and summery or slinky for evening with killer heels. Finish with bias binding on the neck, armhole, and back.

TIP

Try not to overstretch the seams when sewing on the bias. Hold in place with a long basting stitch.

Creating the pattern

Starting with the Darted Dress sloper:

Front bodice

1. Close the shoulder dart and open at the waist.
2. Draw in a smooth curve from the shoulder dart point to the armhole (ab).
3. Decide how low you want the neckline and mark on the CF (d) (5 in./13 cm is a good starting point). Widen at the neck by ½ in. (13 mm) (c) and draw in a V neckline (cd).
4. Draw a line from the bust point to the CF (ef). Cut along this line from the CF to ⅛ in. (3 mm) from the bust point.
5. Pivot the whole bodice away from the CF until the bodice overlaps the waistline by 1 in. (2.5 cm). This creates a space for the gathers at the CF bust and tightens the waist dart.

Back bodice

6. Draw a line across the bodice from the armhole point, stopping ¾ in. (2 cm) from the CB (gh). Extend the back waist dart to meet this line.
7. Narrow the waist by 1 in. (2.5 cm) from the CB and join to the top corner of the bodice (hi).
8. Join the new waist point to the CB hem (ij). Cut and separate, discarding the rest.
9. Cut into the side back bodice along the dart leg and waistline to within ⅛ in. (3 mm) of the waist dart. Pivot this section away from the CB to tighten the waist dart until it overlaps the waistline by 1 in. (2.5 cm) to match the front. Smooth the top line of the bodice.

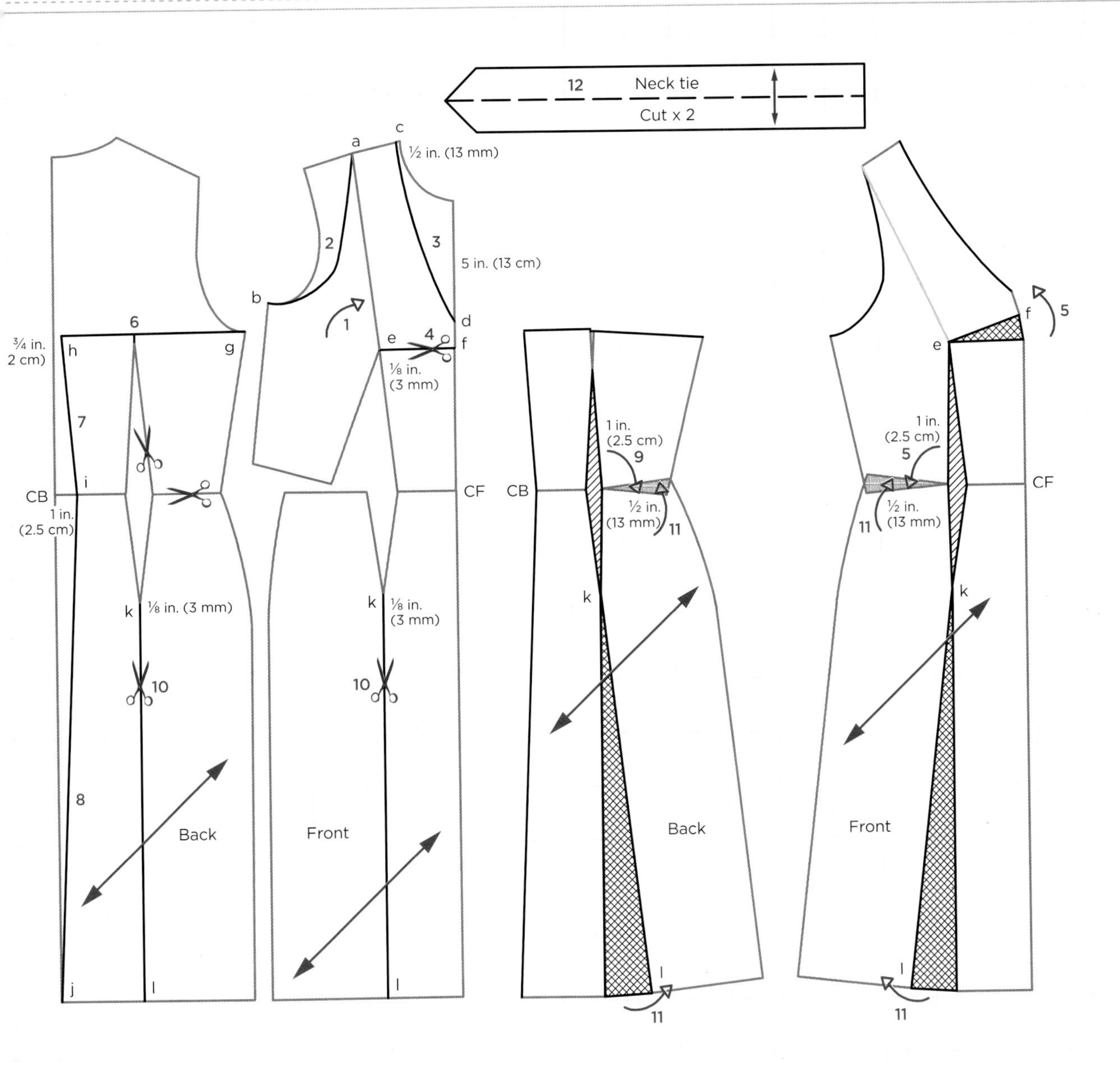

Skirt, front and back

10. Draw a line from the bottom of the skirt waist dart to the hem and cut along to within ⅛ in. (3 mm) of the bottom of the dart (kl).

11. Keeping the CF/CB straight, pivot the side section of the skirt from the bottom of the waist dart (k) until it overlaps the waistline by ½ in. (13 mm). This tightens the skirt waist dart and creates an A-line shape with a slight curve to the hem.

After all this pivoting, be sure to check that your front and back side seams match—they should be the same distance from armhole to hem.

Neck tie

12. Draft a neck tie double the width of the shoulder (ac) and long enough to tie in a bow behind the neck. Finish with a tapered end. Cut two.

Bubble Dress

Forget the 80s—this bubble shape makes a lovely modern party dress. The bodice alone would make a great top. This dress is at its most elegant in a soft, draping fabric. When creating your pattern, pivot open more for fine fabric, less for bulky fabric. Experiment with the amount of fullness you create—try more in the front, less in the back.

Creating the pattern

Starting with the Darted Dress sloper:

Front

1. Close the dart at the shoulder and open at the neck dart position, which lets you redraft the armhole by moving the bust shaping.

Working on the front and the back:

Bodice

2. At the shoulder, widen the neckline by 1 in. (2.5 cm) and lower by 1 in. (2.5 cm) at the CF and CB.
3. Lower the armhole:
   ▸ Front—Divide the section of the new neckline that runs from the shoulder seam to the neck dart (ab) in half and mark (c). Measure ½ in. (13 mm) down at the armhole (d). Join these two points (cd) with a line that sweeps under the armhole.
   ▸ Back—Divide the new neckline into thirds and mark the point closest to the shoulder seam (c). Measure ½ in. (13 mm) down at the armhole (d). Join these two points (cd) with a line that sweeps under the armhole.

Skirt

4. Mark a point two-thirds of the way down the skirt seam from the waist (e).
5. Mark 1 in. (2.5 cm) toward the CF on the hem (f).
6. Draw a long arc from the armhole through the side seam to the hem (def).

Bubble front

7. Draw a line from the center of the neck dart (g), through the center of the waist dart, to the hem (gh). Cut down this line to within ⅛ in. (3 mm) of the hem.
8. Keeping the CF straight, pivot the whole side of the dress away from the CF from the hem

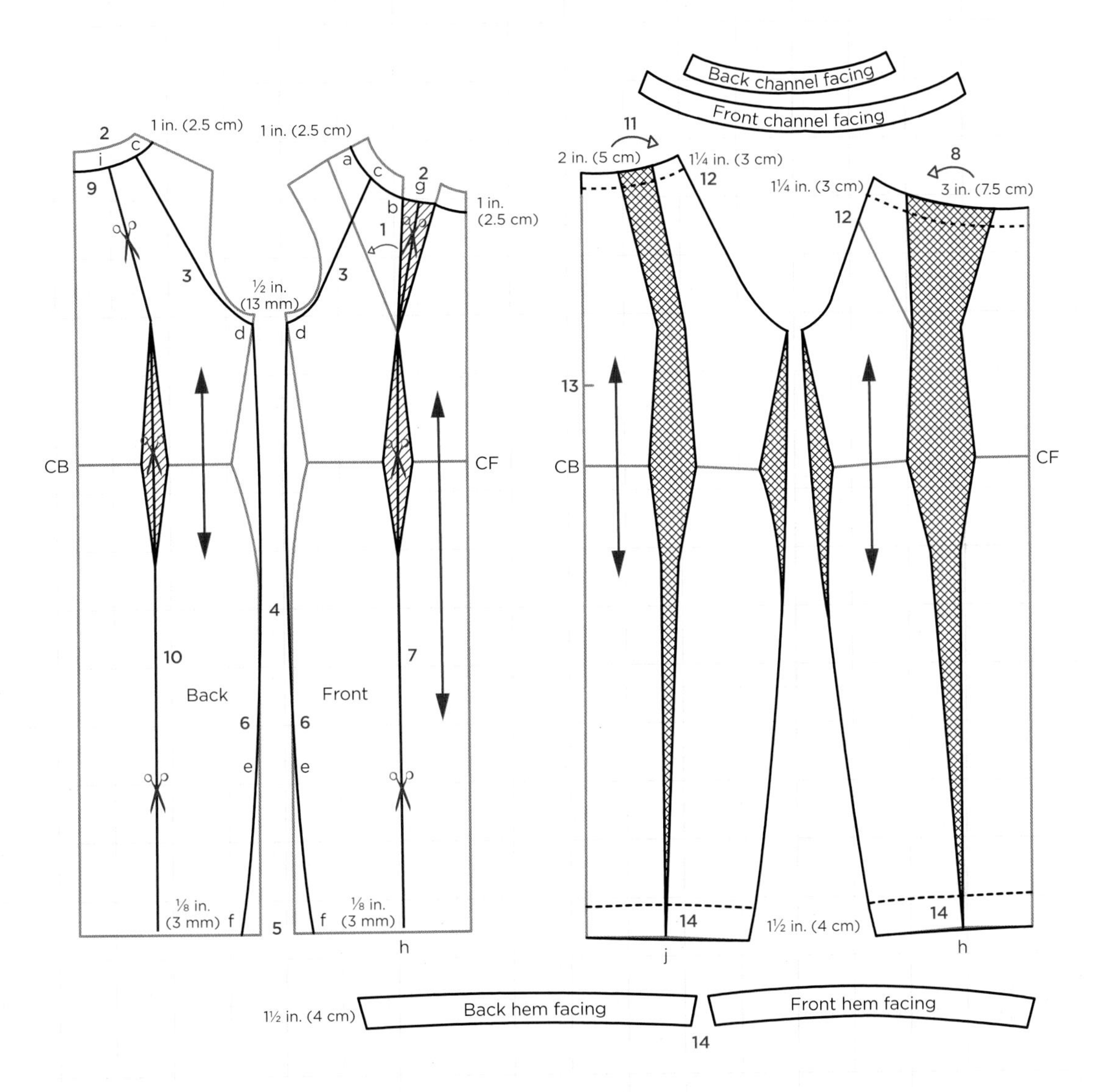

until you have roughly a 3 in. (7.5 cm) gap at the neck. This adds extra fabric to create the gathers at the neck.

Bubble back

9. Mark the center point of the new neckline (i).
10. Draw a line from this point, through the center of the waist dart to the hem (ij). Cut to within ⅛ in. (3 mm) of the hem.
11. Keeping the CB straight, pivot the whole side of the dress away from the CB from the hem until you have approximately a 2 in. (5 cm) gap at the neck.

Facing

Working on the front and the back:

12. Smooth the neckline so you have an even curve and trace off a 1¼ in. (3 cm) facing. This will create a channel for your ribbon.
13. You will need a slit at the neck on the CB seam to tie your ribbon. Mark a notch on the CB seam where you would like the slit to end.
14. Smooth the hemline so you have an even curve and trace off a 1½ in. (4 cm) facing to finish the hem.

Empire Dress

This diaphanous dress is made up in two layers of fabric—try georgette or chiffon with a silky fabric lining. With its raised waistline, this is a great style for a baby bump! It is also popular for bridesmaids.

Creating the pattern

Starting with the Darted Dress sloper:

Front bodice lining

1. Decide where you want the top of the bodice to sit: usually 5–6 in. (13–15 cm) from the neck point. Measure this distance down from the CF neck point and draw a straight line across the bodice to ½ in. (13 mm) from the armhole (ab).
2. Lower the armhole by ½ in. (13 mm) and draw a curve to the new top line of the bodice, parallel to the armhole (bc).
3. To make the bodice lining fit closely, widen the bust dart by ¼–½ in. (6–13 mm) on each side of the dart, depending on your bust size.
4. Draw a line under the bust where the bodice will finish (de). Bodice length can vary, depending on bust size and shape. A full bust might give a bodice length of 14½ in. (37 cm); a small bust might be 12 in. (31 cm).
5. Trace off to form your fitted bodice lining in two pieces (abcde).

Back bodice lining

6. Lower the armhole by ½ in. (13 mm) to match the front bodice and draw a line across the top of the bodice to the CB (fg).
7. Mark the back bodice side (fi) seam to match the front (cd). Draw a straight line across.
8. Trace off and pivot the pieces together along the dart to form one piece (fghi).

Front bodice top layer

Trace off the front bodice lining and slash and spread to make a gathered top layer—about double the width through the bust point:

9. Double the width of the center bodice panel along the bust line by extending toward the CF (ej).

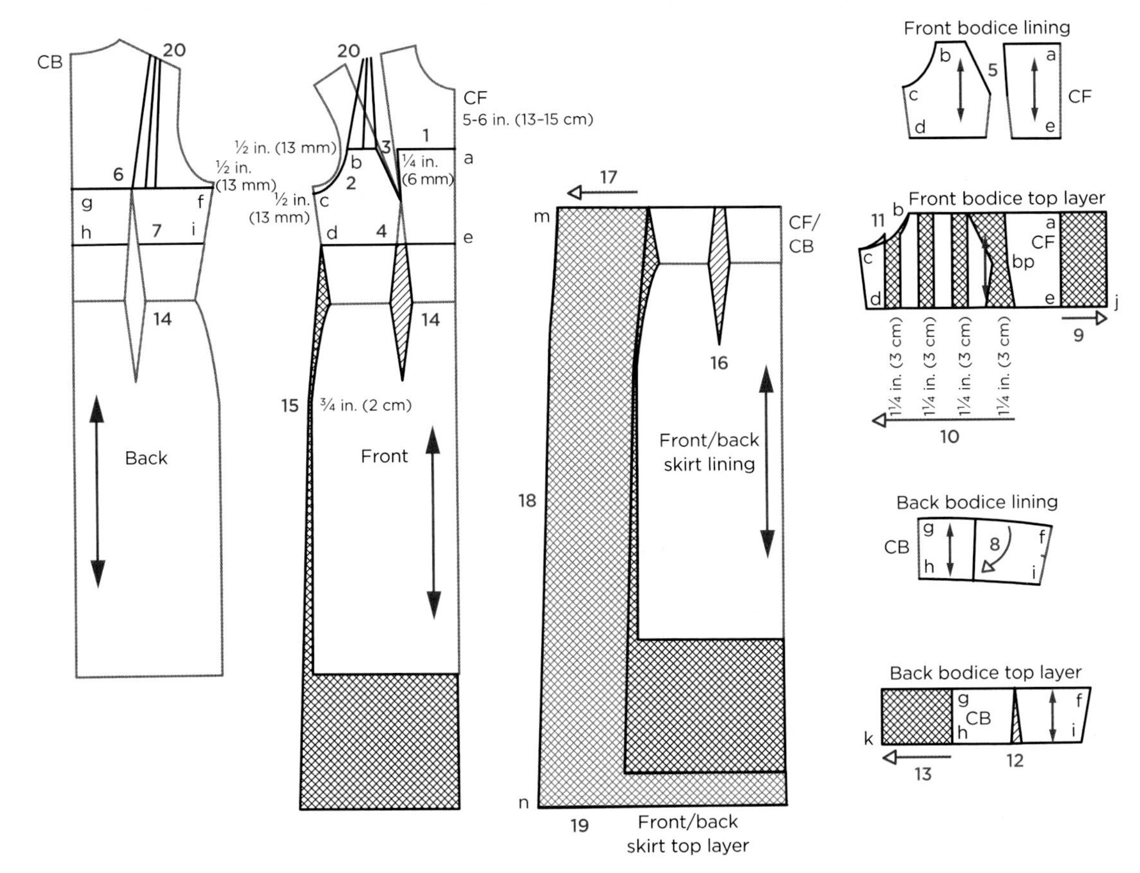

10. Slash the side bodice panel into four roughly equal parts. Spread apart with gaps of about 1¼ in. (3 cm) through the bust point.

11. Smooth out the armhole (bc).

Back bodice top layer

12. Trace off back bodice lining panels, retaining the dart.

13. Measure from CB to the dart (including the dart) and add to CB along the bust line (hk).

Skirt

Using the Darted Dress sloper, front only (front and back are the same), make the skirt lining:

14. Omit the waist dart.

15. From the bottom of the bodice on the side seam, draw a slight A-line to the hem (dl), ignoring the waist and skimming the hips by about ¾ in. (2 cm). Finish 1–2 in. (2.5–5 cm) above the finished dress length.

16. Trace off to form the skirt lining.

Working from the skirt lining:

17. Measure from the center of the (omitted) bust dart to the side seam. Extend the side seam by this amount along the skirt top (m).

18. Extend from this point to the hem at the desired length, following parallel to the A-line side seam of the skirt lining (mn).

19. Trace off to form the skirt top layer.

Straps

20. Cut six rouleau straps and mark positions as shown, using the sloper as a guide for length.

Maxi Dress

This design is a winning combination of comfort and class. It needs a stretch fabric with some weight to make the most of the back cowl and swishing godets—try a heavy viscose jersey. You can leave out the asymmetrical curved panels if you prefer, but you only have to draw one curve and the rest is traced off from that. Why not give it a try?

MAKING A COWL

> This dress uses the scarf method—imagine a classic square headscarf folded in half diagonally and draped around your neck. Sew this into the back V of the dress.

Creating the pattern

Starting with the Dartless Dress Stretch sloper, extended to full length:

1. As this is an asymmetrical design, you need to trace off a whole front and back. The front and back are arranged on opposite sides to the usual layout so you can see how the panels match up on the side seams.

Front

2. Draw in a wide, low V-neck, starting from a point approximately halfway along the shoulder line. Measure down the CF from the neck to the lowest point of the neckline (about 5-6 in./13-18 cm). Be conservative, as you can always cut more off later. Draw one side and mirror on the CF (ab). A slight curve on the V gives a more flattering line.

The back

3. Draw in a low V-neck: Matching the front shoulder point, measure down the CB, stopping 1-2 in. (2.5-5 cm) above the waistline (cd) and mirror on the CB.

Skirt front and back

4. Beginning just under the widest point of the hip, draw in a new side seam that curves out 1 in. (2.5 cm) at the knee to approximately 2½ in. (6.5 cm) at the full-length hem (ef). To ensure even seams on all sides, draw once and trace off or mirror on all the rest. You can now choose whether to leave the skirt plain or add asymmetrical curved panels as shown.

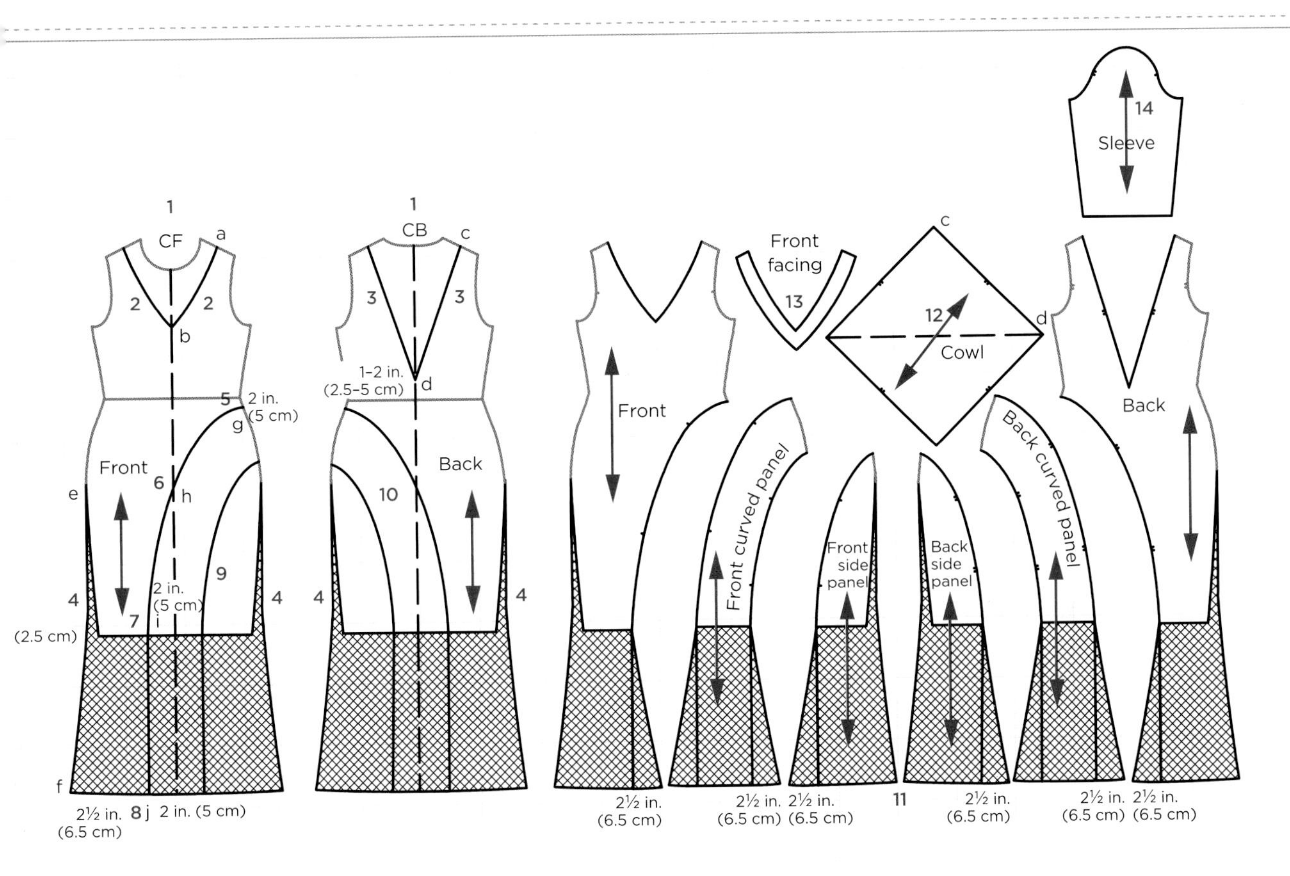

Panels front

5. Mark a point (g) 2 in. (5 cm) below the waist on the left-hand side seam.

6. Mark a point (h) on the CF line at about the level of where you started to draw in the new flared side seam (e).

7. Mark a point (i) about 2 in. (5 cm) from the CF at the knee.

8. Draw a curve through all these points, continuing in a straight line from the knee to the hem (ghij).

9. Make a second curve, parallel to the first, equidistant to the CF at the knee and hem. This forms your asymmetrical panel.

Panels back

10. Trace off and mirror the front skirt panel onto the back skirt, making sure the panels line up on the hip at the side seam.

Panels front and back

11. Cut out the panels and insert a half-godet in between each panel from the knee to the hem. Match the width to the side seam hem extension—2½ in. (6.5 cm). As before, draw one and trace off or mirror as necessary.

Cowl neck back

12. Measure the length of the back V-neck from the shoulder point to the waist point (cd). Draft a square with sides equal to this distance. Cut on the bias and insert at the shoulder points, folding horizontally to create the cowl.

Facing

13. Trace off a facing to finish the front V-neck.

Sleeve

14. Trace off the Three-Quarter-Length Sleeve sloper.

Gown

This beautiful gown looks far more complicated than it is! It is made up of a fitted camisole, a lace dolman-sleeved overbodice, and a double-layered skirt. With a full gathered skirt, it would make a fancy ball gown or even a wedding dress. You can play with alternative skirt patterns: Try a velvet pencil skirt with lace godets for a glamorous cocktail dress!

TIPS

> If using a fine fabric for the underbodice, cut double and bag out to give a neat finish.

> Gather or pleat the skirts separately to fit the waist. If using a fine fabric, a wide hem will give a good weight.

> You may need to tighten the side seam and underarm on the Dolman Sleeve sloper; this will depend on the weight and stretchiness of your lace. Start with the sloper as it is; cut, baste, and try on; then pin in any fitting adjustments.

> To fasten at the back, place the top of the zipper in line with the top line of the camisole, leaving a slit in the lace overbodice layer from the top of the bodice to the neck. Fasten with a button and loop or a hook and eye at the neck.

Creating the pattern

Starting with the bodice section of the Darted Dress sloper:

Underbodice front

1. Decide where you want the top of the bodice to sit, measure this distance down from the neck on the CF (approx. 4 in./10 cm), and draw a straight line across the bodice, stopping at the bust dart (ab).
2. Widen the bust dart by ¼ in. (6 mm) on each side of the dart to create a snug fit for the underbodice.
3. Lower and narrow the armhole by ½ in. (13 mm) and draw in a smooth curve from the armhole to the outer leg of the bust dart (cd).
4. Complete the bodice with a new side seam from the lowered armhole to the waist (de).
5. Trace off the front underbodice in two panels.

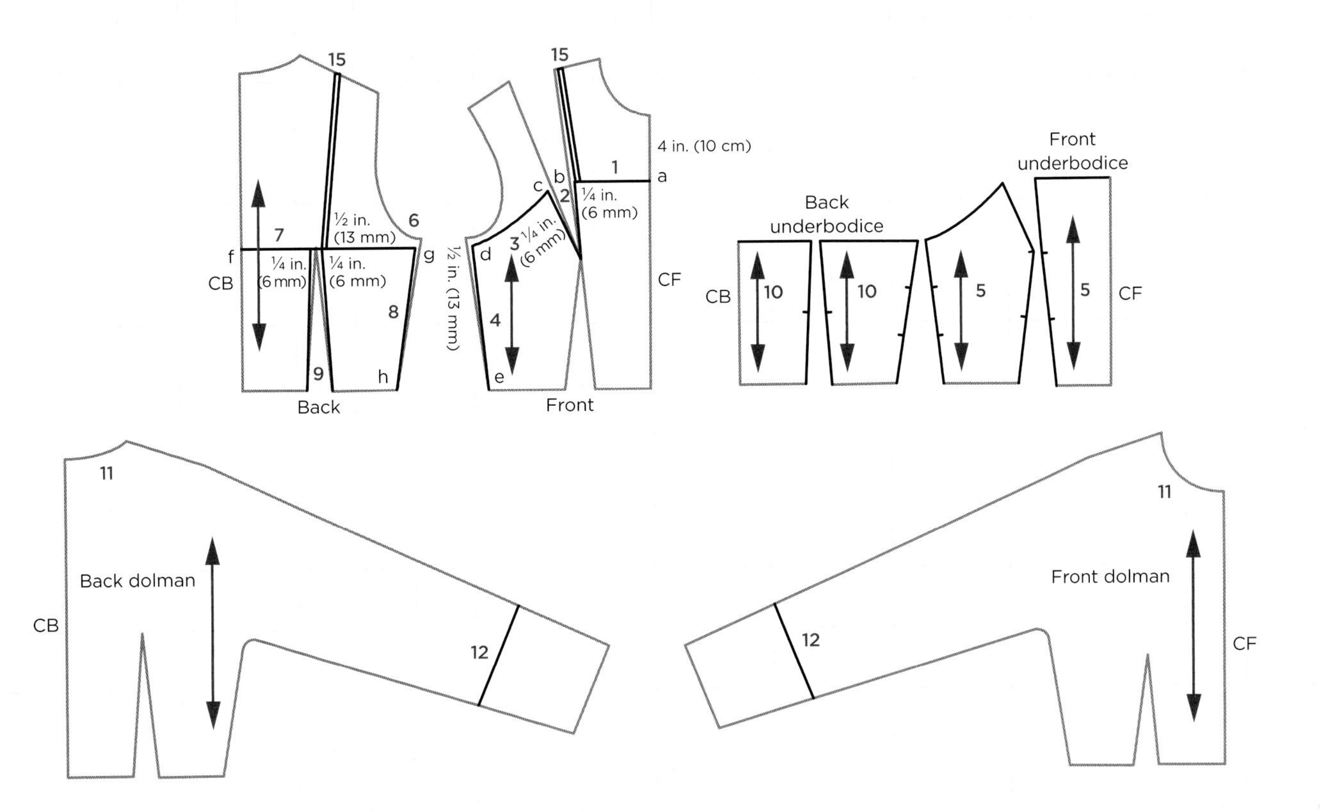

Underbodice back

6. Lower and narrow the back armhole by ½ in. (13 mm) to match the front.
7. Draw a line across the top of the back bodice to match the front bodice (fg).
8. Narrow the back bodice side seam from the new armhole point to the waist (gh).
9. Widen the back dart by ¼ in. (6 mm) on each side at the top line of the bodice.
10. Trace off the back underbodice in two panels.

Lace overbodice layer

11. Trace off the Dolman Sleeve sloper, front and back.
12. Trim the sleeve to three-quarter length.

Skirt

Front and back are the same. For the skirt, you need to draft two large rectangles:

13. Underskirt:
    - Width = 4–6 in. (10–15 cm) bigger than your hip measurement.
    - Length = waist to final skirt length minus 2 in. (5 cm).
14. Overskirt:
    The overskirt can be full as you like.
    - Width = at least 1½ x hip measurement.
    - Length = desired final length of the skirt, measured from waist to hem.

Straps

15. Make two rouleau straps for the underbodice.

Chapter 6

Finishes for Dresses

Necklines

A change of neckline can turn a pattern into a whole new style. To alter the neckline on a pattern, simply draw a new one in with a pencil and ruler or a French curve. Don't forget you can alter the back neckline as well as the front—they don't even have to be the same shape, but make sure the shoulder seams are the same length. Unless it's an asymmetric design, just draw one side of the neckline from shoulder to center and then mirror on the other side.

Here are some ideas to get you going.

Scoop

A low scoop neckline makes a garment look summery or sexy. Play with the depth and the width to get the shape you desire.

SCOOP NECK TIP

Scoop necklines can easily become baggy—this can be rectified by pinching out a section from the bust point to the neck edge (see step 4 of the Wrap Dress, page 98).

Boat

Show off your collarbones with a boat neckline. This is particularly flattering if you are blessed with square shoulders, but is best avoided if you have a full bust.

BOAT NECK TIP

If you're worried about your bra straps showing, take a measurement from strap to strap and make that the width of your "boat."

V

This is similar to the scoop neckline, but it ends in a point. It works just as well on the back as on the front. Experiment with the proportions—how low can you go? A V-neckline is very flattering for larger busts.

V-NECK TIP

As with the scoop, a low V-neckline may need tightening. Try a stay stitch, or pinch as for the scoop neck. A slightly curved line is more flattering than a ruler-straight one.

Square

Often overlooked, a square neckline can be smart or summery. It is a good choice if you want to show off your straight top-stitching. Buttons on the shoulder will give a crisp, nautical look.

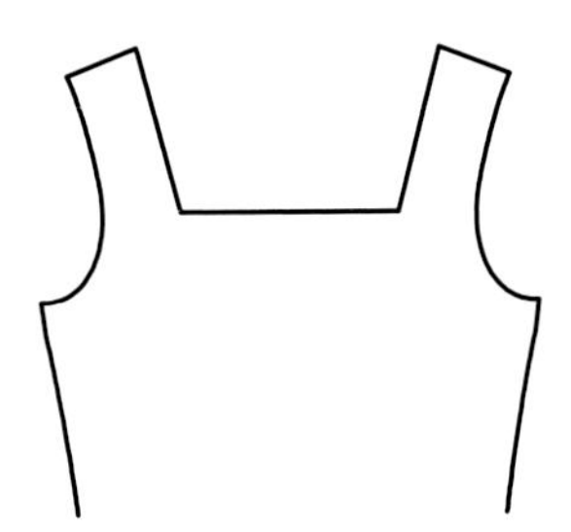

SQUARE NECK TIP

Check where the corners sit so you don't expose your bra.

Sweetheart

A sweetheart neckline says vintage style—why not add diamanté clips in the corners of the curves? This neckline can be cut for modesty or seduction; add piping or a lace trim for extra sweetness.

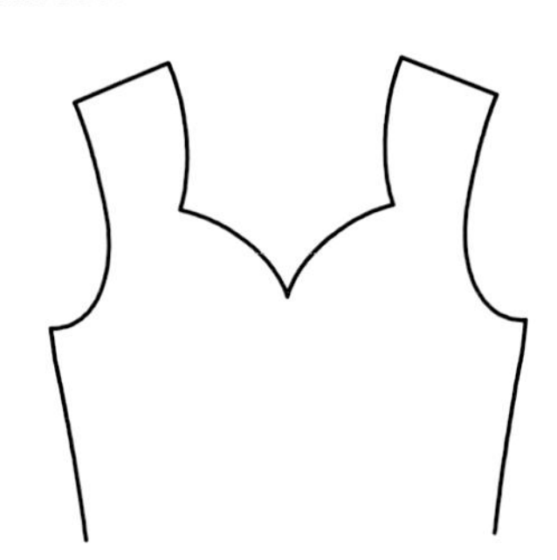

SWEETHEART NECK TIP

This style is best finished with a facing to give your curves a smooth outline.

Asymmetric

Turn a classic into something unusual with a quirky, asymmetric neckline. Sharpen your pencil and go freestyle!

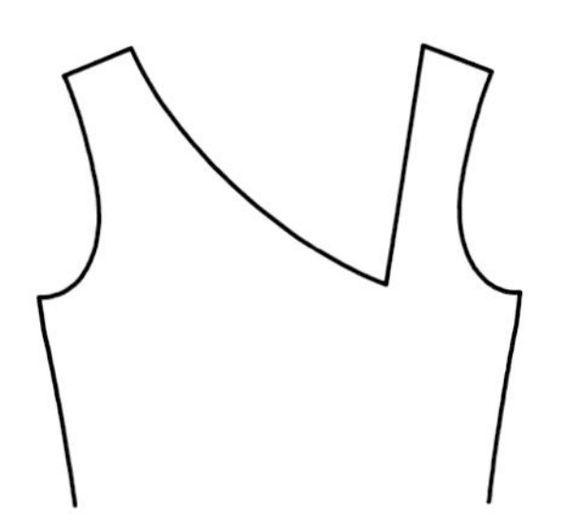

ASYMMETRIC NECK TIP

This neckline is best finished with a facing. Alternatively, go for a raw edge to enhance the cut.

Collars

The following instructions show how to adapt the downloadable collar slopers into these variations.

Standing Collar sloper to Soft Roll Collar variation

You will notice that the Standing Collar sloper on page 30 is slightly curved on the neck and leaf edges. This is to follow the shape of the neck. By contrast, the Soft Roll Collar variation has a folded top, so it needs to be straight on the leaf edge. Unless you are using a soft knit fabric, create the slouch by cutting it on the bias.

TIP

If you are not using stretchy fabric, make sure the collar is big enough to pull over your head!

Starting with the Standing Collar sloper:

1. Measure the circumference of the neckline—a slightly lower and wider neckline will look more relaxed.
2. Draft a rectangle with the long edge equal to the circumference of the neckline. Measure and double the desired height for the collar.
3. Add notches for the shoulder seam points.

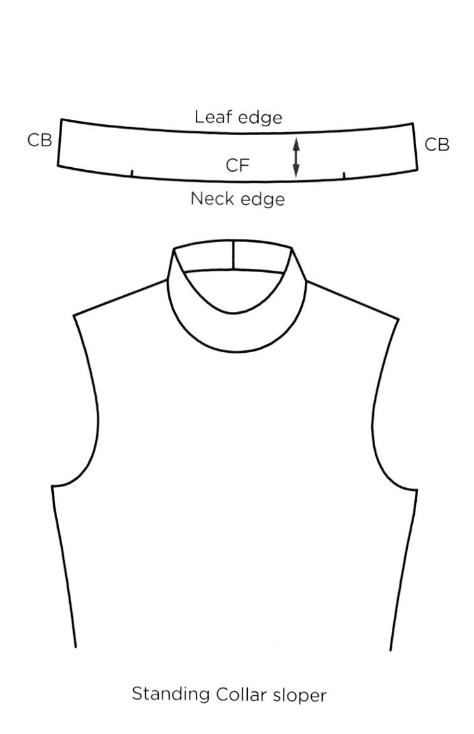

Standing Collar sloper

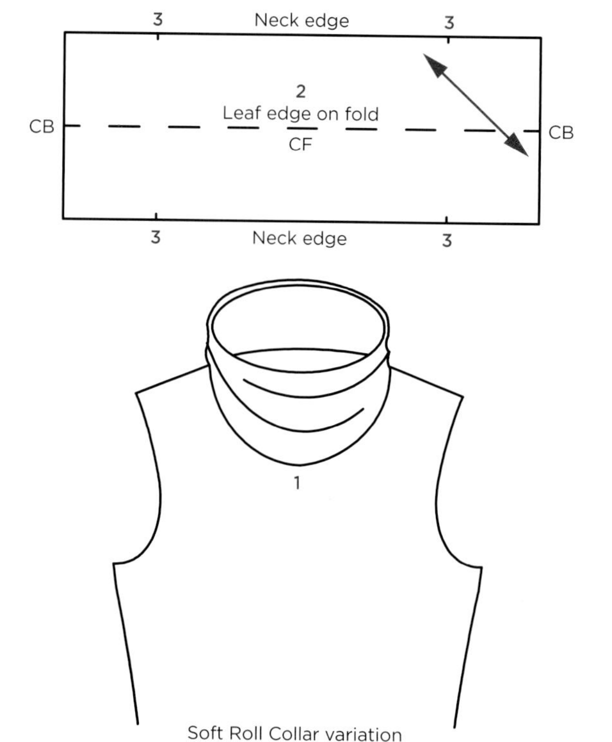

Soft Roll Collar variation

Shirt Collar sloper to Scalloped Edge variation

There are two edges on a collar that have very different functions. The neck edge must be drafted to fit the measurement of the neckline, but the outer or leaf edge is yours to shape as you wish. In this example, a piecrust scallop transforms a shirt from unisex to feminine. If you are not confident in your freehand drafting, make a template for the scallop curves.

Starting with the Shirt Collar sloper (page 29):

1. Redraw the leaf edge of the collar with a scalloped edge.

> TIP
>
> Trim close to your stitching on the scalloped edge and clip into the curves to turn neatly.

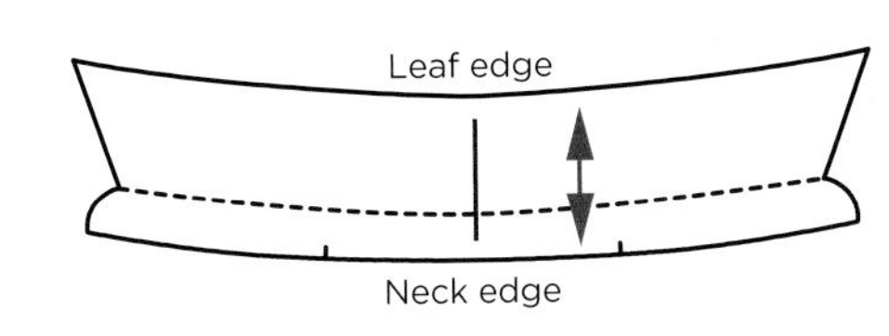

Shirt Collar sloper

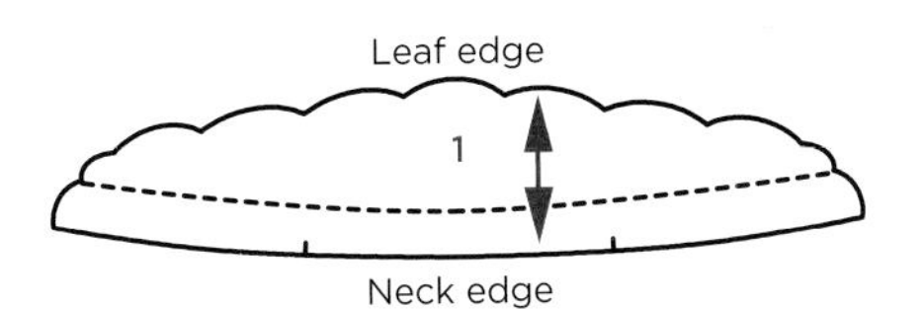

Scalloped Edge Collar variation

Soft and Fluid Collar sloper to Off-the-Shoulder Collar variation

Embrace your inner señorita by adapting the Soft and Fluid Collar into a dramatic off-the-shoulder version.

Starting with a bodice sloper and the Soft and Fluid Collar sloper (page 30):

1. The diagram shows the Darted Dress sloper bodice with the shoulder dart closed and opened at the waist, but you could also start with the Dartless Stretch sloper bodice. On the front and back bodice, draw in a wide V-neckline starting ½ in. (13 mm) from the shoulder point to about 4–5 in. (10–13 cm) down from the neck on the CF/CB (ab, cd).
2. Measure the length of the off-the-shoulder neckline from CF to CB (ab + cd).
3. Trace off and slash into the Soft and Fluid Collar sloper in two (or more) places and spread apart until the neck edge equals the measurement taken in step 2.

TIP

For extra ruffle, cut two—make the top one slightly narrower for a staggered flounce.

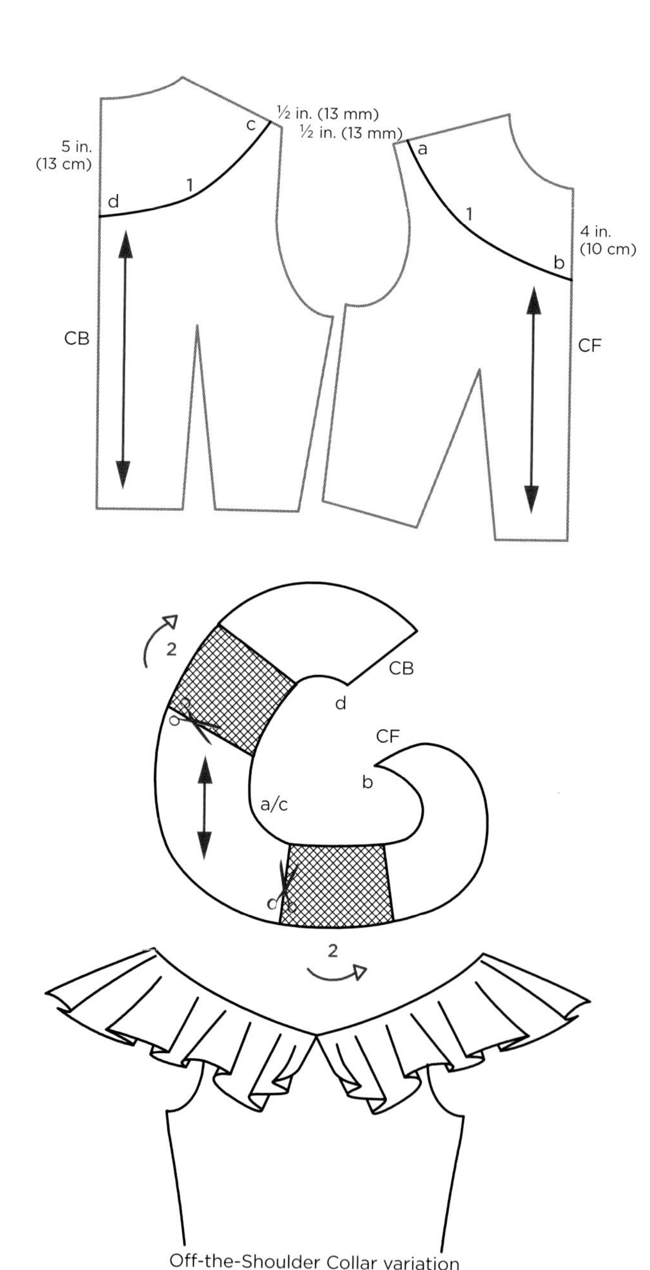

Off-the-Shoulder Collar variation

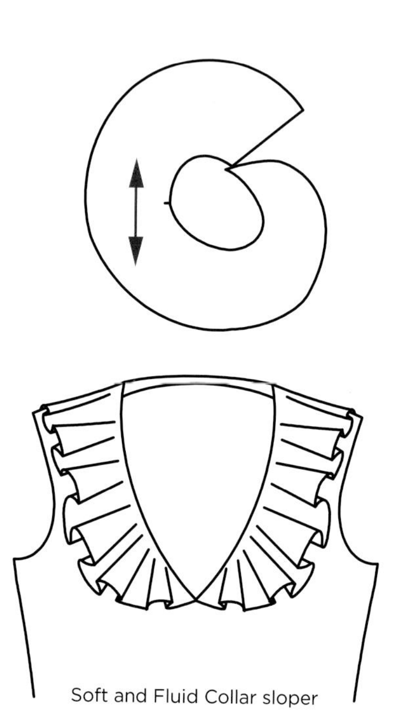

Soft and Fluid Collar sloper

Peter Pan Collar sloper to Sailor Collar variation

Like the Peter Pan Collar, the Sailor Collar sits flat on the shoulders. It needs to be drafted from the bodice of the Darted or Dartless Dress slopers.

Starting with a front and a back bodice sloper (close the front shoulder dart if using the Darted Dress sloper):

1. Draw in a V-neck on the front bodice (see page 120).
2. Join the back and front slopers at the neck point then pivot and overlap by about 1 in. (2.5 cm) at the shoulder point. The more you overlap, the more your collar will roll at the neck edge.

> TIP
>
> Cut the under collar slightly smaller on the outer edge so that the seam rolls underneath.

3. At right angles to the CB edge, draw a line (ab) to the back bodice armhole.
4. At right angles to line ab, draw a line toward the CF, stopping 1 in. (2.5 cm) from the tip of the V-neck on the CF (bc).
5. Extend the end of the collar into a triangular shape that you will be able to tie at the neck.
6. Trace off, mirror on the CB, and cut double.

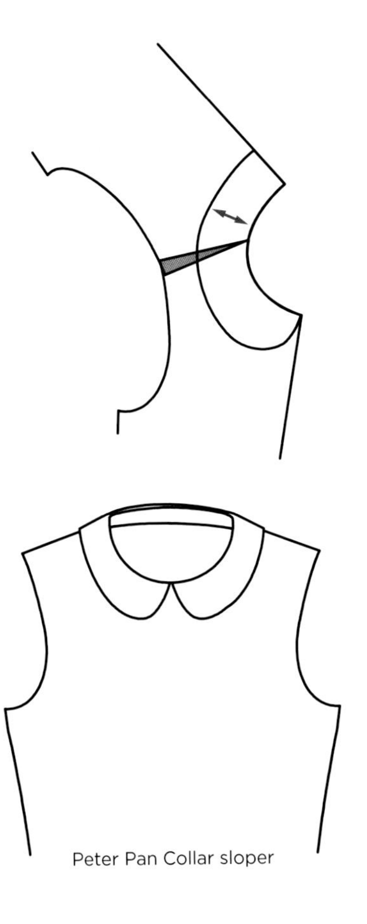
Peter Pan Collar sloper

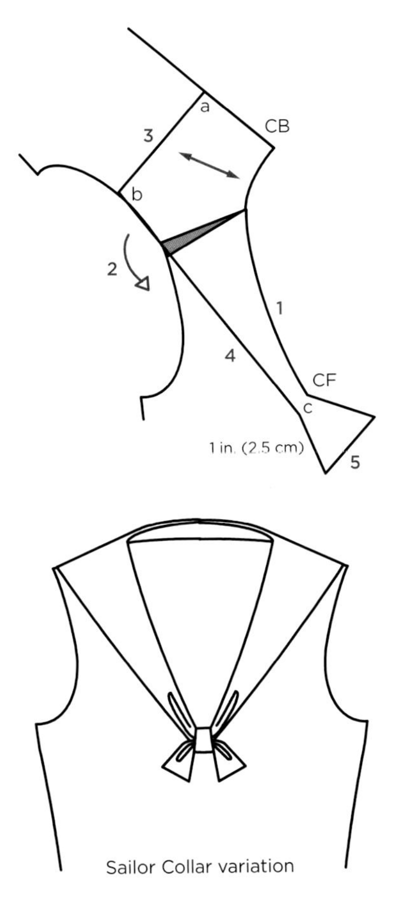

Sailor Collar variation

Sleeves

Dolman Sleeve sloper to Batwing Sleeve variation

Add a touch of drama to your dress with a batwing sleeve. If you use a soft, draping fabric such as jersey or silk, the sleeve will fall in elegant folds. You could also try something stiffer, such as brocade or firm wool, which will give you interesting sculptural shapes.

Starting with the Dolman Sleeve sloper (page 28) and working on the back and the front at the same time:

1. Draw a line from the neck point to the underarm and cut from the armhole to within ⅛ in. (3 mm) of the neck point.

> TIP
>
> There is plenty of room to experiment here—if you pivot the sleeve until it is almost vertical, you will get a very dramatic effect!

2. Pivot the sleeve from the neck away from the CF/CB to open at the armhole—the more you pivot, the bigger the wings.
3. Draw in a new underarm seam from the waist to the wrist.

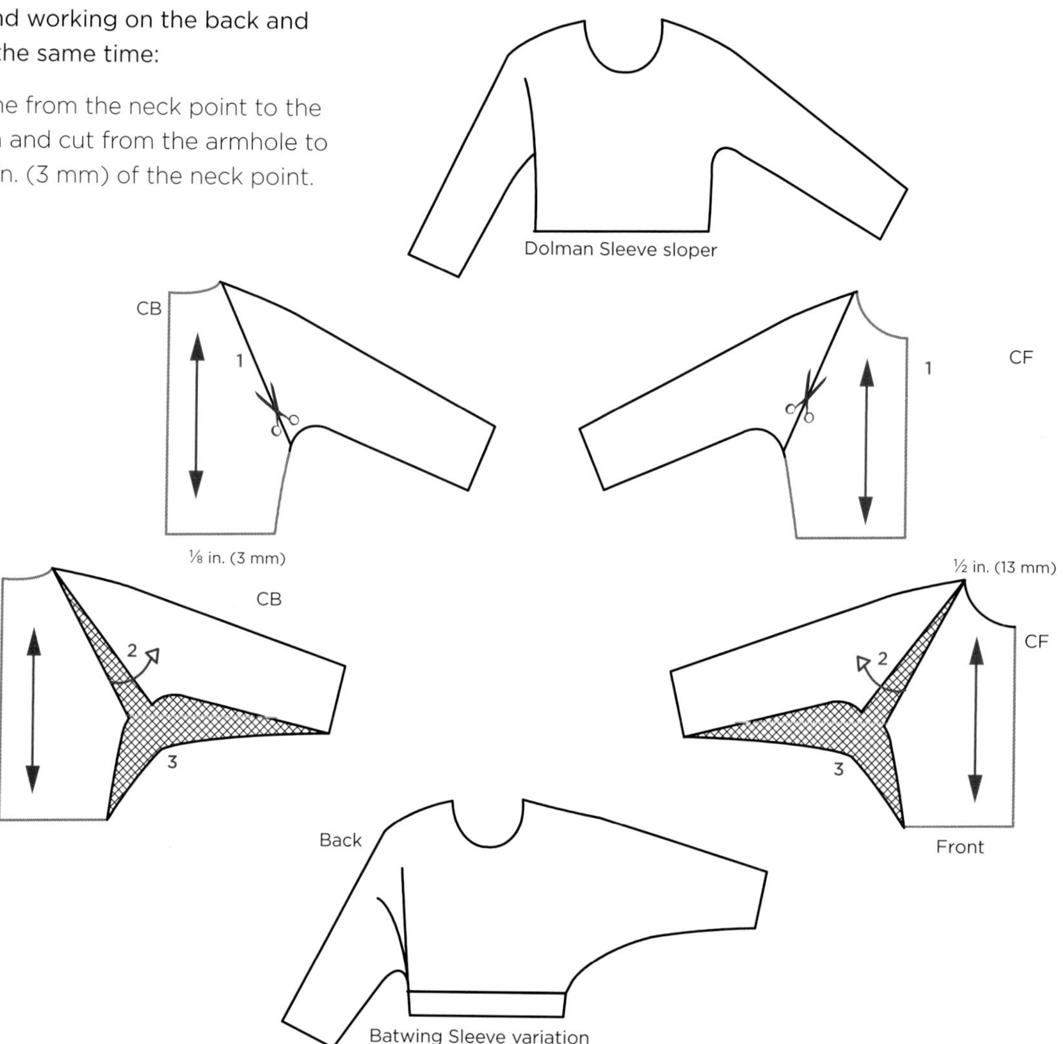

Raglan Sleeve sloper to Ruched Sleeve variation

Ruche up your raglan sleeve with this fun slash and spread technique. It works well in a soft satin fabric with a sheen, as it creates lots of light and shadow in the folds of the fabric.

Starting with the Raglan Sleeve sloper (page 28):

1. Draw a straight line down the center of the sleeve from the bottom of the shoulder dart to the wrist (ab). Cut and separate into two sleeve panels.
2. Divide both panels evenly into about eight equal sections. Cut down each line from the center to within ⅛ in. (3 mm) of the underarm seam.

> TIP
>
> There are three ways to ruche:
>
> > Add a casing to the top edge of the sleeve to thread a ribbon or tape through.
>
> > Stretch ¼ in. (6 mm) elastic into the top seam as you sew it.
>
> > Use the gathering method described for the Tiered Skirt on page 64.

3. Pivot each section away from the wrist until you have approximately doubled the length of the center seam.

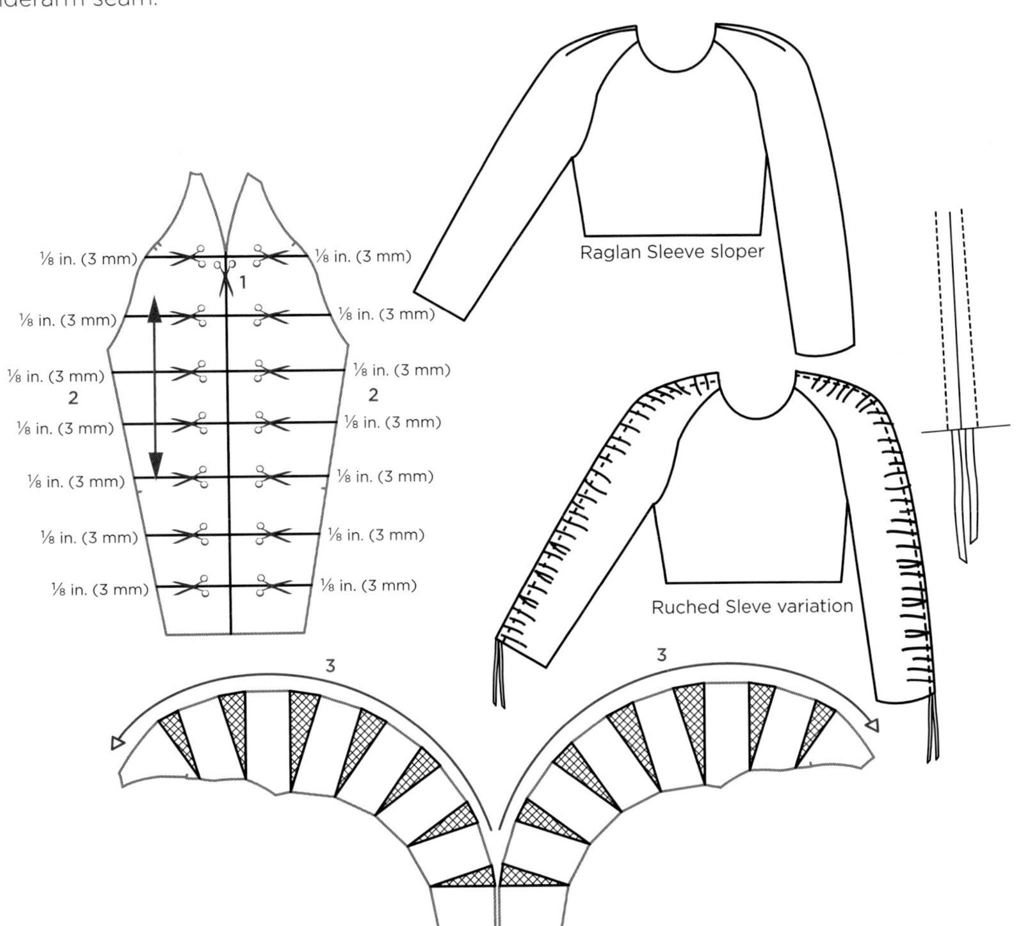

Full-Length Sleeve sloper to Fluted Cuff variation

A fluted cuff has a romantic look—just don't dangle it in your soup! This is another use of the slash and spread method—the more you spread, the more fluted your cuff.

Starting with the Full-Length Sleeve sloper:

1. Mark the length at which you want the fluted cuff to start. Cut and separate into two pieces.
2. Divide the cuff into about five equal sections and cut down these lines from the cuff hem to within ⅛ in. (3 mm) of the cuff seam.
3. Pivot each section from the cuff seam to open at the cuff hem according to how full you want the cuff to be. Add extra on the side seam for a really full look (Example 1).

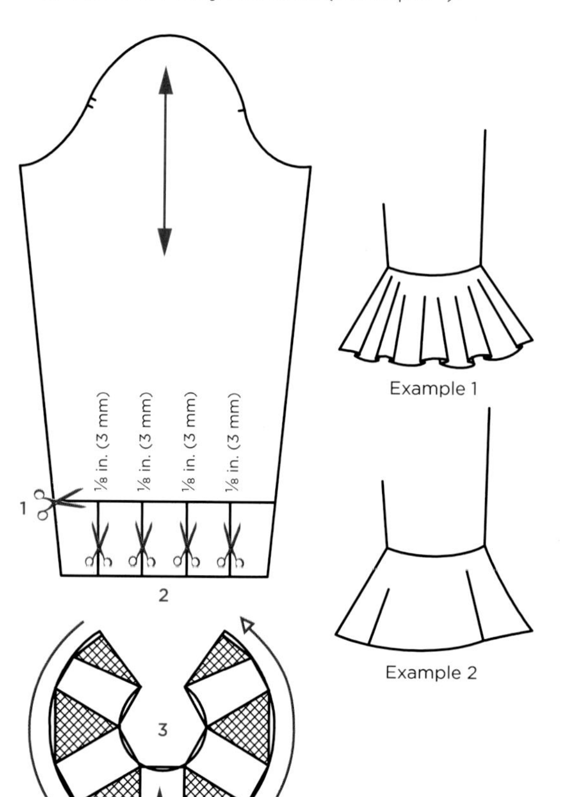

FLUTED CUFF TIP

Cut double and bag out to get a neat finish on the curved hem. Make a feature of the inside of the cuff by using a contrasting fabric or statement lining.

Full-Length Sleeve sloper to Shirt Cuff variation

A shirt cuff is a classic finish for a full-length sleeve and would be a good alternative for the Shirt Dress (page 88). Try it in different fabric and button combinations, such as sheer chiffon with diamanté studs or crisp cotton with a contrast-color button.

Starting with the Full-Length Sleeve sloper (page 27; and see diagrams opposite, above):

1. Draft a rectangle to form the cuff:

   Length = circumference of the wrist + 1 in. (2.5 cm) for ease + 1 in. (2.5 cm) for overlap

   Depth = desired depth of cuff x 2

2. Trim the length of the sleeve by the finished depth of the cuff (remember, your pattern piece is double) minus 1 in. (2.5 cm) for drape.
3. Widen the shortened sleeve at the cuff hem by 1 in. (2.5 cm) on each side and slide up to the armhole.
4. Make an opening in the back side of the sleeve in line with the back armhole notches.
5. Mark your tucks to fit the cuff on either side of the opening. It is normal to have one tuck at the back and the rest at the front.

SHIRT CUFF VARIATION TIP

Remember to match the opening of the cuff to the slit, not the underarm seam (ab-ab).

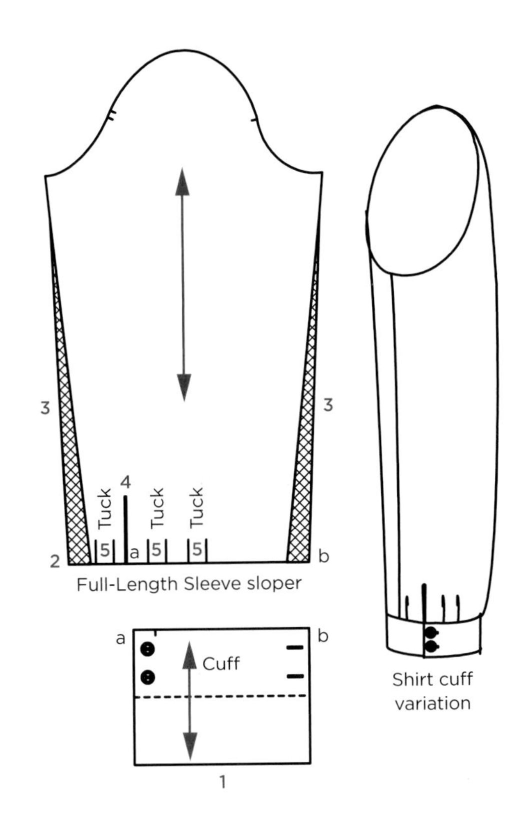

Three-Quarter Length Sleeve sloper to Kimono Sleeve variation

The kimono sleeve is wide and deep—perfect for cool summer evening dresses, cozy winter knits, or nightwear. Try it on the Negligee pattern on page 104.

Starting with the Darted Dress Sloper, back only (front and back are the same), and the Three-Quarter-Length Sleeve sloper (page 27):

1. Draw a straight line parallel to the CF/CB 2 in. (5 cm) beyond the underarm point, finishing ½ in. (13 mm) above the shoulder point.
2. Redraw the shoulder line from the neck point to meet the line drawn in step 1.
3. Draw a rectangle to form the kimono sleeve, as deep and long as you like, with the fold along the top edge.

Front only:

4. Shorten the waist dart if you want to use it.
5. This step is optional. Draw a diagonal line from the neck point to the opposite waist dart to form a wrap.

KIMONO SLEEVE TIP

Add a contrast band or a deep hem to finish the sleeve.

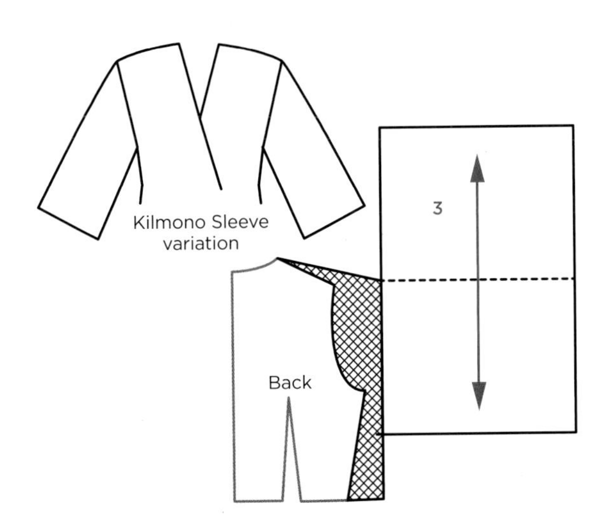

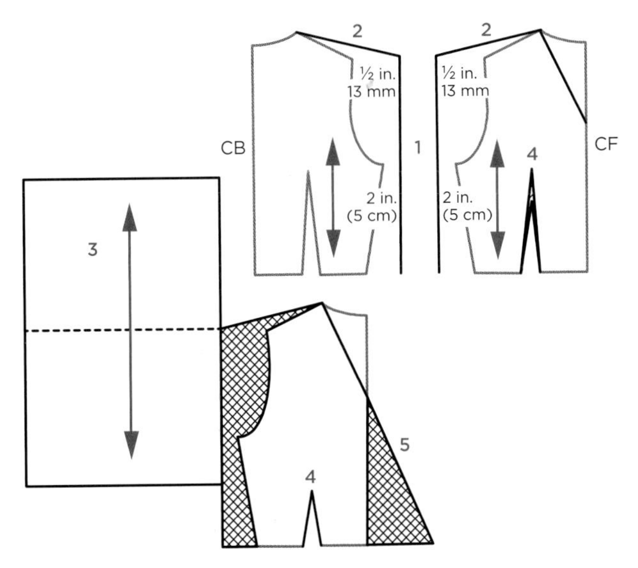

Three-Quarter-Length Sleeve sloper to Split Sleeve variation

A split sleeve is a great addition to a summer or evening dress. Buttons and loops at the sleeve hem add an extra flourish.

Starting with the Three-Quarter-Length Sleeve sloper (page 27):

1. Draw a line down the center of the sleeve, cut, and separate into two pieces.
2. Add a self-facing to both sides of the center seam.
3. Mark on the fold line how long you want the open split to be.
4. Miter the corner of the center seam hem edge.

> TIP
>
> Use a decorative stitch to hold the facing down along the split.

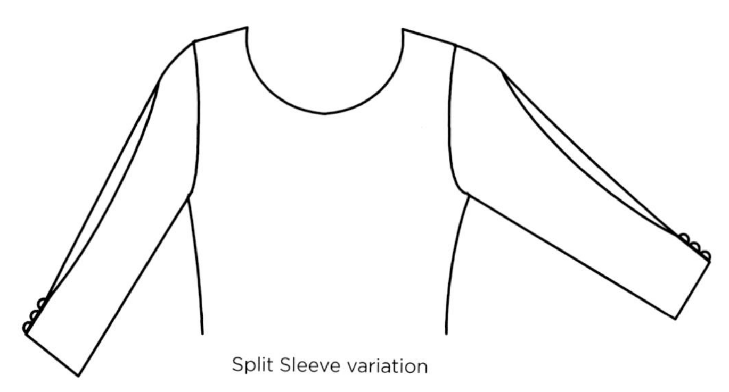
Split Sleeve variation

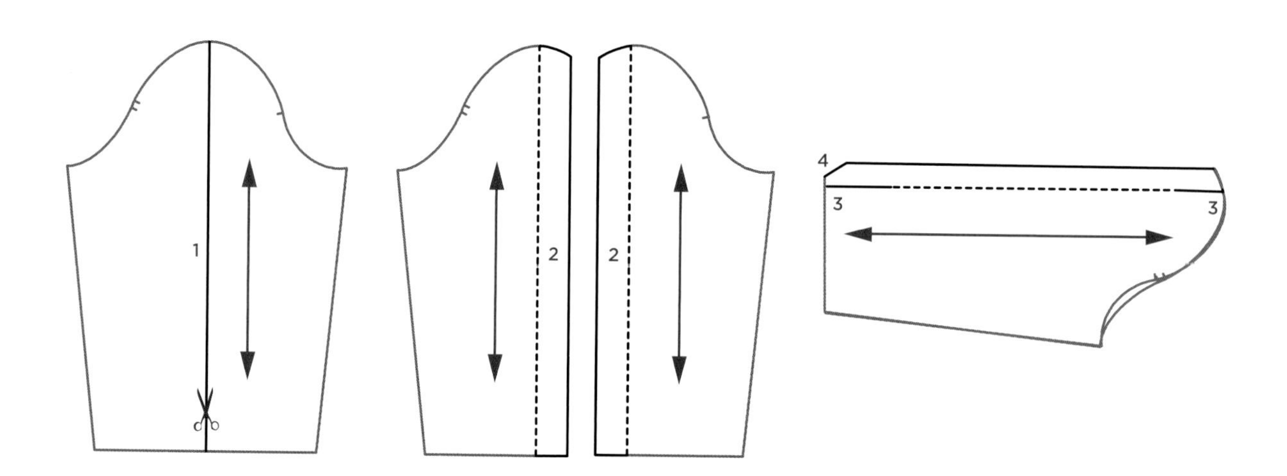

Short Sleeve sloper to Cape Sleeve variation

Smooth at the top and fluted at the hem, the cape sleeve is floaty and flattering. Try it as a cap sleeve with a small flutter, or down to the elbow and bell-like. This style is good for covering the arms without adding warmth.

Starting with the Short Sleeve sloper (page 27):

1. From the center point of the sleeve head, divide the sleeve into five sections with the outer two sections slightly wider at the hem.
2. Cut down each line from the sleeve hem to within ⅛ in. (3 mm) of the sleeve head.
3. Pivot away from the center to add the desired fullness to the cape sleeve. The more you pivot, the fuller the effect will be.

TIP

Try adding this sleeve in a color matching the dress but in a contrasting fabric, such as a silk bodice with chiffon sleeves.

4. As you pivot, the center point on the sleeve head will sink. Redraw in a smooth curve between the notches.
5. Smooth the curve on the hem.

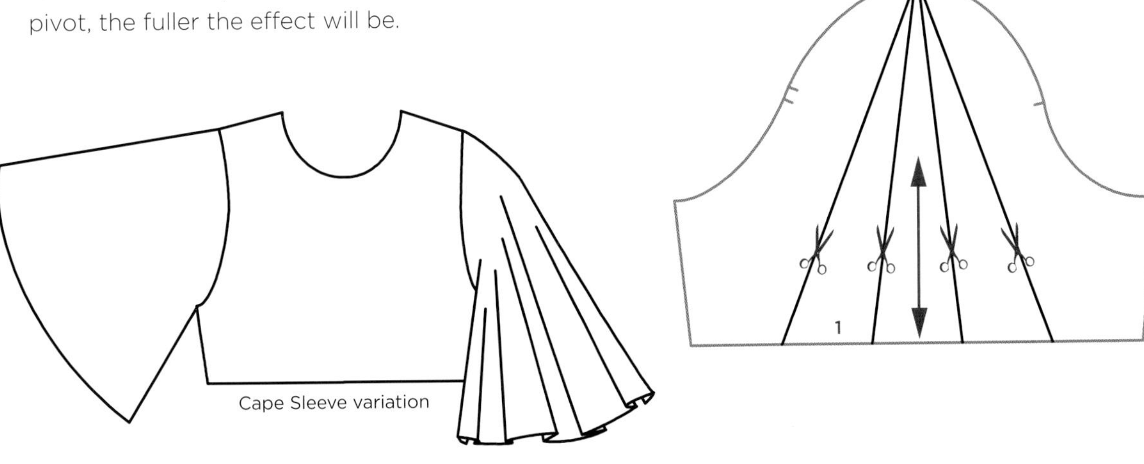

Cape Sleeve variation

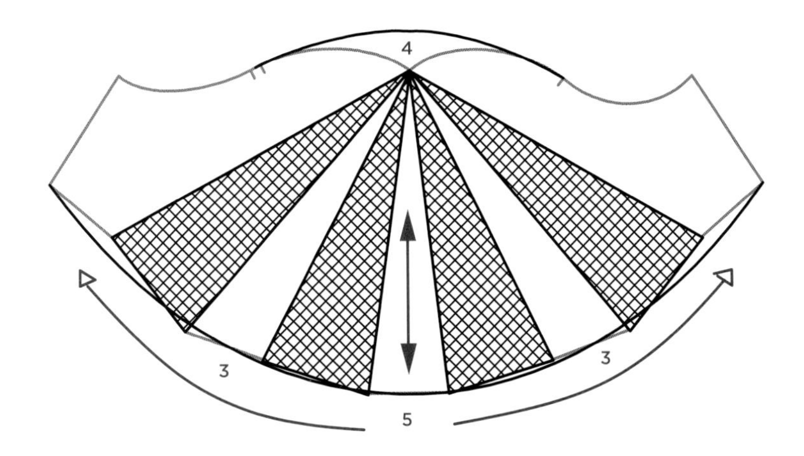

Short Sleeve sloper to Pleated Sleeve variation

The pleating at the crown of this sleeve adds height and definition to the shoulder and would look best in a crisp fabric such as cotton, linen, brocade, or taffeta.

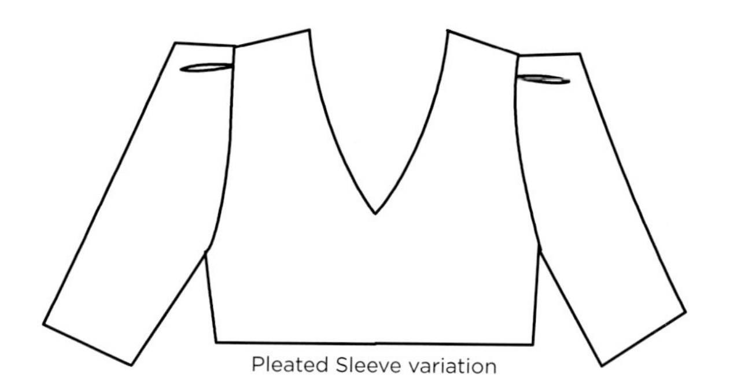
Pleated Sleeve variation

TIP

To increase the structure of the pleated crown, add a square-ended shoulder pad inside the sleeve.

Starting with the Short Sleeve sloper (page 27):

1. Draw a line across the top of the sleeve head just above the notches and divide the top section into three equal wedges (a, b, c).
2. Cut out the top wedge (a) completely and cut from the tip of the wedge to within ⅛ in. (3 mm) of the sleeve-head edge on either side.
3. Pivot open the lower two wedges (b, c) until you have raised the center point by about 2 in. (5 cm). Raise the top wedge (a) so the points of the wedges are equally spaced at the center.
4. Mark the gaps on the sleeve head as pleats with "hats," as you would a dart.

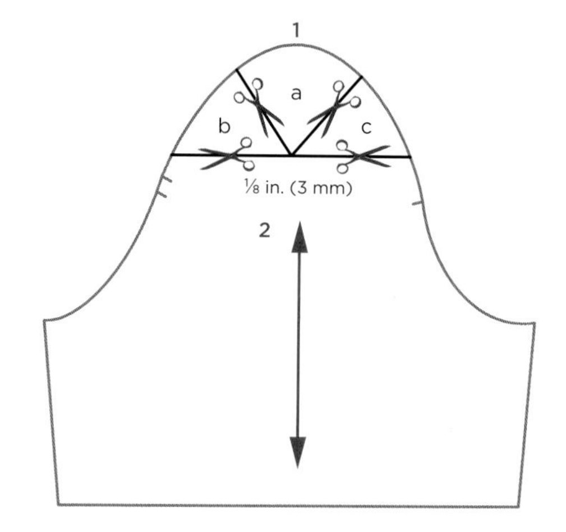

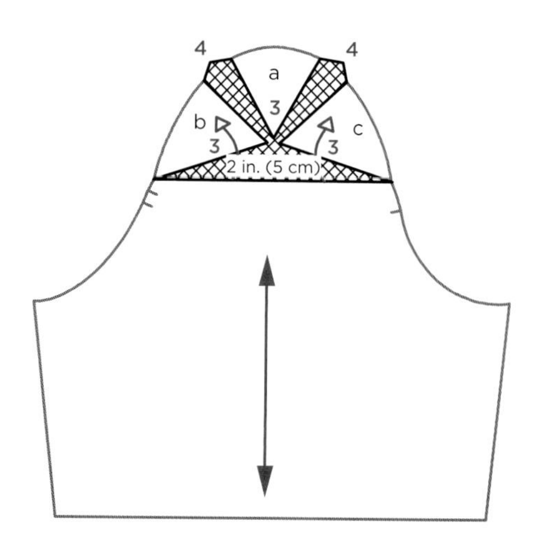

Short Sleeve sloper to Puff Sleeve variation

The puff sleeve is not just for little girls' party dresses. Make it in velvet or silk satin for '40s glamour, or bring out your inner milkmaid in a cotton print or broderie anglaise.

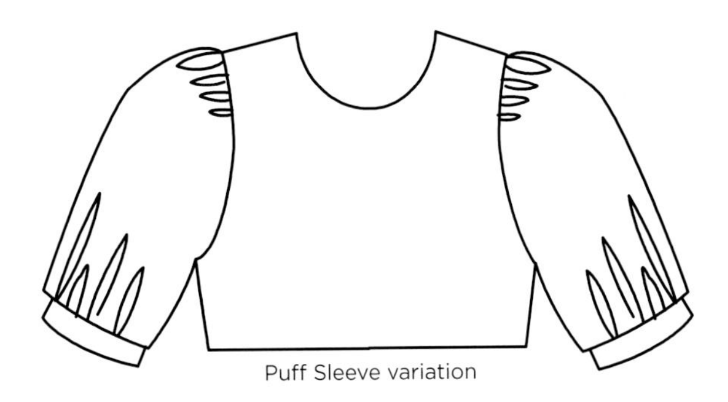

Puff Sleeve variation

TIPS

> Experiment with raising or lowering the sleeve head in relation to the amount added to the width.

> Add a stiff net frill inside at the sleeve head to inflate the puff.

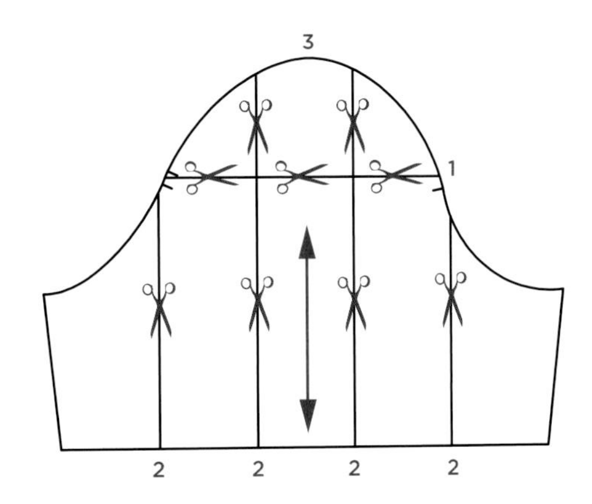

Starting with the Short Sleeve sloper:

1. Draw a horizontal line across the sleeve head at notch level.
2. Divide the whole sleeve into five sections vertically.
3. Cut across all lines and separate.
4. Spread all the sections apart equally by about 1 in. (2.5 cm), or more if you want a puffier effect.
5. Smooth the curved lines of the sleeve head.
6. Draft a band to fit your arm plus 1 in. (2.5 cm) or so for comfort—it should be double the finished depth, with a lengthwise fold. Gather the sleeve between the notches on the sleeve head and along the hem.

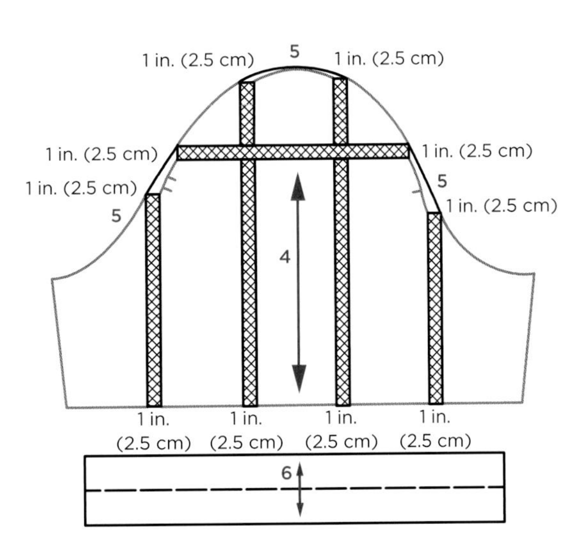

Chapter 7

Fit Solutions

Common Fit Problems and Solutions

The word "sloper" comes from the slopes of your body, and bodies vary, so if your slopes differ a little from the regular ones, don't worry—you just need to make a few adjustments. When you have a perfectly fitting sloper, the idea is that all the patterns you draft from it will include these adjustments and will fit perfectly. In reality, the variables of design, fabric, and pattern-making skill mean you sometimes still need to make small fit adjustments to your patterns. Try on your muslin sloper and arm yourself with a tape measure, pencil, pins, and a mirror. Your measuring buddy may come in useful again here!

Does the neckline fit smoothly and snugly around the neck?

Neckline too tight

1. Bring the front and back bodices together at the neck point (see bottom right).
2. Draw in a new neckline starting at the original CB (it is important to keep this point; otherwise, the neckline will fall backward), going through the shoulder seam and finishing at the CF.

TIP

Trim a small bit at a time until you are happy with it.

Neckline too loose

1. Draw a line from the bust point to the neckline, approximately one-third of the way from the CF (see below).
2. Cut down this line from the neck to within ⅛ in. (3 mm) of the bust point.
3. Pivot and overlap at the neck edge until it feels snug.
4. Smooth out the neckline.

TIP

This is very useful for low necklines so that they don't gape—see the Wrap Dress on page 98.

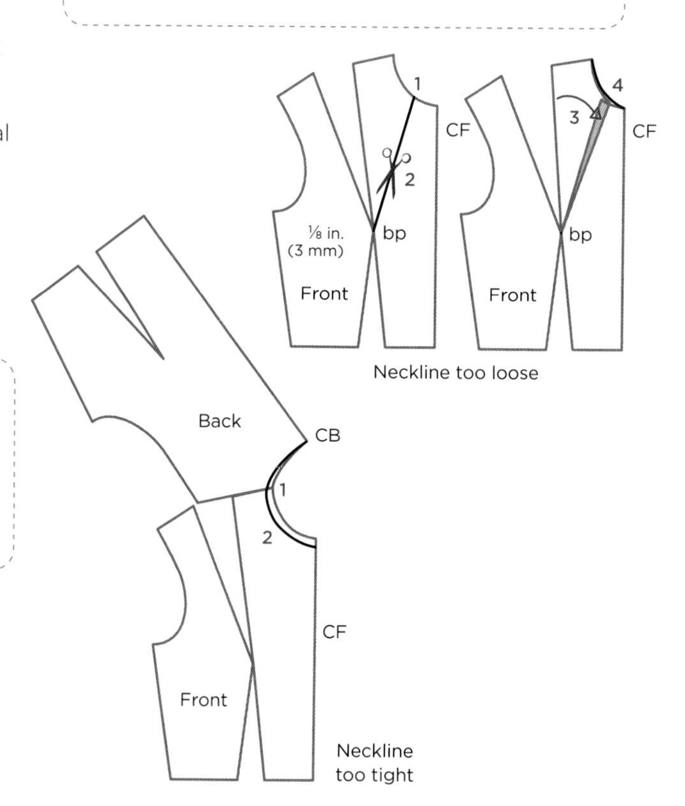

Neckline too loose

Neckline too tight

Do the shoulder seams match the length of your shoulders and sit flat to the body?

Shoulder seam in wrong position (too far forward/back or wrong angle)

1. Close the shoulder dart and open at the waist.
2. Bring the front and back bodices together along the shoulder seam.
3. Draw in your new shoulder line where you want it to be, recut, and separate into your newly aligned back and front bodice pieces.

TIP

You only close the shoulder dart to match up the shoulders while making this adjustment. Pivot back into sloper or style position as required.

Shoulder seam too short

1. Close the shoulder dart and open at the waist.
2. Bring the front and back bodices together along the shoulder seam.
3. Extend the shoulder seam to the required length and fill in to smooth out the armhole.

Shoulder seam too long

1. Close the shoulder dart and open at the waist.
2. Bring the front and back bodices together along the shoulder seam.
3. Shorten the shoulder seam to the required length and smooth out the armhole.

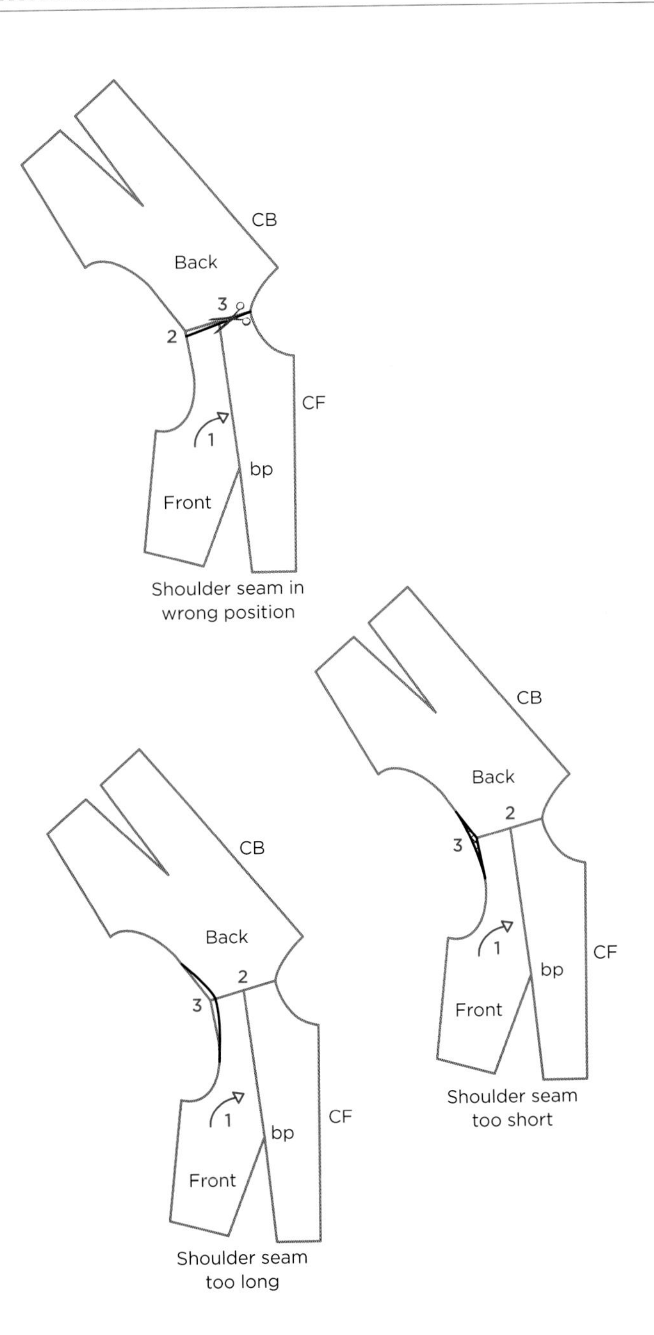

Shoulder seam in wrong position

Shoulder seam too short

Shoulder seam too long

TIP

Don't go too far down the armhole when redrafting, or you will distort it and your sleeve won't fit into it.

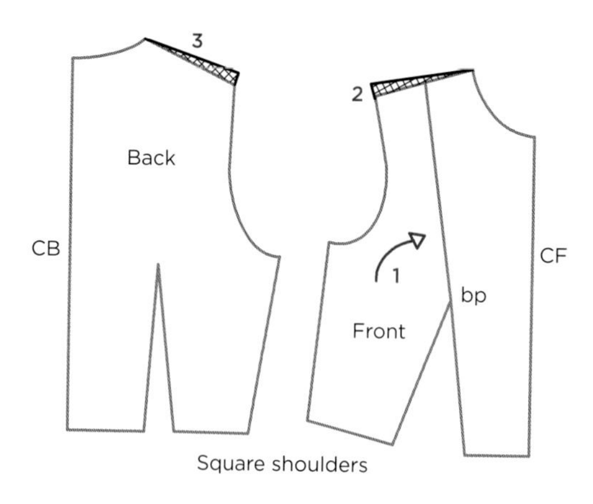

Square shoulders

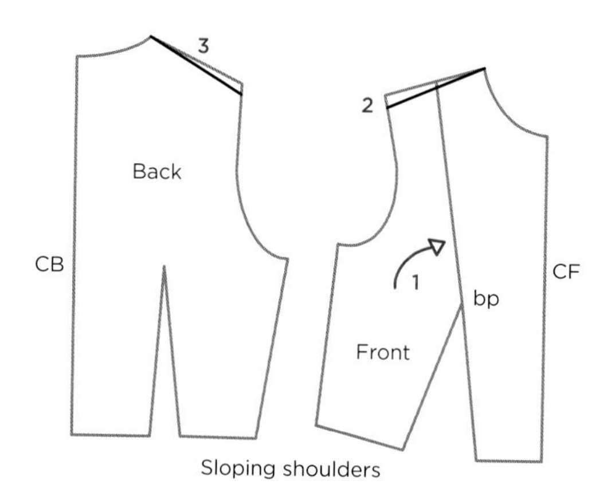

Sloping shoulders

Square shoulders

Front bodice

1. Close the shoulder dart and open at the waist.
2. Add a wedge to the outer edge of the shoulder by raising the shoulder point by the required amount and drawing in a new shoulder seam to the neck point.

Back

3. Trace and mirror the raised front wedge onto the back bodice shoulder seam.

Sloping shoulders

Front

1. Close the shoulder dart and open at the waist.
2. Remove a wedge from the outer edge of the shoulder by lowering the shoulder point by the required amount and drawing in a new shoulder seam to the neck point.

Back

3. Mirror the lowered front wedge onto the back bodice shoulder seam.

For the square shoulders and sloping shoulders adjustments, you may also need to adjust the sleeve head slightly—see the armhole adjustment opposite.

TIP

An alternative adjustment for sloping shoulders is to insert a small shoulder pad, which will fill the shoulders and reduce creases at the armhole.

Are the armholes comfortable, and can you move your arms easily?

Armhole too loose

Front and back bodice

1. Raise the armhole on the side seam and join with a curve into the original armhole.

Sleeve

2. Draw a line down the center of the sleeve from the sleeve head to the wrist. Cut and separate.
3. Overlap the sleeve down the center by approximately the same amount that you raised the armhole on the bodice.

Armhole too tight

Front and back bodice

1. Lower the armhole on the side seam and join with a curve into the original armhole.

Sleeve

2. Draw a line down the center of the sleeve from the sleeve head to the wrist. Cut and separate.
3. Spread and fill down the center of the sleeve by approximately the same amount that you raised the armhole.

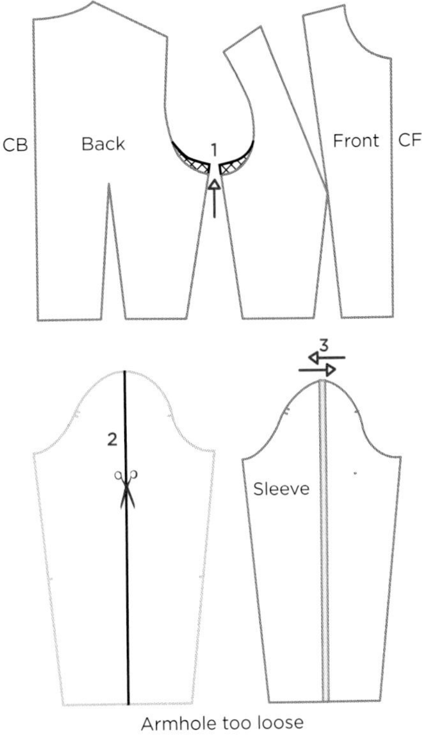

Armhole too loose

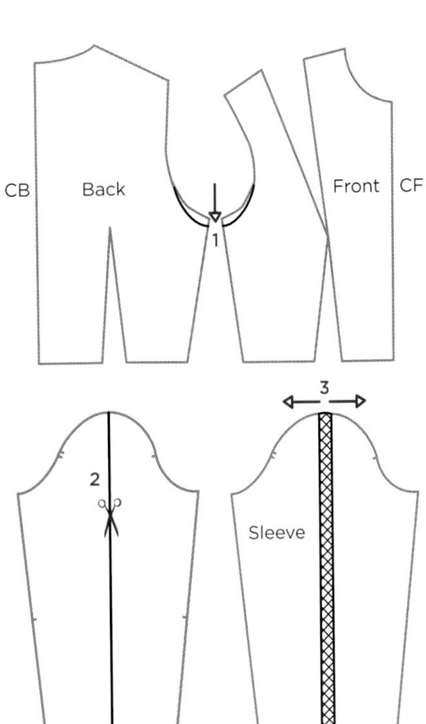

Armhole too tight

TIP

If you don't need the alteration through the whole sleeve, just cut down the center of the sleeve to within ⅛ in. (3 mm) of the wrist and pivot to open or overlap at the sleeve head to fit the adjusted armhole.

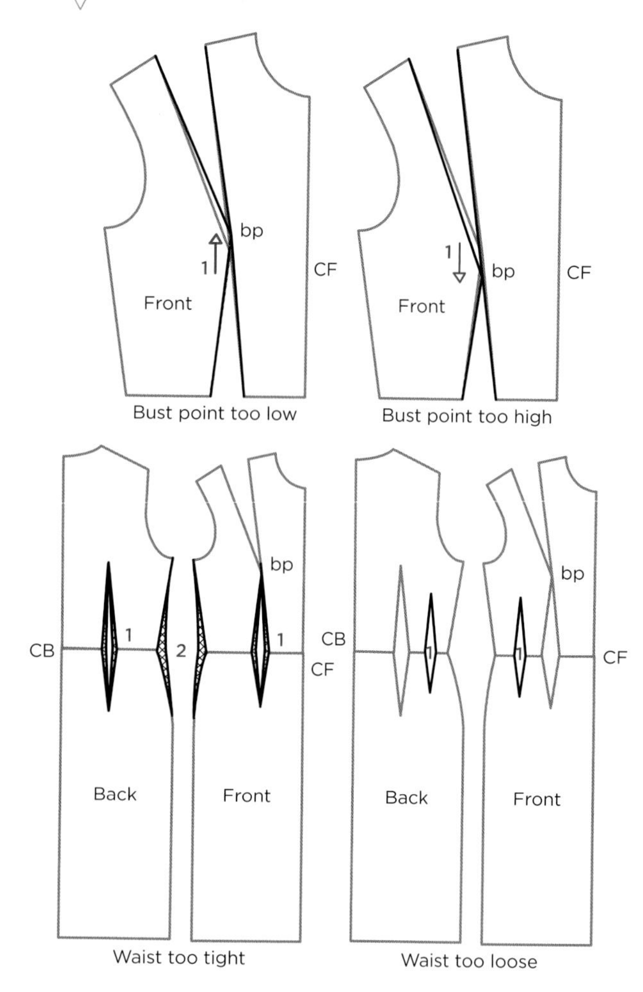

Bust point too low

Bust point too high

Waist too tight

Waist too loose

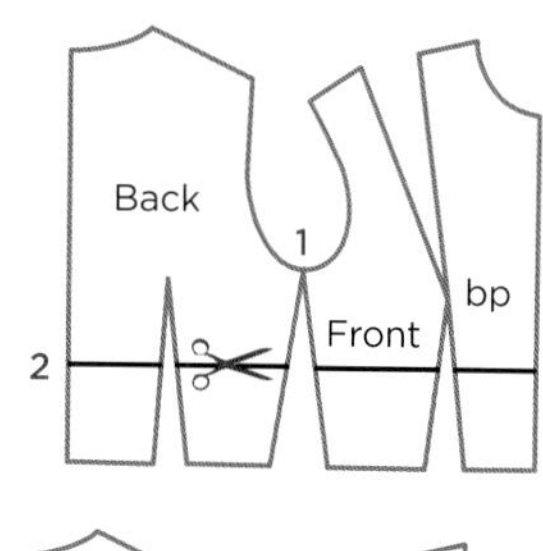

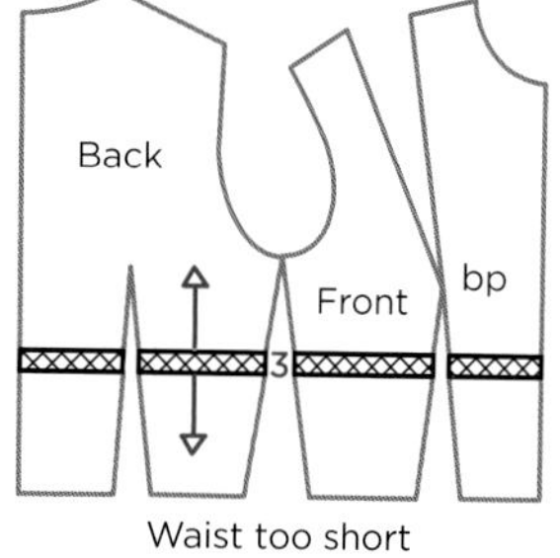

Waist too short

Is the bustline flattering, with the bust point at the apex of the bust? Does it sit well across the back?

Bust point too low

1. Raise the bust point so it is sitting at the apex of the bust and redraw the shoulder and waist dart legs to meet the new bust point.

Bust point too high

1. Lower the bust point so it sits at the apex of the bust and redraw the shoulder and waist dart legs to meet the new bust point.

Is the waistline comfortable and sitting in the right place on the front and back?

Waist too tight

Front and back

1. Narrow the waist dart at the waistline.
2. Extend the waistline and redraft the side seam from just below the armhole to the widest point of the hip.

Waist too loose

Front and back

1. Draft an extra waist dart between the existing sloper waist dart and the side seam. Make it slightly shorter at both ends for an elegant line.

Waist too short

Front and back

1. Align the front and back bodices at the underarm point.
2. Draw a line across the front and back bodices under the bust point across the rib cage area of the bodices. Cut and separate.
3. Spread apart vertically until the bodice reaches the required length.

Waist too long

Front and back

1. Align the front and back bodices at the underarm point.
2. Draw a line across the front and back bodices under the bust point across the rib cage area of the bodices. Cut and separate.
3. Overlap until the bodice reaches the required length.

Do the side seams skim the hips at the widest point without pulling or gaping?

Hips too tight

Front and back

1. Trace off the side seam line from the waist to the hem. Pivot from the side hem point until it is wide enough to fit your hips.
2. Repeat on the side seam of the bodice, pivoting from just below the underarm point until it meets the new waist point.
3. If your sloper is now too loose in the waist (because you have curvy hips and a small waist), remove the excess by adding an extra dart to fit.
4. You can also experiment with shortening the skirt waist darts.

Hips too loose

Front and back

1. Trim the excess on the side seam from the waist to the hem.

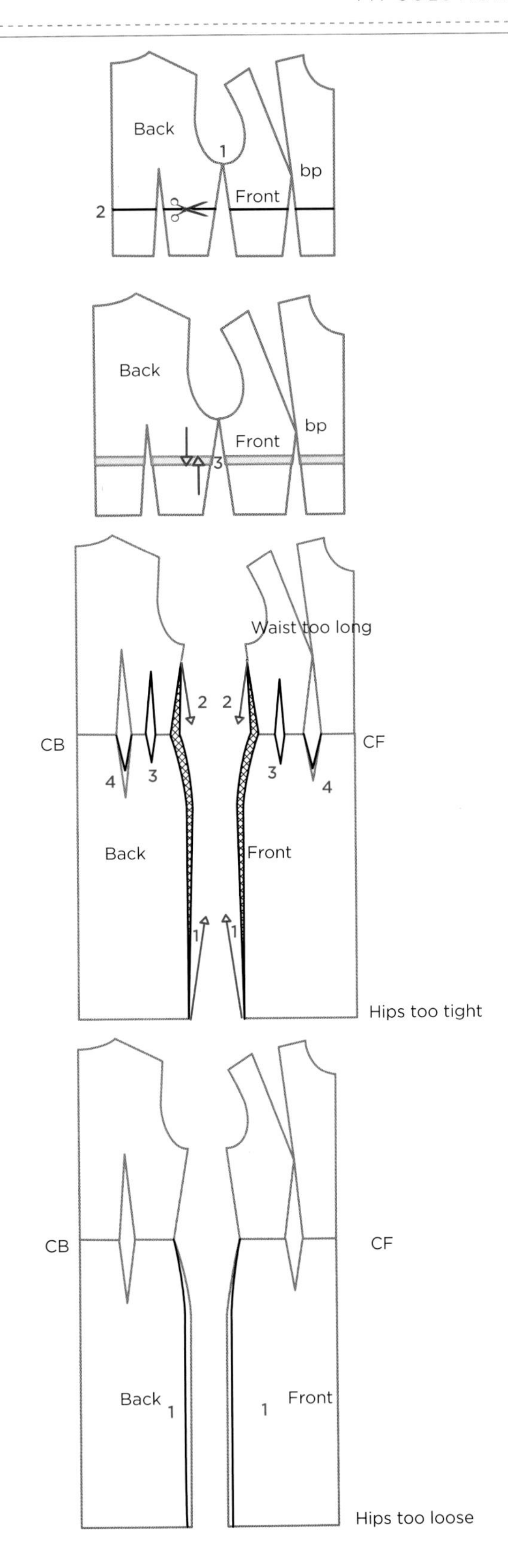

Index

Acknowledgments

A pincushion full of thanks goes to:

Lilia, for co-authoring the book and offering her expertise at the photoshoot;

Nigel, for cocktails and catering;

Sophie, for editing and encouragement;

Stephen, for additional editing;

Singh, for sewing;

Anastasia and Telestia, for inspirational pattern-making techniques;

Rachel and Ray Stitch, for first introductions and moral support; and

PatternMaker, for drafting software with patient help.

Author Biography

Alice Prier has over 30 years' experience working in fashion design and education. She is responsible for teaching pattern cutting classes at London fabric shop Ray Stitch (raystitch.co.uk). She has also founded her own company—Alice & Co (aliceandco.co.uk).

Lilia Prier Tisdall is a Costume Mounting Specialist at the Victoria and Albert Museum, and a freelance writer and theater reviewer (liliapt.tumblr.com).

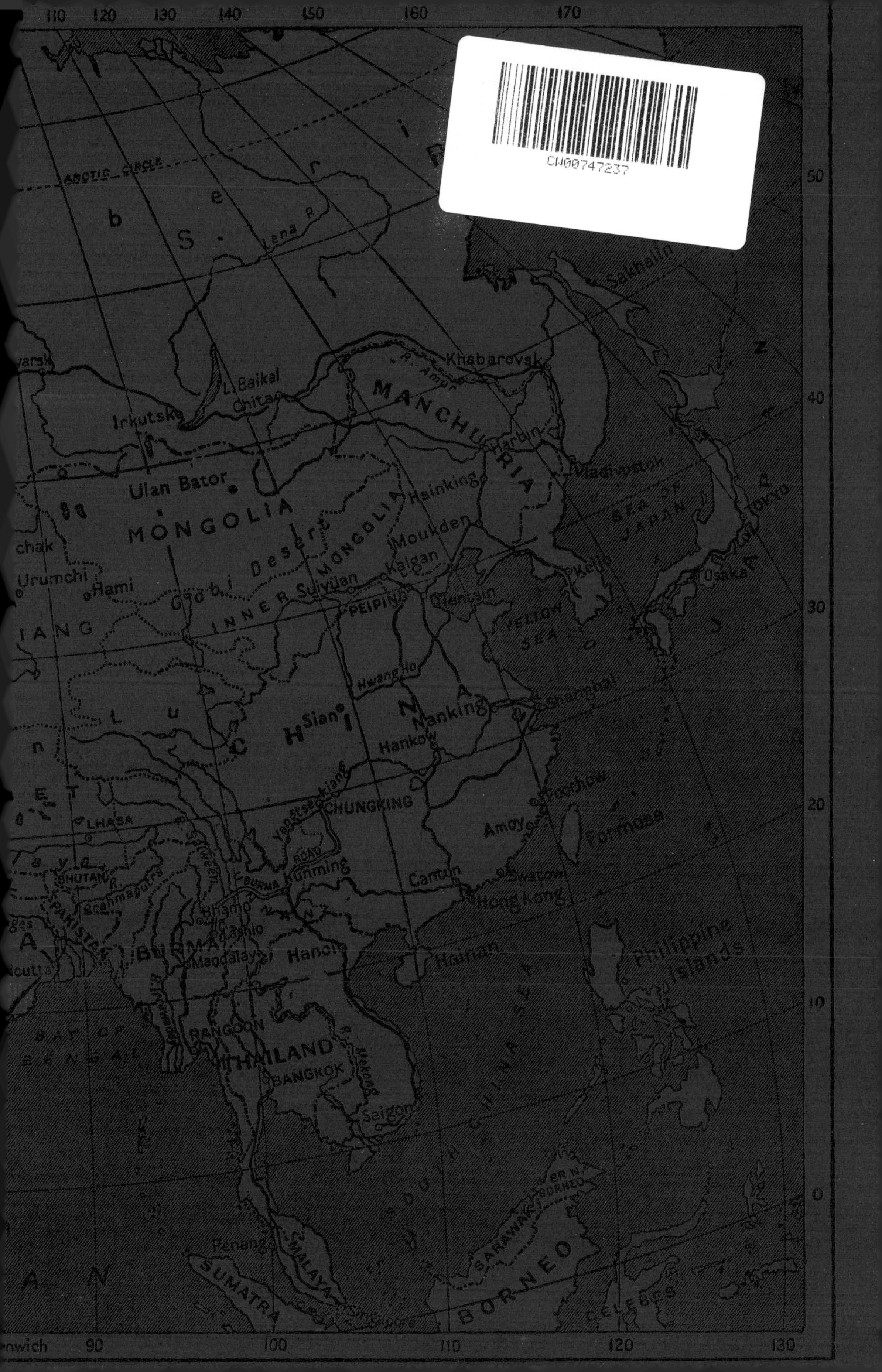

CN00747237
ARCTIC CIRCLE
Lena R.
S i b e r i a
Sakhalin
Khabarovsk
R. Amur
L. Baikal
Chita
Irkutsk
MANCHURIA
Harbin
Vladivostok
Ulan Bator
MONGOLIA
Hsinking
Moukden
SEA OF JAPAN
TOKYO
Gobi Desert
INNER MONGOLIA
Kalgan
Suiyuan
Urumchi
Hami
PEIPING
Tientsin
YELLOW SEA
Osaka
Hwang Ho
Shanghai
Nanking
Sian
CHINA
Hankow
Yangtse Kiang
CHUNGKING
Foochow
Amoy
Formosa
LHASA
BHUTAN
Brahmaputra R.
BURMA ROAD
Kunming
Canton
Swatow
Hong Kong
PAKISTAN
Bhamo
Lashio
BURMA
Mandalay
Hanoi
Hainan
Philippine Islands
BAY OF BENGAL
RANGOON
THAILAND
BANGKOK
R. Mekong
Saigon
SOUTH CHINA SEA
BR. N. BORNEO
SARAWAK
BORNEO
Penang
MALAYA
SUMATRA
Singapore
CELEBES
110 120 130 140 150 160 170
50 40 30 20 10 0
90 100 110 120 130

STROLLING ABOUT ON THE ROOF OF THE WORLD

This volume covers the first one hundred years of the Royal Society for Asian Affairs, formerly the Royal Central Asian Society. It traces its *fons et origo* within the Central Asian Question, and continues through the two World Wars to the present day. Throughout its pages are glimpses and vignettes of some of its extraordinary, even eccentric, members and their astonishing adventures. The wealth of historic, and often amusing, detail makes it a lively account. With its considerable factual content it will become a work of reference for all interested in Asia. This book is generously illustrated and includes many of the Society's unique archival photographs not previously published.

Tibetan Boy with head of Ovis Poli, 1904

[*Frontispiece*] [*RSAA Archives*]

STROLLING ABOUT ON THE ROOF OF THE WORLD

The First Hundred Years of the Royal Society for Asian Affairs (Formerly Royal Central Asian Society)

Hugh Leach

with

Susan Maria Farrington

LONDON AND NEW YORK

ILLUSTRATIONS

The map of Asia on the inside covers is that used in the Society's *Journals* until 1969

FOREWORD

by The Rt Hon. Lord Hurd of Westwell, CH, CBE

As the wheel of history turns images familiar from the past reappear. As I write this foreword a handful of British troops are camped outside Kabul. Our newspapers day after day carry photographs of bearded warriors who rule Herat and Kandahar. Many of us have been re-reading *Kim*.

Behind the news of the day lie themes which go deeper than entertainment or immediate information. Successful policy making, in Asia as elsewhere, depends on informed opinion. We British have been fortunate in the last two centuries, in the number of our countrymen who have studied and travelled through Asia. To be fully valuable such experiences should be shared. That in brief was the purpose of the Royal Society for Asian Affairs when it was founded one hundred years ago. It is timely in Hugh Leach's History to remind ourselves how this came about. Then the focus was on Central Asia, but Lord Curzon quickly endorsed a wide definition of that phrase. At the Society's second Annual Dinner he said that: 'Central Asia is not merely a geographical formula, but a comprehensive phrase opening up a political problem of the first magnitude. These countries . . . form a part of what seems the most complex and intricate, and also the most important political mosaic to be seen on the face of the globe.' Few of us would write in such grandiloquent prose, but the thought remains valid, even though the Indian Empire which Curzon ruled has gone. Through the years the Society and its *Journal* have brought experience to bear on many of the problems which still vex us, for example Kashmir, Palestine and now again Afghanistan.

As in the past we have to wrestle not just with geographical issues, but with problems of principle. A hundred years ago a question mark began to gather over the principle of empire. Members of this Society asked what would be the outcome of the rivalries between the empires which had taken shape in the nineteenth century, and what would happen if these empires relinquished their grip. That grip was indeed relinquished in the twentieth century, but a new problem now arises. In a world of post-imperial nation states in what circumstances are more orderly and successful countries entitled to intervene when particular states decay and fail? This is the old imperial problem in a new guise. Professor Yapp told the Society nearly ten years ago 'the delusion that one can bring about a just order through international intervention in the internal affairs of states is one of the most dangerous follies of our times'. Our present Prime Minister proclaims and acts on the opposite view, both in the Balkans and in Afghanistan. History suggests that there is no absolute answer to this question. The empirical solutions on which we fall back depend on the kind of accumulated and shared wisdom of which this Society and its *Journal* provide such a strong example.

ACKNOWLEDGEMENTS

The first shall be first and these few words are insufficient to record my debt to Sue Farrington for all her help. The book could not have been written without her and is as much hers as mine. She has typed up innumerable drafts, deciphering my dreadful hand with astonishing patience, made numerous sound suggestions and shown an uncanny and determined nose for research.

My kind neighbour, Miss Averil Hughes, has been the first to wield the 'red pen' on my initial drafts. Miss Marinel FitzSimons, MBE, has read and checked all the chapters, drawing on her retentive memory of twenty-seven years of service as Secretary to the Society. The Hon. Ivor Lucas, CMG, has laboured through the whole work, tightening it as necessary; Ms Carol Gardiner has given it the final necessary polish with her professional editing and Mrs Merilyn Hywel-Jones has helped in more ways than there is space to record. To these my especial thanks.

I am grateful for the assistance with specific chapters received from Mr Michael Pollock and Mr Murray Graham (The Library); Mr St John Armitage, CBE, the Society's acknowledged expert on matters 'Lawrentian' (The Lawrence of Arabia Medal); Dr Ina Russell, OBE, and Sir James Craig, GCMG (A Role in Education); Colonel Tony Fowle, MC, (The Dinner Club); Mr Adrian Steger (The Junior Membership); The Hon. Ivor Lucas, Ms Susan Pares and Mrs Kay Beckett (The Journal). Mr John Shipman has checked the historical accuracy of external events in the first three chapters and written that on The Archives.

Sir Denis Wright, GCMG, and Mr Michael Noël-Clark of the Iran Society have made some helpful contributions, especially relating to Sir Percy Sykes. Colonel Gordon Neilson and Mr Antony Wynn have also assisted over the Sykes material.

Personal recollections have been valued, especially from Colonel Tom Walcot for memories and a photograph of his guardian, Geoffrey Stephenson; Captain P. E. I. Bailey, RN, of his uncle Lieut Colonel F. M. Bailey; and Mr James Nash, MBE, for access to his father's papers and photographs of the Malleson Mission.

Others who have been helpful in various ways, responded to the Society's circular asking for contributions, or provided photographs include Professor Hugh Baker, Mr Jonathan Black, Mr Michael Blyth, Mr Richard Burges Watson, CMG, Mr Michael Caroe, Mrs Virginia Dimsey, Mrs Frances Dransfield, Patricia East, Lady Fenn, Mr Christoher Gibb, Mr Neville Green, OBE, Mr Peter Hopkirk, Dr Philip Horniblow, Mrs Eileen Humphreys, Ms Mishal Husain, Miss Leila Ingrams, Major Roddy Jones, Mrs Mary Mackay, Mr John Massey-Stewart, Daphne, Baroness Park of Monmouth, CMG, OBE, Mr Roger Perkins, Professor Colin Platt, Mrs Jean Rasmussen, Mrs Peggie Robertson,

Mr Stephan Roman, Mr Charles Sandeman, Mrs Isobel Shaw, Colonel David Smiley, LVO, OBE, MC, Mr Tristram Sykes, Mr Ken Walton, Mr Bill Wedge, Rebecca Wilmshurst, Mr Hugh Wingfield-Hayes, Mr Francis Witts, Mrs Ingrid Woodburn, BBC World Service, Canning House, the Imperial War Museum, Jacobs Gibb Ltd, the MacRobert Trusts, the National Army Museum, the School of Oriental and African Studies, The East London Mosque Trust (Mr Chowdhury Mueen Uddin and Mr N. Haque) and Tower Hamlets Borough Local History Library (Mr Christopher Lloyd). Illustrations also come from the Society's various collections, the authors themselves and due acknowledgement is made to any others not listed individually. Similarly, whilst every effort has been made to trace, where applicable, copyright holders of photographs, apologies are made to any who might have been inadvertently omitted.

David McCarthy and his team at LaserScript have shown great ingenuity in the layout of the text and photographs and infinite patience in dealing with amendments.

I am grateful also to the Society's hard working Assistant Secretaries, Jane Young, Morven Hutchison, MBE and, previously, Yolande Whittall, who have all carried out miscellaneous areas of research for me.

There are many others who have helped but to avoid a near-endless list I ask their forgiveness by thanking them collectively for their contributions.

Above all, the Society is profoundly indebted to Shell International for their most generous contribution to aid the publication of this work.

INTRODUCTION

Whilst searching through some old boxes in the Society's offices, I came across a rather curious ink-stained note. It read: 'I was asked by General Sir Richard Gale in 1963 to write a history of the Royal Central Asian Society. Finding it impossible to do this at the same time as my Library work, I asked Sir Richard to relieve me of this task, which he did on 30 September 1964. Frank de Halpert.' As any soldier who has served under him will know, it took a brave man to stand up to the General. But de Halpert was eighty-one years old at the time and so perhaps felt seniority was on his side.

The only other archival reference to a history was made in a quip by Sir Edward MacLagan, one time President of the Royal Asiatic Society and guest speaker at the Society's Annual Dinner in 1935. He teased Sir Percy Sykes, then an Honorary Secretary, to write a poetic History of the Society. However he warned: 'It would, like Firdausi's work, have to be done in 60,000 couplets; but, if so, your Treasurer should be warned that when the poem is complete he will demand in payment an elephant with a load of 60,000 gold coins.' The Society's Treasurer may be relieved to learn that I shall lay no such demand upon him.

The Society's centenary was a milestone that inescapably demanded a history, and I was asked by the current Chairman, Sir Donald Hawley, if I would undertake the task. I agreed with some trepidation, knowing that no two people would tackle the work in the same way and that an approach that might please some would draw criticism from others. This early trepidation soon turned to a feeling of humility as I came to appreciate both the antiquity of the Society and the great men and women, statesmen, soldiers, explorers, engineers, authors and scholars, who had made up the Honorary Officers and the membership.

An outsider might conceive of a learned society dealing with Asia as being somewhat abstruse. But, as I have attempted to show, with regard to the Royal Society for Asian Affairs, nothing could be further from the truth. Its activities have negated Kipling's dictum 'East is East and West is West, And never the twain shall meet.' My aim has been to bring the Society alive, to indicate its role in Britain's imperial past and its function after that era, and to show that its tryst with Asia has been a genuine love affair.

My task has been hindered by the dearth of certain archival material which was destroyed during the 1939–1945 war. Most acute in this respect was the loss of the Society's original *Golden Book*, a record of its great events and office holders. For the most part I have had to rely on the minute books, until the mid-1960s mostly handwritten and not always in easily legible script, the *Journals* and various loose papers and documents. Some of this extant material is contradictory, especially regarding dates. But heeding the

Part One

THE CHRONOLOGY

I

GENESIS, BIRTH AND CONSOLIDATION 1901–1907

Students of history are well aware of the obscurity which veils the origins of many institutions which have made their mark on the world.

Lieut Colonel A. C. Yate, Hon. Sec., writing on the origins of the Central Asian Society in the weekly magazine *The Near East*, 25 April 1919

The Pindar river drains from the southern peaks of the Nanda Devi massif in the Kumaon Himalaya and is a source of the Ganges. At its head lies the Pindari glacier, a tangle of massive ice chunks. At the 17,700 ft crest of the glacier lies Traill's Pass, so named after the first British commissioner in Kumaon, G. W. Traill, who crossed it in 1830. The pass divided the ancient kingdoms of Kumaon and Garhwal. Further north, close to the Tibetan border, lies the remote Hindu Bhotia settlement of Milam and above it a glacier of the same name which feeds the Gori Ganga river, another source of the Ganges.

It was at these two remote spots that in 1866 Alfred Cotterell Tupp first became interested in Central Asian questions. At the time of his visit Tupp would have been twenty-six and on leave from his post as Assistant Magistrate at Fatehpur in the North West Province of India. The idea of forming a Society for others interested in Central Asian subjects gestated for some thirty-four years. During this period he had collected a large library dealing with the Himalayas, Tibet, Russian and Chinese Turkestan, and Afghanistan. He had read everything relating to Central Asia that he could lay his hands on. Tupp retired from the Indian Civil Service in 1889 aged forty-nine, having served twenty-seven years, sixteen as a magistrate and judge, before entering the Financial Department. His final post was Comptroller-General to the Government of India, and in this he became known affectionately as 'Tottle it up'. In retirement Tupp saw more precisely how his ideas for such a Society might be developed. World events, especially in Tsarist Russia, had evolved dramatically since those visits to the Pindari glacier and Milam in 1866. Russia had completed her conquest of the Turkestan Khanates and had annexed most of the Pamirs, before concluding an agreement with Britain in 1895 on stopping further advance into Afghanistan.

At the turn of the century, Dr Cotterell Tupp LLD (as he now was) canvassed his friends. They were in common agreement that 'the new overland contacts between Russia, China and British India; between the civilizations of China, India, orthodox Christianity and the West; between Buddhism, Christianity, Confucianism and Islam, would have a profound effect on all the countries of Asia and the world in general. All these new contacts were by land, assisted by new railways and new roads over Central Asia.' Many of Tupp's friends, though not he himself, were members of the Royal Asiatic Society (RAS), a learned body that was precluded from discussing politics. The proposed Society would have a different remit. The problem was to find people of influence willing to support its formation.

It happened that at this time Captain Francis Younghusband, freshly returned from travels around the northern frontiers of India, in Manchuria and across China, was beginning to think along similar lines to Tupp. Younghusband had already made a reputation for himself as an explorer, and was the holder of the Royal Geographical Society's Founder's Medal. Hearing of each other's plans 'through a mutual friend', Tupp and Younghusband met briefly in February 1901 to exchange ideas. On 14 March 1901 Tupp received a letter from Younghusband saying he would be happy to join him in setting up a Society where those who had travelled in Central Asia or were interested in Central Asian questions could meet one another and discuss such subjects. During the next two weeks Younghusband called three times on Tupp at his London home at 17 Devonshire Terrace, Lancaster Gate. Shortly afterwards Younghusband left London, not returning until October of the same year when discussions between the two were resumed. They were now joined by Colonel Algernon Durand, who had made his name in the Hunza Nagar campaign of 1891, though he is better known for his book *The Making of a Frontier* (1900). At this point they drew up a prospectus stating the objects of the proposed Society and circulated it among a few friends who they thought might be interested. This October

Tupp's home at 17 Devonshire Terrace as in 2001

Younghusband's home at 27 Gilbert Street as in 2001

meeting is reckoned to mark the actual birth of the Society although its exact date has been lost to history.

Early in November a meeting was held in Captain Younghusband's house at 27 Gilbert Street, Grosvenor Square, to discuss the response to that first circular. This was attended by Tupp, Durand and General Sir Thomas Gordon, a veteran of the Indian Mutiny and Afghanistan, who had served with the Forsyth mission to Yarkand in 1873–4 and later in Persia. The four agreed there had been sufficient response to the circulation of the prospectus to distribute it more widely in printed form. It read thus:

A Proposal to Establish a Central Asian Society

At present there is in London no society or institution which is devoted entirely to the consideration of Central Asian questions from their political as well as from their geographical, commercial or scientific aspect, though Societies such as the Royal Geographical and Royal Asiatic Society discuss these subjects incidentally.

It is therefore proposed to establish a society to be called the Central Asian Society, with rooms, where those who either have travelled in Central Asia, or are interested in Central Asian questions, could meet one another. At present such persons have no recognised place of meeting or means of communication with each other, and consequently they often cease to take an active interest in the very questions to which they have previously devoted much time and attention. Those who have worked in one portion of the field will, it is thought, be glad to exchange views with others who have worked in different fields or at different times; while those who are interested in Central Asia, but have not had the opportunity of travelling, might be glad to meet those who have.

Meetings for this purpose might take place at stated intervals (say the first Wednesday in each month), when either a Paper might be read or some subject be put forward for discussion.

It is believed that at first a permanent office will not be required; but it has been ascertained that a room in a central position can be hired for the purpose of these meetings.

For the hire of the room and for incidental expenses a small subscription, not exceeding one pound per annum, is proposed. If the present proposal meets with support, it is hoped that in time a permanent home for the Society may be established which will serve as a place of meetings for Members, where a library may be formed and a bureau for the collection and distribution of information on Central Asian subjects be established.

It is proposed to hold the first meeting on December 13th at 5 p.m. at the rooms of the Royal Asiatic Society, 22 Albemarle St. W., to discuss the constitution of the proposed Society and to hear the views of intending members.

This circular was signed by eleven names. In addition to Tupp, Younghusband and Durand they were: Colonel Mark S. Bell, VC, a Central Asian explorer and formerly Younghusband's immediate superior in the Military Intelligence Department of the Indian Army; Captain H. H. P. Deasy, who had just been awarded the Royal Geographical Society's Gold Medal for exploratory and survey work in Central Asia; Colonel Sir Thomas Holdich, an eminent Frontier surveyor of India and neighbouring territories; Sir Evan James, an Indian Civil Servant, who had explored Manchuria with Younghusband in 1886; Mr John Murray, the publisher, who had just brought out the autobiography of the Afghan Amir Abdur Rahman; Henry Norman, MP, a former Indian

Army officer; Mr Henry Spenser Wilkinson, a military historian and journalist; and Mr Robert Yerburgh, MP. In addition to those signatories the names of the Earls of Dunmore and Ronaldshay were listed on the back of the circular as having expressed a willingness to join. Along with Gordon all thirteen can be regarded as the Society's Founding Members.

The embryonic Society had, as the circular suggested, approached the Royal Asiatic Society (RAS) through its secretary, Professor T. W. Rhys Davids, for the use of one of its rooms at 22 Albemarle Street. A handwritten minute of the RAS dated 14 January 1902 reads:

> On the motion of Mr Irvine it was resolved to let one-third of the small room on the first floor to the Central Asian Society for £20 a year. Payment for the use of the larger rooms of this Society's tenancy to be extra, at the rate of one guinea per room per meeting held in such rooms. This letting not to interfere with previous lettings of one-third share of the same room to the Dante Society and the Oriental Translation Trust respectively. The contract on either side to be terminable by six months notice to expire on any date, and payments to be made on the quarter days.

Office space must have been limited but most of the clerical work was done by Miss C. S. Hughes, the Assistant Secretary of the RAS, who threw herself into the new venture with enthusiasm. As recalled fifty years later: 'She realised that there were people among the membership of the RAS – an incredibly learned Society – who did not wish to be learned all the time, but would like opportunities to be a little outspoken and a little critical, particularly in the forbidden realm of politics.'

The constituent meeting of the Society was duly held on 13 December in the rooms of the RAS. General Sir Thomas Gordon presided and was elected the first 'President'. Although the term 'President' was used at the time for the first five holders of that office, this was changed retrospectively to 'Presiding Chairman' on the grounds that there was no President as such until Lord Curzon held that office in 1918. Major (now) Francis Younghusband was elected Honorary Secretary and Dr Cotterell Tupp Honorary Treasurer. The first Members of Council elected (apart from the two Honorary officers) were Major General Sir Edwin Collen, a veteran of wars in Abyssinia, Afghanistan and the Sudan, and later Military Secretary to the Indian Government, who became Presiding Chairman in 1906; Colonel Algernon Durand; Colonel Sir Thomas Holdich, who soon became one of the stalwarts of the Society and its Chairman in 1904; William Irvine, a former member of the ICS and a scholar of Mogul history; Mr F. Gillett; and Mr W. E. Jardine, a serving member of the ICS on leave from India.[1]

General Sir Thomas Gordon

Following this December meeting the number of those expressing a willingness to join the fledgling Society had increased to thirty. They included the Marquess of Breadalbane, the Earl of Dartrey, Lord Elphinstone and the Central Asian explorer and RGS Gold Medallist, St George Littledale. Another who joined shortly after was Sir Henry Drummond-Wolff, son of the Reverend Joseph Wolff, who in 1843 set out in vain to rescue the ill-fated Colonel Stoddard and Captain Conolly from the clutches of the Amir of Bokhara. With this encouragement it was decided to issue a second circular in early January 1902, along the lines of the first but reporting on the success of the December meeting. It added that the first lecture would take place on 15 January when Mr H. F. B. Lynch would speak on 'The Persian Gulf'.[2] The annual subscription was fixed at one pound and it was agreed that each member could bring two friends to the meetings. The circular ended by inviting others to join the Society.

Younghusband's office as Honorary Secretary was short-lived. In January 1902 he returned to India to take up an appointment as Resident in the Princely State of Indore. As a Vice President he remained titulary on the Council and continued to take an interest in the Society. Summoned to Delhi the following year to attend the Durbar to commemorate the coronation of King Edward VII, he found himself at lunch one day sitting next to the Viceroy, his old friend Lord Curzon. Younghusband recalled that the Viceroy talked to him 'literally the whole time' about the frontier, local problems at Indore and the newly formed Central Asian Society.[3] But other than such conversations he was unable to give any practical assistance until his return to England in 1910 when he was appointed also to the Council of the Royal Geographical Society (RGS), becoming its President in 1919. In 1914 Younghusband (now Sir Francis) rejoined actively the Society's Council, often deputising for the Chairman. He graduated to Vice President again in 1920 and on retiring from that post by rotation rejoined Council as an ordinary member. He was offered the position of Chairman in 1923 but was unable to accept it due to his other commitments. In 1934 he was made an Honorary Vice President and held that office until his death in 1942.

Francis Younghusband

That Cotterell Tupp was the true founder of the Central Asian Society, formulating its nascent philosophy and practice, there is no dispute, whereas Younghusband was from the outset Tupp's main supporter, and his name attracted early interest. Although 'Tottle it up Tupp' and the explorer-mystic Younghusband appear different in temperament they became close friends. While we know too little about Tupp, we know a lot about Younghusband and little more need be said here. Biographies have been written and his own literary output was prodigious.[4]

Tupp, on the other hand, comes across as quieter and more self-effacing though, as we shall see, no political dove. Younghusband described him as 'a thoughtful Indian civilian'. His career centred around the legal, financial and statistical and his publications reflect this.[5] It was as a result of his papers on bimetallism (the monetary role of gold and silver) that the University of St Andrews conferred on him the degree of LLD. His principal work, *The Indian Civil Service and the Competitive System*, had a major effect on the recruitment and promotion process in the Indian Civil Service, which, prone to mistakes, had led to unjust blockages in the system. It is clear from the Preface that he wrote this seminal work during a year's sick leave from India in 1875: 'Written on the very eve of departure for India under great disadvantages of ill health ... and pressure for time ... If it should contribute to awaken in England any interest in the noble Service of which it treats, I shall feel that it will not have been written in vain.' Even in retirement Tupp devoted much energy to besieging officials at the India Office to promote his cause, and his lectures to learned societies ranged from Women's Suffrage to British campaigns in Asia and South Africa to the Silver Question. He became a Life Governor of both the School and College of the University of London, his *Alma Mater*. In *Who's Who* he listed his recreations as 'In early life cricket and racquets; later economics and Asian politics'.

In his work for the Society Tupp was ably supported by his wife, Jean, the daughter of a clergyman, who joined in her own right in 1903 and continued to attend the Society's dinners until the mid-1930s, long after his own death in 1914. A colleague recalled fifty years later: 'He was always accompanied by his wonderful wife, distinguished in appearance and each the complement of the other, gracious and friendly to all. Her lovely head of white hair moved among the members of Miss Hughes' adroit pre-lecture teas. These two did much to create the social atmosphere that gave the Society its early tone.'

THE

INDIAN CIVIL SERVICE

AND THE

COMPETITIVE SYSTEM,

A DISCUSSION ON THE EXAMINATIONS AND THE TRAINING IN ENGLAND; AND AN ACCOUNT OF THE EXAMINATIONS IN INDIA, THE DUTIES OF CIVILIANS, AND THE ORGANIZATION OF THE SERVICE,

WITH A LIST OF CIVILIANS AND OTHER APPENDICES.

BY

ALFRED COTTERELL TUPP, B.A.,

BENGAL CIVIL SERVICE.

LONDON:

R. W. BRYDGES, 137, GOWER STREET.

1876.

Younghusband's successor as Honorary Secretary in January 1902 was Edward Penton, Jnr, who gave over fifty years' service to the Society in one position or another. At the time of the Society's inception he had been travelling in parts of Asia, but on return immediately stepped into Younghusband's shoes. The exact history here becomes confused. According to General Sir John Shea, speaking as President at the Society's Golden Jubilee Dinner in 1951, at which Penton was present, it was always intended that the latter should take the Honorary Secretary post on return from his travels and that Younghusband's position was known to be temporary. But Sir Percy Sykes, later to become a long-term and influential Honorary Secretary himself, in his obituary of Younghusband in 1942, gave a somewhat different, though probably more correct, story. 'I first met Younghusband at Rawal Pindi in 1889 ... We did not meet again until 1901 when, after my return from the Boer War, where Younghusband had been acting as a correspondent, we met in London. He informed me of plans to found what is now the Royal Central Asian Society; that he intended to retire from the army to take up the post of Honorary Secretary; and that he hoped to be elected to Parliament. I was shocked at a man of such parts giving up his career until he had reached high office, and, partly owing to my being able to propose a suitable Honorary Secretary in the person of (Sir) Edward Penton, he finally agreed to my advice.'

Either way the choice of Penton, at twenty-six, was propitious and the initial fortunes of the Society lay in both his and Tupp's hands. As the Earl of Ronaldshay said at the AGM in 1912: 'If it was not for Mr Penton we would find considerable difficulty in carrying on at all.' Educated at Rugby and Oxford he became head of a firm of leather manufacturers and from1912 to 1913 Mayor of Marylebone. During the First World War he joined the Royal Army Clothing Department, where he persuaded Britain's boot-makers to mechanise manufacture utilising imported Indian leather. The impact of his innovations was appreciated by both British and allied forces and his efforts were recognised by a knighthood in 1918. When Chief Inspector of Clothing during the Second World War he received, *inter alia*, the Order of Leopold of Belgium. Honorary Secretary until 1919, he took over the post of Honorary Treasurer which, due to pressure of government work, he had to relinquish in 1939. After the war he became a Society Trustee and died in December 1967 aged ninety-two: an amazing record of service.

Following the initial lecture on the Persian Gulf, there were six further lectures in 1901 and by the end of 1907 a total of forty. Many were illustrated by lantern slides, thanks to the services of Mr Simpson of the RGS. Some were well attended, others less so. The former included a talk on 24 April 1903 by T. Gibson Bowles, MP, entitled *The Baghdad Railway*. Over two hundred people were present, including many non-members and journalists. It was fully reported in *The Times*. A lecture by George Macartney on 20 May of the same year, entitled *Kashgaria*, was attended by the legendary Swedish explorer Dr Sven Hedin, who also spoke. General Sir Edwin Collen's paper in March 1906 on *The Defence of India* was reprinted by the War Office for internal circulation. The lectures were held in the rooms of the RAS and as a result of the, at times, overcrowding, the Secretary was asked to 'make as much room as possible by taking off the doors and reducing the size of the Chairman's table'.

Although the *Journal* was not constituted as such until 1914, these early papers were printed and circulated to members. The public could buy them at 2/6d each. There is no record of printed papers for the period January 1902–May 1903, probably because the Society lacked the funds to cover printing expenses.

A study of the titles of the initial forty lectures shows that only a minority were in fact dedicated strictly to Central Asian subjects. Indeed the first, as we have seen, was on the Persian Gulf, there were four more on Persia, one on the colonial policy of Japan in Korea, and one in 1906 by Tupp himself on Indo-China. Five were on communication routes in Asia generally, mostly railways. One of the Society's early strengths was its ability to cater for changing political priorities. But several were quintessentially Central Asian, for example, *Bokhara*; *Impressions of the Duab, Russian Turkestan*; *Chinese Turkestan and the Oxus River.*

Here a word must be said about the Society's geographical remit, a subject of continuing debate given the Society's then name. From the start Professor Rhys Davids, Secretary of the RAS, described the Society as 'Central Asia Unlimited'! In 1908 Tupp wrote: 'It may be thought that we have roamed too widely and that many papers have had little relation to Central Asia; but we have had good papers offered us, which only a narrow interpretation of our Rules would exclude, and we have come at last to practically include in our sphere all Asia except Siberia and the internal affairs of India.' Internal Indian affairs, i.e., 'the plains' rather than 'the frontiers', were excluded because it was felt that this would poach on the province of other societies such as The East Indian Association, The Indian Empire Society, The South India Association and The Royal Indian Society. For the same reason lectures on both Japan and China, each of which had dedicated societies in London, were also precluded. However, these rules were soon broken. There were several early lectures on China, Japan and three on Siberia. Internal India, however, did remain an exclusive zone for many years – strangely, since the Secretary of State for India had been an *ex-officio* member of the Society since 1906.

If the name 'Central Asian Society' was chosen, at least partly, to differentiate it from the Royal Asiatic Society, the choice was best clarified by Lord Curzon in his Annual Dinner speech in 1908. Emphasising that the defence of India was the main focus of the Society's discussions and influence, by Central Asia was meant all those nations and powers which affected in any way her security or determined her future. These he listed as extending from Turkey to China. The phrase 'Central Asia' was not so much a geographical formula, but one defining a political problem. Penton later described 'The Central Asian Question' as the *fons et origo* of the Society.

Retrospectively, several prominent members of the Society have enlarged on these themes. Lord Peel, President at the 25th Anniversary Dinner in 1926 explained: 'Defining our area of interest was always a problem, but we are almost conterminous with the Moslem world . . . and regard the Red Sea as a very unnecessary geographical limit to our studies.' From its early years the Society declared it would always be interested in the development of Islam in Egypt and in other countries outside its geographical area.[6] Sir Ronald Storrs, at the Annual Dinner in 1928, stated: 'The Society's remit is that great triangle based on Constantinople, Cairo and Calcutta from which have been produced three, or if we include Buddhism four, of the great religions of the world.' Sir Arnold Wilson, speaking at the Annual Dinner in 1931, after the Society had received its Royal Charter, suggested, ingeniously, that the problem was the positioning of the adjective 'Central': 'We are in reality the Royal Central Society for Asia.' But perhaps a more compelling view was expressed by Professor Charles Beckingham in 1986: 'I think what our Founders had in mind then was probably what would now be the five Soviet Republics of Central Asia [Turkmenistan, Uzbekistan, Kazakhstan, Kyrgyzstan and Tajikistan], Afghanistan, Sinkiang (then called Chinese Turkestan), Mongolia, Tibet, Nepal, Kashmir and Ladakh. But one thing leads to another. If you take an interest in Tibet, you become involved with China: if with China, then Korea, Japan etc. As time went on the Society found itself taking an interest in virtually any part of Asia.'

By 1903 the Society appeared to be running smoothly under the 'Presiding Chairmanship' of Sir Alfred Lyall. His appointment must have given considerable prestige to the embryonic society for he was both a renowned statesman and a man of letters. He had served for thirty-one years in India, including the post of Foreign Secretary under Lord Lytton and the Marquis of Ripon. Subsequently he became Lieutenant Governor of the North West Provinces. On return to England he served for fifteen years as a member of the Council of India in London. He was a founder member of the British Academy and a poet; his little volume *Verses written in India* is a delight. A friend and biographer of Tennyson, he was on a visit to one of his sons in the Isle of Wight in 1911 when he died of a heart attack aged seventy-six.

Of relevance to the history of the Society is the unusual stand Lyall took regarding Britain's relations with Russia. This was influenced by his experiences during the Indian Mutiny when he narrowly escaped with his life at Meerut. He regarded the behaviour there, and elsewhere, of the Muslim insurgents as cruel and savage and saw the fall of Constantinople to Islam as Europe's greatest tragedy. Thus he strongly supported Russia in her conflict with Turkey, whereas most in India, even the Hindus,

Sir Alfred Lyall

Younghusband with John Claude White. Joint Commissioners for the Tibet Expedition. Giantse Dzong, 1904
[RSAA Archives]

supported Turkey. Lyall considered that Russia had a legitimate interest in extending her power to the borders of British India. He maintained that the British would have done the same to bring the tribes to order. The important thing was to ensure that the Russians went no further, and this could only be achieved, he argued, by an agreement which he was confident they would keep. His stand had influenced the Anglo-Russian agreement on the Pamirs in 1895 and the Anglo-Russian Convention of 1907.[7] But, as we shall see, his was something of a lone voice among the hawkish majority of the Society's 'inner cabinet'.

A letter from Tupp to Younghusband written in early September 1903 gives a clear idea of both the hawkish attitude towards Russia prevalent at the time and offers some intriguing comments on several of the Society's leading members.[8] It also reveals something of Tupp's own personality. By the time the letter arrived Younghusband would have been engrossed in preparations for the British invasion of Tibet the following January.

> My dear Younghusband,
>
> I have been intending to write to you for a long time, but I put it off ... thinking you might have difficulty in getting letters. ... We have heard very little about your mission, but I am very glad that it was created and that you accepted it, for it may mean a great deal in the future; and any stirring up of the waters on the Tibet frontier is a good thing, after our years of inaction. Have you been allowed to go much beyond our frontier and is there any hope of opening up the country in any way or of forestalling Russia? Of course anything you tell me I will keep rigidly secret, but you know how interested I am in the question ...
>
> I gave a lecture on Tibet at the Central Asian Society and I got Sir A Lyall to back me up in saying that whatever happened we must never allow Russia to take Tibet. All

the newspapers reported it and I think it did some good in attracting attention to the subject, but I was very disgusted with Macartney of Kashgar when he lectured, for he said openly (he being our Political there) that we would have to let Russia take it. I say certainly not. Without any war, we can let Russia know that we will not let her have either Tibet or Chinese Turkestan; and we can agree on her taking Mongolia and Zangaria and leaving us the former two. The only way with Russia is to tell her what you mean to do and that she will have to fight if she opposes it. She never fights when warned beforehand, but she will encroach and break Frontiers ad infinitum. I hope you will be able to adopt a forward policy as regards Tibet. The Russians are undoubtedly intriguing with Tibet thro' the Mongolians, Buriats etc; and it is quite time we took action from the South.

Of course I know that you know much more about all this than I do; but I have read a good deal more since you left and I remember you once saying that you did not see how we could hold Chinese Turkestan. I hope your new experience may have changed your views and that you now agree with me and that we should draw the line at the Thian Shan Mts and tell Russia she shall not come south of that.

The Central Asian Society has gone on very well and we have had some very good lectures, notably T. G. Bowles, MP [on The Baghdad Railway] which was crammed and we had 20 reporters. I sent you out 100 copies of our new Rules and List of Members, addressing them to Lahore...

I enclose you a copy of the Memo which I drew up on the Progress of the Society. Penton makes a very good Secretary in most respects, but he is rather too young and flighty for it. He sometimes makes extraordinary proposals which we have to sit on. Sir A. Lyall is of course a tower of strength in name as our Chairman and it has done us good publicity to have him, but he is not an ideal Chairman. He is very impatient and always wants to get away as quickly as he can, so that he cuts speakers short and often prevents men who are shy from speaking at all. Sir Thos. Gordon does not show much interest in it and hardly ever comes and that lazy beggar Algy Durand hasn't shown his face once this year. He is too busy admiring his new uniform as one of the King's bodyguard. Collen, Irvine and Gillett are the most useful members of the Council. I suppose you will be back in India by November and I hope when you can make time you will send me a few lines saying what has been the result of your mission.

'... too busy admiring his new uniform ...'

If there is any part of what you tell me which I may mention to the Society or otherwise, please tell me clearly which it is – all the rest I shall regard as confidential ... Have you formed any plans about coming home again? I would not stay out too long if I were you. Nothing makes up for being away from England ... With kind regards to Mrs Younghusband.

Yours sincerely,
A. Cotterell Tupp

Lyall's stand on Tibet was perhaps surprising given his policy of entente towards Russia. But when it came to the 1907 Anglo-Russian Convention he was at odds with most of the Society's prominent members. The Convention was drawn up by Sir Edward Grey, Foreign Secretary in the Liberal government of Sir Henry Campbell-Bannerman. Grey and his Russian counterpart were determined to limit the rivalry between the two empires in Asia. This, with particular reference to Tibet, Afghanistan and Persia, was deemed crucial to India's defence. It was signed in St Petersburg on 31 August. In essence both sides agreed to refrain from interfering in Tibet's internal affairs and Afghanistan was confirmed as lying within the British sphere of influence. Persia was to be divided in three ways: Russia in the north, Britain in the south (covering access to the Gulf), with a neutral zone between. A secondary, but undeclared, aim of the Convention was to check German ambitions eastwards.

It was the Persian aspect of the agreement which most incensed the hawks on both sides of the government and in the Society itself. They regarded it as a sell-out since most of the major cities lay within the Russian sphere. In July 1907 the Society, learning of the draft agreement and determined to show it had some political influence, addressed a lengthy memorandum to the Foreign Secretary. It expressed in strong terms its concern that the proposed Russian zone was crossed by caravan routes conveying British and Indian merchandise to the cities of Persia, and that it threatened the great trade route between Teheran and Baghdad via Kermanshah. The note concluded: 'The Council ... desires to place on record that it is not aware of any consideration of general policy in Asia or elsewhere, which should induce us to give up any established British interests to Russia without receiving an established Russian interest in return.'

The wording of the memorandum implied that Council knew its business – many of its members were 'there' – and that the government did not and were not! It is hard to imagine the Society proffering such political advice today. There is no archival record of any government reply to this memorandum, but it is clearly not one to which Lyall would have put his name. But by 1907 Lyall was no longer Chairman, having handed over to Colonel Sir Thomas Holdich in 1904. He was succeeded in 1906 by General Sir Edwin Collen. In 1907 the Society's new Chairman was Mr (later Sir) Valentine Chirol, a celebrated traveller and influential journalist who in 1903, whilst Foreign Editor of *The Times*, wrote *The Middle East Question and some Problems of Indian Defence*.

As we have shown, from its outset the Society was determined to cover Asia as a whole, and there are today members of the Society who regard as romantics those believing that its origins lay in what has become known as the 'Great Game'. But the real concern was the security of India and many of its founding members did distrust Russian intentions and felt that the public should be warned of the dangers to come. One of the last lectures in this period under review was *The Strategic Position of Russia in Central Asia*, and retrospective statements confirm this early fear. At the AGM in 1915 Sir Thomas Holdich said: 'The war is having a great effect on Central Asia ... The matter which concerns us most, and which we think about most in this connection, is the speed and influence of Russia through regions which lie southward of her present borderland.' (Later Holdich became as dismissive of Russia's ability to invade India as he was of Germany's to move eastwards at the close of the First World War.[9]) In the same year Sir Mortimer Durand commented: 'One of the objects with which the Society was originally formed was to study the progress of Russia in Central Asia.' At the Annual Dinner in 1953 the Chairman, Admiral Sir Cecil Harcourt, reminded his audience: 'This Society was founded at a time

Valentine Chirol in Persia, 1902, en route to India for the Delhi Durbar

when Russia appeared to be threatening India, and it was founded to draw attention to that part of the world and what went on there.' Even as late as the mid-1950s, a circular advertising the Society stated: 'In the present century, the growing development and speed of means of communication of all kinds are making the influence of the great inland powers, the USSR and China, equal to or surpassing that of maritime powers.' True, this was the 'Cold War Game' rather than the 'Great Game' but none the less it shows the Society's continuing concern about Russian intentions.

On 16 May 1907 the Society, now feeling itself firmly established with 107 members, held its first Annual Dinner at the Imperial Restaurant, Regent Street. Twenty-four members attended. The two guests of the Society were, appropriately, the Presidents of the two related senior societies: Lord Reay of the Royal Asiatic and Sir George Goldie of the Royal Geographical. The dinner henceforth became an annual event.

Nothing conveys more the atmosphere of the early years of the Society than the speech made by Sir Edward Penton at the Golden Jubilee Dinner in 1951. He was the only one of the original members who was still able to attend. He described Tupp as the Society's 'Godfather' and Miss Hughes (later, on marriage, to become Mrs Frazer) as the Society's 'Nanny'. 'A brilliant Secretary ... she forged a link which did much at its foundation to make the Society possible. The Society's rooms, those of the RAS, were incongruously situated over Asprey's Albemarle Street

'... incongruously situated over Asprey's Albemarle Street shop ...'

shop. I notice that the door and staircase, which then led to our rooms, is now closed, so that nothing so indiscreet should ever occur there again.' Penton continued:

> Among its founders were Francis Younghusband – a veritable Mahatma – with his legendary reputation as traveller, political officer and author; the soldiers Thomas Gordon and Edwin Collen; the politicals Algy Durand – more like an ambassador than any ambassador could ever have been – and Lepel Griffin, always gay and debonair; Lord Zetland – Lord Ronaldshay as he was then – fresh from service on Lord Curzon's staff, with his distinguished career ahead of him; and many others whose names can be traced in the Society's records. But there are two whose boldness of conception and courageous outlook are engraved on my memory: Sir Thomas Holdich, the geographer and engineer, and Sir Alfred Lyall, the statesman.
>
> At its start many of the Founders read papers, sometimes more than once ... for the Society was not well enough known to attract lecturers who had something to say and wanted a platform to say it from. Besides, it was embarrassing to ask eminent travellers, and others possessed of unique knowledge, to risk addressing a very sparsely attended meeting ... I lived in agony for the last thirty minutes before every lecture, watching the empty chairs fill, and trying to induce latecomers to occupy the vacant front row ... I shall never forget how at one of our early meetings a disappointed speaker, himself a member of the Society, who instead of empty chairs had anticipated an audience eager to absorb his views, forced me to accompany him up Bond Street to listen to his vituperations, until at last, having led me into his tailors, he switched his wrath on the cutter because his trousers did not fit to his liking!
>
> But what was the reason for founding the Society and courting those early struggles? There are doubtless many versions ... But I have a conviction, bred of long observation, that the Society was founded by men who through a lifetime's experience, recognised the constant conflict of the peoples of the Heartland and the sea-going nations on the perimeter. You may particularise it if you like as 'the integrity of India': but instinctively those founders realised the wider dangers, and it was because of their fervent anxiety to preserve their work that they founded the Society to warn their countrymen of the perils to come.
>
> Some wanted to preserve the *status quo* at all costs – by which they meant to prevent Russian access to the Persian Gulf. But there were others, notably Sir Alfred Lyall, who realised that coming events could not be merely resisted, but had to be accepted and moulded to our advantage. I remember an argument at a Council meeting specially convened to discuss the Berlin to Baghdad Railway, the bogey of the moment. There were several notable members present. Sir Alfred, by that time a very old man, sat apart, a gaunt solitary figure, his head bent forward with his chin resting on his chest, neither moving nor speaking and looking like a moulting bird. An unconstructively hostile resolution was ultimately accepted, but as other members rose to go and I was completing my notes, Sir Alfred's hand shot out to seize me by the wrist: 'See that I am not associated with that resolution,' he hissed. The wise old statesman's final protest. Impossible as it may sound now, Sir Edward Grey in 1907 reached an agreement with Russia over spheres of influence in Persia.
>
> You might imagine that the Society would have been delighted at his success, but instead its first reaction was 'what are we going to talk about? Was it the Society's

death knell?' But that impression was momentary. There was still a wide scope for discussion!

Aficionados of the 'Great Game' hold that the era finally came to an end with the 1907 Anglo-Russian Convention. But of course it was all torn up when the Bolsheviks came to power in 1918 and a new 'Game' started when, in the best tradition of those Founding Fathers, many colourful members of the Society took part in it. There was, indeed, 'a wide scope for discussion'.

ANNEX TO CHAPTER I

The following, who joined the Society in 1901 and 1902, are listed as the Society's 'Original Members'. Those marked with an asterisk may be considered the Founding Members.

Captain A. Aglionby
Charles Barrington Balfour, MP
*Colonel Mark S. Bell, VC
T. J. Bennett
The Marquess of Breadalbane
Lieut Colonel C. D. Bruce
W. A. Buchanan
Major General Sir Owen Tudor Burne, GCIE, KCSI
Stephen Bushell, CMG, MD
A. D. Carey, ICS
Lieut General Sir Edwin Collen, GCIE, CB
Mrs F. A. Crow
The Earl of Dartrey
*Captain H. H. P. Deasy
The Rt Hon. Sir Henry Drummond-Wolff, PC, GCB, GCMG
*The Earl of Dunmore
*Colonel A. G. A. Durand, CB, CIE
Lord Elphinstone
Terrell Garnett
*General Sir Thomas Gordon, KCB, KCIE, CSI
Major General Sir William Green, KCSI, CB, DL
Sir Lepel Griffin, KCSI
Field Marshal Sir F. P. Haynes, GCB, GCSI
General Sir J. Hills-Johnes, VC, GCB
*Colonel Sir Thomas Holdich, KCMG, KCIE, CB
Major J. D. Inglis
William Irvine, ICS
*Sir Evan James, KCIE, CSI
Mrs Jardine
W. E. Jardine, ICS
James Kennedy, ICS
Sir H. Seymour King, KCIE, MP
St George Littledale
The Rt Hon. Sir Alfred Comyns Lyall GCIE, KCB, DCL, LLD
H. F. B. Lynch, MP
Sir G. S. Mackenzie, KCMG, CB
*John Murray
*Henry Norman, MP
A. W. Paul, CIE, ICS
Hon. W. Peel
E. Penton, Jnr
Woolrych J. T. Perowne
Lieut Colonel H. P. Picot
Baron George de Reuter
*The Earl of Ronaldshay
Colonel A. E. Sandbach, DSO, RE
Sir Edward Sassoon, Bart
Colonel F. Spratt-Bowring, RE
Sir Douglas Straight, LLD
Miss Ella E. Sykes
*A. Cotterell Tupp, ICS, LLD
Joseph Walton, MP
S. H. Whitbred
*Henry Spenser Wilkinson
Lieut Colonel Arthur C. Yate
*R. A. Yerburgh, MP
*Major Francis E. Younghusband

II

THE YEARS OF STRUGGLE 1908–1919

So far as the future of the Society is concerned there is no means of saying what its prospects may be; they must be more or less on the knees of the gods.
Colonel Sir Thomas Holdich, AGM, 1915

In March 1908, as part of a planned recruiting drive, Cotterell Tupp was asked to write a brief history of the Society up to that date. Having extolled its successes, he concluded: 'We are now in our seventh year and it will hardly be denied that we have justified our existence; but we have not met with as much support as we might reasonably have anticipated. Our numbers hover about the round hundred and unless we can increase that number, we cannot print all our papers and we cannot even begin the formation of a Library.' Six hundred copies of this history were printed and distributed. Messrs King and Co. were asked to arrange its circulation among 'Residents and Chief Political Officers in India; Chief Political Officers in the Persian Gulf and Turkish Arabia and to Consuls and Vice Consuls in China and Persia'.

In the same year the Chairmanship was passed to the Earl of Ronaldshay, MP, later to become the Marquis of Zetland, at the young age of thirty-three. A Founder Member, he served the Society continuously through various offices until his death in 1961 at the age of eighty-five. His great interest in life was India and he was an expert on the Hindu and Buddhist religions. He served as Governor of Bengal from 1916–1922 and later as Secretary of State for India from 1935–1940. His writings included the official three-volume biography of Curzon. Before Ronaldshay, each Chairman had held office for one or two years only, though the rules stated he could be re-elected annually. But his tenure was popular and lasted six years during which he actively supported Tupp and Penton's recruiting drive.

The Earl of Ronaldshay travelling in China as a young man

The Society's Rules

Before continuing further it may be useful to pause here and study how the Rules of the Society evolved. This should make it easier to follow the subsequent appointments of the various office holders and other developments in the chronology.

From the outset rules were drawn up to regulate the affairs of the Society. They defined and directed its aims; charitable status; management of properties and assets and action thereto in the event of dissolution; appointment of Council and its officers; categories of membership; payment of subscriptions and other such matters. The details changed over the years as the Society became more established and increased its membership.

The President, once that office was established, and Chairman were both elected by Council each holding office for a set period, thence eligible for re-election. Vice Presidents, up to a maximum of ten, were similarly elected, two retiring by rotation. The tradition gradually evolved whereby the two senior members of Council automatically progressed to that position. However, the office was abolished as nugatory in 1997. But that of Honorary Vice President continued, the appointees being elected by Council for their 'meritorious service'.

Council itself, originally comprising ten members, eventually increased to twenty, was elected at the Anniversary Meeting (AGM), again each member holding office for a set period and only eligible for re-election after a year's interval. The offices of Honorary Secretary, Treasurer and, on the formation of the Library in 1922, Librarian were proposed by Council and similarly elected at the AGM. Three Trustees were also appointed for the purpose of vesting in their name the property, funds, deeds of title and documents of the Society.

Both sexes were eligible for ordinary membership from the start. Other membership categories that subsequently evolved were Affiliate, Corporate and Junior Members. Honorary members, up to a maximum of ten, have also been elected for 'distinguished service in, or knowledge of, Asia'. At the time of the Society's centenary they numbered six.

Despite the recruiting drive by 1912 attendance at some lectures was disappointingly low. At first this was put down to a preoccupation with the Balkan War. In June 1913, with the membership still only around 120, Council considered some urgent measures, such as the possibility of an amalgamation with the Persia Society or some arrangement with the Royal Asiatic Society (RAS) whereby the Society became its 'Political Branch'. It even considered obtaining a list of members of the China Society with a view to some poaching. No firm decisions were made until the next meeting when the following was decided: (a) meetings of the Society should be advertised in the Athenaeum, Travellers, East India and United Service Clubs as well as one of the Ladies' Clubs and the Royal Geographical Society (RGS); (b) any member of the above could attend a lecture of the Society on presentation of a visitor's card; (c) the Society's publications should be made more encompassing by listing a diary of associated events, new books and articles of relevant interest in other magazines and quarterlies; and (d) overseas members should be asked to give news of the countries in which they were living, which could also be used in this way. This was before the birth of the *Journal* in 1914; previously lectures, progress reports and other news had been published in off-prints entitled *Proceedings of the Central Asian Society*.

One reason for the slow increase in membership was that many resigned on being posted abroad during the war, and some were killed in action. But a good number of overseas members did stay. For example, in 1919, the end of the period under review, there were 139 members in the Society. Of those, 35 lived overseas, of whom 25 were in India (their subscription was 12 rupees p.a.). Many of the new members in India were recruited by virtue of their office, rather than their person. These included the Agents, or Residents or Secretaries to the Governments of Delhi, Quetta, Peshawar, Bangalore, Rajputana, Bombay, Bahrain and Kuwait. Clearly Messrs King & Co. had done their job well.

Some interesting new members joined during this period, many of whom we shall meet again later: Sir Percy Cox; Major Percy Sykes; Captain F. M. Bailey; Lieut P. T. Etherton; Colonel J. G. Kelly, known as 'Chitral Kelly' due to the part he played in the relief of the Chitral Fort in 1895, who became an active member of Council serving from 1913 to 1919; George Macartney of Kashgar, who joined the Council in 1919; Dr Aurel Stein; Lieut Colonel J. K. Tod; Major Reginald Teague-Jones, who served with General Malleson's Mission in Transcaspia; and the Arabian explorer Mr H. St J. B. Philby. The Society's first Asian member, Bahadur Sahibzada Abdul Qaiyum Khan, CIE, Assistant Political Agent, Khaiber, NWFP, joined in 1910 and the second, Sirdar Ikbal Ali Shah, joined in 1918. Ikbal became a frequent lecturer and was probably the first Afghan to address an audience in London. Some overseas members had rather exotic addresses: Mr H. G. G. Perry-Ayscough gave his as c/o The Chinese Post Office, Shanghai, China, via Siberia; and Captain J. W. Watson as HBM Consulate, Tarbat-i-Haidari, Meshed, via Askabad, Transcaspia, Russia. But if the membership continued low in number, it was high in quality. As Sir Thomas Holdich said in 1914: 'If [we are] a comparatively small society, numbered among its members are men having the right to say they know at first hand more about Asia than anyone could tell them in any other society.'

Apart from the varying lecture attendance there was also the problem of finding lecturers, especially when some speakers suddenly found themselves posted abroad at short notice. But the talks continued to cover topics of interest, some with appealing titles: *Gun Running in the Persian Gulf*; *A Typical Day's March in Eastern Bokhara*; and *Adventures with Armoured Cars in Russia and the East*. There were several on Afghanistan; indeed in the history of the Society there have been more lectures on this subject than any other. As Lord Curzon said at the Annual Dinner in 1908: 'If the Central Asian Society exists and is meeting fifty or a hundred years hence, Afghanistan will be as vital and important a question as it is now.' There were several more on China, despite the supposed restriction, one being delivered by 'a Chinese gentleman holding high office in Peking,'[1] and others on Asian Communication Routes, especially railways, still a favourite topic. Some covered the war – *Japan's Part in the War*; *Turkey the War and Climatic Influences in Turkey* and *The Near East and the War*. This latter was attended by the modernist Indian Shiite Muslim thinker, Syed Ameer Ali, a former High Court Judge and Privy Councillor. He rose from the audience at the end of the talk to say, 'We Indian Moslems are British citizens and we love the British Empire.' Just as well, if true, for at that moment the Germans were planning a *Jihad* of Indian Muslims against the British via Afghanistan. In 1918 Syed Ameer gave the Anniversary Lecture entitled *Persia and Her Neighbours* when he listed 'Romanoff' atrocities in the region, emphasising Britain's lack of wisdom in signing the 1907 Convention with Russia.

The Anniversary Lecture the following year, 1919, was given by Sir George Macartney on *Bolshevism as I saw it at Tashkent in 1919*. Publication of this lecture in the *Journal* was delayed until 1920 – 'until it was known that Lieut Colonel F. M. Bailey was out of reach of Bolshevist animosity'. In the autumn of 1919 Bailey, in order to effect his escape from Tashkent, whence he had been sent to report on Bolshevik activity, had disguised himself as an Albanian army clerk. In a brazen scheme he had got himself recruited by a branch of the General Staff, *Voinye Kontrol*, recently separated from Cheka, the Bolshevik Secret Service. Its role was to track down foreign spies. Bailey's brief was to report on British

Sir George Macartney and General Ma Titai at Kashgar, 1918 [RSAA Archives]

activity in Bokhara, including any information on a British officer named Colonel Bailey! The Society had to wait impatiently until 1921 for Bailey's own account of his experiences.

The Society, keen to make its influence felt as widely as possible, became involved in a number of minor extra-mural issues in this period. In December 1911, Sir Thomas Holdich and Dr Tupp represented the Society in a joint deputation with the RAS to the Board of Education over the appointment of an expert to supervise the Indian Section at the South Kensington Museum. In March 1914 it accepted an invitation from the Organising Committee of the Oriental Congress to send a representative to its meetings. Next came an unexpected development concerning Chinese astronomical instruments. On 11 December 1918 Mr J. O. Bland delivered a lecture on China.[2] It was chaired by Sir Edmund Barrow, who had been General Sir Alfred Gaselee's Chief of Staff on the expedition sent to Peking in 1900 to relieve the Legation beleaguered by the Boxer rebels. During the course of the lecture questions were asked about the rare astronomical instruments that had been taken by the Germans from Peking to Potsdam, and later moved to Berlin. A correspondent of *The Times*, present at the talk, had taken notes. The following day an article

Bailey's escort in the Karakum Desert between the Oxus and the Murghab rivers during his escape from Bokhara to Meshed, December 1919. Left to right: Awal Nur and Kalbi Muhammad (NCOs in the Corps of Guides) with (?)Haider, Bailey's Punjabi servant [RSAA Archives]

appeared in that newspaper, quoting the lecture, about the German looting of the Chinese instruments, some of Mongolian origin. This sparked a public outcry and in March 1919 the Germans agreed to return them to China. This was a plus for the Society, albeit more by accident than design.

In 1914 Lord Ronaldshay was posted to India and the Chairmanship passed to Sir Mortimer Durand, who held it for the next four years. Sir Mortimer was the brother of Algernon, one of the Founding Members. He is best remembered for what became known as 'the Durand Line', demarcating the border between Afghanistan and the NWFP of India. (Confusingly, it was Algernon who wrote the book entitled *The Making of a Frontier.*) His mission as Foreign Secretary to the Amir Abdur Rahman in Kabul in 1893 paved the way for that ruler's relative co-operation and the Anglo-Russian agreement of 1895. In 1894 Durand was sent as Minister to Teheran and subsequently held high diplomatic posts in Europe and America.[3]

Sir Mortimer Durand

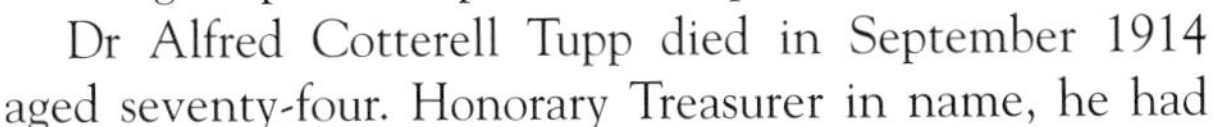

Dr Alfred Cotterell Tupp died in September 1914 aged seventy-four. Honorary Treasurer in name, he had been the Society's 'God-father' and guiding hand since its inception. He had become ill the previous year and, unable to attend meetings, asked to be relieved of his duties. But his role was so crucial that he was persuaded to continue work from home. By March 1914 he was unable to do even that and instead accepted a nominal position as Vice President. Meanwhile, Sir Evan James, another Founder Member, took on the post of Honorary Treasurer.

The Annual Dinners continued. In 1908 Lord Curzon, a member but yet to become President, was the guest speaker. Invitations to attend the dinner were sent to the *Morning Post*, the *Daily Telegraph*, the *Standard*, *Daily Chronicle* and the Press Association. In 1909 Dr Aurel Stein was the guest speaker and the Russian Ambassador was invited. The dinner proposed for 1912 was cancelled for lack of support and in 1914 the venue was changed from the Imperial Hotel, Regent Street to the Savoy. There were no dinners during the war; they recommenced in 1920.

The expenses and accounts of the Society in its early years look modest enough at this distance, though no doubt at the time they were critical. The annual balance sheet in 1908 totalled about £150 and by 1918 had only increased to just over £200. Subscription rates remained at £1 (compared to the £4 levied by the RGS at this time) and the Annual Dinner cost was pegged at 10/6d. Rent for the office was £20 and the Secretary's annual salary was £25. In 1908 the Honorary Treasurer was delighted to be able to report that there was £44 lodged in the bank, which was considered 'very satisfactory and will last for the next six months'. With some reluctance it was agreed to pay £2 each year to the RAS for the use of their telephone. One of the most expensive items was the hire of the slide lantern from the RGS for £9.9.0. Some of these figures rose considerably with post-war inflation.

In 1917 Lieut Colonel Sir Henry Trotter was appointed Chairman. A Royal Engineer, he had gone to India in 1860 and joined the Trigonometric Survey. He accompanied Sir Douglas Forsyth on his famous mission to Yagub Beg in Yarkand and Kashgar from 1873 to 1874, after which he was employed on 'Special Duties' in China. Subsequently he served as an additional Military Attaché in Constantinople to cover the Turko-Russian war, travelling with the Turkish army to do so. This was followed by appointments in Kurdistan, Constantinople again, Syria and Romania: a total of forty-six years' Crown Service. Above all he was a great sportsman and was the first European to have shot an *Ovis Poli*, the wild sheep of the Pamirs, later to become the Society's emblem. On retirement he busied himself not only with the affairs of the Society, but also with the RGS, RAS and the Society for the Propagation of the Gospel. For much of his term of office he was terminally ill and Sir Francis Younghusband virtually took his place.

Transcaspian Episode

One of the most significant events of the war period in which existing or future members of the Society took part became known as the Transcaspian Episode. The Russian Revolution in 1917 and the rapid spread of Bolshevik influence to many parts of the Russian empire raised the likelihood of a peace treaty between the new Russian regime and Germany. This could lead to a Turkish or German advance on India via the Caucasus, Transcaspia or Persia, where hitherto Imperial Russian forces had blocked the way. Germany had its eye on Baku oil and Turkestan gun cotton, and Enver Pasha dreamed of a Pan-Turanian empire spreading eastwards over most of Central Asia. The Brest-Litovsk Treaty of March 1918 confirmed the worst fears of British strategists, and four British missions were organised to counter the threat. One mission under General Lionel Dunsterville (Kipling's 'Stalky'), known as Dunsterforce, was despatched from Mesopotamia to Enzeli on the southern shore of the Caspian with a view to bolstering local defences in Baku or destroying oil facilities there in the event of a Turkish or German victory in the Caucasus.[4] Another, under General Wilfred Malleson, known as Mallmiss, was sent from India through eastern Persia to Meshed, south of Ashkabad and the Transcaspian railway.[5] The third, under Commodore David Norris, was detailed to establish a flotilla on the Caspian to back up both Dunsterville and Malleson.[6] A fourth, under Major F. M. Bailey was, as mentioned, dispatched to Tashkent via Kashgar to assess the intentions of the new Bolshevik regime in that region.[7] In addition Colonel Denis Knollys commanded the British Indian contingent that was deployed inside Transcaspia.[8]

Dunsterforce eventually reached Baku in stages from Enzeli only to find local troops too involved in nationalist politics to offer any serious resistance to the Turks. By dint of subterfuge and with the help of Norris's Caspian flotilla, Dunsterville managed to evacuate his forces to Enzeli, whence he was redirected to Krasnovodsk. Meanwhile, Malleson was ordered to carry out intelligence and military operations across the Russian frontier to prevent the Transcaspian railway being taken over by Turkish or Bolshevik forces. However, the collapse of Germany and her allies, and the temporary reoccupation of Baku by British forces, changed the strategic situation, and by March 1919 all British and Indian troops were withdrawn from Transcaspia either to Meshed or to Baku. In addition to the officers mentioned above, others involved in this military 'sideshow', who were later to recount their experiences either in lectures to the Society or in books and articles, included Captain Edward Noel, Major L. V. S. Blacker, and Captain C. H. Ellis.[9] But one officer, Captain Reginald Teague-Jones, remained silent throughout his life. Teague-Jones joined the Society in 1919, only to rejoin it in 1921 in the name of Major Ronald Sinclair, an identity which he maintained until he died in 1988. He was Malleson's liaison officer with the Menshevik government in Ashkabad, which had revolted against the Bolshevik

Commodore Norris and General Dunsterville on the Caspian

Drilling Armenian troops at Baku

Armenian soldiers, having abandoned their rifles, fleeing the front

General Dunsterville with an Armenian soldier

The Staffordshire Regiment recovering the situation at Baladjar Station following the Armenian withdrawal to Baku

DUNSTERFORCE – 1918 [RSAA Archives]

Soviet in Tashkent but whose position remained precarious. Malleson had agreed to supply Ashkabad with military support, equipment and finance in return for their co-operation against the threat of a Turkish advance across the Caspian or potentially hostile moves by the Tashkent Soviet. Teague-Jones was the lynchpin of Malleson's highly efficient intelligence network: 'There was hardly a train on the Central Asian railway which had not one of our agents on board, and there was no important railway centre which had not two or three men on the spot.'

Menshevik supporters at Ashkabad [Colonel W. Nash]

In September 1918 twenty-six Bolshevik Commissars led by Stepan Shaumian, escaping from Baku across the Caspian, ended up in Krasnovodsk where they were arrested by the local anti-Bolshevik Commandant, Kuhn, who then asked the Ashkabad authorities what should be done with them. The latter referred the matter to Malleson for advice. The accepted version of events, recorded in lectures to the Society by Malleson and others, and in British official sources, is that Malleson proposed that the Commissars should be sent direct from Krasnovodsk to him in Meshed for onward transmission to British India, where they could be held hostage against the return or release of British officers, including Bailey and Noel, who had disappeared. However, by the time Malleson's reply reached Ashkabad, Kuhn had already arranged for all twenty-six Commissars to be shot in a remote spot along the Transcaspian railway, east of Krasnovodsk. The Soviet government made great play of blaming the British for complicity in the massacre, even accusing Teague-Jones of having had a direct hand in it. The incident became a *cause célèbre* between Moscow and London, the more so because Shaumian had been a personal friend of Lenin. Trotsky's violent and quite unjustified denunciation of Teague-Jones in May 1922 gave the latter good reason to take seriously the threat of Soviet reprisals but by then he had changed his name to Ronald Sinclair.

Years later, a letter was published in the *Observer* from a former officer on Malleson's staff in Meshed, Colonel William Nash. As Captain Nash he was ADC and Staff Officer to Malleson and had left India for Persia with him in June 1917. Writing on 4 March 1956, Nash declared that 'to the best of my recollection' the Ashkabad authorities' request for advice as to what to do with the Commissars had come in the form of a telegram which he had personally taken to Malleson – 'at that time in bed with a severe attack of malaria' – to ask him what reply he should send. 'He told me that it was essentially a matter for the Russian authorities, and that he did not see his way to interfere. I therefore had a telegram put into Russian to the effect that they must dispose of the Commissars as they thought

General Malleson (centre) with members of his Mission [Colonel W. Nash]

fit.' However, when Malleson was informed of the massacre he sent a further telegram instructing Teague-Jones to inform the Ashkabad authorities of his horror at what had happened.[10] A current member of the Society, Mr James Nash, recalls his father, Colonel William Nash, speaking of the affair. At the time of writing he is in contact with a Russian film editor researching for a documentary on the incident. This illustrates well the Society's continuing links with notable Asian events of the past.[11]

Star of Bokhara, 3rd Class, awarded to Captain William Nash

In 1918 Lord Curzon accepted the invitation, arranged through his friend Sir Francis Younghusband, to become the Society's first President, a post he held until his death in 1925. Curzon had joined the Society in 1907. In May 1909 he declined the offer of Chairmanship but agreed to become a Vice President. The weight of his name undoubtedly gave prestige and influence to the Society. At the Annual Dinner in 1920, the first since his appointment, he said: 'I regard the Society with great interest and peculiar affection. I do so because during the greatest part of my life Central Asia has been my study, I might almost say my hobby ... I regard my invitation to become your Honorary President ... as a culminating point in my study of Asia.' His obituarist in the *Journal*, anxious to play down the popular myth of his supposed arrogance, wrote: 'Socially no one could be more agreeable and interesting, whilst officially no one could be more impressive and inspiring.' He gave many illuminating and amusing addresses to the Society, especially at the Annual Dinners. Two of his daughters followed him into the Society: the Baroness Ravensdale, his eldest, in 1935, who was closely involved in Younghusband's 'World Congress of Faiths', and Lady Alexandra Metcalfe in 1939. The latter was awarded the Sir Percy Sykes Memorial Medal in 1988 for her work with the Save the Children Fund in Asia.

Lord Curzon

Copy.

CENTRAL ASIAN SOCIETY,
22, ALBEMARLE STREET,
LONDON, W.

Letter from Sir Henry Trotter to the Rt. Hon. Earl Curzon of Kedleston.

18 Eaton Place.
17th December, 1917.

Dear Lord Curzon,

The Council of the Central Asian Society at a recent Meeting authorized me as their Chairman to write to your Lordship to invite your Lordship's consent to your nomination as Honorary President of the Society.

This is a new Office which it is proposed to create and it is felt that the efficiency of the Society would be increased and its status raised by having so distinguished a statesman at its head.

The duties of the post would be nominal. The President would of course preside at any ordinary Meeting which he might desire to attend, also (if present) at the annual dinners, (which however have been discontinued during the War).

Your Lordship is already a Vice-President of the Society and it would be a great pleasure to the Council and to myself personally if so high an authority on Central Asia would honour us by accepting the post of Honorary President.

If I had thought that the work would have taken any appreciable portion of your valuable time I would not have ventured to make the proposal, but having done so I trust that your Lordship's reply may be favourable.

Believe me
yours very truly
Henry Trotter.

Copy.

CENTRAL ASIAN SOCIETY,
22, ALBEMARLE STREET,
LONDON, W.

The Rt. Hon. Earl Curzon's reply to Sir Henry Trotter.

1 Carlton House Terrace.
S.W. 1.
Dec. 21st, 1917.

Dear Sir Henry Trotter,

I cannot resist so high a compliment as that which is offered me by a Society with whose work and aspirations I have so much sympathy as the Central Asian Society, the more so as your Council have so considerately safeguarded me against calls which in the existing condition of affairs it would be impossible for me to meet. Some day I hope we may all have more leisure.

Begging you to thank your Council for the honour,
I am,
Yours very truly
Curzon.

Exchange of letters between Trotter and Curzon

With the death of Sir Henry Trotter in 1919, Lord Carnock took over as Chairman. As Sir Arthur Nicolson he had held diplomatic posts in Berlin, Constantinople, Teheran, Budapest, Tangier, Madrid and finally as Ambassador in St Petersburg. Like Sir Alfred Lyall, his policy towards Russia was one of entente. On return to England in 1910, he was appointed Under Secretary of State at the Foreign Office until his retirement in 1916.

In the same year the Society moved its offices, along with its RAS host, to 74 Grosvenor Square. This time the agreement was to hire a room jointly with the Anglo-Italian Literary Society for £50 a year, of which the Society paid £30. This sharing did not prove entirely satisfactory.

Lieut Colonel Arthur Campbell Yate's Bookplate

However, the most important event in 1919 was the appointment of a new Honorary Secretary. Due to pressure of other work Sir Edward Penton had asked to step down, but agreed to replace Sir Evan James in the less onerous post of Honorary Treasurer, which he held until 1939. Another change was caused by the resignation, on marriage, of Miss Hughes, the Society's 'Nanny'. Her place as Secretary was taken by Miss L. B. Phillips, the new assistant secretary at the RAS. But who was to be the new Honorary Secretary in this game of musical chairs?

The Society was still ailing in the sense that its membership had climbed to only 139, an increase of a mere thirty in twelve years. The appointment of Lieut Colonel A. C. Yate to fill the post gave it a much needed impetus and saved it from possible extinction.

Arthur Campbell Yate was the son of a clergyman. Like his brother, Colonel Sir Charles Yate, also a member of the Society, he was educated at Shrewsbury. He entered the army in 1875 serving with the 1st West India Regiment before transferring to the Bombay Staff Corps. He took part in the Second Afghan War and the Burmese Expedition of 1886. In 1903 he took command of the 129th (Duke of Connaught's Own) Baluchis. During his time in India, and later, he wrote various books and contributions to reviews, magazines and newspapers. His knowledge was refreshed by constant travel. At his home at Beckbury Hall, Shifnal, Shropshire, he had one of the finest private libraries of books on Central Asia in Britain. Many of these came to the Society's Library on his death in 1929 aged seventy-six, only four days after that of his wife.

Though an original member of the Society, Yate did not retire from the Indian Army until 1905, when he became a regular attender at the Society's functions. In 1911 he was elected to the Council on which his brother was also serving. He took a hand in editing the embryonic *Journal* in 1914. There were few stalwarts left behind during the Great War to manage the affairs of the Society but Yate was certainly one of them. However, his great work came on his appointment as Honorary Secretary. Although he lived in Shropshire he rarely missed a meeting and commuted weekly to the Society's offices. It is not surprising that on his death in 1929 his *Journal* obituarist was moved to write: 'Never has an institution existing for the study of current Eastern affairs had more devoted service from an Honorary Secretary than that which was given to this Society by Lieut Colonel Arthur Campbell Yate'. His obituary in *The Times* added 'The advancement of the Central Asian Society was his ruling ambition in later years ... he was unwearied in the recruitment of both lecturers and members, and never lost an opportunity of seeking the co-operation of anyone who had been associated with travel, adventure or diplomacy in the wide regions covered by the proceedings of the Society.' Yate himself, when praised for his endeavours, would shrug his shoulders and say, 'I undertook to do the thing and when I do that, I do not let myself fail if possible.'

Yate's achievement belongs to the next chapter. But it may be said here that he had the foresight to see that the war had introduced Asia to many thousands of men and women who would not otherwise have gone to that continent. The trick was to get them to join the Society on their return and, as he wrote, 'thus bring double grist to the Society's mill: the grist of brain to the lecture field and the grist of funds for the production and maintenance of a Central Asian Journal, such as the Society may regard with pride.' Perhaps even Yate would have been surprised at the results of his labours.

III

FROM LEAN YEARS TO GOLDEN YEARS 1920–1939

The fact is we want members, we want strength, we want money, otherwise we cannot carry on.

Lieut Colonel A. C. Yate, Hon. Sec., 1920

What I may call in these days of film stars the Society's glamorous period . . . a list of Presidents with whom every schoolboy should be familiar.

Sir Edward Penton, Jubilee retrospective

We now reach a turning point in the history of the Society – from a time when the Society was struggling for its very existence to a period of steady growth, optimism and fulfilment when many of its most interesting and memorable characters joined. Some told of their experiences and adventures during the Great War, others of their explorations after it. Several gave their services to the Society as its Honorary Officers.

Penton and Yate, supported by Lord Carnock, concentrated on their recruiting campaign. Both the RGS and RAS were asked to circulate leaflets about the Society, and Centres of Asian Studies in British universities were successfully lobbied for recruits. In June 1920 Yate was able to announce a 70 per cent increase in membership: 'The old school of Central Asians know quite well that a new era has commenced and welcome to their ranks the younger generation who have problems to face which differ essentially from those which were the framework of what was known for a good half century as the Asian Question.'

In 1921 the membership had climbed to 415, more than doubling its numbers in just twelve months. 'The Society now numbers amongst its members two Secretaries of State and the pick of great administrators and soldiers of the Empire and also the elite of that younger generation which holds the future destinies of that Empire in our hands . . . Our *Journals* record the ability, prowess, courage, resource and endurance of men, and occasionally of women, who are an example and incentive to those who will come after them.' By 1922 the Society had nearly 600 members, of whom 143 had overseas addresses – 68 in India – and 25 were, separately, Asian members. The membership was top-heavy in senior military ranks with 3 Field Marshals and 37 Generals. It also included the Duke of Devonshire and Winston Churchill, who joined in 1921 when he was Secretary of State for the Colonies.

In April 1920 Mr H. St J. B. Philby was elected to Council. Impatient to get back to the Arab World he resigned after only five months having found a position under Sir Percy

Photograph taken at the Cairo Conference in 1921. Sir Winston Churchill, then Colonial Secretary, is seated between Sir Herbert Samuel (later Lord Samuel) and Sir Percy Cox, with Lawrence of Arabia behind Sir Percy. This was the year in which Sir Winston became a member of the Royal Central Asian Society.
[RCAS Journal, April 1965]

H. St J. B. Philby, '. . . one of the Society's most colourful if provocative characters . . .'

50 years ago...

The Daily Telegraph

July 10, 1937

MR. PHILBY'S GRIEVANCE

MR St. John Philby's lecture at Burlington House to the Royal Central Asian Society on his latest explorations in Southern Arabia generated, I hear, an atmosphere of liveliness unusual at a meeting of a learned society.

After commenting rather severely on the inadequate surveillance exercised by the British authorities over the hinterland of the Aden Protectorate, Mr Philby criticised Lt.-Col. M.C. Lake, the Political Secretary, who at the time was Acting-Governor.

When Mr Philby reached the Indian Ocean he informed the Residency in Aden of his presence, asking also for spare motor parts. The parts were sent. At the same time he had an official reminder from Col. Lake that he had acted contrary to the regulations in entering Shabwa without the permission of the British Government.

Mr Philby's diffuse but uncompromising condemnation of Col. Lake's attitude caused restiveness in the hall. This was finally voiced by Sir Percy Sykes, who rose and declared, amid applause, that the lecturer should know better than to use such language.

Upon this Sir Denison Ross, the chairman, who had been following the lecture, which was illustrated with lantern slides, from the body of the hall, returned to the platform.

Saying that it was time for him to remind everybody that he was arbiter of the proceedings, which he would now bring to an end, he declared that the British authorities in Aden were all honourable men and that Mr Philby was an explorer of genius. The resulting clash might therefore, in his opinion, be considered discreditable to neither party.

This diplomatic enforcement of the closure enabled the members to adjourn for refreshment in a spirit of détente.

. . . and his 'grievance'

Cox in Iraq. Philby was one of the Society's most colourful if provocative characters. Although he remained a member until his death in September 1960, more than once he threatened to resign, complaining that everyone running it was 'too old'. His place on Council was taken by Captain Geoffrey Stephenson and in April 1921 Yate enrolled him as joint Honorary Secretary. As Yate lived in Shropshire he felt it useful to have a London-based assistant. The choice marked almost as important a milestone in the history of the Society as the appointment of Yate himself. After serving as a French and German interpreter with the BEF in France in 1915, Stephenson was transferred to Mesopotamia to work under Sir Arnold Wilson and subsequently as Agent in London for the Mesopotamian administration. In later life he retired to live in a wooden bungalow on Lock Island, Marlow. A delightfully eccentric bachelor, he was in the habit of smoking his pipe whilst swimming in the Thames. A current member of the Society, Colonel Tom Walcot, was Geoffrey Stephenson's ward and from 1948 lived with him in that bungalow. Walcot recalls life there and how he would quite often telephone the railway station to hold the 'Marlow Donkey', the local train, for when his guardian travelled to London for Society, and other, meetings. Stephenson maintained his interest in the Society until his early eighties when he was still an Honorary Vice President.

Geoffrey Stephenson

As Sir Edward Penton remarked after Yate's death, he and Stephenson would walk daily round St James's Square with a bundle of banker's orders and would compel everyone they met interested in the East to sign up at the nearest lamppost. They made the United Service Club yield its quota of great soldiers and would then go across the road and recruit distinguished pro-consuls at the Athenaeum. Yate would say: 'Whenever I am brought into touch with people interested in Asia I speak or write to them; about eighty per cent then join' – and looking at his audience he would add: 'Go and do thou likewise.' Between them they recruited 300 new members in just two years and by the time Stephenson retired from his position in 1927 he had the satisfaction of seeing the membership reach the long-desired figure of a thousand. He had recruited 400 members off his own bat, a hundred in a single year, Winston Churchill amongst them.

Council itself continued to think up new recruiting ideas such as sending a free copy of the *Journal* 'to all Members of Parliament who might be considered imperially inclined'. One of the problems faced was the large number of losses from both resignations and deaths, some through such unlikely incidents as being mauled by a tiger! Although the subscription was still only one pound many members resigned on being posted or leaving for some assignment abroad, often to rejoin later. Another problem was the rival attraction of the Persian Society and the recently inaugurated Near and Middle East Association.

Yate was not in good health when he took on the position of Honorary Secretary in 1919 at the age of sixty-six. By 1923 he was seriously ill and was forced to resign. He died six years later. On his retirement the Society thanked him for his outstanding work and presented him with a silver-mounted mazer hardwood drinking-bowl as a token of its appreciation.[1] Yate's place as Honorary Secretary was taken by Lieut General Sir Raleigh Egerton, whose army career had been spent mostly in India, including a period as ADC to the Governor of the Punjab.

The loss of Yate in 1923 was compounded by that of Lord Carnock the same year, having completed a five-year term as Chairman which had seen the Society's membership grow from 130 to 700, an increase which the AGM was informed that year 'has enabled us to carry on rather than put up the shutters'. Carnock was replaced for a year by Sir Maurice de Bunsen[2] before Viscount Peel, who had just relinquished his post as Secretary of State for India, took over in 1924. An original member of the Society, Peel became President two years later on the death of Lord Curzon, the title no longer being labelled 'Honorary'. He returned to the India Office in 1928 while still holding the Presidency.

There were further changes in the Honorary Secretaries. The pattern was now established where there would be two, and sometimes three, covering differing geographical areas. Egerton, too busy with his Service charities, was replaced briefly by Major General Sir William Thompson and then more substantively in 1926 by Major General Sir William Beynon, who held the position for six years. Beynon, a well-decorated soldier, had been Staff Officer to Colonel Kelly during the celebrated forced march to relieve the Chitral garrison in 1895, and subsequently served with Younghusband in Tibet. After further service in Somaliland, Europe and Afghanistan he joined the Royal Observer Corps in the Second World War at the age of seventy-seven.

Major General Sir William Beynon

Meanwhile Stephenson's position was eventually taken by Mr Emanuel Gull, whose career had been in the Chinese Customs Service, during which he had travelled extensively in Mongolia and the Gobi desert.[3]

On Peel's elevation to the Presidency in 1926 his place as Chairman was taken for a year by Sir Michael O'Dwyer, a former Lieutenant Governor of the Punjab.[4] He was succeeded in 1927 by Field Marshal Viscount Allenby, who in 1930 was also elevated to the Presidency. Allenby's nine years in office, both as Chairman and later (1930) as President, saw some of the most important events in the Society's history. During these years the Society received its Royal Charter and, appropriately, the Lawrence of Arabia Memorial Medal was inaugurated. Allenby was in harness almost to the time of his death in 1936 when members subscribed to the fund for ex-servicemen opened in his memory.

Field Marshal Viscount Allenby

Lord Lloyd of Dolobran succeeded Allenby as Chairman and President. Lloyd was in Cairo with Colonel Gilbert Clayton and T. E. Lawrence, and later on Allenby's Intelligence Staff. Towards the end of that war he was appointed Governor of Bombay. He then resumed his career in Parliament before following Allenby as High Commissioner in Egypt. A born imperialist, Lloyd loved the pomp and circumstance of high office, his last being that of Secretary of State for the Colonies. He gave eleven years' service to the Society as Chairman and President, finally relinquishing the latter post in 1941.

Meanwhile Sir Horace Rumbold, a diplomat who had served in Persia, Japan and Turkey, took over the Chairmanship from Lloyd for three years. He in turn was replaced by

Field Marshal Lord Chetwode, who had served as a Corps Commander under Allenby in Palestine and later as Commander-in-Chief in India.[5]

Beynon retired in 1932 and was replaced by Brigadier General Sir Percy Sykes, who did more for the Society in its middle years than anyone. He held office for thirteen years and was the mainstay of the Society during the Second World War, giving lectures at short notice when speakers at that time were hard to find. The details of his life are given in the chapter on the medal inaugurated in his memory.

Perhaps because of the Society's prestigious office holders, the membership continued to climb steadily. By 1930 it had reached 1,300, and in 1939 with Sykes and Gull now in their eighth year as joint Honorary Secretaries (a team similar to that of Yate and Stephenson), 1,800. At this time there were 502 overseas members, of whom 130 were in India, 83 in Iraq, 45 in Palestine, Syria and Jordan, 38 in Persia, 18 in Arabia and 31 in the United States. There were relatively few living in the Far East: 12 in China, 5 in Burma and 1 each in Singapore and Malaya.

The increase in membership meant a greater workload for the Secretary. In 1921 Miss M. N. Kennedy, a niece of the Society's founder Dr Cotterell Tupp, had taken over from Miss Hughes. The Secretaries worked 'in that little box on the third floor of 74 Grosvenor Street from where hundreds of letters, circulars and Journals are despatched all over the world'. Their conditions were relieved somewhat the following year when the Persia Society, which occupied larger rooms within the RAS building, agreed to an exchange. But the need for yet larger accommodation remained pressing until the Society secured its own premises, independent of the RAS, at nearby 77 Grosvenor Street in 1929. Here there was a room large enough for board meetings and another for use as a reading-room. Eight years later the Society was warned that the building was shortly to be demolished, which precipitated a move to 8 Clarges Street where there was space for the Society's embryonic library. The additional expense entailed in the move was made possible by generous donations from an American member, Mr Charles Crane.

Left-right: 74–77 Grosvenor Street, 2001

All these problems had overtaxed Miss Kennedy and in January 1937 she was ordered to take six months unpaid leave and given £100 towards travelling expenses for a Middle East study tour. Her place was taken, temporarily, by Miss Rachel Wingate, sister of Orde Wingate who was later to gain fame as the Chindit leader in Burma. On Miss Kennedy's return, Rachel Wingate stayed on to help, eventually taking over as Secretary in 1944. When Miss Kennedy retired that year she could look back on twenty-four years of outstanding service. Sir John Shea, a later President, recalled: 'Never was a society better or more effectively served ... If anybody came back from abroad and could possibly conduct a lecture she was waiting either at Waterloo or Tilbury to catch him.'

Another important change in Honorary Officers occurred in 1939 when Sir Edward Penton was forced by pressure of government work to retire from his post as Honorary Treasurer. He had served the Society non-stop for thirty-eight years. His place was taken by Major Edward Ainger, a former cavalry officer and army interpreter in Russian and

Japanese. He held the position almost until his death thirty-seven years later. These long terms of office were essential for the Society's 'tribal memory'.

Another innovation in this period was the creation of local Honorary Secretaries abroad, whose role was to propagate information about the Society and encourage recruitment. By 1939 there were such representatives in Syria, Iraq (both Baghdad and the RAF base), Egypt, and the NWFP of India.

The Persia Society

The Central Asian Society (CAS), ever mindful to increase its membership, kept an eye open for suitable amalgamations, or better absorptions, of other like-minded societies which had an interest in Asia. In 1921 it turned down an overture from the Anglo-Russian Society as being unsuitable, but considered making an approach to the Japan and China Societies. In 1923 the question of a merger with the Persia Society was discussed but it was decided to wait until the latter became the supplicant. In 1929 it did, realising it could no longer survive on its own.

The Persia Society was founded in 1911 by Lord Lamington, Mr H. F. B. Lynch and Professor E. G. Browne.[6] It was supported by the Persian Legation, whose Minister became, *ex-officio*, its Honorary President. The Society's aims were to promote sympathy between the peoples of Britain and Persia through personal intercourse, the study of Persian literature, and the promotion of joint interests in the fields of arts, science, industry, economics and education.

In 1929 the Persia Society had some 250 members, many of whom also belonged to the CAS. In the event, with resignations, the net gain of new members was only 83. The Persia Society's funds, about £375, were placed in a separate trust administered by a special committee, most of whom were old Persia hands.

There was a problem over the name of the amalgamated Society. Most CAS members of Council felt the Persia Society should expire gracefully. However, its original members, foremost amongst whom was Sir Arnold Wilson, did not want to see the title 'Persia' disappear. After animated debate and an Emergency General Meeting, when the suggestion 'Asian Society' was rejected as being too close to that of the Royal Asiatic Society, the formula 'The Central Asian Society in which is incorporated the Persia Society' was decided upon. The Persian Minister in London became an Honorary Vice President of the amalgamated Society, Lord Lamington (an early member of the CAS) a Vice President, and the two Honorary Secretaries of the Persia Society joined Council.

In theory all should have worked well but the older members of the Persia Society, not least Lord Lamington, were loath to lose their total independence. They insisted on the funds remaining separate and used for financing such events as a yearly lecture on Persia, an occasional dinner, support for archaeological projects through the Gertrude Bell Memorial Fund, and the purchase of books on Persia for the Library. In July 1934 the funds were used for a 'Firdausi Millenary Luncheon' at the House of Lords. Anthony Eden, then Lord Privy Seal, who had taken a degree in Oriental languages at Oxford, was the guest speaker. The Persian Minister, presiding, was so impressed by Eden's erudition that he described him as 'a mesmerizing personality, with all the attributes of youth, beauty and eloquence. He knows, moreover, a great deal about the East, its literature and culture.' The Aga Khan was also present and spoke.

The additional title was eventually quietly dropped for everyday use as being too cumbersome. But the problem of the separate fund account continued for another thirty years, involving much legalistic argument. The Society's Treasurer, Ainger, wanted to incorporate this money into his main account, one reason being that in 1936 the Society had reworded its Charter so that it was recognised as a Charity, thus entitling it to a refund of tax. The Persia Society, before amalgamation, had made no such provision. This was resolved in 1946 by making the Society Trustees of the Persia Fund, but the account remained separate until the 1960s.

The Iran Society, which had no direct genesis in the Persia Society, was established in 1935. In 1953, when its membership stood at over 100, of whom 59 were members of the Royal Central Asian Society (RCAS), there was an experimental affiliation between the two Societies. This was prompted by Dr Moussadeq's nationalisation of the Iranian oil industry and the consequent break in diplomatic relations in 1952. Thereupon the Iran Society suspended its activities and sought a temporary alliance in the RCAS, whilst retaining its own identity. With the restoration of relations in 1954 the Iran Society was able to resume its activities and went its own way again. However, in 1967 it asked the RCAS to undertake, for a fee, its secretarial work. This situation remains though the Societies function separately.

The Society's Royal Charter and Coat of Arms

In May 1921 the Duke of Connaught was asked if he would be the Society's Patron. He was unable to accept. On 4 March 1931 the Society, under the Presidency of Viscount Allenby, aimed higher and applied for a Royal Charter. This was granted by King George V on 15 April of the same year when the Society was renamed the Royal Central Asian Society. In February 1937 the Palace confirmed that the Charter held good indefinitely without the need for a further application on the accession of a new Sovereign.

In June 1933 the Society decided that this honour should be commemorated by a Coat of Arms, a crest and a motto. The choice of the horns of the Marco Polo Sheep, or *Ovis Poli Ammon*, as the Society's crest has its origins in 1930. In June that year Sir Percy Sykes presented the Society with the horns and head of an *Ovis Poli* which he had shot in the Pamirs in 1915. He said at the time that should the Society ever adopt an emblem this would be the most fitting, being the representative game of the very heart of Asia. He quoted Marco Polo: 'One ascends so high that they say it is the highest place in the world. It is called Pamier [*sic*] ... There are wild sheep of very great size. Their horns reach a length of quite six spans.' This is the first known description of the

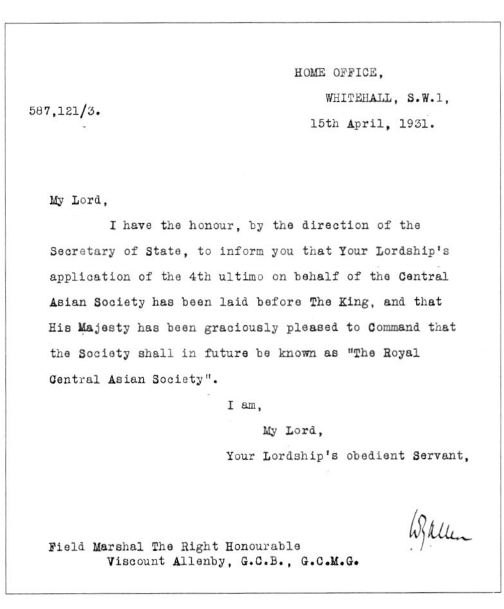

HOME OFFICE,
WHITEHALL, S.W.1,
15th April, 1931.

587,121/3.

My Lord,

I have the honour, by the direction of the Secretary of State, to inform you that Your Lordship's application of the 4th ultimo on behalf of the Central Asian Society has been laid before The King, and that His Majesty has been graciously pleased to Command that the Society shall in future be known as "The Royal Central Asian Society".

I am,
My Lord,
Your Lordship's obedient Servant,

Field Marshal The Right Honourable
Viscount Allenby, G.C.B., G.C.M.G.

Letter Granting Royal Charter

celebrated animal, which bears his name. A member of the Society, the Italian explorer Sir Filippo de Filippi, also wrote at the time: 'The *Ovis Poli* is as much the heraldic beast of Central Asia as the white bear is to the Arctic or the lion to Africa.'

Having decided upon the horns as the Society's emblem, Sir Percy Sykes wrote to Lady Roberts, widow of Field Marshal Lord Roberts of Kandahar, to ask if the head in the possession of her late husband could be used as the design artist's model. This head, with its record span of 75 inches, was given to Lord Roberts by the Amir of Afghanistan. Lady Roberts agreed. The motto chosen to appear beneath the emblem was *Cornua levat super Terras*, loosely translated as 'He raises his horns over the Roof of the World'.

The Society's Blazon of Arms, 1933

The Coat of Arms incorporated those from the shields of the Society's President, Viscount Allenby of Megiddo and Felixstowe and of its Chairman, Lord Lloyd of Dolobran. A member of the Society, Mr Omar Ramsden, offered his services in preparing the necessary designs and working drawings of the shield. A fund was opened to cover the fee of £50 required by the College of Arms. The response was generous and the final sum raised was over £120. The surplus was used to institute a Golden Book, whose purpose was to record the great events and names of the officers of the Society. In 1934 Sir Percy Sykes wrote: 'It is hoped that this will be of interest to present members and be of especial interest to the generation which will celebrate the Centenary of the Society in October 2001.' Tragically, that Golden Book and the original Coat of Arms were destroyed by enemy action during the Second World War. In June 1945 an application was made for the renewal of the Grant of Arms and a new Golden Book was established.

In 1944 Field Marshal Viscount Wavell, then Viceroy of India, a member since 1934 and at the time a Vice President, informed the Society that he was sending it a pair of *Ovis Poli* horns. This fine pair, with a span of 70½ inches, thought to be the fourth largest recorded, had been given to Lieut Colonel E. H. Cobb, Political Agent at Gilgit, at the latter's request, by the Amban (magistrate) of Tashkurghan, Mr Wang Ying-Chu'an, in 1943. The head had been found in the Kukturuk Valley of the Taghdumbash Pamir and it was believed the twelve-year-old ram had been killed by wolves.[7] The horns of

Head and horns of Ovis Poli presented by Viscount Wavell displayed in the Society's Library

A mature Ovis Poli ram shot by Lieut Colonel Evelyn Cobb, Taghdumbash Pamirs, 14,000 ft, 1943 [RSAA Archives]

the head were similar to those of Lord Roberts's animal used as the model for the Society's emblem. Colonel Cobb sent the head on to the Viceroy in Delhi with the proposal that he should present it to the Society. It eventually arrived from India in July 1945, shipped by Messrs Thomas Cook for £2. Customs valued the head at £100 and wanted £10 in dues but after argument this was waived. The taxidermist firm of Roland Ward cleaned and mounted the head, though the skin mask itself was so badly decayed that it had to be mounted as a skeletal exhibit. This is the pair of horns currently displayed in the Society's Library. It was exhibited at the International Big Game Fair at Düsseldorf in 1954.

In 1955 Lieut Colonel Cobb wrote: 'It is not surprising that our crest and motto should excite our admiration and stir our imaginations. If we may think of the achievement of this Society since its foundation and of its ever-increasing scope, are we not also tempted to think that Marco Polo's sheep still looks down from High Asia upon the world with the destinies of the great civilizations of Western Nations, Great Russia and China's millions, supported in the weight and balance of those massive horns?'

In March 1956 the Society was offered the head that had belonged to Lord Roberts but had to decline it for lack of space. In April 1968 a member, Dr Howard Harper, offered to send from Kabul another set of *Ovis Poli* horns. This again had to be declined. And finally in January 1975 Lord Lovat let it be known he was most anxious to buy, on behalf of the Shikar Club, the pair of horns presented by Viscount Wavell at their market value. Council rejected the offer!

The Assyrian Problem

Throughout its history the Society has never been slow to interest itself in the political issues of the day and to highlight the cases of people or communities perceived to be the victims of injustice or mistreatment, the more so in its earlier years when it felt it had political influence.

The plight of the Assyrian Christians, or Nestorians, exercised the Society during the 1920s and 1930s and was the subject of some thirteen lectures and several articles during this period.[8] The Assyrians had sided with the Russians and turned against their Ottoman overlords in the 1914–1918 war. With the collapse of Tsarist Russia in 1918 they turned to the British who encouraged those tribesmen living in the mountains north of the Mosul Vilayat to rise against the Ottoman Turks. The rebellion failed. After the resulting massacre those who had escaped sought protection with the British forces in Persia. With the fall of Baghdad to the British they were transferred to a nearby refugee camp and after the armistice became a minority problem in Iraq.

The Assyrians had a rightful claim to British gratitude. During the war they had been known as 'Britain's smallest ally' and after it their flag appeared with those of the other allies at the Cenotaph.[9] They gave loyal support during the post-war mandatory period. Many enlisted in the locally-raised Levies and generally allied themselves to the British cause. As a result they became estranged from the Arab and Kurdish communities and in 1933 there were further massacres. The problem was handed to the United Nations for a solution with a suggestion that they should be moved out of Iraq and later, in 1939, 12,000 were resettled in Syria.

In 1933 the Assyrian Patriarch, the Mar Shimun, joined the Society. In 1934, Sir Percy Sykes, the Honorary Secretary, was asked to look into the Assyrian question and wrote to the Secretary of State for Foreign Affairs, Sir John Simon, on behalf of the Society, enclosing a copy of his own recent article on the subject in the *Journal*.[10] He suggested, *inter alia*, that the Assyrians should be resettled in Eastern Canada, adding that the Mar Shimun agreed. Sir Percy concluded his letter: 'It is difficult to see how they can be secured the treatment they undoubtedly merit outside of the British Empire.' A sympathetic reply was received from Simon mentioning that Brazil was another possibility.[11]

In his Annual Dinner speech in 1934 Lord Lloyd said: 'We have had several lectures on the Assyrian problem and I do not believe there is anyone in this country who is aught but ashamed and unhappy at the fate of a minority for whose welfare we are completely and admittedly responsible ... Their very espousal of our cause in the war made it impossible for them to live in their homeland save under our guarantee – and we have failed them.' In 1936 the Archbishop of Canterbury used the Society's *Journal* pages to raise funds for the Assyrians' plight, reminding readers they were the Nestorians of antiquity. Two members, Major D. B. Thompson and Captain G. Gracey,[12] were especially active in their refugee camps and Miss Kennedy, the Society's Secretary, during her six-month study tour of the Middle East, reported to Council on the unsatisfactory state of that at Khabbur. Another member, Major A. D. W. Bentinck, who had served for a year with the Assyrian Levies, was a prolific lecturer on their history and plight.

The problem of the Assyrians dragged on into the mid-1940s when they were again recruited into the locally-raised Levies to provide guards for the Habbaniya airbase. This was a vital role at that period of the mandate: most of the British army had been withdrawn and it was left to the RAF to maintain the peace. But again there were problems. In 1944 a meeting of interested parties was held at the Society's offices and in 1953 the English-educated Assyrian Patriarch, Mar Eschai Shimun, lectured to the Society on the current situation regarding his widely dispersed people.[13]

2nd Battalion Assyrian Iraqi Levies, 1925

Assyrian Levies, South Kurdistan, 1928

The Asyrian Patriarch Mar Shimun XXI (2nd from left) with his Aunt Lady Surma Khanim
[RSAA Archives]

Palestine

Another subject that received attention was Palestine, which at the time was under the British mandate. There were twenty-seven lectures and *Journal* articles during the period under review. (Surprisingly only seven were given during the years 1940–1960 when the State of Israel was being created.) The Society has always claimed neutrality in political debate. With regard to Palestine its reputation can best be attested by the fact that during the Mandate there were among its members some of the Husseini family and leading Jewish advocates of the Zionist cause. Sheikh Hafiz Wahba, Saudi Arabian ambassador to London, the Iranian ambassador and the Israeli ministers in Washington and London were all members, many of them of long standing. The lecture programme was thus well balanced, giving opportunity for both the Zionists and the Arabs to give their points of view. Dr Chaim Weizmann gave two separate lectures presenting the Zionist case and a number of Palestinian Arabs including Jemal Bey Al Husseini, Fakhri Bey Nashashibi, and Miss Nabiha Nasir gave theirs. Other lecturers were given by British administrators, whilst the Chair at meetings was taken by Members of Council such as Sir Ronald Storrs and Sir Horace Rumbold, who had deep experience of the country.

After the speakers had made their opening addresses many of the lectures took the form of a discussion with members from the floor joining in at times animated debate. Again there was a balance between the pro-Zionists arguing that Zionist immigration brought benefit to the country as a whole, and the Arabs expressing concern at their loss of lands and identity. At Fakhri Nashashibi's talk on *The Arab Position in Palestine*, when Storrs took the Chair, the lecturer pointed out that if Britain gave support to the unlimited immigration of Jews then the Arabs would find it difficult to support Britain's imperial interests – and vice versa. Both the Muslim scholar Mr Marmaduke Pickthall and the Arabist Mr St J. Philby spoke from the floor. Mr Archer Cust, both in his own lecture and from the floor in others, pressed his case for cantonisation. The guest speaker at the Annual Dinner in 1937 was Lieut Colonel Sir John Chancellor, a former High Commissioner in Palestine. Both he and Sir Horace Rumbold spoke for the Arab cause. In April 1939 the Society convened a special discussion group at its offices to study the latest Palestine proposals.[14] At the Annual Dinner that year the guest speaker was the Rt Hon. Malcolm MacDonald, Secretary of State for the Colonies. His portfolio included responsibility for Palestine and he devoted virtually the whole of his speech to the growing problems there. The writer and broadcaster, Mr Nevill Barbour, was a valued interpreter of Arab Affairs until his death in 1973, as was the Arab writer Mr George Antonius. Lectures on the Palestine issue continue to the present. In April of the Centenary year Mr Afif Safieh, Palestinian General Delegate to the United Kingdom, spoke on *What has happened to the Middle East Peace Process?*

These subjects apart, the lecture programme in this period roamed far and wide – for some too wide. Members made no complaint about talks on Albania and Tunisia. But in 1922 a lecture entitled *The Cape to Cairo Railway from the point of view of African Development* drew criticism as being just too far outside the Society's remit.

The Society's explorers returned to tell their tales. Mr Bertram Thomas and Mr H. St J. B. Philby lectured on their crossings of the Empty Quarter and then exchanged acrimonious (though possibly tongue-in-cheek) correspondence in the *Journal* over the spelling of place names, for example Wabar/Ubar and its exact location. Praise was heaped upon them at the Annual Dinner speeches stressing the prestige they brought the Society. Other travel lectures were given by Sir Eric Teichman, Peter Fleming and Ella Maillart. Sir Aurel Stein spoke at the Annual Dinner in 1929 and two years later the Society sent him a telegram of support when he was facing bureaucratic obstruction in China. Captain Frank Kingdon Ward, the explorer and plant collector, delivered seven talks in this period.

Sir Aurel Stein

There were three consecutive lectures on Wahhabism given in 1929–1930, the first by the Saudi Arabian envoy Sheikh Hafiz Wahba. There were more talks on railways, the Society claiming that 'Railway enterprises in Persia is a subject that CAS has made its own', and subsequently some on Air Routes. Lectures on internal India remained a problem, though the Society reached an agreement with the East India Association that they could be given 'jointly'. Some lectures had alluring titles – *The Freeing of Russian Slaves at Khiva*; *Sport on the Snow Line*; *With the Calipers on the Roof of the World* and *The Reindeer Tungus of Manchuria*.

Many of the lectures, such as those by Major General Dunsterville on his Caspian mission; Lieut Colonel F. M. Bailey on his adventures in Central Asia; Sir Arnold Wilson on the future of Asia and Mrs Rosita Forbes on the Senussi of North Africa, proved so popular that members had to be turned away at the door through lack of space. Having no lecture premises of its own the Society used, variously, those of the Royal Society and the Royal Astronomical Society, both in the Burlington House complex, the RUSI in Whitehall and the Royal Society of Arts in John Adam Street.

Dinners took place annually, either at the Victoria and Cecil Hotels, Claridges or Grosvenor House. In 1923 the price was raised to 11/6d. Lord Curzon presided in 1924 and gave a memorable speech, extolling the appeal of Central Asia: 'the appeal to the spirit of service and duty more than any corresponding area of the globe... [which] holds us by the magnificence of its surroundings and by the splendour of its surface.' But he also welcomed unreservedly the wide remit the Society had now adopted. At the Silver Jubilee Dinner in 1926 the Presidents of both the RGS and RAS were welcomed as guests. In his 1927 dinner speech, Field Marshal Lord Plumer suggested to his audience that when young officers came on leave from parts of Asia, worn by the discomforts of government service in exacting conditions, members of the Society should endeavour to show them some private hospitality, such as 'weekends in the country, fishing and shooting parties and dinners in London with a play to follow': a splendid reminder of a more leisured age.

Viscount Allenby, on assuming the Presidency from Lord Peel in 1930, reminded the Society that it still had a political role by quoting from a speech made by Sir Francis Younghusband in 1910. 'It is not sound business to be continually at the mercy of events ... Events can be largely foreseen and if troubles are coming they can be provided for by those who know the countries and their peoples.' Allenby enlarged: 'We who have served in the East have all suffered because this dictum was not heeded... If this Society can make known the judgements of the men who know best what should be done; if we can save our Eastern dependencies and friends from legislation passed by politicians with their eyes directed towards voters, instead of honest considerations of the questions in hand ...

then we shall surely have done something to help our countrymen who are working under such great difficulties.'

The Amir Saud, Crown Prince of Saudi Arabia, attended the dinners in 1935 and 1937. He made short speeches in Arabic, which were translated by Sir Ronald Storrs and Mr Mahmood Zada of the Saudi Legation. Mr Philby complained to Council that a small piece of bacon had been served with the quail at the 1935 dinner. Claridges were most apologetic.

Over the years speeches at the Annual Dinners have entertained as well as informed. In 1925 Mr Leopold Amery, Secretary of State for the Colonies, told of how thirty years earlier he and the Earl of Birkenhead had been travelling in a remote part of Asia Minor. Benighted in the wild mountains their only refuge lay in a hut occupied by some villainous-looking brigands. Awakening from a deep sleep he heard one of the outlaws say: 'Let's kill the little one first.' Recognising himself as the victim he fumbled for his revolver, realising just in time it was a question of which chicken was to be sacrificed for the breakfast of the visitors.

In 1990 Mr Shaharyar Khan, High Commissioner for Pakistan, related how an Ambassador to one of the monarchies of Europe was rehearsed on how to present his letter of credentials. The moment the horse-drawn coach stopped he was to alight, bow three times and say to the Marshal: 'Allow me to present my letter to His Majesty.' On the day the coach was held up by traffic. Thinking he had arrived the Ambassador acted as he had been instructed. Bowing in the precincts of a fish and chip shop the owner telephoned the police to say that a lunatic had escaped. Meanwhile the coach arrived at the Palace empty.

Dinners apart, there were a number of receptions held in the period: in March 1928 for the ladies of the Society to meet the Queen of Afghanistan; in June 1936 for the Sheikh of Bahrein, Hamid bin Isa Al Khalifa; in May 1937 one was held for the Amir Abdullah of Jordan, and in April of the following year one for the Sultan of Muscat and Oman, Saeed bin Taimur. He was described afterwards as 'shrewd and energetic and speaking excellent English'.

By the close of the period the Treasurer's accumulated balance sheet had risen from a modest £200 in 1919 to £2,000. Salaries had risen to £450, *Journal* expenses to £695 and the annual rent of the office to £250. Even the telephone costs had grown from £2 to £13! Investments and cash assets stood at £685 and the separate Persia Fund at £354. In 1932 Life Membership was fixed at 15 guineas. Amazingly, the annual subscription had remained at £1 since the inception of the Society. In 1928 there was a proposal to raise it but because of the economic situation this was abandoned. In 1939 it was raised to 25/- for new members. Existing members were asked to pay the same if they could; 243 did so. Everyone was encouraged to take out a covenant, but the threat of war discouraged people from committing themselves.

So passed what many considered to have been the golden years or, as Sir Edward Penton put it in his retrospective at the Golden Jubilee Dinner, 'The Society's glamorous period . . . with a list of Presidents with whose names every schoolboy should be familiar.' A period when its members included some of Britain's leading explorers who returned to tell the Society of their discoveries and when the Society felt it still had sufficient influence to write to Secretaries of State – some members had previously held their posts. There were others, no less distinguished, such as missionaries, doctors, scholars, archaeologists and

Annual Dinner, 14 July 1937, The Ballroom, Grosvenor House. Standing: The Emir Saud, to his left, standing, Lord Lloyd, to the Emir's right, sitting, Mr Mahmood Zada
[RSAA Archives]

engineers and these have been detailed in a separate chapter. The war and the gradual dismemberment of Empire inevitably pushed the Society in a different direction, as we shall see.

When war did break out in September 1939 the Chairman, Field Marshal Lord Chetwode, girded his military loins and in Churchillian mode issued a notice to all members: 'The wickedest war in history has come upon us; we are fighting a cunning man and an evil mode of life. We are the leaders of the world in the struggle for everything we think worth living for and we have no choice but to see the thing through to the end, and in the end we shall win ... Let us keep a high heart and a good courage, believe no rumours and do, each one of us, what we can to help, knowing well we never offered service in a better cause and one which must triumph.'

IV

FROM EMPIRE AND BACK TO TRADE 1940–1959

In ten years time there will be few, if any, administrators joining our Society . . . we can expect the principal connection we shall have with Asian countries will be where we began – trade.

Earl of Scarbrough, Annual Dinner, 1959

With a strong military component on the Council, described as 'looking like a page from the Army List', the Society faced the War with a determination to proceed as near to normal as possible. Even at the height of the blitz the lecture programme was maintained, though timings were arranged so that no one need be out after dark. Only the Annual Dinners and meetings of the Dinner Club were suspended.

In November 1940 Field Marshal Sir Philip Chetwode, busy running the War Organisation of the British Red Cross, was replaced by another robust soldier, General Sir John Shea. Coincidentally, both officers had served under Allenby in Palestine, Shea receiving the surrender of Jerusalem in December 1917. Shea's early military service had been in India, taking part in the relief of Chitral in 1895, and after the First World War he returned there. He was the ideal Chairman during the War; at the height of the London bombing he never missed a meeting. It was largely due to his example that the Society continued to function and produce its *Journal* in those difficult years.

One of Field Marshal Chetwode's last duties was to write to another Field Marshal, the Finnish statesman, soldier and Central Asian traveller, the Baron Carl Gustav von Mannerheim, who had been a member of the Society since 1928. Mannerheim's great feat was to ride from Osh, in Southern Kyrghizia, and then across Sinkiang and China to Kalgan north of Peking. A journey of 14,000 kilometres, it took two entire years, from 1906–1908, to complete.[1] As a young officer Mannerheim had served in the Russian army and taken part in the Russo-Japanese war. His Chinese journey, ostensibly part of an archaeological mission, had been sanctioned by the General Staff in St Petersburg and was in reality as much to collect military information as to pursue Mannerheim's own anthropological and philological interests. His achievement ensured promotion in the Russian army, but in 1918 he led the Finnish resistance against the Bolsheviks, and against Russia herself in 1939. He later became his

Baron Carl Gustav von Mannerheim

country's President. The Society now offered Mannerheim Honorary Life Membership, a gesture of respect for that gallant military leadership as much as for his Central Asian endeavours.

The war caused a problem in recruitment. Many members resigned, especially when posted abroad. This had a serious effect on the Society's finances; the overheads had still to be paid. A circular urged everyone to do their utmost to bring in more members and as a recruiting incentive the joining fee was waived for those in the armed services and the Merchant Navy. Another recruiting aid was the circulation of the *Journal*, together with an introductory letter, to Officers' Messes and Military Hospitals. As a result of these measures, the steady loss of members was halted. By the end of the war membership stood at 1,672, compared with 1,827 at its start. Sir Percy Sykes prophesied that after the war, as had occurred in 1918, those who had for the first time experienced Asia would join and the membership would soon reach two thousand. Although that figure was never achieved it was not too far off.

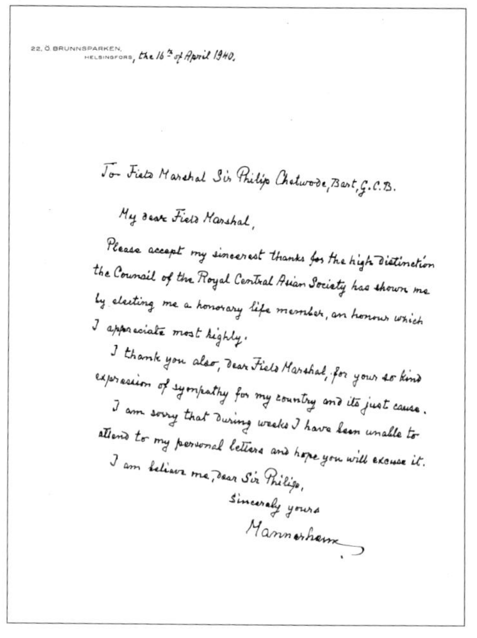
22, Ö. BRUNNSPARKEN,
HELSINGFORS, the 16th of April 1940.

To Field Marshal Sir Philip Chetwode, Bart, G.C.B.

My dear Field Marshal,

Please accept my sincerest thanks for the high distinction the Council of the Royal Central Asian Society has shown me by electing me a honorary life member, an honour which I appreciate most highly.

I thank you also, dear Field Marshal, for your so kind expression of sympathy for my country and its just cause.

I am sorry that during weeks I have been unable to attend to my personal letters and hope you will excuse it.

I am believe me, dear Sir Philip,

Sincerely yours

Mannerheim.

Mannerheim's letter to Chetwode, April 1940

The Caxton Hall Incident

Early in the war, though unconnected with it, one of the most extraordinary, yet largely forgotten, incidents in the history of the Society took place. On 13 March 1940 at a joint meeting of the Society and the East India Association, Sir Percy Sykes, the Honorary Secretary, spoke on *Afghanistan: The Present Position*. The other speakers, all distinguished members of the Society, were Sir Michael O'Dwyer, a former Chairman, Lord Lamington, Sir Louis Dane and Lord Zetland. As the meeting drew to a close a member of the audience, an Indian Sikh, Udham Singh, walked to the front of the hall and fired six shots from a large-calibre revolver, killing Sir Michael O'Dwyer and injuring Lamington, Dane and Zetland. Fatalities might have been greater had Udham not been using thirty-year-old cartridges.

As the assassin sought to escape from the Hall several of the elderly members present shouted for him to be stopped. Miss Bertha Herring, a volunteer wartime ambulance driver and long-serving member of the Society, then in her sixties, with great presence of mind put out her foot causing Udham to stumble. Upon this she, Captain Binstead, Mr Claude Riches and Flight Lieutenant W. V. Emanuel all pinned the murderer to the floor, whilst Miss Mary Rowlatt ran into the street to find a policeman. Meanwhile, three doctors present, Colonel C. H. Reinhold, IMS, Dr M. R. Lawrence (a brother of T. E. Lawrence) and Dr Grace Mackinnon gave aid to the wounded. Miss Herring was awarded an MBE for her action. Those other members mentioned received letters of appreciation from the Council.

Sir Michael O'Dwyer

Miss Bertha Herring receiving her MBE from King George VI

[Courtesy of Roger Perkins]

There is not space here to enlarge upon the incident, its aftermath and causes. These issues have been covered elsewhere.[2] Suffice it to mention that Udham Singh as a young man had been wounded at the Jallianwala Bagh massacre at Amritsar on 13 April 1919. Along with other Sikhs in the Punjab, he had held O'Dwyer as much responsible for the incident as Brigadier General Dyer himself. Dyer, also a member of the Society, had died in 1927. O'Dwyer, Lieutenant Governor of the Punjab at the time of the massacre, had condoned Dyer's action and subsequently defended him against charges of brutality. Though that may have been sufficient reason for wanting to seek revenge on the British administrators, whom Udham blamed for the incident, there are some strange twists and turns to the story, such as his contact with revolutionary leaders in Britain, including the IRA. The Scotland Yard file on the incident has been closed until 2016 and the Home Office one to 2040. This has led to speculation that since arriving in England in 1934 and adopting an alias, Udham may have been used by the security services in some way.

Udham Singh was speedily brought to trial on 4 June of the same year, found guilty and sentenced to death. In the aftermath of Dunkirk and the need for maximum support from Indian servicemen, the press was discouraged from making him appear as any sort of martyr. As a result of pressure from the Indian government, his body was exhumed from Pentonville Prison in July 1974 and returned first to Delhi and thence, in triumph, to Amritsar and on to his birthplace at Sunam. His portrait adorns the museums of both the Bagh and the Golden Temple with the inscription *The Great Revolutionary Shahid Udham Singh who shot O'Dwyer, the butcher of Jallianwala Bagh and embraced martyrdom.*

Another shock befell the Society early in the war. At its outbreak, the more valuable books of the Library were farmed out to the homes of members living in the country, while the remainder were placed in the cellars of the offices at Clarges Street. But the most rare volumes, together with the Society's Coat of Arms, its 'Golden Book', collected treasures, archives, pictures and only complete set of *Journals*, were placed in the cellars of its printers,

Golden Jubilee Dinner, Claridges, 11 October 1951.
Top Table left to right: Admiral Sir Howard Kelly, –, Lord Scarbrough, – , Sir John Shea, Sheikh Hafiz Wahba, – , – , – , Sir Edward Penton(?)

[RSAA Archives]

1948 the Treasurer, Edward Ainger, warned Council that during the next ten years there had to be a change in the character of the Society to attract substantial income through extended membership of commercial firms working in Asia. Already nearly two hundred members were employed in oil companies and an increasing number of young members were going out East as engineers or in business.

In 1953 the Chairman, Admiral Sir Cecil Harcourt, said: 'Up to a short time ago a large proportion of our membership and higher officers of the Society sprang from the great administrative services in Asia. Our members included ex-Viceroys, Provincial governors and so forth ... that source has now ceased ... A large proportion of our Society live and work in Asia and the greater part of them now are representatives of our big commercial undertakings.'[5] In 1956, for the first time, the guest speaker at the Annual Dinner, Lord Godber, Chairman of Shell, was a leading figure in the oil industry. Harcourt repeated his previous theme adding: 'Now members who go to work in Asian countries are on the staffs of our great industries, including oil and engineering. These industries have recognised the work done by the RCAS and have helped us by means of finance and other encouragements.' In 1959 the Earl of Scarbrough put it more bluntly: 'In ten years time there will be few, if any, administrators joining our Society ... we can expect the principal connections we shall have with Asian countries will be where we began – trade. And it is to the younger members of our great firms, which do business in the East, that the Society will be useful.' It was no real innovation: the first lecture on the subject *Our Commercial Policy in the East* was delivered in December 1903 by General E. F. Chapman. All this was a long cry from 1921 when the Society proudly boasted it had 'the elite of that younger generation which holds the future destinies of Empire in our hands', and when it sent free copies of the *Journal* 'to all members of Parliament who might be considered imperially inclined'.

Whilst thematically those statements made at the dinners in the 1950s were true, they failed to recognise that even if administrators no longer ruled and 'trade was of the essence', a large proportion of the Society was still coming from members of the Diplomatic Service, the remnants of the Colonial Service, the British Council and members of the armed services either stationed in Asia, or as loan personnel helping to build emerging forces there. All of these services provided a continuing source of membership.

Euphoria over the Jubilee period also hid the fact that the Society was on the point of facing its worst financial crisis yet. At a Council meeting in February 1952 the Treasurer warned that there was a danger of imminent bankruptcy. A circular signed by the three Honorary Secretaries was sent immediately to all members. While pointing out that the membership was being sustained, the Society was facing greatly enhanced expenditure in the cost of producing the *Journal* and paying its staff 'a rise in whose salaries was long overdue'. An increase in subscriptions was considered but meanwhile: 'If in the Jubilee year each member would recruit one or more members most of our financial troubles would be solved ... The question that everyone has to ask himself, or herself, is whether any institution of which he is a member is worthy of continued support ... If Britain herself is to survive as a great country she must have continued and increasing relationships with the Asian continent; and the Royal Central Asian Society provides an essential and irreplaceable means to this end.'

In June of the same year the subscriptions were raised; to £2 p.a. for members resident in London and within 50 miles of Charing Cross and £1.10s for country and overseas members. Remarkably, in fifty years the membership subscription had risen by only £1! This action was followed by an appeal to sixty-nine firms working in Asia. Those that responded resulted in a gain of £913. This strategy continued for the next ten years and by 1962 had resulted in a total of £10,056. Despite this bankruptcy scare, by the end of 1959 the balance sheet was in the black once more.

In 1953, amidst all this activity, Miss Rachel Wingate the Society's capable secretary died suddenly as a result of complications following a common cold. She had given twenty-eight years of service to the Society. Her place was taken by Mrs K. G. Putnam. Like her predecessor Mrs Putnam had had an interesting Asian career. She joined the WAAC, under age, straight from school in the First World War. After marriage to Lieut Colonel W. A. Putnam, she lived in India for over fifteen years, taking opportunities to trek in the Himalayas. In 1942 after her husband was killed in the Middle East commanding a battalion of the 14th Punjab Regiment, she returned to India to join the WAC. In charge of the Casualty Directorate at GHQ, she rose to the equivalent rank of Lieut Colonel and was awarded the MBE. Her picture, painted by Simon Elwes, hung in the WAC Mess at Delhi until 1946 when it was presented to her on departure. She served as the Society's Secretary until 1960 when she was forced to retire on grounds of ill health.

In 1955 the Earl of Scarbrough replaced General Sir John Shea as President. He had devoted a large part of his life to India, including six years as Governor of Bombay, before becoming its Secretary of State in London. He is perhaps best known for the Scarbrough report concerning Oriental Studies in Britain. In 1957 Sir Hugh Dow replaced Sir Cecil Harcourt as Chairman. Dow was an Indian Civil Servant, crowning his career with appointments as Governor of Sind and Bihar and after leaving India as Consul General in Jerusalem. He was succeeded in 1959 by Sir Philip Southwell. His career being in the oil industry, he was the first 'non-establishment' figure to hold the position since Valentine Chirol in 1907.

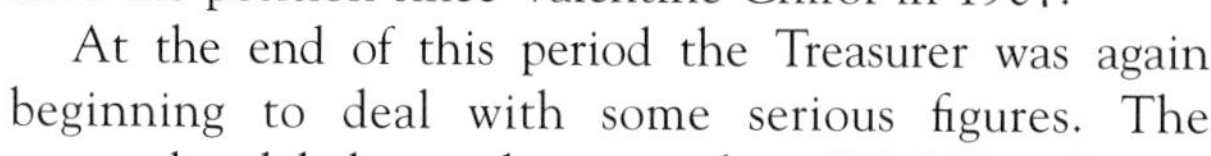

The Earl of Scarbrough

At the end of this period the Treasurer was again beginning to deal with some serious figures. The accumulated balance sheet stood at £13,000; salaries now accounted for £1,680, the rent of premises £201 – the cleaning and upkeep of which cost £260 – and the telephone bill had risen to £28. The largest single item was the cost of producing the *Journal*, now £1,527.

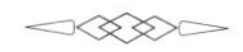

We can close this chapter with a vignette showing the continued vitality, and indeed good humour, of the Society. In September 1958 the redoubtable Honorary Secretary, Group Captain 'Chips' Smallwood, then aged seventy-five, was visiting a remote part of Western Mongolia with Dr Charles Bawden of SOAS, a Mongolian scholar and himself later a member of Council. They were, to the best of their knowledge, the only two Englishmen in that country. Visiting an archaeological dig at Kiltegen, under Czech and Mongolian supervision, they were invited into a nearby yurt. Toward the end of the meal one of those present lifted his Chinese bowl full of Russian champagne and said in broken English that he wished to propose the health of the English Queen, whom he admired greatly. Translated into Mongolian the toast was enthusiastically joined by all present. Thereupon

Smallwood sent a telegram to Her Majesty informing her of such loyal sentiment in far-off Asia. This story encapsulates the spirit of the Society. It has a Royal Patron and there is no part of Asia to which members do not penetrate. It also demonstrates the friendship which the Society endeavours to promote between Britain and the peoples of that great continent.

Sir Edward Penton closed his Jubilee retrospective speech by speaking about the second half of the Society's century. 'The road will be the same, the method will differ. We may not get the flow of distinguished and experienced members from the same source as hitherto. But that does not mean that there are not thousands of people who are necessarily interested in the area we cover. On the contrary, the sources are possibly less restricted today. From these our membership must be drawn: residents in the countries which already correspond with us; visitors travelling for information who will want to tell the Society what they have found; businessmen who trade in Central Asia (as interpreted by the Society) and, above all, the politicians who need such a repository of knowledge.' We can now turn to see how the Society did fare in the next forty years.

V

SETTLING TO A BALANCE 1960–2001

There is a balance in our affairs we must always bear in mind. It is the balance between the cultural, historical and archaeological content on the one hand and the current affairs content on the other.

Sir Arthur de la Mare, Chairman, AGM, 1981

We now enter an extended period when the 'Great Game' has long since gone, the Empire gone and some would argue the day of seminal exploration also gone. Members no longer returned from India to become its Secretary of State in London. Indeed, few in government had the sort of expertise that could point out, as did Sir Olaf Caroe, that President Yahya of Pakistan was not a Pathan, as commonly reported, but a Qizilbash. The days of the plenipotentiary were all but finished, the mandarin in Whitehall now acted on his own whim. Sir Esler Dening, Chairman, posed the question at his dinner speech in 1967: 'The Society was founded sixty years ago when the British Empire was still at its zenith ... it would be legitimate to ask whether today it is a declining relic of our imperial past or whether it is a living organism with a part to play in the day and age in which we now live.' He answered it: 'I suggest it is the second which is the truth.'

More than ever there was a need for a repository of knowledge about Asia that could be made available to those who needed it. The Society could supply that better perhaps than any other organisation. As the new Chairman, Sir William Dickson, pointed out, the Society now had a more enhanced role than in the past when there was no lack of statesmen and administrators in the East to keep its problems in everyone's mind. Most had now come home and there was thus a danger of a serious ignorance about the area among the current generation. This viewpoint was reinforced by Lord Home in 1977: 'Your Society exists and is composed of individuals who have known Asia, who have lived in Asia, and who have traded in Asia and who understand what significance Asia holds for the rest of the world ... We shall need to rely on that kind of experience more and more as political and diplomatic knowledge of that continent becomes scantier. An ounce of experience in these matters is worth one ton of theory.'

As noted at the close of the last chapter, the Society would ignore interest in trade, and links with those doing business in Asia, at its peril. But this did not mean that it was turning into some sort of mercantile advisory organisation. On the contrary, as will be seen by the end of this chapter, its vitality over a broad range of subjects and activities remains as great as ever. To quote Sir William Dickson again: 'Today our contacts are less and less through government and more and more through the medium of business and trade. We have, nevertheless, a full appreciation of the importance of language, literature, art, history, religion, antiquities and customs. How often is it not necessary to understand these if we are to understand the peoples of which they form a part?' But the Society had to adapt, not only to abide by its charter but in order to survive. Like similar societies, some of which were forced to 'put up their shutters', there were hard times ahead. Economic realities and the changing interests of a younger generation meant an inevitable drop in membership with concomitant financial anxieties.

In 1960 Marshal of the Royal Air Force Sir William Dickson replaced the Earl of Scarbrough as President. After service as a pilot on the North West Frontier during the First World War, in the Second he rose to become C-in-C of the Middle East Air Force and after it Chief of the Defence Staff. The following year, General Sir Richard Gale succeeded Sir Philip Southwell as Chairman. He had been a member of the Society since 1931. After the First World War, Sir Richard spent eighteen years in India, where he took part in several Himalayan climbing expeditions; in the Second he is best remembered for his role in training and commanding airborne forces. He was recalled from retirement to succeed Lord Montgomery as Deputy Supreme Allied Commander in Europe. Renowned for his bluff exterior, inside lay a kindly soul.

In 1961 Mr Colin Rees Jenkins succeeded Colonel Routh as Honorary Secretary, serving for twenty years. His background, useful at this stage of the Society's development, was in the oil industry, his career culminating as a Director of Shell-Mex. In the same year Miss Margaret Marsh became the new Secretary. Like her two predecessors, she had an Asian career behind her. Born in Shanghai, after schooling in Europe she returned there as a secretary in the Consulate General during the Sino-Japanese hostilities. In 1940 she was commissioned into the ATS holding various staff appointments in the Middle East, and after the war in South East Asia. In 1957 she transferred to the Foreign Office retiring to take on the Secretaryship of the Society where she was known, not unkindly, as 'the Colonel'.

In 1960 the Palestine Exploration Fund, under whose roof the Society was lodging, unashamedly increased its rent to gain more money for its own activities. That increase could not be met and again the question of an amalgamation was discussed. The Royal Asiatic Society (RAS) was the obvious choice but that proving impracticable, others were considered: the Iran Society, the Anglo-Malayan, the Anglo-Arab and the Anglo-Iraqi among them. But the RCAS was supra-national and nervous about the nationalistic attitude of these one-nation organisations.

The problem of accommodation unresolved, in July 1961, the Society's Diamond Jubilee year, an experimental afternoon tea party was held at the Hurlingham Club to which members of the Anglo-Iraqi, Anglo-Arab and China Societies were invited. It was an opportunity to get to know each other should any amalgamation take place. Tickets cost 10/- while the charge for car parking was £5. Over three hundred members of the four societies attended and the Saloon Band of the Royal Air Force played. The occasion became a permanent feature, though after 1965 the venue was moved to the Terrace of the House of Lords, for RCAS members only.

In 1961 the Society found new premises at 12 Orange Street off the Haymarket. Its congested office space, poor approach and general dingy air scarcely gave the right image to the new commercial firms the Society was hoping to attract and the lease was cut short. Meanwhile, Council began to implement a policy that would both attract and benefit those large firms, which later became known as 'Corporate Members'. Some became generous and valuable benefactors.

Leaflets describing the Society's activities were sent to organisations engaged in banking and shipping, to the Middle East Association and the London Chamber of Commerce. The prevailing recession curtailed the outcome: 6 firms had joined by 1965, 22 by 1975 and in 2000 the number stood at 31. The benefits to the 'Corporates' were the increased number of lectures dealing with topics of interest, and the influential speakers at the Society's Annual Dinners. These included Ministers of Trade, Bank of England Governors, Chairmen of Oil Companies and large organisations trading in Asia. In addition there were similar speakers, together with serving and retired ambassadors, at the confidential Dinner Club (an adjunct of the Society covered in Chapter XI) and special luncheons for Corporate Members to meet ambassadors from Asian countries.

Sir William Dickson's speeches set the theme for the coming period. The lecture programme and the Society's activities settled to a balance. The past was not ignored for it was the way to understand the future, but current affairs, economics and trade gained a new importance. As early as 1963 from a total of 22 lectures in the year, 5 were on trade and economics and 5 on current affairs. The base from which lecturers were drawn changed also. The range had always been wide: administrators, diplomats, international civil servants, architects, soldiers, schoolmasters, churchmen and missionaries, museum staff, explorers, travellers, broadcasters and scientists. This continued, but increasingly there were more academics and scholars (in 1981 six out of eighteen speakers came from faculties of Asian studies in British universities), reliable journalists, businessmen and authors, most of whom were younger people. Council was keen to get Asians to speak and the Foreign Office and British Council were asked to look out for likely candidates coming to Britain.

Mr Shaharyar M. Khan, High Commissioner for Pakistan in London, guest speaker at the Annual Dinner in 1990, commented that 'the Society has the most wonderful list of lecturers that I know of ... doing an amazing job to extend the frontiers of knowledge for people interested in Asia. The range of talks each year is remarkable.' That was true. In 1965, for example, individual countries covered were China, the Gulf States, Israel, Pakistan, Mongolia, India, Malaysia, Burma, Ceylon, Uzbekistan and Afghanistan. Juxtaposed in each year's programme was a wide spectrum of subjects ranging from Japanese Industry, Persian Society under the Qajars and Israel's Search for Identity to Mongolian Wild Flowers, Arabian Date Cultivation and Working Elephants in South India. Despite the drive to have more lectures on current affairs and economics, the Honorary Secretary in his report for 1972 had to admit, as did a predecessor in the 1920s, 'judging by audience attendances the most popular lectures are those on travel, especially if illustrated'.

In May 1965 the lecture venue moved across the courtyard of Burlington House from the rooms of the Royal Society, which since 1921 has been one of the most used premises, to those of the Society of Antiquaries, where they have been held ever since, an arrangement that is gratefully acknowledged. In 1970 evening lectures, which had been stopped during the war, were restarted, many young members having found lunchtime attendance difficult. These were held initially at the Council Chambers of the Law Society in Chancery Lane before moving to Burlington House.

In 1964 Sir Gilbert Laithwaite became Chairman. He had served in the India Office for twenty-eight years, seven of which were spent as Private Secretary to the Viceroy, and after independence as High Commissioner to Pakistan. He remained a Vice President of the Society until his death in 1986, aged ninety-four. The following year Mr Hubert

Evans, a former administrator in India, and after independence an Ambassador in Korea, became an Honorary Secretary. In 1966 Miss Marsh retired as Secretary after seven energetic years; her place was taken briefly by Miss E. Kirby.

Visiting Asian scholars have always been welcomed at the Society's offices, when relevant members of the Foreign Office and British Council were invited to join them. For example, in 1960 Mr K. M. Abdullaev, an eminent geologist from Uzbekistan, met the Society's own Central Asian experts. In 1968 Dr Nirmal C. Sinha, Director of the Mangah Institute of Tibetology and Professor Dr Bazary Shirendev, President of the Mongolian Academy of Sciences, were entertained and in 1969 Dr Soewondu and Mr Saing Silalahy, Vice Governor and Deputy Mayor of Djakarta. From 1970 to 1972 there were visits from Mr Abdul Haw Waleh, an Afghan newspaper editor, Dr Seong Hi Yim of the Korean National University, General Musa Ogun, Director of Turkish Radio and Television and Dr V. N. Nikiforov, of the Institute of Eastern Studies in the USSR. An authority on Chinese history, Dr Nikiforov had an especial interest in the kidnapping of Sun Yat Sen in 1896 by the Chinese Legation in London. By coincidence that incident took place outside the very offices of the Society, then in Devonshire Street, where Dr Nikiforov was being entertained. And it was Sir James Cantlie, the father of a member, who had been instrumental in rescuing him.

The Society was less kind to Soviet officials who showed an interest in actually joining. In 1976 an application from the Russian Assistant Naval Attaché was turned down by the Society's then President, Lord Greenhill who, only five years previously when Permanent Under Secretary at the Foreign and Commonwealth Office, had expelled one hundred and five Soviet officials for spying. Nor was a Soviet member of the International Wool Council any more successful in January 1982. Just as well for, despite his persistence, shortly afterwards he was also expelled from the country. Ironically, at this period there were more than a dozen *Journal* subscribers in the USSR. There was, perhaps, more chivalry at the tail end of the 'Great Game' than at the height of the Cold War: in 1909 the Russian Ambassador was an invited guest at the Society's Annual Dinner.

The Society has performed some unusual roles. Perhaps none more so than when in 1965 the Honorary Secretary, Group Captain Smallwood, with the help of Mr Reginald Hibbert, a member who was then Chargé d'Affaires in Ulan Bator, was assisting the Royal Horse Guards (The Blues) to obtain a supply of yak hair for their helmets.

In 1966 the Earl of Selkirk replaced Dickson as President. An early career in the Royal Air Force was followed by various government posts, including UK Commissioner for Singapore and Commissioner General for South East Asia. He gave much of his time to the Society and was active in its affairs to within a few days of his death. He was well known for his Scottish grace, said to have been written by Robert Burns for one of his ancestors.[1]

In January 1967 there was a move from those unsatisfactory quarters off the Haymarket to more spacious ones at 42 Devonshire Street. That year Sir Esler Dening took over as Chairman. Joining the Japan Consular Service in 1920, he returned there as Ambassador in 1952. His understanding of the Japanese was such that a Prime Minister once complained, 'He not only understands what we say but what we think.' In 1967 Mr James Fulton became an Honorary Secretary, a post he held for twenty-five years. A former diplomat, he also brought Far Eastern experience to the Society.

Throughout the 1960s, the membership was maintained at around 1,600, dropping in the 1970s because of inflation and an inevitable increase in subscriptions. Reasons given

Members of the RCAS entertain an eminent geologist from Uzbekistan. Left to right: Miss M. K. Marsh (Secretary); Sir Clarmont Skrine, OBE; Lieut Colonel G. Fox Holmes; Russian Interpreter; Mr K. M. Abdullaev; Lieut Colonel G. E. Wheeler, CIE, OBE, and Group Captain H. St C. Smallwood, OBE

42 Devonshire Street, 2001

for resignation were most often 'retired to the country', 'too many commitments', 'reduced circumstances' or 'old age'. When such distinguished and long-serving members as Field Marshal Sir Claude Auchinleck, Lieut General Sir John Bagot Glubb and the missionary doctor Sir Henry Holland claimed such plight, they were invariably offered Honorary status.

With the end of Empire as such, there was an increasing membership from the Diplomatic Service, many of whom brought similar Asian expertise as had those from the Indian Civil Service. But there appeared to some members an imbalance, especially in those serving on the Council. In 1983 the Chairman, Sir Arthur de la Mare, felt obliged to state that there was no formal connection between the two organisations 'except that our purpose which is to maintain a good understanding with and among the peoples of Asia is also the purpose of the F.C.O.'.

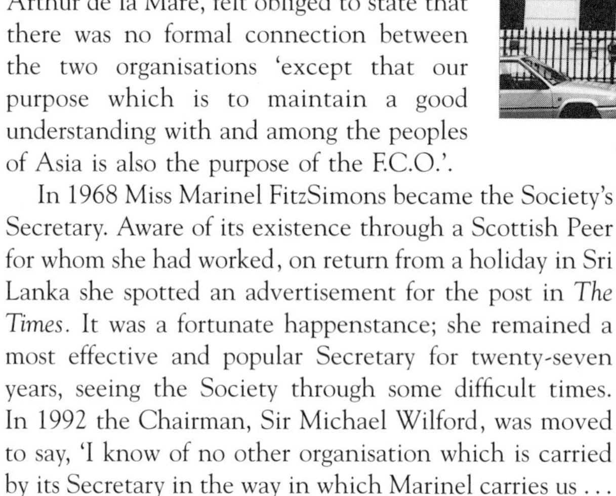

Miss Marinel FitzSimons

In 1968 Miss Marinel FitzSimons became the Society's Secretary. Aware of its existence through a Scottish Peer for whom she had worked, on return from a holiday in Sri Lanka she spotted an advertisement for the post in *The Times*. It was a fortunate happenstance; she remained a most effective and popular Secretary for twenty-seven years, seeing the Society through some difficult times. In 1992 the Chairman, Sir Michael Wilford, was moved to say, 'I know of no other organisation which is carried by its Secretary in the way in which Marinel carries us . . . She virtually *is* our Society.' In 1993 she was awarded an MBE for her work.

Sir Norman Brain had a similar career to Sir Esler Dening, whom he replaced in 1971, both in the Japan Consular Service and as Minister at the Embassy in Tokyo, before becoming Ambassador in Cambodia.[2] During his tenure of office an important sub-committee under Sir Robert Black, a former Governor of Singapore and Hong Kong, was appointed to look into the whole future direction of the Society. After much deliberation it concluded that the members, lecturers and *Journal* contributors were changing in their identity: 'The end of Empire means we can no longer call on men and women in overseas government service, with knowledge of, and ready and authoritative access to, the people, their customs, languages and cultures.' The sub-committee suggested that measures were needed to counter this. These included more social activities in connection with distinguished Asian visitors and exhibitions; the Society's financial situation required taking a further look at an amalgamation with another, or other, societies and there was a need to attract more affiliate members from amongst corporate institutions, educational as well as commercial, including Oriental Departments in European Universities. In addition a joint approach might be made with other similar societies to the government, via the Royal Society, for financial aid, or a direct approach made to a Charitable Trust.

Simultaneous with the Society's own review, the Royal Society and the British Academy were conducting their own exercise examining the financial and other problems of some three hundred learned societies. The Society appointed a liaison officer but apart from the Treasury cutting the VAT paid by such societies little else of benefit ensued.

Sir Stanley Tomlinson, who succeeded Brain as Chairman at the end of 1974, also came from a background of the Japanese Consular Service and South East Asia, before becoming High Commissioner to Sri Lanka. The following year Mr Edward Ainger was replaced as Honorary Treasurer by Mr Peter Rees. Their joint tenure coincided with one of the Society's periodic financial crises. Inflation and rising *Journal* costs had caused a deficit. The loyal world-wide membership once more responded to the Chairman's *cri de coeur* that the finances were in a 'desperate state' and the resulting donations eventually wiped out the deficit.

Change of the Society's Name

The change of the *Journal's* title to *Asian Affairs*, made in 1970, was the precursor to changing the name of the Society. A Council minute at the time noted: 'If the Society should change its name in future the title *Asian Affairs* should be borne in mind'. The decision to make such a change and rename the Society 'The Royal Society for Asian Affairs' (RSAA) was taken in December 1973. As we have seen, from its inception the Society's remit extended beyond the narrow confines suggested by the original title. But since the end of the war few people outside the Society understood its origins, and the narrowness suggested by its appellation was becoming a positive hindrance to recruitment, especially of those in business and academic circles who felt they had no real connection with Central Asia *per se*.

There were legal procedures to overcome. Application had to be made to the Charity Commissioners and the Home Office and permission sought from the Queen. This was received in October 1974 and an Emergency General Meeting was held on 10 December so that members could endorse the decision. The change became effective from 1 January 1975. Maximum publicity was sought with letters to the press, government departments, institutions and universities to the effect that the Society was interested in Asia as a whole, that it dealt with the contemporary economic, political and social developments of every country in Asia but in no way competed with the Royal Asiatic Society.

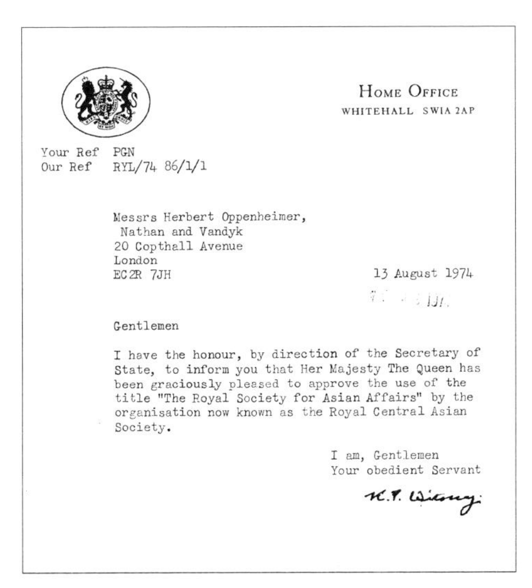

HOME OFFICE
WHITEHALL SWIA 2AP

Your Ref PGN
Our Ref RYL/74 86/1/1

Messrs Herbert Oppenheimer,
Nathan and Vandyk
20 Copthall Avenue
London
EC2R 7JH

13 August 1974

Gentlemen

I have the honour, by direction of the Secretary of State, to inform you that Her Majesty The Queen has been graciously pleased to approve the use of the title "The Royal Society for Asian Affairs" by the organisation now known as the Royal Central Asian Society.

I am, Gentlemen
Your obedient Servant

K.T. Wilcoxy

Letter agreeing change of Society's name

Old British Consulate, Chini Bagh, Kashgar
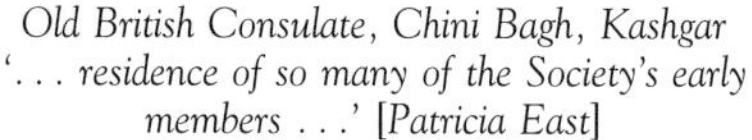
'. . . residence of so many of the Society's early members . . .' [*Patricia East*]

'Dr Dennis Duncanson made a stirring speech . . .'

There were, of course, renegades upset by the disappearance of this perceived romantic link with the past. When, in 1993, the Chairman, Sir Michael Wilford, said at the Annual Dinner: 'One result of the collapse of communism in Central Asia has been to bring very much more into focus our original title of the Central Asian Society – and there are indeed some renegades in the Society who feel that our new title of the RSAA is actually a step backward. . .', some of the audience broke into applause. Later the same year the Society's Annual Tour took place in Chinese Central Asia. A banquet was given by the Chinese in what had been the old British Consulate at Chini Bagh in Kashgar, residence of so many of the Society's famous early members. Dr Dennis Duncanson, an Honorary Secretary, made a stirring speech at this historic moment. A toast was drunk to Sir Francis Younghusband and, overcome by the nostalgia of the moment, some members proposed the old name of the Society be restored. However, such revisionist sentiments were probably made more with good humour than serious expectation.

In 1977 Lord Greenhill of Harrow, a former Head of the Diplomatic Service, became President. Apart from war service his direct experience of Asia was in Singapore. But he brought to the Society a knowledge of the Whitehall machine, sound common sense and a dry humour. He had started his working life as a railway apprentice and, like Sir Frederick Burrows an early post-war Governor of Bengal, he would say proudly he had spent more time 'shunting and hooting than hunting and shooting'. In the same year Dr Dennis Duncanson became an Honorary Secretary. His career in the Far East was involved in the fight against communist terrorists in Malaya and in Vietnam. On retirement from government service he established a Centre for South East Asian Studies at the University of Kent. Ten of his seventeen years in the post saw a happy partnership with Mr James Fulton with whom he shared a common Asian background.

Sir Arthur de la Mare

In 1978 Sir Arthur de la Mare became Chairman, again with service in Japan before becoming Head of Mission in Afghanistan, Singapore and Thailand. With his inimitable jovial style he was a popular Chairman. In 1981 he recruited to the Society Mr J. F. N. (Bill) Wedge to take over as Honorary Treasurer, a post he held for fourteen years. With a career in Barclays International, during which he had travelled extensively in Asia, he was an ideal choice to see the Society through a period when the finances were again under strain. This latest problem was caused by the coming expiry of the lease on Devonshire Street, the purchase of which had entailed exhausting the Society's reserves. This time serious money was involved; at least £100,000 was required, otherwise, as the Chairman put it bluntly, 'we shall be broke and homeless'. In March 1984 an appeal circular and various fund-raising schemes were launched. An auction of members' Asian artefacts – 'look in your attics' – organised by Mr J. B. da Silva, and held at no commission by Christies, was the initial success. A world-wide approach under Mr Maurice Smith, aided by Mr Frank Steele, brought in munificent contributions from the Sultans of Oman and Brunei, an anonymous Saudi donor and Mr Ahmed Farid. Thanks to these and to the generosity of members, the target figure was reached. No doubt the Society's change of name helped; some of these donors might have asked what connection they had with Central Asia.

In 1984, in the midst of this fund-raising activity, Sir Michael Wilford took over as Chairman, holding the position for ten crucial years. He was the fifth consecutive Chairman with a Far Eastern background, ending his diplomatic service career as Ambassador to Japan. In the same year Lord Denman became the new President and remains in that position in the Society's centenary. After war service in India and the Middle East, he has been engaged in business, commerce and overseas banking, especially in the Arab world. He has been the first President to have participated actively in the Society's Asian tours.

The financial position temporarily eased, the next problem was to find fresh accommodation. Members of Council were looking actively at a variety of options, one at least in a most unsavoury area of Kings Cross! Rooms in the basement of the Travellers Club was another possibility. In the event Mr Frank Steele negotiated and secured quarters at Canning House, Belgrave Square. The move was made in December 1985 and it is where the Society remains happily housed.

Canning House, 2 Belgrave Square
[© Canning House]

In July 1986 HRH The Prince of Wales accepted the invitation to become the Society's first Patron. (A proposal to ask the King to take that position when a Royal Charter was bestowed in 1934 had been considered too precipitate.) In 1987 he was Guest of Honour at the Annual Dinner. Over four hundred members and their guests were present. Before addressing weightier issues, the Prince put his audience at ease: 'I must say that in the context of the Royal Society for Asian Affairs I am all in favour of personal contacts. I have always heard that the best way to learn a foreign language was to have a foreign mistress. To have a special society to encourage Asian Affairs, established by Royal Charter, shows particular imagination.' The Prince then dealt with the problem of the teaching of Oriental languages, referring to the recent government report of a member, Sir Peter Parker.[3] This was especially apt because the subject was one of the first the Society dealt with after its inception.

The Annual Dinners continued throughout the period. The cost in 1960 was £2; in 2000 nearer £50. Coincidentally, that cost has always equated approximately the annual subscription. There was a move from the Hyde Park Hotel to the Savoy in 1972. The dinners were held in the winter which could cause problems. In 1962 there was such dense fog that forty-seven members had to cancel on the night. In 1991 the snow was so deep no trains and few buses were running and taxis were at a premium. One Council member remembers running four miles across London in black tie to greet the guest speaker. In 1998 the dinners were moved to June, close to the Annual General Meeting.

In 1982 HRH Crown Prince Hassan of Jordan as the guest speaker reminded his listeners that the leader of the Arab Revolt of 1916 was his great grandfather and added, 'I find it tragic that religion and ethnic break-up endangers the entire Middle East today.' In 1992 the Aga Khan, as guest speaker, attracted a large number of Ismailis to the dinner. The following year the Foreign Secretary, the Rt Hon. Douglas Hurd, recalling the Society's founding interests, remarked on how Central Asia itself was returning to a world of manoeuvre and intrigue conducted almost as in the days of the 'Great Game' except that the peoples of the area were now involved in their own destiny. Looking to the Society's future he saw that 'new forms of effort will require just as much energy as the Viceroys and the Consuls and the District Commissioners had to exercise in the past', but he foresaw also 'new forms of reward and new forms of satisfaction'.

In 1994 the Princess Royal impressed her listeners by her very personal account of the recent travels she had made in Mongolia, Kazakhstan, Uzbekistan and Vietnam as Patron of the Save the Children Fund. She gave a graphic account of those countries' problems in the aftermath of the Russian withdrawal. 'We need to know more about their culture and that is where the RSAA has an enormous role and influence, particularly in education.'

Relations with the Royal Asiatic Society

As we have seen, whenever the Society faced a move or a financial crisis, the possibilities of amalgamation with other societies were considered. And other societies in a like position acted similarly. In 1967 the RCAS made an offer to take over the Anglo-Mongolian Society, which was rejected. In 1973 Lord Inchcape, Deputy President of the Royal India, Pakistan, and Ceylon Society, proposed a merger 'so long as its Journal *South Asian Review* could be kept'. That was unacceptable. But the really serious proposals have centred, periodically, around a merger with the Royal Asiatic Society (RAS), which had been the Society's host in its formative years. When in 1929 the Society moved for the first time to its own quarters, it publicly acknowledged its 'thanks to the RAS under whose roof the Central Asian Society was fledged and for the constant kindness and the help their Secretaries have so kindly given'. At the Annual Dinner in 1935 Sir Edward MacLagan, twice President of the RAS, remarked: 'The two Societies are sisters. The RAS is by far the elder sister [it was founded in 1823] and she is, perhaps, more wrinkled, but she watches with the greatest pride the vivacity and the social success of her younger sister. She looks also, I am afraid, with great envy on the large number of her young sister's admirers. Both Societies have one object, to make the East better known to the West and vice-versa, but we go about that work in a different way.'

It was that 'different way' which in the event always thwarted an amalgamation. Sir Robert Black had written in his 1974 Review: 'The RAS is unwilling to entertain a closer association with us because the nature of their interests calls for an emphasis on a scholastic method in studying their concerns, whereas we seek to interpret the contemporary problems of our area of interest against the background of its history and culture.' However, from 1981 to 1984, and again in 1989, when the Society was facing further financial difficulties, a merger with the RAS was considered in earnest. At that latter date the President of the RAS was Mr Frank Steele, also a member of the Society and one who had been a most active member of its Council. He was sympathetic to a union; if ever there was to be one that was the time. But whilst Council saw financial advantage in the longer term, when put to the vote the majority felt strongly that the two societies were of such a different nature that a merger would devitalise them both.

In all these merger exercises the Society has always been the supplicant and the RAS, with its freehold premises and sound financial footing, has held the more advantageous position. From this standpoint an ink-stained letter unearthed in the Society's archives, written in November 1940 by the then President, Lord Lloyd, and addressed to the Secretary, appears in retrospect fanciful:

> Dear Miss Kennedy
>
> If and when the time comes for any negotiations with the Royal Asiatic Society, I do hope you will let me know. I believe that we are in the major position and that there can be no question of amalgamation on equal terms. If we handle the thing right, we can absorb the Royal Asiatic, and this is what I think we should do. . . . What we want is their building and library, if it remains standing at the end of the war.

Lord Lloyd may have felt that the Society, with a membership at the time of around 1,700, compared with less than 800 for the RAS, was in the stronger position. In 1989 the figures were more equal: the RSAA at just over 1,000, the RAS still around 800, some 300 of whom were also members of the former.

There were new Honorary Secretaries to replace the partnership of Fulton and Duncanson. In 1988 Lieut Colonel A. P. H. B. Fowle, who had served with Indian Mountain Batteries on the Frontier and instructed at the Pakistan School of Artillery at Nowshera, took the position. His service on the Council and as Honorary Secretary totalled, at the centenary, over twenty-five years. Dr Ina Russell joined him in 1993 after a career with the Board of Trade, concerned mainly with South East Asia. She was replaced in 2000 by Mrs Merilyn Hywel-Jones, who has had many years experience of Arabia following her soldier husband.

Along with similar Societies, the 1980s saw a fall in the ordinary membership and in the mid-1990s, for the first time since 1927, it was below a thousand. This caused new membership drives with letters to the Heads of Diplomatic Missions in Asian countries and to the Board of Trade; renewed contact with British universities and from the early 1990s a special effort to bring in more Junior Members. At the end of the year 2000 the membership had climbed back to 1,128.[4]

Lord Denman and Sir Donald Hawley (*President and Chairman at the time of the Society's Centenary*) *beneath the horns of an Ovis Poli, Chitral Fort, Pakistan, 1995* [*Ingrid Woodburn*]

In 1994 Sir Donald Hawley became Chairman. After legal training he joined the Sudan Political Service, transferring to the Foreign and Commonwealth Office on independence. He bridged the Middle and Far East with Head of Mission posts in Muscat and Kuala Lumpur. In 1997 he inaugurated a five-year plan to review the Society's primary aims, increase its membership and ensure its future financial stability. He also saw the Society through its centenary celebrations.

The following year Mrs Helen McKeag replaced the long-serving Miss FitzSimons as Secretary. After two years she was succeeded by Mr David Easton, whose career in the Diplomatic Service saw postings in the Middle East and India. He held the position for four energetic years during which time he introduced several innovations to the Society's working structure. In particular he oversaw the computerisation of the office procedures. While in some ways this has eased, in others, because of broadening the Society's overall exposure through such as the Internet, it has increased the burden on its small and admirable administrative staff. In November 2001 Mr Norman Cameron, with a similar Diplomatic Service background in the Arab world, took his place. There were further changes also in the Honorary Treasurers, a post, as we have seen, not without considerable importance to the Society's very existence. In 1996 Mr Francis Witts briefly replaced Mr Wedge before Mr Neville Green took the post. An Arabist, with service in overseas banking, he holds the position in the centenary.

David Easton

'. . . *its small and admirable administrative staff* . . .' – *Jane Young and Morven Hutchison*

Three significant innovations in the Society's programme were made during the period. In 1971 a series of yearly tours to Asian countries was started, some of which have been both unusual and adventurous. In the early 1990s the Junior Membership was revived with expeditions to the north of the sub-continent and annual meetings held when Junior Members themselves gave talks about their own experiences. Both these subjects have been dealt with in separate chapters. In 1996 a programme of one-day visits to exhibitions of Asian interest, both in the United Kingdom and nearby Europe, was started, as recommended in the Black Report.

In 1997 and 1998 the Society, conscious of its historical roots in the sub-continent, hosted separate receptions to celebrate the fiftieth independence anniversaries of India, Pakistan and Sri Lanka. Each was followed by a talk by the respective High Commissioner.

In June 1999 HRH The Duke of York agreed to become the Society's Patron in succession to the Prince of Wales. The Society is indebted to His Royal Highness for the immediate interest he has shown.

The Society depends for its smooth running not only on its Honorary Officers but on other Members of Council – and indeed on voluntary ordinary members. At the start of the period under review Council was especially rich in those having Indian experience. Lord Birdwood, after service in the Indian army, espoused causes of the sub-continent, especially Tibet. Lord Gore-Booth, who had been High Commissioner in Delhi from 1960 to 1965, and later Head of the Diplomatic Service, joined the Council in 1970. Later, in 1995, Sir Nicholas Barrington, with service in Afghanistan, Japan, Vietnam, Iran and Egypt, before becoming High Commissioner in Pakistan, brought to the Council wide Asian experience and contacts. An unusual testimony to him stands at the British Mission in Islamabad in a fine marble statue of a young Queen Victoria which he rescued from a garden in Rawalpindi, although sadly she lost both hands during the Suez crisis. Air Chief Marshal Sir John Whitworth-Jones, who served on the Council from 1959 to 1972, was especially active. He organised the Society's first Annual Tour to Anatolia in 1971, established a working relationship with the Centre for International Briefing at Farnham Castle and actively encouraged a younger generation to join.

Dr Violet Conolly, who served the Council from 1963 to 1977, was a descendant of Captain Conolly, who was imprisoned and executed by the Emir of Bokhara in 1842. A Sovietologist of repute, she was a prolific lecturer and book reviewer, a member of the Editorial Board and a holder of the Percy Sykes Memorial Medal. Petite, frail-looking and of obvious intellect, her approach was invariably announced by the jingling of bracelets. An inveterate traveller, at the age of eighty-seven, she was preparing for yet another venture 'when a greater journey intervened'.

Nubar Gulbenkian, who served on the Council in the 1960s, was another valued committee man. A colourful character, changing his place of abode as often as his nationality (Persian, Turkish, British) and of his speech (Armenian, French, English) he will long be remembered for his burly figure, cigar, orchid and opulent dinner parties. His contacts in the oil industry were especially useful at that period of the Society's development.

Members of the Society are of long-lived stock. At the Annual Dinner in 1994 the Chairman, Sir Michael Wilford, reminded diners that it was the ninetieth birthday of Lady Alexandra Metcalfe, daughter of Lord Curzon, and the ninety-first of the Swiss traveller Mlle Ella Maillart. The following year Sir Michael mentioned that it was Dame Freya Stark's one hundredth. In 1997 Mrs Doreen Ingrams, joint Lawrence of Arabia Memorial Medal holder with her husband, Harold, in 1939, died aged ninety-one. Several

Mlle Ella Maillart [Isobel Shaw]

Dame Freya Stark still travelling in her 80s, Yemen Tihama, 1976 [Hugh Leach]

members of the Society whom we met in Chapters I and II continued into this, the final part of our chronology. The Marquis of Zetland who, as Lord Ronaldshay, was a founding member in 1901 and Chairman from 1908 to 1913, continued as a Vice President until his death in 1961. Sir Edward Penton, the first substantive Honorary Secretary in 1902, likewise remained a Vice President until his death in 1967 aged ninety-two.

The Society has had many explorers and venturers throughout its history but it has never been in a position to finance or organise expeditions of its own, apart from the annual Asian Tours and the more recent Junior Member excursions. In 1922 the Royal Geographical Society suggested that the two Societies should finance a joint expedition 'through an unknown part of the Arabian desert'. There is no record of any such undertaking, though it may have led to the subsequent explorations of Mr H. St J. B. Philby and Mr Bertram Thomas. However, the Society has been asked continuously for help from individuals and young groups, but in each case it has had to limit its assistance to the use of the Society's Library for research, introductions to members with expertise on the areas concerned and written introductions to local Honorary Secretaries and those of influence en route. By 1972 the number of such submissions had increased to such an extent that the Society felt it necessary to clarify its policy by joining a working party of representatives from the Royal Geographical Society, the Foreign and Commonwealth Office, the Ministry of Defence and the British Council, set up to discuss the issue.

Yet, as the following examples show, individual members, singularly or in small groups, have continued to set off on their own ventures and projects, especially to those areas which the Society has loosely regarded as the essence of Central Asia. During the Civil

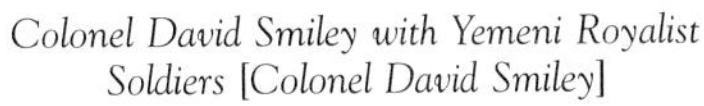

Colonel David Smiley with Yemeni Royalist Soldiers [Colonel David Smiley]

Lake Shiwa

War in the Yemen (1962–1968) some intrepid members travelled with the Royalist Forces across previously little explored Arabian territory; Lieut Colonel Gerald de Gaury, Colonel David Smiley, Mr Wilfred Thesiger, Lieut Colonel Neil McLean, Dr Philip Horniblow and Major Bernard Mills among them.[5] Dr André Singer has made journeys to Afghan border areas to study tribal anthropology.[6] Mr Hugh Leach visited a remote corner of Afghan Badakhshan in 1971 to explore how the waters of Lake Shiwa reach the Oxus, concluding work started by the Central Asian explorer Ney Elias in 1865, thus enacting Sir Olaf Caroe's edict that a purpose of the Society was to keep green his memory.[7] Mrs Isobel Shaw has crossed countless passes in Northern Pakistan with her son, researching for her guide books on that country.[8] Miss Susan Farrington has travelled widely throughout the sub-continent recording the cemeteries and remote graves of past British residents and soldiers.[9] Major E. R. L. Jones has made journeys into the Panjsher Valley in north-eastern Afghanistan to supervise, with the co-operation of the Swedish Committee for Afghanistan, the building of a local maternity clinic for the use of followers of the late Afghan leader Ahmed Shah Masoud. One such visit was made in October 2001 during the confrontation between the Northern Alliance and the Taliban. Mr John Hare has travelled to some of the most inhospitable areas of the Mongolian and Chinese Gobi in pursuit of his project to assist the Chinese authorities in establishing a reserve around Lop Nor for the remaining wild Bactrian camels of Tartary.[10] Professor John Carswell has explored archaeological sites as far afield as Inner Mongolia, returning to enthral the Society with his findings.[11] Those graduating through the rank of the Junior Membership have, similarly, been drawn by the lure of Central Asia. Captain Charles Timmis, a young

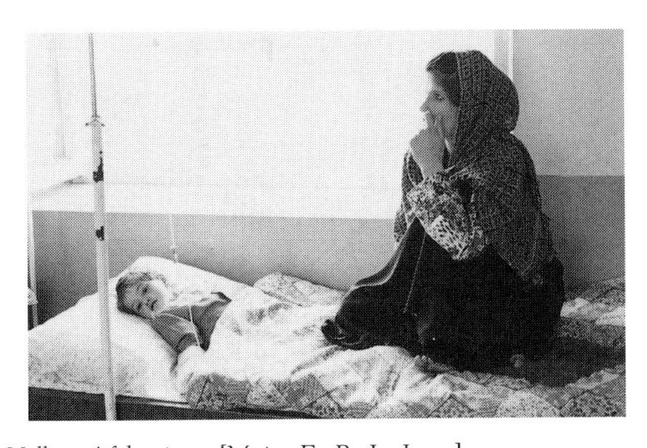

Mother and Child Clinic, Rokha, Panjsher Valley, Afghanistan [Major E. R. L. Jones]

peers. Others became involved on reaching the end of their Asian careers, enabling them to recall past days and keep in touch with subsequent developments.

This diverse membership brought to the Society an immense and varied wealth of understanding of Asia. Sir Edward Penton, recalling how in the early days of the Society some fifty chairs might accommodate the average audience, added 'but measured by knowledge the Albert Hall would not have been sufficient'.

In this chapter brief pen-sketches are given of archetypes from a selection of those who made up the membership; not just the well known, but rather those whose achievements, often as great, have been hidden from public view. The dates given in parentheses indicate the year of their joining the Society. Some entries have been expanded upon, and yet others freshly included, in Chapter X.

Long-standing Members and Generation Links

At the start of the Society's centenary year the individual membership stood at 1,128, the longest serving of whom was Mr Paul Ensor, who joined in March 1934; a continuous membership of sixty-seven years. Sir Roderick Sarell joined in 1939, his father Mr Philip Sarell in 1929; both started their careers in the old Consular Service.[1] The longest serving overseas member was Dr Ercument Ataby (1943) from Istanbul. Of the lady members, Mrs Eileen Humphreys joined in 1944 (her father, Captain Harry Partridge, in 1933) and Mrs Jean Rasmussen in 1945. She had been married to the renowned explorer and plant collector, Captain Frank Kingdon Ward, whose links with the Society went back to 1924.

Mrs Eileen Humphreys

Similar to the Sarells, there has been a long tradition of links between generations. The publisher Mr (later Sir) John Murray was a Founding Member. His great nephew, the 'sixth John Murray' joined in 1939. Colonel John Tod, who had an adventurous career in the Indian Army, including serving in Malleson's Transcaspian Mission, joined in 1908; his son, Captain Norman Tod, RN, joined in 1950 three years after his father's death, narrowly impairing a ninety-three-year continuity. Both the sons, Hugh and William, of Colonel E. F. Norton (1929), leader of the 1924 Everest expedition, remain members. Captain Godfrey Meynell (1927) won a posthumous Victoria Cross campaigning in the Mohmand tribal area of the NWFP in September 1935; his son, Godfrey (1958) was also a Frontier Officer in the Aden Protectorate. The Revd H. W. Funnell (1938) was one of several members who served in the China Inland Mission where his son, Dr Victor Funnell (1956), who became Editor of the *Journal* in 1992, was born. A father and son team in the Diplomatic Service was Sir Christopher Summerhayes, a member of Dunsterforce in Baku in 1918 before joining the Levant Consular Service, and his son David, both of whom joined in 1946. A prominent Parsee, Mr K. A. Marker, author of *A Petal from the Rose*, joined in 1929 and his son, HE Mr Jamsheed Marker, Pakistan's ambassador to the United States, in 1964. These are to quote but a few examples.

Agents and Adventurers

The Society was famed in its early years for having among its members many who had been engaged in a variety of clandestine and adventurous activities. These have been chronicled in a number of works written either by themselves, their biographers or historians, not least the series of enthralling books by Mr Peter Hopkirk (1975), himself a holder of the Sir Percy Sykes Memorial Medal.[2] Best known of these adventurers is Lieut Colonel F. M. Bailey (1910) whom we met in Chapter II whilst escaping from Tashkent disguised as an Albanian army clerk and employed by a branch of the Russian General Staff to hunt for his own person. He has told the story of his adventurous life in a number of books, enlarged upon by his biographer. A member of the Indian Political Service, Bailey was a man of diverse parts, soldier, explorer, intelligence agent and naturalist – a Himalayan blue poppy is named after him. He was the Society's last remaining link with the 'Great Game' and thus, to some, embodied its quintessence. On retirement he served both on the Society's Council and as Librarian. He died in 1967 aged eighty-five. It was fitting that his nephew, Captain P. E. I. Bailey, RN was able to attend the Society's Centenary Dinner. He remembers especially his uncle's tremendous sense of fun. His security consciousness, however, meant that stories of his exploits had to be dragged out of him, but they were always accompanied by the assertion that nothing should ever be taken too seriously, particularly officialdom, which he described as 'The Mugwumps'. In the family he was called 'Hatter', a reference to the 'mad one'!

Bailey was accompanied on that historical mission to Tashkent by Major L. V. S. Blacker (1920) though he returned early because of sickness. Relations between them were strained and Blacker in his own *Journal* account of the mission,[3] and in his book *On*

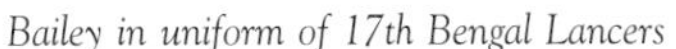
Bailey in uniform of 17th Bengal Lancers

Lieut Colonel F. M. Bailey

[Captain P. E. I. Bailey, RN]

'Breakfast in the Taghdumbash Pamirs'. Bailey's party near the Mintaka Pass on its way to Kashgar, 23 May 1918. Left to right: believed to be Major P. T. Etherton and Major L. V. S. Blacker [*RSAA Archives*]

Secret Patrol in High Asia, failed altogether to mention Bailey even though he was the leader. Subsequently, Blacker joined Malleson in Meshed. But Blacker was an adventurer. Despite suffering a broken neck from a flying accident during the First World War, in 1932 he made the first aerial photographic survey of Mt Everest, flying at 31,000 ft in temperatures of minus 45°C.

Another legendary member whose adventurous life paralleled that of Bailey was Major Reginald Teague-Jones (1919), whom we also met in Chapter II when he was General Malleson's chief agent in Transcaspia at the close of the First World War. In the early 1920s he changed his name to Ronald Sinclair, remaining in the Society under that alias and giving an address care of his London Club. His professionalism ensured that his membership as Teague-Jones overlapped that of Sinclair, whose date of joining he placed back to 1921. In 1975 he changed his address to Marbella, Spain, presumably reckoning that by then the Soviets had lost interest in a punitive reprisal for his believed involvement in the murder of the twenty-six Baku Commissars in 1918. A book of his memoirs, *Adventures in Persia*, was published when he was aged ninety-nine, shortly before his death in 1988. A further book, *The Spy who Disappeared*, based on his diaries, was published posthumously.[4]

Major Reginald Teague-Jones

Several members from this period were involved with the agent Herr Wilhelm Wassmuss, the 'German Lawrence'. Having effected Wassmuss's capture when serving in Persia in the First World War, Lieut Colonel Edward Noel (1920) was himself captured in 1918 and held chained in a vermin-infested prison whilst on his way to join Dunsterforce,

Herr Wilhelm Wassmuss

with which he subsequently served in Baku. A man of singular enterprise he twice cycled from London to India staying in tribal tents on the way. He died in 1974 aged eighty-eight.

Others involved with Wassmuss came from a more prosaic background. Major E. B. Soane's (1921) entry to the East was as an accountant with the Imperial Bank of Persia in Yezd. At the outbreak of the First World War he was representative of the Anglo-Persian oil company in Baghdad. Made prisoner by the Turks, he was marched across the Syrian desert to Mersin and imprisoned. On release he joined the Mesopotamian Political Department and was sent back to Iran. There, disguised as a Persian and guarded by six cut-throat Kurds, he travelled throughout the deserts of Arabistan and Bakhtiaristan living in a black tent and tracking down the seditionist agents of Wassmuss. Later he held administrative appointments in some of the wildest parts of Iran and Iraq, always guarded by his faithful Kurds. He died in 1923 on board a ship destined for North Africa, whence he was bound in order to restore his health, damaged by those adventures.

Colonel F. H. Bell's (1931) experiences began as a youth in China in 1891. He served in the Chinese Imperial Maritime Customs, spending his leave periods walking vast distances across the country. In 1905, whilst on leave from China, he joined the South African Police, fought in the Zulu insurrection and then walked across Madagascar. He was twice wounded during the War in Europe, after which he returned to China where he held posts in Macao, Chefoo, Kowloon and Canton, followed by Manchuria and Tientsin. Having to outwit the intrigues of the Chinese War Lords, he faced great personal danger. In 1936, as Defence Security Adviser in Singapore, he warned of the dangers to which the island was exposed if war came. No one listened and in 1939, labelled a scaremonger, he was sent home. He joined the RAF the following year when well into his sixties.

Roving agents apart, many members held overt appointments in Intelligence Bureaux throughout Asia and Sir Maurice Oldfield (1950), after war service in the Middle and Far East, rose to become Head of Britain's Secret Intelligence Service. Not only were such individuals great characters but their activities had a direct bearing on the way in which the British government formulated its policy. Their exploits still captivate, especially when seen from the perspective of a more technical age.

Explorers and Archaeologists

Many, if not most, of the great explorers and archaeologists of Asia were members of the Society, which thus enabled it to fulfil one of its early objects 'to catch the expert and the explorer when they are fresh from their most recent triumphs and to induce them to give at once to the world their experience and knowledge which otherwise might remain for years hidden away'. Amongst those who did so lecture the Society were such well-known names as Sir Aurel Stein (1909), Mr H. St J. B. Philby (1919) and Sir Wilfred Thesiger (1934). Others may be less familiar.

Sir Filippo de Filippi (1926), an Honorary KCIE, gave up the study of medicine for exploration and travelled in Russian Turkestan at the turn of the twentieth century. In 1909, accompanied by the Duke of Abruzzi, he explored the Baltoro glacier in the Eastern

Sir Aurel Stein's grave in Kabul, restored by British members of ISAF, March 2002

Karakorum, and in 1913 led an expedition to Baltistan, Ladakh and Chinese Turkestan under the patronage of the Italian and Indian governments. When news of the outbreak of war reached the party those members who were officers in the British and Italian armies made their way back to their respective regiments, whilst Filippi went on to Russian Turkestan. He subsequently became Secretary General of the Italian Geographical Society and was awarded the Mussolini Prize for Science.

Mr Douglas Carruthers (1935), a Sykes Medal winner, was an explorer and naturalist who, after joining a British Museum team in Central Africa in 1906, concentrated his exploration in Arabia, Central Asia and Mongolia bringing back fine head specimens of wild oryx and sheep. His knowledge of the Arabian deserts was exploited by the War Office during the First World War when he was engaged in preparing maps for the Arabian campaign. The Society inherited part of his valuable collection of books and charts.

Douglas Carruthers in the Arabian desert on Sharari

Captain Frank Kingdon Ward was not only a great explorer but also a leading plant collector and author. We owe to him a number of rhododendrons now found in Britain. The son of a botanist, in 1904 he took up a teaching post in Shanghai but soon engaged in Himalayan expeditions and continued plant collecting and exploring for the next fifty years in China, Tibet, Burma and India. In the First World War he served in the Indian Army and in the Second with the Special Operations Executive in Burma. His most notable expedition was from 1924 to 1925 when, with Lord Cawdor (1925), he explored the world's deepest gorge along a

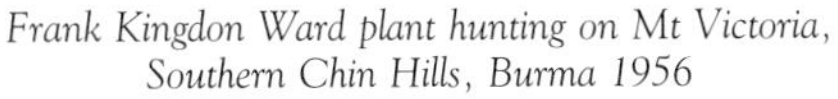

Frank Kingdon Ward plant hunting on Mt Victoria, Southern Chin Hills, Burma 1956

Jean Kingdon Ward changing plant presses at Mindat, Southern Chin Hills, Burma, 1956

[Mrs J. Rasmussen]

tributary of the Brahmaputra river in south-east Tibet. On return he wrote *The Riddle of the Tsangpo Gorges*.[5] He was helped by Major F. M. Bailey, then Political Officer in Sikkim. In 1947 he married, as his second wife, Jean Macklin (1945), thirty-six years his junior, who accompanied him on most of his subsequent expeditions and who, as Mrs Jean Rasmussen, was mentioned at the start of this chapter. She retains vivid recollections of the period which appear in her own book of memoirs in the Society's Library.[6] In 1950 reports that both had been killed in an earthquake in Burma turned out to be untrue, and in 1954 he gave the Anniversary Lecture when he was described as 'without doubt the greatest living plant collector'. He died in 1958, aged seventy-two, planning his next visit to what is now Vietnam. He was one of the most prolific lecturers in the history of the Society, his first being in 1924. He was made an Honorary Member in 1947.

Lieut Colonel R. C. F. Schomberg first joined the Society in 1921, but subsequently resigned and rejoined at least three times, in keeping with his impulsive nature. He led a life of unusual variety as a soldier, explorer and finally Catholic priest. He is best known for his travels in the Karakorum mountains described, with his often acerbic pen, in four books. His papers and slides are in the Society's archives; a fuller description is given in that chapter.

Other European members included Captain Henning Haslund Christensen (1934), who led two of the Royal Danish Geographical Society's expeditions to Mongolia, one before, and the other just after, the Second World War. He died in Kabul of a heart attack part way through the second journey in 1948 aged fifty-two. The ambition of Dr Emil Trinkler (1929), from Germany, was to follow in the footsteps of those great explorer-archaeologists of the Chinese Central Asian deserts, Sven Hedin, Aurel Stein and von Le Coq. He fulfilled this in an expedition he led to the Taklamakan desert from 1927 to 1928 when, like those earlier explorers, he dug up buried treasures, now in the Bremen Museum. He was killed in a motor accident in 1931 at the young age of thirty-five.

Prince Peter of Greece and Denmark (1942) was an explorer and anthropologist who had gained first-hand knowledge by rides across Central Asia and Tibet in the 1930s. He was a regular lecturer to the Society on Tibet, Afghanistan, the Oxus, Sinkiang and the Danish expeditions to the sub-continent. His grandfather was King George I of the Hellenes, but the crown passed down through his uncle and cousin and for dynastic reasons he was obliged to live in exile in London, Paris and Copenhagen.

Members serving in remote parts of Asia were fortunate in those less hurried days in being able to combine their military and civilian functions with their passion for exploring. Many left their records behind in government reports; Sir Francis Younghusband himself is an example.

Frontier Officers

If the Society had a spiritual home in Central Asia it had another on the North West Frontier of pre-independence India. A glance through the early membership lists shows many addresses there: even the 'Office' of the Chief Commissioner of the Province joined in 1916. For those fortunate enough to serve on the Frontier it was a venturesome life. As Sir Olaf Caroe wrote: 'The Indian Political Service [which provided the Frontier's Political Officers] was probably the most colourful and adventurous service to be found anywhere in the world.' The obituary of one famous Frontier Officer, Major General Sir Arthur Parsons, which read 'He never married; the Frontier and his friends on the Frontier were wife, child and home to him' could have applied to many, married or not. Other obituaries frequently carried such depictions as 'They were the happiest years of his life, in contact with those fine rough men of the Frontier', or 'He could keep up with a Pathan youth on his own hills'.

Sir Olaf Caroe

Three great names stand out. Sir George Cunningham (1926) spent thirty of his thirty-five years of service in India on the Frontier or involved with its problems. He had the unparalleled distinction of being asked by Mohammed Ali Jinnah to return as Governor of the NWFP in independent Pakistan. Sir Olaf Caroe (1928) spent fourteen years there between 1923 and 1937 before returning in 1946 to see the region through the final stages of the transfer of power. But allegations by Congress of his partiality to the Muslim League caused him to step down before the crucial referendum on the future of the Province. In retirement he wrote copiously on the history of the area. But his interests ranged wider and included both Tibet and Soviet Central Asia. In 1951 he founded the Turcological Centre, which transformed into Lieut Colonel Geoffrey Wheeler's

Sir George Cunningham

Central Asian Research Centre. Caroe became one of the great pillars of the Society, serving as its senior Vice President for many years, and he was a prolific obituarist of his many departed friends.

Sir Evelyn Howell (1908) died in 1971 aged ninety-four after sixty-three years in the Society. He combined remarkably the role of scholar (he once returned the draft of a subordinate leaving only one word of the original) and man of action. In 1905 with firmness and courage he staved off a potential mutiny following the murder in his presence of a Militia Commandant by a rebellious sepoy. Again in 1930 his firm action quelled the Peshawar riots after a regiment mutinied. His monograph *Mizh* is a classic of the deep knowledge officers developed of the tribal peoples amongst whom they worked – as was Caroe's *The Pathans*. Long service on the Frontier seems to have gone hand-in-hand with long life and long service to the Society. Lieut Colonel W. Elliott-Lockhart (1931), who spent virtually his entire working life on the Frontier, was a member for sixty-two years, dying in 1993 aged eighty-seven.

Sir Robert Sandeman was perhaps the most revered of all Frontier officers. His administration of Baluchistan was a model for others to follow, eschewing the previously adopted 'Close Border Policy'. On 25 February 1935 a combined Society and East India Association luncheon was held at the Criterion Restaurant in honour of the centenary of his birth at which seven members who had had connections with him gave short speeches in his memory. They included Field Marshal Sir Claud Jacob, Sir Henry McMahon, Lieut Colonel C. E. Bruce, Sir Francis Younghusband and Sir Hugh Barnes. It is not surprising that both the current President of the Indian Army Association, Captain Sir Charles Frossard, and its Chairman, Major John S. Hewitt, are members of the Society.

'. . . deep knowledge officers developed of the tribal peoples . . .'. Photograph by Sir Evelyn Howell of South Waziristan Scouts on patrol, 1934 [RSAA Archives]

Sandeman Centenary Luncheon. Insert: Sir Robert Sandeman [RSAA Archives]

Scholars

The Society's scholars were manifold; some were academics by profession, others became so as a by-product of their occupations. Several were holders of the Sir Percy Sykes Memorial Medal.

Sir Archibald Creswell (1930), a scholar on Muslim architecture, was without peer. Largely self-taught, his first experience of Egypt was service there with the Royal Flying Corps in 1916. He returned in 1920 and surviving the many rifts in Anglo-Egyptian relations, lived there henceforward, for many years as Professor of Islamic architecture at Cairo University. He described his large library, later bequeathed to the American University in Cairo, as 'my harem'. While he never married, as the Egyptian press stated in their fulsome tributes on his death in 1974, aged ninety-four, 'to the last he had an eye for a pretty girl'.

Foremost among the great professors of Arabic and Islam was Sir Thomas Arnold (1924). In 1888 he joined the Indian Muslim College at Aligarh when Sir Syed Ahmed Khan, its founder, was still preaching his liberal interpretation of Islam and his pro-Western views. Arnold adopted Muslim dress and was much revered by his Indian students. He later taught in London and Cairo. His gentle nature and obvious empathy for Islam made him as great an ambassador for Britain as anyone in Muslim countries.

Other Islamic scholars included Professor D. S. Margoliouth (1927); Sir Hamilton Gibb (1927); Professor Reynold Nicholson (1927); Professor A. S. Tritton (1938) and Professor Bernard Lewis (1939). The Society has lost in recent years two others; Professor R. B. (Bob) Serjeant (1942), who had an especial interest in South Arabia, and Charles Beckingham (1942), Professor Emeritus of Islamic Studies at London University and an active member of Council and Sykes Medallist.

The old Consular Services, invented by Britain for her extra-territorial role in those countries not part of her empire, offered adventurous and romantic-sounding careers with time to travel and absorb the local culture. As Sir Denis Greenhill said at the Seventieth Anniversary Dinner, 'One can only look back with nostalgia at the galaxy of distinguished scholars produced by the old specialised Consular Services in the various parts of Asia . . . when our members could find time to produce dictionaries and monumental histories.'

Others became scholars as a consequence of the opportunities their careers furnished. For there is, seemingly, a difference between those who travel especially to obtain knowledge and those who acquire it through osmosis, a result of sustained residence. Lieut Colonel Gerald de Gaury (1923) learnt Arabic whilst recovering from wounds sustained at Gallipoli and this led to a remarkable career. He was the last of a band of Englishmen who played an active role in the creation of contemporary Arabia, knowing personally both Ibn Saud and the Hashemite Kings of Iraq. Later he became Political Agent in Kuwait. His last twenty years were spent in Brighton writing of his long experiences and passing them on to a younger generation. He died there in 1984 aged eighty-seven.

Gerald de Gaury

Persian scholars have included Dr L. Lockhart (1934) whose mentor was the great Edward G. Browne; Mr Peter Avery (1956); Professor Ann Lambton (1964), Emeritus

Denis Wright when Vice Consul, Trebizond, 1941

Professor of Persian, University of London and Sir Denis Wright (1945) who first joined the Foreign Office as a temporary war-time recruit with Consular posts in Romania and Turkey, finishing his diplomatic career as Ambassador to Iran. He has written books and articles on Anglo-Persian relations during the Qajar period and, uniquely, twice delivered the Society's Anniversary lecture, as well as being a Sykes Medallist.

Sir Clarmont Skrine (1922) is best known as an authority on Chinese Central Asia stemming from his time as Consul General in Kashgar. Less well known are his thirteen years of service in Iran. His command of Persian was such that when Consul General in Meshed during the war he and his wife put on a local production of *Charley's Aunt* in that language. He died in 1971 aged ninety-four having been a member for sixty-four years.

Professor Zekin Velidi Togan (1957) had a singular life. Born in 1881 in Bashqurdistan he studied classical Arabic and Persian at Kazan University. Determined that Russian Muslims should have a part in the administration he raised the Bashir insurrection against the Bolsheviks. After its failure he fled to Bukhara and joined Enver Pasha in his Basmachi revolt against the Soviets. After Enver's death in 1927 he settled in Turkey becoming Professor of Oriental Studies at Istanbul University. He died in 1971, aged ninety, ending one of the Society's remaining ethnic links with Central Asian history.

Dr Louis Dupree

So many members served in Afghanistan that Lord Curzon remarked: 'If there is one Society that knows its Afghanistan it is the Central Asian.' But for actual scholarship few equalled the American, Dr Louis Dupree (1955), whose monumental work *Afghanistan*, published in 1971, remains a standard textbook.

Of the Society's many distinguished Japanologists, most started their career in the Japan Consular Service. But Professor Richard Storry (1968) started his in 1937 as a teacher of English at Otaru College in Japan's northernmost island of Hokkaido. After intelligence duties in the war he returned to Japan, later settling to a Fellowship at St Antony's Oxford where he wrote *A History of Modern Japan*. Likewise, the Burmese scholar Professor B. R. Pearn (1950) who, in the 1920s, became a lecturer at Rangoon University, remaining there until he was forced to escape from the Japanese by the long march into India. He returned to the university after the war before finishing his career in the Research Department of the Foreign Office when he contributed his knowledge of Burma to many publications, including the Society's *Journal*. Both were typical of other members who joined the Society whilst teaching at academic institutions in Asian countries.

Sinologists, Tibetologists and Mongolists

These disciplines often overlapped; one who embraced all three was Sir Eric Teichman (1919). Traveller, scholar and sportsman, he spoke Chinese as he spoke English. He entered the Chinese Consular Service at Peking in 1907 aged twenty-three when his duties took him frequently to Mongolia. In 1919 he was stationed in Tibet when he rendered a service to the Chinese by stopping an outbreak of fighting on the Sino-Tibetan border. He returned to the British Legation in Peking as Chinese Secretary before retiring eventually in 1936 after an epic journey from Peking to Delhi. Recalled in 1942 he acted as adviser to the British representative in Chunking, making another memorable cross-country excursion to get there. Despite battling with arthritis all his life Teichman was a great sportsman. During the civil war in Peking in 1922 Chinese troops occupied the racecourse. Under a white flag Teichman persuaded the General in charge to allow the October race meeting to occur, offering the Chinese officers places as enclosure guests. In 1944 he became an Honorary Vice President, dying later the same year.

Among the best known Tibetologists were Sir Charles Bell (1921), Sir Basil Gould (1937), and Dr Hugh Richardson (1937), who died in 2000 at the age of ninety-four. He was Britain's last envoy in Lhasa and was probably the greatest living authority on Tibet, his books becoming standard works for students.

The first recorded member sent on an individual mission to Tibet was Lieut Colonel R. L. Kennion (1928) in 1900. In 1912 Brigadier-General M. E. Willoughby (1921) led the commission repatriating through India the Chinese armed force that had been beleaguered in Lhasa by the Tibetans. Shortly before his death in 1939 he presented the Society's library with his well-illustrated report on this unusual mission. Mr F. Williamson (1925) was Trade Agent at Gyantse in 1924 and later Political Officer at Sikkim in 1935. He was to die at Lhasa at the young age of forty-four on the second of two long visits to Tibet.

Officers of the Chinese Troops Repatriation Mission at Gnatong, 1912. Centre front: Lieut Colonel M. E. Willoughby [RSAA Archives]

Other members were concerned with Tibet from positions in the India Office. In 1943 Sir Algernon Rumbold (1934) drafted the text of the British view on Tibet recognising that country as having enjoyed *de facto* independence since 1911, but stressing that Chinese suzerainty could be acknowledged only on the understanding that Tibet was regarded as autonomous.

One of the best-known Mongolists in the Society was Professor Owen Lattimore (1928). Also a Sinologist, on joining the Society he delivered a controversial lecture *The Chinese as a Dominant Race*.[7] During the war he became an adviser to Chiang Kai-Shek and later to the US government. However, his sympathies for the Chinese and Mongol people resulted in his becoming an unjustified target for the cold-war McCarthy witch-hunts. As a result he lost his academic post in the US and moved to Leeds where he founded the first centre for Mongolian studies in this country, remaining there until his retirement in 1970. Professor Charles Bawden (1965), who taught at SOAS, succeeded him as the Society's leading Mongolian specialist.

Although other societies may have made greater in-depth studies of these countries, the Society provided an active forum for presenting its members' research and harbours in its archives some of their results.

Missionaries and Medics

Members with these vocations served in some of the loneliest parts of Central Asia; several joined the China Inland Mission. The Reverend George Hunter (1930), who became known as 'The Apostle of Turkestan', joined it in 1889. He returned to England for furlough only once in the following fifty-seven years. Though essentially a missionary, he was also an explorer and knew Chinese Turkestan (Sinkiang) as well as anyone. But he was reticent about his findings, which made it especially ironic that in the end he was to suffer imprisonment and dreadful torture on suspicion of being a British spy. Exiled from the Turkestan he loved, he died as he lived a lonely man, nursed by Chinese Christians at Kanchow in the Province of Kansu. His personal triumph was the translation of the scriptures into the vernacular of the most remote tribes. We shall cover the activities of that remarkable trio, the Misses French and Miss Mildred Cable, who also worked in the China Mission, in a later chapter.

Revd George Hunter

The Reverend Oskar Hermansson (1947), a member of the Swedish Missionary Society, had, like Hunter, an eventful life at the hands of the local warlords. He reached Turkestan in 1920 after a six-week trek from Kashmir to Yarkand in the depths of winter. During the 1933 civil war in Chinese Turkestan, when local Christians were being executed for their faith, he, along with two other Swedish missionaries, found themselves tied to posts and facing a firing squad armed with muzzle loaders. An additional executioner, armed with a cudgel, stood by in case they missed. Hermansson 'found it difficult to fix his mind on higher things than a wish that the firing squad had Bofors equipment'. They were rescued at the last minute by local Indian *Aqsaqals*. He was interned again in 1938 when nearly every member of the Christian church was murdered. But he had managed to smuggle out to India his manuscript translation of the Bible into Eastern Turki, a work he completed in Bombay in 1946.

Among the medical missionaries the most singular was Sir Henry Holland, who ran his eye hospital in the North West Province of India. His career has been covered in the Lawrence Medal chapter. Another was Lieut Colonel G. Fox Holmes (1958), who worked for seven years in Central Asia before becoming, perhaps uniquely for a former missionary, Consul General in Urumchi where he was also interned by the Chinese. In retirement he became one of the Society's foremost experts on the area.

Several physicians in the Society served in prominent positions in Asia. Sir Harry Sinderson 'Pasha' (1923) arrived in Iraq in 1918. He was to remain there for twenty-eight years, mostly in Baghdad where he organised the Royal College of Physicians. Appointed Physician to the Royal Family, the Amir Abdullah of Jordan conferred upon him the title of 'Pasha'. He died in 1974, a day after the publication of his memoirs *Ten Thousand and One Nights: Memories of Iraq's Sherifian Dynasty*.

Colonel Sir William Willcox (1921) was Chief Consultant Physician in the Mesopotamian Expeditionary Force in the First World War. At its close he visited Northern Russia where he found 10,000 refugees from Baku, who had fled from the Turkish occupation of that city, huddled together, rampant with cholera, typhus and influenza. Recognising the last as an unusually virulent strain, he hastened back to Baghdad in time to initiate precautions before it ravaged Mesopotamia on its westward course.

Dr Oliver Garrod (1945) spent much of the Second World War engaged in medical work among the nomadic tribes of South West Persia, thus keeping them on the side of the Allies when German infiltration was at its height. Able to penetrate deep into Khuzistan, Luristan and the tribal districts of Fars, he collected seminal material on nomadism which he gave to the Society in a lecture on his return in 1946.[8] He accompanied the Society's tour to Iran in 1976 and became an active member of Council in 1980.

Although missionaries may be less in evidence today, there has been a recent emergence of Non-Governmental Organisations (NGOs), many operating in the aid, development and charitable sectors. Several members now belong to these, thus maintaining the tradition of personal involvement in Asian countries.

Journalists and Broadcasters

In 1953 there were thirty-three members actively engaged in journalistic work. Those working in London included correspondents for *The Times*, the *Telegraph*, *News Chronicle*, *Daily Express*, *Daily Mail*, *Daily Graphic*, the *Jewish Chronicle* and the *Church of England Press*, while others were based in the Middle East, Palestine, Turkey, India, Hong Kong and China. Among several from the BBC Overseas Services the most prominent were Mr Evelyn Paxton, of the BBC Arabic Service; Mr Nevill Barbour, a staunch supporter of the Palestinians, who also worked for the BBC Arabic Service, and Mr Eric Robertson who, after a broadcasting career in the Far East, returned home to the BBC Overseas Service. Significantly, Paxton, Barbour and Mrs Peggie Robertson were all involved in the Editorship of the Society's *Journal* as was, briefly, Mr Evan Charlton, once editor of the *Statesman* of Calcutta and Delhi.

The career of another member merits more detailed study. Mr Peter Hume went to Peking as assistant editor of the *Peking Chronicle* in 1937, aged twenty, before Japanese troops occupied the city. He joined the Society the following year. He travelled extensively in Mongolia and Manchuria and acted as Secretary to the Royal Danish Geographical Society's expedition there. During the war he worked with the Malay Broadcasting Corporation in Singapore when, due to the paucity of staff, he had to present the news, read it and then introduce a programme of music, all in different voices. Between the fall of Singapore and his return to restore a British Broadcasting Service there he was attached to the Chinese Ministry of Information in London. Subsequently he joined the BBC's Chinese Service. Most tragic was the manner of his death in 1954 aged thirty-six. He fell from the upper-story ledge of his flat in an attempt to effect an entry having mislaid his key. In the short span of his membership he had lectured the Society

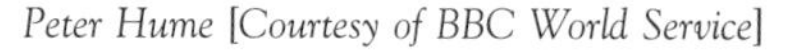

Peter Hume [Courtesy of BBC World Service]

Rupert Wingfield-Hayes and a Northern Alliance Commander, November 2001

and served twice on its Council. His knowledge of the Far East was, at that period, of great value and he was exactly the type of young member the Society wished to, and still needs to, attract. Fortunately the tradition is being maintained. A young member, Mr Rupert Wingfield-Hayes is, at the time of writing, the BBC's correspondent in Peking, transferred temporarily to Afghanistan in October 2001.

Engineers

Outsiders may tend to think of the Society as being composed of soldiers, diplomats, scholars, administrators, explorers and travellers. On the contrary, its diverse membership has included those who have made an impression on Asia through feats of engineering not least in the field of communications. On retirement many served on the Society's Council, ensuring that the lecture programme covered this important aspect of Asia's development.

Among the great civil engineers, one of the earliest to join in 1920 was Sir Alexander Gibb, founder of the firm of consulting engineers that bears his name. His son Alistair, who followed him into the Society and under whose guidance the firm widened its activities in Asia, died in 1955 after a polo accident. Sir Alexander himself died in 1958 aged eighty-five.

Many were involved in Asian communication systems, especially railways. In 1920 the South Manchuria Railway Company joined as a corporate body. Colonel Sir John Ward (1921) was Director General of the Port of Basra when he joined. With a co-post as Director General of Navigation in Iraq, he maintained the Shatt-al-Arab waterway for a hundred miles. By re-building the airfield alongside the port, he helped improve the England to India air route. In 1936 he became Director General of the Iraqi State Railways. A man of many parts, he served also as the non-stipendiary priest for the Anglican community at Basra.

Sir Alexander Gibb

Colonel Alistair Gibb

[*Courtesy of Jacobs Gibb Ltd*]

Mr Leonard Short (1954) was another who contributed to the development of Asian Railways through a career with the English Electric Company. In 1927, as Resident Engineer for the Company at Bombay, he was responsible for the part electrification of the Great Indian Peninsular Railway and later for sections of the network in Iran. During the war and after it he sought contracts for hydroelectric schemes in Asia, often through Portugal, realising the potential of her Asian colonies such as Macao. In a remarkably busy life his electrification schemes and thermal power stations involved many countries in the Far East.

Lieut Colonel Kenneth Cantlie (1959) joined the Jodhpur State Railways in India before going to China in 1929 where he became Technical Adviser to the Chinese State Railways in Nanking. He helped to rebuild the system which had fallen into neglect during the era of the War Lords, though his work was cut short by the outbreak of the Sino-Japanese war in 1937. Cantlie was the godson of the Chinese Dr Sun Yat Sen, mentioned in the previous chapter as having been kidnapped by the Chinese Legation in London in 1896.

Mr Norman Nairn (1923) and his brother Gerald were New Zealanders who had spent the First World War in the Middle East, after which they started the famous Nairn Transport Company whose articulated buses ran across the Syrian and Iraqi deserts from Damascus to Baghdad, running the gauntlet of Druse tribesmen.

In the public mind engineers may not be so romantic as explorers. But they left behind them a more tangible legacy, raising living standards and contributing to the economies of both Britain and the countries in which they worked.

Sir Alexander MacRobert
[Courtesy of The MacRobert Trust]

We have quoted from the lives of a small, but representative, number of the membership. But there were, of course, members from many other professions, which do not fit neatly into the above categories. One of the most remarkable of these was the Scot, Sir Alexander MacRobert (1920). A self-made man, in 1884 he took up an appointment as Manager of the Cawnpore Woollen Mills in India. His business acumen was such he was soon President of the Upper India Chamber of Commerce, attending congresses world-wide, and the benefactor of many charitable projects, including Dr Graham's Homes at Kalimpong. Lieutenant Governors and even Viceroys soon sought his counsel and in 1910 he was knighted. In 1918 he was the guest of the Afghan Amir Habibullah Khan in Kabul. In a lengthy stay the Amir sought his advice on the industrial development of the country and invested him with the Order of Honour. He was one of the last British visitors to have spent time with the ruler before he was assassinated.

After the death of his first wife Sir Alexander married, in 1911, an American, Rachel Workman. She was the daughter of the world-famous American mountaineers, Doctor Hunter and Fanny Bullock Workman. The Workmans, when in England, were frequent attendees at the Society's early meetings and in 1907 Fanny Workman lectured the Society on *Exploration in the Himalayas*. No doubt it was they who persuaded Sir Alexander to join the Society. He died in 1922 three months after being elevated to the Baronetcy of Cawnpore and Cromar, but his second wife, who had borne him three sons (the first union was without issue) survived him by thirty-two years. All three sons died while flying, two on operations in the Second World War. The combined wealth from Sir Alexander's business empire in India and his wife's inheritance enabled the creation in 1943 of the MacRobert Trusts, many dedicated to service causes. Prior to this in 1941 Lady MacRobert herself had donated a Stirling bomber, and later four Hurricane fighters, to the RAF in memory of their sons. An aircraft of the Service still carries the name 'MacRobert's Reply'.[9] Had the Society instigated its Corporate benefactor scheme in Sir Alexander's day, he might well have been in the vanguard, such was his philanthropic interest in Asia and the affairs of the Society.

Other members were businessmen in Bombay, Calcutta and Madras with Sir Thomas Ainscough (1916) as the Senior Trade Commissioner for India to support them. There were representatives also of the great British Trading Houses in Shanghai, Hong Kong and Basra and overseas bankers throughout Asia.

Lady Members

Ladies formed an important part of the Society from the outset, three being among the original members. Many were explorers and travellers of note. In 1913 Miss E. G. Kemp, on joining, lectured on *An Artist's impressions of Western Tibet and the Turkestans*.[10] The title was an understatement; she may have had pen and brush but she carried them on an adventurous journey from Kashmir across Chinese Turkestan and into Tibet. Sir Francis Younghusband, who introduced her talk, said it was a journey 'such as no lady before has ever undertaken'. In 1914 Miss Ella Sykes (1903) (sister of Sir Percy) spoke on 'Persian Family Life'; transcribed, it appeared as the second article in the newly inaugurated *Journal* that year. It was essentially a depiction of the oppressed condition of women in Iran but a reflection of the still prevailing male attitude of some at the time can be seen in the concluding remarks of the Chairman, Sir Mortimer Durand: 'Miss Sykes has got the idea that the position of women in Persia is not altogether desirable. I don't know; that is a woman's point of view. One thing is certain: ladies in England ought to be satisfied with their position.' A strange remark, perhaps, made at the height of the suffragette movement! In 1916 Miss Sykes became the first woman member of Council.

Many were well-known authors and travel writers, Dame Freya Stark (1934), Mlle Ella Maillart (1936), Rosita Forbes (Mrs McGrath) (1920), Mrs Steuart Erskine (1933), Lady 'Peter' Crowe (1947) and the still active Miss Dervla Murphy (1971) among them. Mrs Patrick Ness (1962) was a renowned geographer and author of *Ten Thousand Miles in Two Continents*. Dr Ethel Lindgren (1988), an anthropologist, spent many years in Mongolia and Manchuria studying reindeer nomadism. Others were reluctant to record their adventures. Miss Ada Christie (1918) roamed relentlessly over Asia Minor, the Middle East, Iran, the sub-continent, South East Asia, China and Japan. She had many a tale to tell but was too modest to do so.

Some lectures were directed specifically to Asian feminist issues. In 1931 Miss E. M. Aidin spoke on recent changes in the outlook of women in the Near and Middle East. In 1935 Mrs Guy Innes reported on the Women's International Conference at the Yildiz Palace in Istanbul, lamenting the fact that despite representatives from thirty countries, there was no one from Central Asia.

The Asian Membership

The Society has both valued, and been rich in, its Asian membership. The first to join in 1908 was Nawab Sahibzada Abdul Qaiyum Khan, when he was Assistant Political Officer of the Khaiber, Peshawar. A prominent figure on the Frontier, he became First Minister of the Province in 1932 and co-founder of the Islamia College in Peshawar. He was knighted in 1921. By 1951 there were 105 Asian members. Many who joined were from the sub-continent, some with, to British ears, exotic sounding princely titles: The Hon. Sir Bijay Chand Mahtab Maharajadhiraja Bahadur of Burdwan (1919); HH Maharaj Rana Sri Bhawani Sahib Bahadur of Jhalawar (1920); HH The Maharaja Manikya Bahadur of Tripura (1930) and HH The Maharaja Sir Tashi Namgyal, Gangtok, Sikkhim (1935). Two direct descendents of Shuja-ul-Mulk, the twelve-year-old proclaimed ruler of Chitral by the British in 1895, which resulted in the famous siege there, became members: Shahzada Nazir-ul-Mulk in 1932 and Colonel Khushwaqt-ul-Mulk in 1968. Major General Miangul Jahan Zeb (1963) was the last Wali of Swat and the last ruler in Pakistan exercising absolute power over his people.

There were 'princely' members from other parts of Asia also, including the Princes Chula and Bhidhyalab of Siam (1950). HH The Aga Khan, Sir Sultan Mohammad Shah, was elected an Honorary Member shortly before his death in 1957 and his grandson, Karim Aga, in July 2001. His Imperial Majesty the Shahanshah of Iran became an Honorary Member in 1965. HH Al Emir Haidar al Sherif Muhammad Emin (a son of

Sir Abdul Qaiyum Khan [RSAA Archives]

Major General Miangul Jahan Zeb

Captain Shahzada Nazir-ul-Mulk [RSAA Archives]

Colonel Khushwaqt-ul-Mulk

Sherif Ali Haidar, whom the Turks appointed Grand Sherif in 1916) joined in 1946 from Baghdad. Other members from Iraq included Al Sayyid Murid Hussain Bukhari (1938) who joined from Kerbala, one of the most holy cities in Shia Islam; senior politicians such as Nuri Al Said (1945) and Baba Ali Al-Shaikh Mahmud (1950), a son of the Kurdish leader Mahmud Barzinji.

Other members closely connected with the Kurdish community were His Beatitude the Mar Shimun, Catholicos Patriarch of the Nestorian Assyrians (1933) and Major-General Ghazi Mohammed Daghistani (1944). He was a descendant of the great Sheikh Shamil, who raised the whole of the Caucasus against Imperial Russia. Ghazi was born in Iraq and schooled at the RMA Woolwich and the Staff College, Quetta. He rose to become Chief of Staff to the Allied Arab Command in the Palestine campaign of 1948, and in 1954 was Iraqi Military Attaché in London. He commanded the Iraqi 3rd Division at the time of the murder of King Feisal. Imprisoned and sentenced to death, he was released in 1960 and lived the rest of his life quietly in London.

Syed Waris Ameer Ali (1946) son of the Shia modernist thinker, Syed Ameer Ali, was one of the first Indians to join the Indian Civil Service. Retiring in 1929 he lived in London where, during the war, he was employed by the India Office. He married a daughter of the Earl of Dartrey, one of the Society's original members. Not surprisingly he became a pillar of it, rarely missing a meeting.

Members of interest who joined from Palestine, Jordan and the Levant included Ahmed Sameh Ibn Shaikh Raghib Al Khalidi (1924) who claimed descent from the early Muslim warrior Khalid Ibn Walid. He was a prominent educationalist during the period of the Palestine Mandate and established the only wholly Arabic-speaking school in the Middle East which possessed a sixth form in the style of English Public Schools. Several leading figures from Jerusalem joined during the period of the Palestine Mandate, most prominent of whom was Auni Abdul Hadi Bey (1936). He was an original member of the Young Arab Association, which later became the nucleus of the Arab Nationalist Secret Societies seeking independence from Ottoman rule and which gave rise to the Arab Revolt. He later became a respected Palestinian Arab elder statesman. Another distinguished member was the Christian Maronite Emile Bustani (1954). Arab nationalist, industrialist and philanthropist, had he not been killed in an air crash in 1963 he would probably have become President of Lebanon. The Arab Christian writer Professor Kamal Salibi, whose recent books on the origins of Christianity have caused some controversy, joined in 1950.

Some Asian members joined from their embassies in London. Sheikh Hafiz Wahba, a long-serving member, joined in 1931 when the Saudi Mission was styled the Royal Legation for Nejd and the Hedjaz. The Minister of the Persian Legation became an ex-officio Honorary Vice President shortly after the Persian Society was absorbed in 1929.

Pakistan has had an especially close relationship with the Society, many officers joining from their service on the North West Frontier, some after training at Sandhurst. Two became President of their country: Major General Iskander Ali Mirza, who joined as a Captain in 1938, was deposed by Field Marshal Ayub Khan (1951) in 1958. This must be the only occasion when the Society has had two Asian Presidents, one ousting the other, whilst both remaining staunch members. Mirza spent his last eleven years living quietly in London. General Mohammed Musa (1959) became Commander-in-Chief of the Pakistan Army at this time, and Sir Firoz Khan Noon (1940) Prime Minister in

Iskander Ali Mirza

Field Marshal Ayub Khan

December 1957. Major General Hayaud-din (1949) was a Frontier Force Officer who won a Military Cross in the war and rose to become Chief of Staff. He was killed in an air crash in 1965. Major General Shahid Hamid (1984) was a popular member. After Sandhurst he joined the 3rd Cavalry Division, seeing war service in Burma. At the time of partition he was Private Secretary to Field Marshal Sir Claude Auchinleck, the last British Commander-in-Chief in India and an Honorary Vice President of the Society. The two remained life-long friends. Shahid became Adjutant General and on retirement held ministerial posts. He lectured the Society on the Karakorum and Hunza and wrote five books, including the evocatively titled *So They Rode and Fought*. A Patron of the Adventure Foundation Pakistan, he gave support to the Society's Young Persons' tours in his country. He died in 1993.

Major General Shahid Hamid

Professor Akbar Ahmed (1979), after a career in tribal administration, settled to a university vocation of Oriental scholarship at Cambridge and was for a time Pakistani High Commissioner in London before moving to take the Ibn Khaldun Chair of Islamic Studies at the American University in Washington. He has been an established lecturer, article writer and book reviewer for the Society and was awarded the Sykes Medal in 1994 for his work in creating an understanding of Islam in the West.

The American Membership

The highest proportion of overseas members has come from the United States. The first recorded American member was the Library of the American Museum of Natural History, New York, in 1919, and the second Mr Heyward Cutting of New York (1925). By 1939 there were 39 members with addresses in the United States; in 1951, 45; and in 2000, 72 with 231 *Journal* subscribers.

Mr Paul Knabenshwe was an American diplomat with long service in the Arab world. He was Minister in Baghdad at the time of the Rashid Ali rebellion in March 1941 when he earned the thanks of the British by giving refuge to 150 desperate subjects there, throwing open to them his own house and those of his secretaries. He died shortly after in 1942. The Hon. Cornelius Van Engert (1959) entered the American Foreign Service in 1911, seeing Asian service in China, the Middle East and Afghanistan, where from 1942 to 1945 he was the first US Minister in that country. A regular visitor to the Society's summer activities, his overall contribution to Anglo-American relations was recognised by an Honorary CBE. He died in 1985 aged ninety-seven. Another senior American diplomat, Dr James W. Spain (1963), has published three substantial works on the North West Frontier of Pakistan.[11]

Mr Charles R. Crane (1923) was a generous benefactor to the Society and to educational institutions in Asia. As a young man he lived in Bukhara and Samarkand and later became US Minister in China where he spent much time locating the singers of Chinese songs that were in danger of being lost and making gramophone records of them. He later supported engineering works in Saudi Arabia and the Yemen. Dr George Rentz (1949) was another who spent much of his life in Saudi Arabia as a senior member of the Arabian American Oil Company ARAMCO. As Government Relations Officer he researched for the Saudis their claim to villages in the Buraimi oasis, counter-claimed by the Ruler of Abu Dhabi and the Sultan of Muscat and Oman and backed by the British. A friend of the explorer H. St J. B. Philby, he wrote widely on Arabia. In retirement he became Curator of the Middle East collection of the Hoover Institute at Stanford.

Dr George Rentz

Current American members include the Central Asian specialist Mr Paul Henze (1950) and Ambassador Hermann F. Eilts (1962). A distinguished diplomat with many years' service in the Middle East, he is renowned in the Society for his succinct and penetrating lectures.

Lack of space prevents the inclusion of any more specific biographies or of those from the several other nationalities represented in the Society. Suffice it to mention that glancing along a shelf of books on Asia one is impressed by how many of the authors, or the subject of the work, were members. Likewise many of the same family names continue to appear

Poli horns that now hang in the Society's Library.[4] At those on India and Jordan young people from both countries attended and distributed gifts to the audience.

One of the last lectures in the series also involved audience participation when three members of the Society, who had served in parts of Arabia as Political and Desert Intelligence Officers, gave a presentation of life among the Bedouin. Two were dressed as tribesmen, one as an Omani and another, clad in only a loincloth and blue indigo, as a Mahri from the Hadhramaut. Offering dates and coffee, with full Arabian ritual and conversing in Arabic, the young audience were fooled, though, like the furniture at the Royal Overseas League, many became well covered in indigo![5] Such talks gave an understanding to the audience of the lives lived by others.

Younger speakers themselves started to appear in the Society's calendar in the late 1960s and early 1970s. Members of a Cambridge University expedition to West Pakistan spoke on opportunities for young people to work voluntarily in the area and members of Voluntary Service Overseas encouraged others to follow in their footsteps. The first report on schools' expeditions, entitled *Practical Problems of Asian Exploration for Younger Members*, was given in 1972 by Major Peter Willey, who had led several expeditions of boys from Wellington College to the Alamut valley in Iran. The pattern of the Society's approach to young people was clearly evolving: adventure, education and involvement with encouragement to do the same, rather than mere didactic teaching. However, by the mid-1970s, the first meeting on the lecture calendar in January, that had traditionally been described as the 'Young People's Meeting', became the Christmas Lecture. While usually of an entertaining nature, it was no longer specifically aimed at the younger generation.

In 1962 Council felt there was now sufficient interest to introduce a separate Junior Membership for those under twenty-five at a nominal annual subscription of 10/-. Initially, only eight joined. To encourage recruitment, letters from the Chairman were sent to Parliamentary Parties, University Appointments Boards, the School of Oriental and African Studies, firms interested in Asia and careers masters at schools. By 1972 numbers had grown to twenty-four. As the Society was making a loss on such a small subscription the age limit was later dropped to twenty-one but raised to twenty-five again in 1998, with a further reduced step-membership fee for those graduating from the ages of twenty-five to thirty.

In 1991 an incident took place which changed the whole direction of Young People's activities. That year the Society's Annual Tour was to Siberia. From Gorno Altajsk the party visited the edge of the Balukha range in the Altai mountains. One of its members, Mrs Anne O'Regan, looked longingly at the distant peaks and felt disappointed she was not able to join some others in an extensive walking tour there. On return she raised the matter at Council proposing there should be a tour 'specifically for younger members' – in mind were those under fifty – who felt themselves fit enough to engage in more strenuous activity. She suggested that a member, Mr Hugh Leach, might lead them. Mr Leach responded that it would be more appropriate to organise Society-led tours for those under twenty-five. Council firmly backed the idea. He approached his friend Mr Adrian Steger who agreed to co-lead any such expeditions: a surgeon, there was the advantage he could act also as doctor.

The result was a series of expeditions to Northern Pakistan and North West India, comprising either the Junior Members themselves, schools affiliated to the Society or conducted under its aegis or association. To allow a greater understanding of the peoples to be experienced, those taking part were briefed beforehand on the histories and cultures of the areas concerned. The terrain covered often involved tough walking, so there was the physical challenge as well. Dialogue with the locals was encouraged so that the young participants could investigate and appreciate the differing cultures, religions and value systems themselves. The routes were tailor-made so as to form a link with the early history of the Society and to give a sense of wilderness adventure, yet, where at all possible, to be within a three-day march of a road-head. A further safety feature was to have a doctor with the party who could also treat the local people. This allowed even greater contact between the travellers and the people among whom they were travelling.

The first expedition of six junior members (four boys and two girls) was in 1992 through the remote Ismaili-populated valleys between Naltar and Yasin in North Western Pakistan.[6] The timing was apt since it was HH the Aga Khan who had been guest speaker at the Annual Dinner the previous year and his encouragement and introductions in the area were of great value. On this expedition two 15,000 ft passes, the Naltar and the Asambar, were crossed. This general area, though not those passes, had been explored by Sir Francis Younghusband at the end of the nineteenth century.

For this and subsequent expeditions to Pakistan invaluable help was given by the Adventure Foundation Pakistan (AFP). A charitable organisation, the AFP was founded in the early 1980s by Brigadier Jan Nadir Khan to develop leadership among young Pakistanis, and others from neighbouring Asian countries, through the medium of outdoor education and adventure training. The Foundation has also provided invaluable support to such British-based projects as Operation Raleigh. The AFP provided their own young leaders, principal among whom was Rana Naveed Anjum, who accompanied all the Society-sponsored tours in Northern Pakistan. These young Pakistanis acted as the interface between the expedition members and the locals, few of whom spoke English.

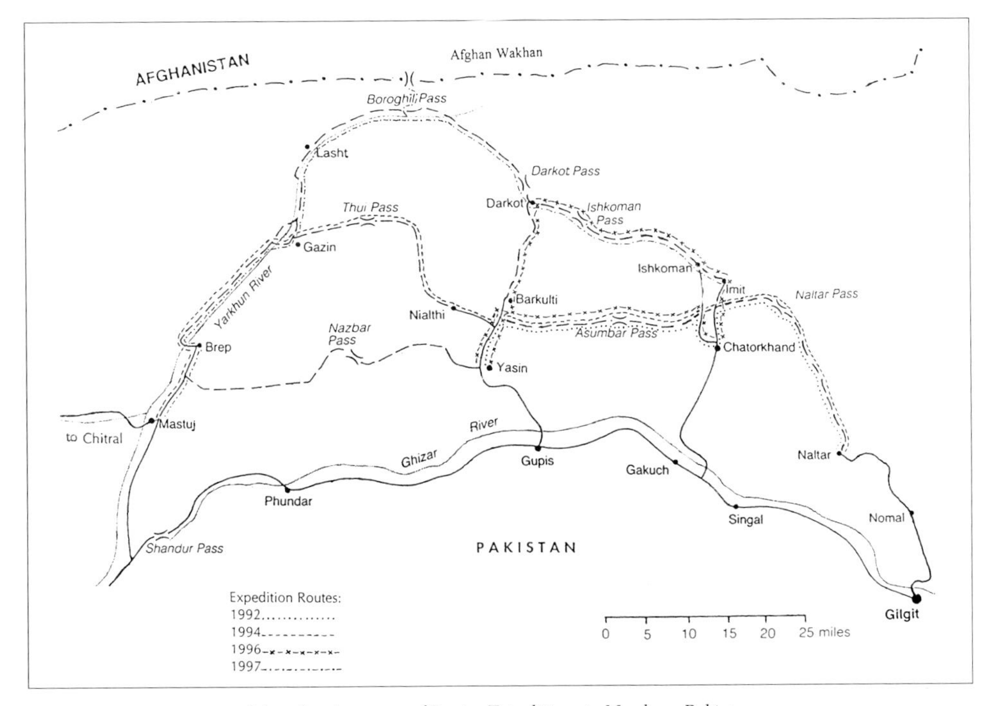

Map showing route of Junior Expeditions in Northern Pakistan

Brigadier Jan Nadir Khan, President, AFP

Naveed Anjum and Uthman Rathore, young AFP leaders

The AFP itself, without whose help these ventures would not have been such a success, became an Affiliate Member of the Society. The use of host country organisations for in-country administration, such as travel, tentage, rations and porterage, allowed greater local contact than would have been possible making such arrangements through commercial companies.

In 1994 a party of twelve boys from Abingdon School made a strenuous expedition crossing three high passes and some 160 miles between Naltar and Mastuj. Though taking a more difficult route, it emulated the first leg of the march made by Colonel Kelly in 1895

Colonel Kelly and his officers on arrival at Chitral Fort, 1895. Six members of this group subsequently joined the Society

Abingdon School Expedition on arrival at Mastuj Fort, 1994. Of these, the School and five individuals are members of the Society

to relieve the besieged fort at Chitral. This traverse, one hundred years after Kelly's historic epic, was singularly tough, but his timing was equalled.[7] In recognition of this achievement the expedition was asked to provide a school flag to hang at the AFP Centre in time for a visit by the Foundation's Patron-in-Chief, the President of Pakistan.

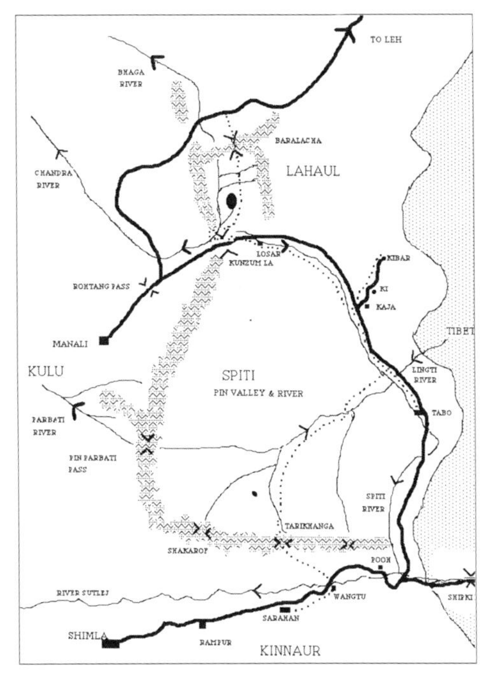

Map of Kinnaur, Spiti, Lahaul Route

In 1995 four Junior Members trekked through Kinnaur, Spiti and Lahoul, an area south-west of Tibet on the Trans-Himalayan plane, only recently opened to non-residents. Starting from Sarahan, they crossed the 15,300 ft Tarikanga Pass into Spiti and the Pin valley. This valley was first visited by Mr Louis Dane, Assistant Commissioner in Kulu, in 1884. He was one of those shot and wounded at the Society's meeting in Caxton Hall in 1940. Spiti, 'where Kim and his Lama walked', was bleak but endowed with unique Buddhist monasteries at Tabo, Ki and Kibar. The onward march entailed crossing the 15,000 ft Kunzum La into Lahoul, two thigh-deep river crossings and the 16,500 ft Baralacha Pass.[8]

Crossing the Tarikanga Pass into Spiti

There were two further expeditions to Northern Pakistan. In 1996, a large mixed party from Culford School crossed the Asambar Pass from Yasin to Chatorkhand, and then over the spur of the Hindu Kush traversing the Ishkoman Pass into Darkot. That pass has been described by Colonel R. C. F. Schomberg in his *Between Oxus and Indus*. An achievement of this expedition was to locate the exact location of the 'Farang Bar', where the explorer George Hayward, on his way to investigate the source of the Oxus, was murdered on the orders of the Mir of Yasin in 1870. At that spot two of the pupils read Sir Henry Newbolt's poem *He Fell Among Thieves* describing, somewhat fancifully, that dramatic event.[9] On reaching Yasin the party visited the rock on which Hayward had carved his initials and an arrow, supposedly indicating his onward route west along the Naz Bar. This has been a point of pilgrimage for those interested in Hayward. The party was disturbed to find that the rock had been drilled for dynamite to clear the land for building. (Four years later two members[10] visiting the site found that the rock had been demolished along with this small piece of British history.) The President of the Royal Geographical Society was informed of these events as they concerned one of its Gold Medallists. This drew an appreciative response.

Rock near Yasin showing arrow carved by George Hayward in 1870

Close-up of Hayward's arrow

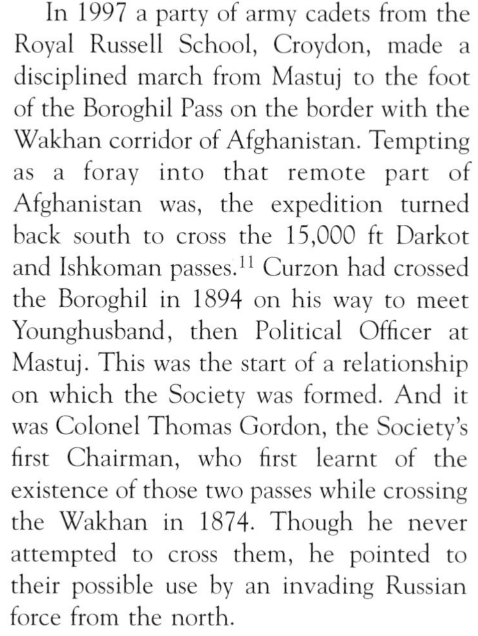

In 1997 a party of army cadets from the Royal Russell School, Croydon, made a disciplined march from Mastuj to the foot of the Boroghil Pass on the border with the Wakhan corridor of Afghanistan. Tempting as a foray into that remote part of Afghanistan was, the expedition turned back south to cross the 15,000 ft Darkot and Ishkoman passes.[11] Curzon had crossed the Boroghil in 1894 on his way to meet Younghusband, then Political Officer at Mastuj. This was the start of a relationship on which the Society was formed. And it was Colonel Thomas Gordon, the Society's first Chairman, who first learnt of the existence of those two passes while crossing the Wakhan in 1874. Though he never attempted to cross them, he pointed to their possible use by an invading Russian force from the north.

Hayward's rock after demolition, 2000

In 1997 a new series of Annual Junior Members' meetings was started. These were organised by Mr Adrian Steger and held at the East India, Sports and Public Schools Club. The format differed substantially from those pre-1970 meetings in that the four to six short talks were delivered by young persons themselves, followed by discussions. They attracted a mixed audience of both young and old, society members and those outside it. After the addresses, the meetings moved on to a dinner, or drinks, allowing experiences to be exchanged, plans for future expeditions

Adrian Steger chairing Junior Members' meeting, April 2001

Junior Members' meeting being addressed by Dr Gareth Jones, April 2001

made and friendships forged. The talks have been a mixture of the theoretical, the academic and the adventurous. They have included such diverse subjects as trekking expeditions in Tibet and the sub-continent; studies of Delhi's slum conditions; research into the Islamic legal basics in Pakistan; working with UNICEF in Afghanistan; the survival of the Asian tiger and life under the China Seas.[12] Some of the talks have been expanded and included as a lecture in the Society's main calendar programme.[13] The ages of the speakers has ranged from thirteen to thirty. Alexander Steger, who spoke on *Trekking with my Family and Other Animals*, a family trek around the Spiti valley, was possibly the youngest to have addressed the Society.

The meetings have been good recruiting grounds; the cry has been 'Bring a friend'. By the end of 1999, there were 29 Junior Members under twenty-five, and 25 who had graduated to the twenty-five–thirty bracket. The majority have continued their membership into the senior category.

These Junior Members' activities, with their broad exchange of ideas and contact, have had an influence on those participating, some even changing their university courses as a result. Others have gone on to organise their own expeditions in Asia, work as trekking guides and even to form a company running both educational trips for schools to India and advising multi-national companies on cultural sensitivities.

General Sir Richard Gale, who chaired Lieut Colonel Fox Holmes's talk on *Youth in Central Asia*, concluded by saying: 'I hope that a sense of adventure will make you want to visit this part of the world. I can assure you that it is only when you have travelled in these wonderful countries and met these astonishing people, that you really taste a breath of life.

You do not do it on the tarmac and pavements of England.' Few of the young venturers who have taken part in those expeditions would gainsay that.

Part Three

THE ACTIVITIES

VIII
THE JOURNAL

It is a Journal of really very great importance and is read all over the world.
Rt Hon. Patrick Gordon Walker MP, Annual Dinner, 1968

The birth of the Society's *Journal* was a by-product of a recruiting drive. In July 1913 Council asked overseas members to write in with news of current events of the countries in which they were living. These items, together with a list of new publications on Asia and lists of relevant articles appearing in sundry periodicals, would be carried in the Society's intermittent printed papers.[1] This, it was hoped, would foster an increasing interest in the Society and thus of its membership. Prior to this the Society published only occasional papers carrying the texts of those lectures deemed by a special sub-committee to be worthy of such treatment. Although the first lecture was delivered on 15 January 1902, the first evidence of one being printed was that by General E. F. Chapman, *Our Commercial Policy in the East,* published in 1904. The publication was headed *Central Asian Proceedings*, amended in the second such paper to read *Proceedings of the Central Asian Society*. It appeared between crimson covers, a colour, with tone variation, held to the present.

These occasional papers numbered between three and seven a year and were combined with periodic membership lists and, from 1908, an account of the Annual Anniversary Meetings and Dinners. They were distributed free to members. Extra copies were available at 1/-. For non-members they cost 2/6d. This arrangement, which continued until the end of 1913, did not constitute a journal. The response from the overseas membership to Council's request, however, was such that it was obvious that their contributions would expand considerably the current printed papers. The Secretary, Miss Hughes, was asked whether she would undertake the editing of such a journal, the first time that term was used. This agreed upon, the first issue was launched in early 1914 under the title *Journal of the Central Asian Society*. Its opening article was *A Visit to Mongolia* by E. Manico Gull. This was followed by several pages headed 'Notes and News'. Items carried varied from 'Captain F. M. Bailey's Latest Exploration', to 'China's Coal Supply' to 'Turkish Boy Scouts'. Also included were lists of 'Recent Books on the East' and 'Publications of the Central Asian Society'.

In March 1915 booksellers were asked to take the *Journal* and display it in their windows. In 1917 Sir Francis Younghusband, then back on the Council, wrote to the Viceroy in India asking that the *Journal* be taken by different departments of the Indian government. In 1918 the first photographs appeared. In 1920 a proposal was put to the

Persia Society that both societies combine their magazines, but the idea was rejected. By 1921 500 copies of the *Journal* were being printed at a cost of £200; that number increased to 620 the following year. During the war it had not always been possible to keep to the number of proposed publications, but the quarterly editions were achieved from 1921 for the next twenty years.

As the number of transcribed lectures increased, the volume of 'Notes and News' decreased until these were occasional items only. In 1921 the lists of books gave way to actual book reviews (despite a decision the previous years not to include any) when Sir Percy Sykes's *A History of Persia* was reviewed by Sir Mortimer Durand, reprinted from the *Journal of the Royal Asiatic Society*. In 1922 there were three reviews. By 1925 they included several on works in foreign languages. By 1929 the book review section had become a major feature of the *Journal* occupying 54 out of 160 pages in Part I of that year. But the reviews were long, four and a half pages being common. In 1935 a review of *The Transformation of Nature in Art* by Ananda K. Coomaraswamy occupied ten pages and *The Spirit of Zen* by A. W. Watts, reviewed by Bishop A. Lea, eleven and a half: a record.

Reviewers pulled no punches. One 'H.W.', reviewing in 1931 *A Tour in the Himalayas and Beyond* by Lieut Colonel Sir Reginald Rankin, Bt wrote: 'The author set out with practically no knowledge of any Indian language, with an indifferent camp outfit and a bad lot of servants and blames everyone but himself for the troubles and difficulties that arose and which fell heavier on his unfortunate wife, whose pluck is the only bright feature of this book ... It would have been much better if it had not been written at all.'

Especially vicious were those experts on Arabia who were critical of any daring to trespass upon their territory. In 1925 the Arabian explorer Mr H. St J. B. Philby reviewed a somewhat lightweight work, *Through the Inner Deserts to Medina* by the Countess Donshka Malmignati, suggesting it was largely a work of fiction: 'A careful reading of the book forces one instinctively to echo a question asked of herself in the closing paragraph "those last three months were they but a dream?" One is tempted to answer in the affirmative.' The Countess, in a spirited reply, retorted: 'I am not the *De Rougemont* Mr Philby makes me out to be ... my book is true ... But as such known Arab travellers as Palgrave and Mr D. Hogarth had also to undergo the critical doubt of Mr Philby, I should not mind being added to victims so highly esteemed and distinguished.' The correspondence continued in this vein over two years.

In 1933 there was another prolonged correspondence battle between those two Arabian Titans, Mr Philby and Mr Bertram Thomas, who had reviewed each other's books and were especially critical over the respective locations and spelling of the 'lost city' of Wabar/Ubar. Philby had the advantage of being able to head his letters as written from 'Mecca, Arabia', whereas Thomas had to be content with Trinity College, Cambridge. Arabia seems to attract a peculiar possessiveness. In 1993–1994 a not dissimilar correspondence ensued between Mr H. St J. B. Armitage, an acknowledged authority on Arabia, who had known the great Philby himself, and Mr Leslie McCloughlin, an accomplished

'Philby ... [was] able to head his letters as written from Mecca...' where he photographed the King's Palace and Jebel Ghurur in 1933 [RSAA Archives]

Arabist, over their respective articles, books and reviews relating to Saudi Arabian history. Invariably, this type of correspondence had to be closed by the well-tried Editor's formula.

Criticism by reviewers of the English spelling of vernacular names was another repeated source of irritation to authors, who regarded this as unnecessary pedantry. Such a view was aired in 1935 by Mr H. C. Armstrong in defiance of remarks made by a reviewer over the spelling of place names in his book, *Unending Battle*, about the Georgian struggle for independence. 'Mr Allen criticises my spelling of Akalzika for Akhaltzikhe. This is the old quarrel between the pedants and those who, like myself, believe that a name should show easily to the eye and sound easily to the ear and not be spelt in accordance with some rigid rules of transcription laid down by Professors . . . No Georgian, however full of drink, ever made a noise like Akhaltzikhe. He would have to gargle himself into apoplexy before he got anywhere near it.' Others took the reverse view. In 1932 Philby wrote: 'I will content myself with deprecating the deplorable fact that a Society like this should tamely follow the fashion set some years ago by Colonel Lawrence of spelling Arabic words just anyhow.'

The *Journal* frequently advertised books written by members which had been reviewed in that same issue. A delightful illustration of this in 1935 was a book *The Peshawar Vale Hunt* by Captain and Brevet Major G. S. Hurst, MFH, Royal Signals – illustrated by Snaffles and Major H. M. Tullock of the Poona Horse. 'A book that almost makes you hear the cry of hounds in full chase across the green fields of Peshawar.' The reviewer, Sir Evelyn Howell, 'Whipper-in 1904–1908', who had served many years on the North West Frontier, and who became one of the great names of the Society, enlarged upon this notice by making the reader feel he was riding to hounds himself.

Apart from acrimonious conflict between author and reviewer, the letters section of the *Journal* also carried practical advice. In 1928 a correspondent wrote: 'Members who are returning to Iraq and Persia in their own cars may be interested in the following account of a 12 H.P. touring car crossing the Syrian desert to Baghdad . . . over soft sand and camel thorn.' And subsequent advice on continuing to Persia: 'For the remainder of the journey from Khanikin to Duzdab a big 29 horse power car is advisable, enough to carry 700 lbs of luggage and 56 gallons of petrol.' For the final leg from Duzdab to Meshed, a further 553 miles, the advice was to take a tennis racquet: 'The European communities in the towns passed through are most hospitable and will swallow with relish anything new in the tennis line.'

Three pages of notes by Mr Edward A. Waters on equipment and supplies taken by him and his wife on a journey from Bandipur to Kashgar and back in 1932 show how

'. . . over soft sand and camel thorn.'

'. . . a big 29 horse power car . . . enough to carry 700 lbs of luggage . . .'

Nairn Motor Route, 1933 [*RSAA Archives*]

lightweight travel was not yet in vogue. 'We took with us a Shikari, cook and bearer, tiffin coolie, an assistant cook, a coolie who was a good pony man. A sweeper is a great convenience. Heavy Gilgit boots and fur coats make the evenings bearable on the Pamirs and several times we slept in them. Take folding camp cots and folding canvas wash basins and a bath tub ... a rifle, gun and pistol, the latter useful for the feeling of assurance it might give one.'

This wide spread of articles, book reviews and letters enabled Sir Arnold Wilson to say of the *Journal* at the Annual Dinner in 1931: 'The articles are of quite exceptional interest and value. Indeed we have received special praise at the hands of *The Times Literary Supplement*, than which there is no higher authority or praise.'

It was not long before there were subscribers to the *Journal* outside the individual membership. By 1922 there were 12, their numbers shortly to include the Russian Consul in Tabriz. By 1948 this had reached 89, including the U.S. Central Intelligence Group, Washington. Ten years later the figure had reached 336; there were 120 in the United States (the Georgetown University handbook mentioned the RCAS *Journal* as 'one with which each student is advised to make himself or herself very familiar'), 31 in China, 17 in the USSR and 7 in Japan. An indication of the regard in which the *Journal* was held is shown by the fact that even when the individual membership of the Society decreased the number of *Journal* subscribers actually increased. By 1964 there were 454 subscribers in fifty different countries, including 135 in the USA, 35 in Iran (24 of which were subscribed by CENTO), 23 in India, 25 in Pakistan and 14 in China. In 1975 the number had reached 577, requiring 2,500 copies of the *Journal* to be printed. In 2000 there were 431 such subscribers in some thirty countries when a total of 1,600 copies of the *Journal* were required for each issue. The cost per annum for subscribers (it was always free to members) rose gradually from 25/- in 1961 to £9 in 1977, £30 in 1991 and £40 in 2000.

In 1939, prior to the outbreak of war, free copies of the *Journal* were sent to the RAF Cadet College at Cranwell, the Royal Naval College, Greenwich and the Imperial Defence College. In the early years of the conflict extra copies were required for circulation to army messes and hospitals both to make the Society better known and for their educational value. A problem arose in 1941 when, as part of war-time economy measures, the Society's paper allowance was cut by 50 per cent, making its consequent quota of 5 cwt of paper, and that of poor quality, sufficient only for 1,750 copies at three issues a year, each of 120 pages. As about half the Society's membership was then abroad, there was concern lest the reduction of this, their only link, should result in resignations. A petition was made to the Government Paper Controller asking for the cut to be reduced to 25 per cent. The submission pointed out that the *Journal* helped the war effort in respect of both the morale of troops and of the propaganda resulting from the prestige it portrayed of the British Empire. 'If copies were sent to Air Force and Army messes in the Middle East and the Burma Front, it would be good for the morale of young officers in those places, both as relieving boredom and in helping them to find an interest in the part of the world in which they were serving.'

Meanwhile, to abide by those economy measures, the number of issues per year was cut from four to three, combining parts III and IV. This was, perhaps, not such an inconvenience, as during the war it proved difficult to sustain high-quality articles. In fact the *Journal* never returned to four separate issues. This practice was kept until 1965 when it settled to three straight issues with no pretence at a combination.

APOLOGY

It is very much regretted that, owing to printing difficulties resulting from the serious flooding experienced in southern England this autumn publication of the *Journal* has been delayed, for the first time in office memory.

September 1968 at our printers, Billing & Sons Limited of Guildford.

As we have seen, when the *Journal* was instituted as such in 1914 the Secretary, Miss Hughes, as other secretaries after her, became effectively its editor. Miss Hughes was helped by Lieut Colonel A. C. Yate, then a member of Council prior to his becoming Honorary Secretary in 1919, and successive secretaries by Mr Edmonds from the Society's printers, Billing and Sons. In 1924 a separate sub-committee was formed under the title 'Journal and Details and General Purposes Committee'. Its records are scant but it seems it was concerned mostly in choosing lecturers and selecting articles for the *Journal* rather than having any editorial role. It was disbanded in 1934 and its duties reverted to the main Council.

It was not until July 1961 that an Editorial Board was established, consisting of at least two members of Council, the remainder from the Society at large. Its first members were Lieut Colonel Geoffrey Wheeler, who became the Board's Chairman, Sir Gilbert Laithwaite (later to become the Society's Chairman), the journalist and broadcaster Mr Neville Barbour, Miss Violet Conolly, Colonel C. H. Ellis and Mr E. H. Paxton. The original concept was that individual members of the Board should retire after three years to give way to others with similar area expertise. This held under Wheeler's chairmanship but subsequently lapsed.

An editor was appointed in October. Amongst those considered were Mr Stewart Perowne (husband of Freya Stark) and Colonel C. H. Ellis. In the event Mrs K. E. West, who had worked for Wheeler at his Central Asian Research Centre, took the position.

The choice was ideal: she had wide literary experience, having served on the editorial staff of the *Encyclopaedia Britannica*'s Research Bureau, as sub-editor of *International Affairs,* and during the war in the Press Department of the British Embassy in Moscow.

Mrs K. E. West

Prior to Mrs West's appointment, the *Journal* was something of a house periodical; Colonel Wheeler, not a man to mince his words, described it as 'rather parochial'. However, as it was essentially the only British periodical concerned with current Asian affairs, it did now require development on more comprehensive lines, not least the section dealing with book reviews. A growing number of books on Asia were being offered and discipline was required for limiting their treatment; there was no longer space for eleven-page reviews. Also, whereas previously most articles in the *Journal* were transcripts of lectures delivered at the Society's meetings, not all such lectures, especially those illustrated, were now of sufficient substance to be included. The new format was to include articles submitted by individuals, many of them well-known scholars. A few received a small honorarium, though most were content with the prestige it bestowed. As a result the *Journal* soon reached an even greater status within academic circles and was regarded as having the finest book reviews on Asian subjects anywhere. To recognise this, in 1982 the British Academy made a grant of £1,000 towards its costs.

Wheeler, in his initial enthusiasm, considered the possibility of merging the *Journal* with that of the Royal Asiatic Society. However, similar to other amalgamation schemes with that Society, this proved impracticable, their respective approaches differing too broadly. But he did publish in the *Journal* a number of articles on Soviet writings on Central Asia, whose provenance was his own Research Centre. He resigned from Chairmanship of the board in January 1965; subsequent holders of that office are given in the Annex.

Lieut Colonel Geoffrey Wheeler

At the start of 1970 the *Journal* was given a new title, *Asian Affairs*, and new serial numbers. The previous title, *Royal Central Asian Society Journal*, was misleading over the area covered and was limiting its appeal. In any case it was not the *Journal*, but the Society, that was Royal!

In February 1969 Mrs West resigned; three short-term editors replaced her, none lasting the course, and under her new married name, Mrs K. Beckett, she had repeatedly to be recalled to fill the gaps. In October 1975 Mrs Peggie Robertson settled to the position for six years. In October 1984 Mr Robert Longmire, after a career spent mostly in the Foreign and Commonwealth Office, became editor. In his tenure of eight years he raised the standing of the *Journal* to an even higher internationally acknowledged level. He fought a terminal illness to see his last edition through the press days before he died, a moving example of his steadfast devotion. Dr Victor Funnell and Mr John Shipman followed for short periods before Ms Susan Pares became editor in January 1997, holding the position to June 2001, when Mr Michael Sheringham took her place. Thanks to a generous donation of £5,000 from Shell in 1997, the editing system for the *Journal* was computerised and all material sent to the printers, Santype International, on disk. The Editorship and membership of the Board are responsible positions. The content of the work they supervise has had countless readers in over fifty countries and the international standing of the Society lies to a large degree in their hands.

There is no space here to detail the vast range of subjects relating to Asia that have, during a century, appeared in the *Journal*. Virtually every country has been covered but with a preponderance on Arabia, Soviet Central Asia, South East Asia, China and Tibet, and always the Society's choice subject, Afghanistan. But the smaller countries have not been neglected; there have, for example, been at least three articles on the Maldive Islands. The content indexes themselves make fascinating reading and show a coverage of articles on such diverse subjects as exploration, mountaineering, archaeology, anthropology, religions (especially Islam), history and the 'Great Game', education, technology, rail and air routes, natural history, Asian feminism, current affairs generally, oil, industry, trade and economics. Since 1960 there has been some increase in the last five subjects but the balance has been kept. In 1939 there were 109 book reviews, and in 2000 161. As a consequence the articles became shorter and fewer in number.

In January 1963 a copy of an article on Tibet was sent to His Holiness the Dalai Lama, which brought a grateful reply. In January 1965 copies of the *Journal*, with articles on Iran, were sent to His Imperial Majesty the Shahanshah of Iran; as a result he became an Honorary Member the same year. Articles on Islam, transcribed from lectures, have been a prominent feature of the Society's publications from the outset and have evoked interest in the Muslim world. In 1906 Valentine Chirol lectured on Pan-Islamism at a time when Sultan Abdul Hamid was still seated on the Ottoman throne.[2] Other early articles were by such well known Islamic scholars as Professor D. S. Margoliouth,[3] the Afghan writer Sirdar Ikbal Ali Shah,[4] and Professor H. A. R. Gibb.[5] In 1931 a series of three lectures on Islam 'From the Sudan to Western China' was proposed with Mr Mohammed Ali Jinnah, King Feisal of Iraq and the British Muslim Mr Marmaduke Pickthall as speakers. In the event only the latter spoke.[6] Another British Muslim, Lord Healey, wrote in 1924 of his experiences in performing the *Haj*.[7] Lectures on Islam, written up as articles, have been carried regularly in the *Journal* ever since. In 1989 an advance copy of an article by Mr Hugh Leach on contemporary Islam was sent to the Society's Patron, the Prince of Wales, because of his known interest in the subject.[8]

A popular feature of the *Journal* is the obituaries; an enthralling volume could be made from a collection. They were written by friends, most often former colleagues, of the deceased, who brought out less-known aspects of a person's life. They were not drawn from *Who's Who* entries. The first obituary, that of the Society's founding chairman, General Sir Thomas Gordon, appeared in 1914, followed in 1915 by that of the Society's founder, Dr Cotterell Tupp. The nine-page obituary of Viscount Allenby, written by Sir John Shea, one of his Divisional Commanders in Palestine, is the longest any member of the Society has received,[9] though as pertinent to the understanding of his character was Field Marshal Lord Chetwode's address at the Annual Dinner in 1937. Sir Henry Dobbs, who replaced Sir Percy Cox as High Commissioner in Iraq, rated nine pages and the Arabian explorer Mr H. St J. B. Philby five, written by four separate Arabian scholars who knew him and could interpret his complex character.[10] There have also been obituaries of many prominent Asian rulers and statesmen.

Some obituaries were especially dramatic, others entertaining. That of the Reverend Oskar Hermansson describes how in 1933 he narrowly escaped execution by a Chinese firing squad at Yarkand,[11] and the obituary of Lieut Colonel John Inglish Eadie by Professor Charles Beckingham conveys the delightful eccentricities developed by many members after long years of bachelor service in the East.[12]

The *Journal* is essentially the Society's 'Flagship'. It is the vehicle by which the Society is known both nationally and internationally and links the large overseas membership to the parent body. As the Chairman, Sir Arthur de la Mare, said at the 1980 Annual Dinner: 'If we did not have the *Journal*, we would be a very small society, able to cater only to those members who live either in London or near enough to London to be able to attend our lectures. It is entirely because of the *Journal* that we are able to get members literally in all five continents.' And a study of the *Journal* indexes will reinforce a remark made by Lord Curzon in 1924: 'Your *Journal* is a splendid production ... its papers are written by experts and they contain information which could not be found anywhere else in the world.'

IX

THE LIBRARY

Our Library continues to be the jewel in the Society's crown
Lieut Colonel A. P. H. B. Fowle, Hon. Sec., AGM 1993

The idea of a library was announced at the Annual General Meeting in June 1920 by the Honorary Secretary, Lieut Colonel A. C. Yate. 'We have reached a time when we are considering forming a library and a collection of photographs and lantern slides.' This was followed by a circular in November asking for contributions: 'The central subject of the Society's study is the Middle East, which should first and foremost be represented on its bookshelves. The Near and Far East are the complements of the Middle.' 'Middle East', in the Society's terms, then meant the 'centre of the East', i.e. Central Asia.

The first response to this request was received in February 1921 when Major H. L. Haughton of the 36th Sikhs donated a Chinese currency note of the reign of the Emperor Hung Wu, the first ruler of the Ming dynasty. This was followed by a trickle of a dozen or so books. The first substantial gift of 152 books, together with a bookcase, was made by Lady Trotter from the estate of her late husband, Sir Henry Trotter, who had been the Society's Chairman from 1917 to 1919; and the second a contribution from Sir Percy Sykes, which included an autographed copy of Dr Wolff's *A Mission to Bokhara 1843–45*.

This embryonic collection revealed the lack of any substantial shelf space in the modest office at 74 Grosvenor Street, occupied by courtesy of the Royal Asiatic Society (RAS), the Society's hosts. The problem was alleviated, though not solved, by moving to a larger office within the same premises. In 1922 Mr Roland Michell, who had recently joined the Society, volunteered to become the first Honorary Librarian. By 1923 the Library consisted of 485 volumes and 75 pamphlets. There were further gifts in the following two years.[1]

It would be tedious to list all the individual donors, even if there were a complete record, but it seems only right to acknowledge for posterity, either in the text or in the notes, the generosity of those who have made major contributions. This relies on sketchy records and many will be unintentionally omitted.

In June 1925 Mrs R. W. Frazer (formerly Miss Hughes), after retiring as secretary of the RAS, offered to take on the Honorary Librarianship in place of Mr Michell. Cataloguing the growing collection, she found there were some forty books not strictly of Asian interest. These were offered for sale to members at 2/6d, but as there were no takers they were sent to the Prison Library at Wandsworth. Since the collection included such tomes as *The Flora of Niger* by Joseph Hooker, 1849, one wonders how many were read by the inmates. Mrs Frazer was followed in the honorary post of Librarian by Mr A. C. Wratislaw in 1927 and in 1928 by Miss Ella Sykes.

At the end of 1928 a proposal was made that the Society should approach the Carnegie Trust for an allowance over the next five years to establish a proper library. Colonel S. F. Newcombe, a member of Council and a representative of the Trust, advised the Trustees against it, arguing that the Society's Library had yet to carry sufficient books of value. Another member of Council, Sir Arnold Wilson, who had had experience of the Trust, warned against the idea on the grounds that accepting Carnegie money placed restrictions on the use of the library. The idea was then shelved. A letter to Sir William Forster of the India Office Library asked if members could use that library and whether it would lend the Society books for a given period. Sir William stalled the proposal by adopting the useful formula of asking the joint librarians to 'look into it' and the idea does not seem to have been pursued. Rather, Council resolved to continue to build the library as previously, by encouraging the gifts of books, either directly or by bequest, and asking reviewers to return their copies. This has been the policy ever since and in fact relatively few books have been purchased.

In 1929 the Society moved to its own quarters at 77 Grosvenor Street, which provided facilities for a reading room and library. The new shelves were soon filled by 'the most valuable gift of books, almost a library in itself', part of the collection of Lieut Colonel A. C. Yate, the Society's late indefatigable Honorary Secretary, which were presented by his son in his father's memory.

In July 1930 Lieut General Sir Raleigh Egerton became the Honorary Librarian, succeeded in the following year by Colonel J. K. Tod. By the end of 1932 a further surplus of duplicated and irrelevant books had built up. Instead of bombarding prison inmates with obscure florae, this surplus was divided between the Royal Empire Society and the Witwatersrand Library in South Africa.

By 1935 the Library comprised some 2,150 volumes. In June 1940, with the threat of German bombing, the Library was divided up for safekeeping. The bulk was placed in the cellars of the Society's then headquarters at Clarges Street, whilst some of the rarer volumes were stored in the homes of members living in the country. But the most valuable were placed in the warehouse of the Society's printers, Billing and Sons, at Guildford. As mentioned earlier a direct hit by an incendiary bomb destroyed irreplaceable archival material as well as ninety-four of the most precious books.[2]

Council decided that little could be done about this disaster until the war was over. Meanwhile, members were asked to scour second-hand bookshops for replacements and Francis Edwards, the antiquarian bookseller, undertook to value for insurance purposes the books destroyed. As a result over the years many of the books have been reinstated.[3]

In June 1945 the dispersed books were gathered and the Library again functioned normally. In the same year Lieut Colonel F. M. Bailey became Honorary Librarian. It cannot be said that librarianship attracts the prosaic. Both Bailey and his predecessor, Colonel Tod, had had as adventurous lives as any in the Society or outside it.

The end of the war saw more additions to the Library. The bequest of Sir Charles Bell, the famous Tibetologist, added 250 rare books on Tibet; his diaries followed in 1948. A large part of Sir Percy Sykes's library was presented by his widow, Lady Sykes, on his death. In 1950 the Himalayan explorer Lieut Colonel R. C. F. Schomberg gave 50 books and a collection of glass slides, clearing his effects, perhaps, before being ordained as a Catholic priest.[4] There was traffic the other way. In 1950 the Foreign Office Arabic Language School, MECAS, in the Lebanon, which had supplied the Society with a steady stream of recruits, asked that in future they be sent any surplus books.

In 1960 Mr Frank de Halpert took over as Honorary Librarian from Colonel F. M. Bailey, who had retired to Norfolk. He made a detailed survey of acquisitions which, excluding the bound *Journals* and miscellanea, now amounted to 4,052 books. The majority were on India and Pakistan (618) followed numerically by China and Korea, the Middle East and the Arab World, Turkey, Tibet and Central Asia. Advice was sought from a professional librarian, Miss Mary Piggott, lecturer at the School of Librarianship and Archives of University College, London. Her recommendations included the need for more shelves (easier said than done given the limited space); books to be sub-arranged by subject matter within their geographical shelves (this was not adopted, it being preferred to shelve them alphabetically under authors); a classified subject catalogue should be made and, for security reasons, a separate list of books made in addition to the card index. Two student librarians assisted by two lady members worked voluntarily during the summer vacation to put these measures into effect. The Library has always relied upon voluntary help from members and in this respect particular mention must be made of the endeavours in recent years of Mr John da Silva, Mrs Merilyn Hywel-Jones and Mr Murray Graham.

By 1961 the Library numbered some 4,500 volumes, including in this increase 150 books on the Far East given by Brigadier E. V. Bowra 'in memory of his father and grandfather'. In the following year the explorer and scholar Mr Douglas Carruthers left a most valuable collection of 215 books on Central Asia and the Arab world. His modest bookplate will be familiar to borrowers. A note left with the donation read: 'The whole of my collection risked complete destruction when on 30 August 1940 the first enemy bomb to be dropped in Norfolk fell within ten yards of my library room at Barmer Hall, Kings Lynn, the target being Bircham Newton aerodrome one mile away.' In 1962 Sir Roger Hollis presented 85 books on the Far East, and a further 40 on the same area were donated by Mr E. M. Gull. In that year alone 405 books came to the Library from legacies.

In December 1962 the first Library Committee was formed, comprising the Honorary Librarian and initially two or three other members with separate geographical experience. The committee invited Mr S. C. Sutton, Librarian at the India Office Library, to join. On his retirement his place was taken by Miss Joan Lancaster, also a Director of the India Office Library. The committee was authorised by Council to spend up to £100 per annum on new books if it felt it necessary.

In 1963 Sotheby's valued the Library at £8,826, compared with £1,525 in 1947. Bequests continued to add to its numbers and in 1965 a total of 158 additional volumes were received. The time had come for some major weeding and 330 books were removed from the shelves that year and sold.

John Massey-Stewart

At the end of 1967 the stalwart Frank de Halpert resigned on reaching the age of eighty-four. His place was taken by Mr John Massey-Stewart, who approached his duties with zeal. As an experiment he kept the Library open until 6.30 p.m. on the first and last Monday of each month. The trial was not a success, though more books were borrowed than previously, reaching around 300 a year. Undaunted, Massey-Stewart continued with his crusade to put the Society's Library on the scholarly map, pointing out that its collection on Afghanistan, Mongolia, Mesopotamia, Turkestan and Tibet included uniquely rare works, some the envy even of the British Museum. In 1973 he contributed an article to the *Journal* about the twelve volumes of the Hakluyt Society's publications of travel narratives. These had just been presented to the Library by Mrs Elinor Sinclair, daughter of the late Sir Percy Sykes. After his successful tenure of eleven years, Massey-Stewart's place was taken in 1978 by Mr Michael Pollock, then at the India Office Library. He remains in office at the time of writing, serving jointly as Librarian of the Royal Asiatic Society.

In January 1969 Viscount Furness gave on long loan some fifty rare books on Mongolia. But a proposal by the Anglo-Mongolian Society ten years later that the whole of their library should be housed with the Society's, for the joint use of both, was turned down for lack of space.

In the 1980s there were valuable bequests from the estates of three of the Society's foremost scholars. C. J. Edmonds, an authority on the Kurds, left a large part of his library, as did Sir Olaf Caroe, one of the last Pro-Consuls of the former British Indian Empire, and Lieut Colonel Geoffrey Wheeler, the acknowledged expert on Soviet Central Asia.

At this time the Society was facing serious financial difficulties and Council was forced to scotch rumours that it intended to sell the Library to solve the problem. No doubt some saw this as tempting, since in 1980 it had been revalued at between £80,000 and £100,000. But as the Chairman, Sir Arthur de la Mare, made plain, 'to abolish the Library would be to destroy the Society'. He emphasised its uniqueness, pointing out that its collection ranged from the seventeenth century to the present as well as archival material dating back to 1823. That apart, the Library is a factor in the Society maintaining its educational charitable status.

In December 1985 the Society moved its offices from Devonshire Street to its present location at Canning House in Belgrave Square. By then the total number of volumes held, many in boxes, had reached nearly 6,000. As the new premises offered less wall space for shelving another weeding was necessary. A good many books discarded were duplicates, or dealt with areas outside the Society's strict geographical remit. These were sold so that by the time of the move the number had been reduced to about 4,500 volumes, including the *Journals*.

A general view of the Library

Thanks to the generosity of members, gifts and legacies continued. In 1990 Colonel Gerald Morgan, a former member of the Library Committee and biographer of the celebrated nineteenth-century Central Asian explorer Ney Elias, left £2,500 to the Society for the use of its Library, as well as some Tibetan artefacts. In 1992 there were contributions from the estate of Mr Edward Sykes (son of Sir Percy), and a collection of rare seventeenth to nineteenth-century leather-bound travel books was sent from the library in Italy of Major R. C. Murphy shortly before he died. In 1998 Mr Jeremy Wilson, editor of the recently published 1922 text of T. E. Lawrence's *Seven Pillars of Wisdom*, generously presented the Society with one of the limited Collectors' Editions of this work.

The move to Canning House focused the Library Committee on the problem of space and it put forward a proposal to Council that the Society's archival collection (details of which are outlined in the following chapter) should be handed to the India Office Library on permanent loan. The Committee argued that the latter had better facilities for the preservation of such material and that it would be more readily available to the public there. Council rejected robustly this proposal, feeling it to be a surrender of a major asset and that it would dissuade others from leaving material to the Society. It would be better, it argued, to try to obtain a grant from some organisation to fund preservation. A bid to obtain such funds from the Barakat Trust in 1999 failed because that body aids only Islamic collections. Since 1997 members of the National Decorative and Fine Arts Society (NADFAS) have been active cleaning and carrying out minor repairs to ailing volumes. An 'Adopt a Book' scheme was launched for volumes requiring more major repairs, at an average cost to the donor of £30.

A NADFAS team at work

The editor of the Society's *Journal* currently receives some 200 books each year for review, though not all undergo that treatment. Returned review copies, where appropriate, are added to the Library and this provides a steady increase of up-to-date publications. There have been suggestions that the Society's Library should concentrate its collection on such recent works and that the library of the Royal Asiatic Society should be the custodian for the more antiquarian volumes. Three things need to be said here. Firstly, the majority of books borrowed or read *in situ* by researchers are the older volumes, especially those on travel. Secondly, and this may be the reason for that, modern books are available at provincial libraries. And thirdly, not unimportantly, the indigenous wealth of the Library, and thus of the Society itself, rests in its antiquarian collection. A balance must be kept and the Library Committee is active in keeping the shelves stocked with quality modern publications. It is certainly not a 'dead library', but at the same time it cannot ignore the fact that many members do enjoy browsing in antiquity.

At the time of the centenary the Library, all but bursting at its seams, carried 5,320 titles. The coverage includes travel, biography, history, archaeology, religion, current affairs and economics, but not literature. It may well be the Society's 'Jewel in the Crown', but it is an under-used jewel even though non-members may, on recommendation, make use of it. And whilst no armchair traveller could ask for more than to disappear into the vanished world found on its shelves, the serious researcher will find, the books apart, uniquely rich material lying in a century's worth of the *Journals*.

X

THE ARCHIVES

by John Shipman

Our archives date back to 1823 . . . We must never surrender such a major asset.
Sir Arthur de la Mare, Chairman, 1983

The archive derives from the piecemeal accumulation of bequests and donations over many decades. The collection is modest by the standards of other learned societies, but it is rich and diverse enough to intrigue both generalist and specialist. Although the Society's limited means has hitherto precluded the systematic organisation and maintenance of this resource, the Society, until comparatively recently, continued to solicit donations of material from members. However, with the passing of the generation who were born, lived or served in the outposts of empire, the well of benefaction has run dry – or almost dry – and the time has come to concentrate attention on the assets which the Society holds. These, for the most part, are listed, but they remain uncatalogued. Some items are of unknown provenance, while the source of others is only partially known or a matter of conjecture.

It would be tedious to attempt a comprehensive survey of the archive. What follows, therefore, is an impressionistic review, arranged alphabetically, of some of its highlights and curiosities, with notes on the personalities involved.

The Bailey Collection

The Society holds some 300 glass slides of photographs taken by the explorer and naturalist, Lieut Colonel Frederick Marshman (Eric) Bailey (1882–1967). They relate to his travels, on and off duty, in Central Asia. At an early stage in his career, Bailey concluded that 'nothing important happens in India itself. To get on one must learn about the neighbouring countries.'[1] And so he did. He served with the Younghusband expedition to Tibet in 1904, and later, in 1918–1919, travelled via Kashgar to Tashkent and other parts of Russian Turkestan.[2] After the First World War he was appointed Political Officer, Sikkim, when he had the opportunity to revisit Tibet and to explore

Mt Ararat. Watercolour by Sir William Everett, 1880s [*RSAA Archives*]

Bhutan. He was later Resident in Kashmir. Most of the original photographs, together with Bailey's papers, are held in the British Library. Bailey's wife, the Hon. Mrs Irma Bailey, also presented the Society with an album of sketches (and a few photographs) belonging to her grandfather, Lieut Colonel Sir William Everett (1844–1908) who served as Consul-General at Erzerum, Turkey, 1882–1888. Everett had a trained eye and was an accomplished artist; his Turkish sketches and watercolours are of exceptional interest.

The Bell Papers

As Political Officer in Sikkim for most of the period from 1908 to 1920, Sir Charles Bell (1870–1945) was directly responsible for British relations with Tibet. A leading scholar of Tibet's language, history and culture, he was the friend and biographer of the Thirteenth Dalai Lama. The papers bequeathed by his widow – in addition to many of his books – comprise a random collection of photographs, printed material and documents mainly relating to Tibet. They include original correspondence ending with Bell's magisterial letter to *The Times* of 8 August 1935 in which he argued that the authentic Tibetan name for Mt Everest was *Kang Chamolung*. Unfortunately, the most important item, a typescript of the diary which he kept during his Mission to Lhasa in 1920–1921, has disappeared.

Sir Charles Bell with the Thirteenth Dalai Lama (seated) and Maharaja Kumar Sidkeong of Sikkim, Calcutta, 1910 [*RSAA Archives*]

The Bourdillon Bequest

Two albums containing photographs of exceptional size and quality comprise this bequest by the Misses Bourdillon in 1949. They were taken during the Younghusband Mission of 1903–1904 by John Claude White (1853–1918), a Public Works Department engineer on loan to the Indian Political Department. White had been sent to Sikkim in 1888–1889 with a British military expedition tasked to eject an invading Tibetan force. Appointed to the newly created post of Political Officer, Sikkim, he was subsequently given responsibility for relations with Tibet and Bhutan, and assumed he would conclude his career in command of the British Mission to Lhasa. His disappointment at the appointment of Younghusband embittered his last few years in Gangtok.[3]

The Bowra Bequest

In 1961 Brigadier E. V. Bowra[4] donated printed, manuscript and photographic material which had belonged to his grandfather E. C. M. Bowra (1841–1874) and to his father C. A. V. Bowra (1869–1947), both of whom had served with distinction in the Chinese Maritime Customs Service. In 1860 Edward Bowra, as a quixotic, lion-hearted youth of nineteen, postponed getting a job in order to join Garibaldi's Red Shirts in their fight to liberate Italy. Shortly after his recruitment into the Imperial Chinese Customs Service in 1863, he volunteered to join General Gordon in the storming of Soochow, then in the hands of the Taiping rebels. He became a brilliant Chinese linguist and scholar, serving both as interpreter and commissioner in Canton and Ningpo before his sudden death at the age of thirty-three, while on leave in Kent.[5] His papers include his *History of the Kwang-Tung Province of the Chinese Empire* (Hong Kong 1872) with manuscript annotations, and two albums of photographs of China in the 1860s. These contain some striking images of the temples, monuments and other buildings of old Peking, including the then recently sacked Summer Palace, as well as scenes of Ningpo and Canton. Cecil Bowra's unpublished manuscript *Some Episodes in the History of Amoy* is embellished with annotations in his fine Chinese script.

Edward Bowra with son, Cecil, c. 1871 [RSAA Archives]

Ningpo, c. 1867. Edward Bowra's house is the prominent building on the far bank [RSAA Archives]

The Chapman Papers

Shortly before his death in 1962, Sir Richard Maconachie, a former Indian Civil Servant and diplomat, presented a collection of sketches, watercolours and photographs which had been given to him during the Second World War by 'a lady whom I knew slightly' (but whom he did not name); she had told him 'that they had belonged to a relation of hers – a Colonel Chapman ... who had been a member of the Forsyth Mission'.

General Sir Edward Francis Chapman (1840–1926) had an eventful career spent largely in India. As a Captain in the Quarter Master General's Department, Lucknow, he was appointed Secretary of the Forsyth Mission to Yarkand and Kashgar (1873–1874), with responsibility for administration and transport. He faced the daunting task of organising the passage of '300 souls and 400 animals' along the Karakoram caravan route from Leh to Yarkand, across four of the highest passes in the world, in below-freezing temperatures. The ostensible purpose of the Mission, led by Sir Douglas Forsyth and including two future chairmen of the Society, Sir Thomas Gordon and Sir Henry Trotter, was to negotiate a commercial treaty with Yakub

Sir Douglas Forsyth in camp at the border post of Shahidulla, October 1873. Here he was met and escorted to Yarkand by emissaries of Yakub Beg

Officers in the service of Yakub Beg, at ease in Yarkand, November 1873

Snuff and tobacco sellers, Yarkand, November 1873

Women patients outside the Forsyth Mission clinic in Kashgar, January 1874

FORSYTH MISSION – 1873 [RSAA *Archives*]

Pen and watercolour sketches by Chapman of local life in Eastern Turkestan [RSAA Archives]

Beg who in 1867 had established himself as the independent ruler of much of Chinese Turkestan. The unstated purpose of the exercise was to counter the spread of Russian influence in a region flanking India's Northern Frontier. Before joining the Mission, Chapman took a crash course in photography with Messrs Bourne and Shepherd in Simla, where he later sent his negatives for printing (110 in all, including a few taken by Henry Trotter). Chapman's photographs, copies of which were circulated with the Mission's official report (1875), were the first to be taken of 'native' society in Chinese Turkestan, and are of considerable historical and ethnographic interest. They are usefully (and delightfully) complemented by Chapman's watercolour sketches, somewhat naïve in style and execution but with illuminating, often humorous notes in his flowing hand.[6]

The Enriquez Papers

In Upper Burma, in the early 1950s, a French travel writer, Joseph Kessel, visited a retired Indian Army Major at his home on a spur of jungle-covered hillside overlooking the lakeside town and valley of Mogok, famous for its ruby mines. Kessel wrote, 'spread out before us was an enclosed world where everything was orderly, formal, elegant'. On the terrace above a stairway of lawns and flower-beds leading up to the teak-built house, 'we saw a tall, upright old man . . . [wearing] a tweed sports coat, flannel trousers and a woollen tie, as though he was in Surrey or Kent'. Kessel noted that everything inside the spacious, gracefully proportioned house – which, with its contents, had miraculously survived the Japanese occupation intact – was in meticulous order. 'Yet here, just as amid the lawns and flowers of the formal garden, one could sense the pain of solitude and silence.' The Major's knowledge of the land and people 'was something far beyond learning . . . it embraced the customs, the language, the history, the legends, the flora and fauna . . . Between Upper Burma and this old gentleman there was a sort of marriage of the flesh and spirit.' Kessel did not identify the Major, only the name of his house, 'Lone Spur'.[7]

More than thirty years later, at the suggestion of her cousin, Lady Greenhill,[8] Mrs Diana Burnard presented the Society with a collection of printed material and manuscripts which she had been given by an unnamed acquaintance. The papers related to Burma and had been written by a Major C. M. Enriquez. Colin Metcalfe Enriquez was born in 1884, and followed his father, Lieut Colonel Albert Dallas Enriquez (1854–1940), into the Indian Army in 1905, serving with the 21st Punjabis in Northern India and with the Kachin Rifles in Burma. His love affair with Burma began in 1913 with his first posting to the province, and he decided to retire there in 1928. Enriquez's first book was published as early as 1910,[9] followed by numerous articles and short stories on the history, social life and folklore of the Burmese people written in a light, conversational, sometimes moralising vein, under the pseudonym of 'Theophilus'. Why 'Theophilus'? He adopted the name from his mother's grandfather, Sir Theophilus Metcalfe, the British Resident in Delhi at the outbreak of the Indian Mutiny in 1857. In 1930 Enriquez had a son by his Burmese wife, Ma Me Tin. The boy was baptised Theophilus John Metcalfe Enriquez, to whom he dedicated his book *Khyberie in Burma: The*

Lieutenant C. M. Enriquez, 1912 [*RSAA Archives*]

Adventures of a Mountain Pony (1939), as he had an companion volume *Khyberie: The Story of a Pony on the Indian Frontier* (1934) to his daughter Alice Theophila Metcalfe Enriquez.

When the Japanese invaded Burma in 1942, Enriquez was forced to leave Mogok for India. A Japanese linguist, he spent the next three years in Delhi, serving in the Far Eastern Bureau of the Ministry of Information as supervisor of its Japanese Section. Here he befriended a twenty-five-year-old Japanese American from Hawaii, Ernest Sunau Miyabara, whom Enriquez later appointed his literary executor. A visit to Miyabara in Hawaii resulted in an unpublished manuscript, *Hawaiian Interlude* (1948), dedicated to 'Ernie'. Other unpublished manuscripts include an account of Enriquez's time in Delhi, whimsically drafted as the reminiscences of a dog, 'Skipper', and a critique (1946) of Britain's post-war policy in Burma, dedicated to 'our American allies who fought and died for the Liberation of Burma'.

Enriquez joined the Society in 1946, unaware that long after his death these papers would find their way to its archive.

The Fraser Bequest

From 1896 to 1902 Sir Stuart Mitford Fraser (1864–1963) was tutor and mentor to the young Maharaja of Mysore, Krishnaraja Wadiya Bahadur (1884–1940). Fraser was Resident in Mysore 1905–1910, and in Hyderabad 1914–1919. The most interesting of several items presented to the Society by his daughter is a leather-bound volume entitled *Diary of HH The Maharaja of Mysore: Provincial Tour 1901–1902*. This is a detailed account of a fifty-day tour, covering 650 miles, undertaken by Krishnaraja Wadiya (then aged seventeen) accompanied by Stuart Fraser and other officials. The diary, which includes several photographs, is written in Fraser's hand but drafted as if it were the young Maharaja's own personal memoir of the tour. Fraser also drafted for the guidance of his young charge a volume of *Notes on Law*, to which Krishnaraja appears to have made some additional entries in his own hand. In 1902 Lord Curzon visited Mysore to formally invest Krishnaraja with full ruling powers; the latter, as sovereign of the second most important princely state in India, attended Curzon's Delhi Durbar the following year. The Bequest also includes an album of photographs printed to commemorate the visit in 1906 of the Prince and Princess of Wales to see a wild elephant hunt (*kheddah*) in the Kakankota forest of Mysore, and a file of papers relating to Fraser's time in Hyderabad.

The young Maharaja of Mysore, Krishnaraja Wadiyar, 1901. Stuart Fraser and his wife on the Maharaja's left

Violet Fraser accompanied her father (then Resident in Kashmir) on his tour of the Gilgit Agency in 1913. She rode a yak between Hunza and Nagar

[*RSAA Archives*]

T. E. Lawrence: A Sketch Map[10]

Drawn in ink on a fragile sheet of greaseproof paper, Lawrence's sketch map shows a section of the route between Wejh and Aqaba taken by Sharif Nasir's expedition which culminated in the capture of Aqaba in July 1917. It embraced the expedition's route from a crossing of the Hejaz Railway between Dis'ad and Al-Mu'adhdham to Imshash Arfaja in Wadi Sirhan about 60 miles west of Jauf. Lawrence was the first westerner to travel this northward route, during the course of which he crossed the west–east tracks of Guarmani, Carruthers, Musil and Gertrude Bell.

Lawrence had no direct links with the Society, but many of his friends were members, through one of whom, Dr D. G. Hogarth (Lawrence's mentor since his Oxford days and first Director of the Arab Bureau), he established contact with Douglas Carruthers, the probable source of this copy of his traverse. During the First World War, Carruthers, whilst Honorary Secretary of the Royal Geographical Society (RGS), was engaged in map making of northern Arabia. Throughout the Arab Revolt he was in contact with the Arab Bureau in Cairo, which led to his first, indirect, contact with Lawrence. In early 1918 the *Arab Bulletin* noted that data and conclusions about the Sirhan and Jauf depression, which Carruthers had submitted to the Arab Bureau the previous October, might be modified in the light of 'more recent observations by Major T. E. Lawrence'. After the war Lawrence and Carruthers corresponded a good deal, chiefly on geographical matters; Lawrence's last letter to Carruthers was in May 1934.[11]

The sketch map has two annotations by Lawrence. First, a note of identification, the date being that of the traverse rather than that of the sketch itself:

> Hejaz Rly. to Wadi Sirhan 1:5000,000. Compass traverse.
> Names by Auda Abu Tayi. May 1917. TEL

Second, a cautionary note to the user which suggests that it was drawn by Lawrence after April 1918, probably post-war:

> This is the only drawn copy so please do not lose it prematurely. In adjusting it to GSGS 4011 (Nefud Sheet, April 1918 RGS) 1/500,000 it should be swung on Fejr and Affaja: since Rly on this sheet (based on Huber) is too far to the East, in proportion to Wadi Sirhan TEL

In a later reference to the traverse, Lawrence wrote to Hogarth, now Keeper of the Ashmolean, in June 1922:

> You know Carruthers' address . . . Do you think he would like the enclosed? Your copy of the whole will come later, but this covers the scrap of traverse which I once worked out and sent him. If he doesn't want it I'd like it back. I'm conscious of a horrible word about geographers in the middle of it: but perhaps he'll excuse it . . .

'The enclosed' was an extract from the 1922 Oxford text of *Seven Pillars of Wisdom*[12] (Chaps XXXIX–LIV of the 1935 Cape edition); 'the scrap of traverse' is the subject of this note. Although dated 1917, it is not the original sketch. That is to be found in a diary kept by Lawrence from 17 January to 28 June 1917, now in the British Library (Add. MSS

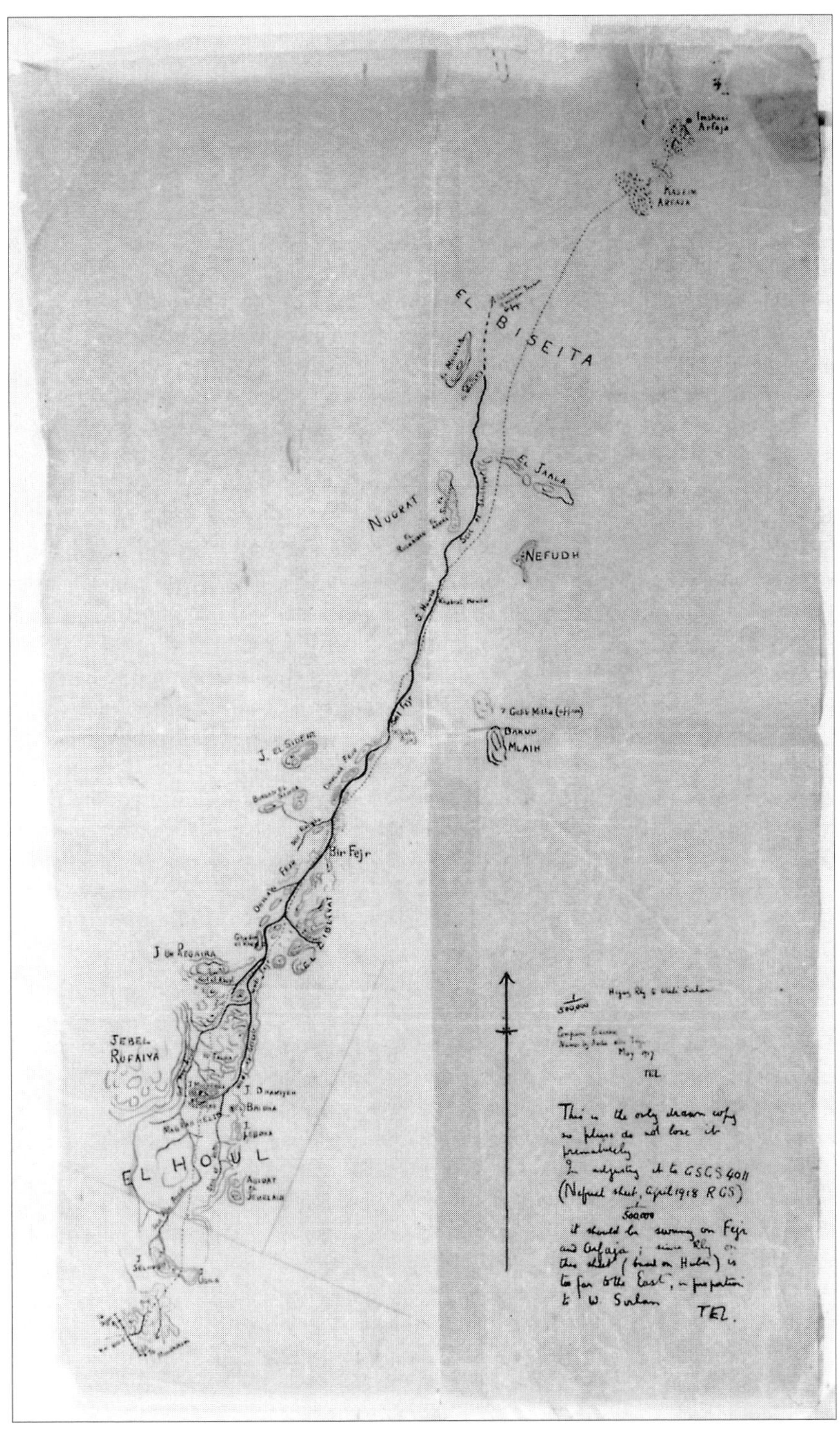

Lawrence's sketch map [RSAA Archives]

45915). Written in pencil on the back of Army Form C2121 Message and Signal pads, the entries record topographical and other details of journeys made by Lawrence in that period. Times of marches and halts, direction and bearings of prominent features are all noted and were later used by Lawrence when he translated the rough sketch into the traverse which he sent to Carruthers. His description of the terrain and notes about his companions are clearly the bare bones of his published narrative.

Carruthers (1882–1963), explorer, naturalist and writer, joined the Society in 1935 and left it a valuable collection of his books and maps. His *Arabian Adventure: To the Great Nefud in Quest of the Oryx*, published in 1935, was the full account of his historic journey in 1909–1910, the aim of which, as he reported to the RGS in March 1910, was 'to travel over and map out the blank that exists between the Hejaz Railway and the Wadi Sirhan, to determine the western limits of the Great Nefud, and to visit the oasis of Taima'.

In his Preface to *Arabian Adventure* Carruthers acknowledged Lawrence's co-operation over many years in an attempt to answer the geographical questions about, and improve the maps of, the area. The End Papers of the book are a map of *The Shararat Wilderness and Western Nefud* and, reflecting Lawrence's contribution, have considerably more detail than the RGS 1910 *Sketch Map of Northern Arabia* showing the explorations by Carruthers.

The Nefud Sheet of April 1918, referred to by Lawrence, was compiled at the RGS, almost certainly by Carruthers, and published by Ordnance Survey in May 1918. It was entered in the Map Room at the RGS in June 1918, and is now indexed under Saudi Arabia. It appears to have been a late wartime addition to the five-sheet GSGS 4011 Ottoman Empire 1:500,000 Series covering Mecca to Aleppo which was published for the Arab Bureau by the Survey of Egypt, under authority from the War Office, in early 1917. Today's maps confirm Lawrence's cautionary note that the Hejaz Railway as shown on the Nefud Sheet (at Kala'at al-Mu'adhdham) was too far East – by about twenty-two miles. However Lawrence's sketch, swung as he suggested, reduces that error by more than half.

Major General Sir Charles MacGregor

MacGregor (1840–1887) rose to become Quarter Master General of the Indian Army (1880–1885) and founder of its Intelligence Department. He proved fearless in battle, and between the Indian Mutiny and the Second Afghan War there were few campaigns in which he did not take part. He was a careerist with a talent for self-advertisement unsurpassed by any of his contemporaries. To bring his name to notice, he bombarded the press with letters, wrote many unsolicited reports, and even invented a new type of saddle; and at the despairing suggestion of his colleagues, he bought his own trumpet and learnt how to blow it! The subjects which he tackled ranged from *Clandestine Prostitution* (which doubtless won him a wide, if surreptitious, readership) to *Notes on Field Equipment of Troops for Service among Mountains*. MacGregor, who had travelled in Baluchistan and Persia in the mid-1870s, became a passionate advocate of a 'forward policy' to counter the perceived Russian threat to British India. In 1883 this led him to write one report too many: *The Defence of India*, a

Sir Charles MacGregor, Quarter Master General of the Indian Army, 1880–1885 [RSAA Archives]

detailed, supposedly confidential, assessment of the likely strengths and deployment of Russian and British Indian forces in the event of an outbreak of war between them. MacGregor concluded that 'there can never be a real settlement of the Russo-Indian question till Russia is driven out of the Caucasus and Turkistan'. To pressurise Calcutta and the Gladstone administration in London, MacGregor imprudently leaked his report to the press. The ensuring furore dashed his hopes of further promotion, and he died a sick and embittered man in 1887.[13]

His diary of the Second (mistakenly entitled 'Third') Afghan War (1879–1880) and other printed papers were presented by his widow[14] in 1923, together with a photograph of MacGregor in full military fig. Lieut Colonel A. C. Yate, then Honorary Secretary of the Society, who had himself served in the Afghan campaign, felt moved to comment on the cover of the diary: 'That any officer should have dreamed of printing such an injudiciously-written diary as this, appears to me inexplicable; and yet here it is in print, and that unquestionably by MacGregor's own order. His own egotism and self-seeking and the way in which he writes about Sir F. Roberts [later Lord Roberts of Kandahar, whom MacGregor served as Chief of Staff] and in the worst taste, jar upon one's sense of what is right and manly and dignified. In fact the man on whom this book reflects the least credit is MacGregor himself...'[15]

The Schomberg Collection

Towards the end of his life, when he was about to train for the Roman Catholic priesthood, Lieut Colonel R. C. F. Schomberg (1880–1958) presented the Society with a collection of diaries, manuscripts, photographs and maps, and a substantial cache of glass slides. Reginald Schomberg won a DSO and Bar with the Seaforth Highlanders in Mesopotamia; but peacetime soldiering had diminishing appeal and he retired from the Army in 1928. During the next twenty years he devoted most of his time and energy to the exploration of remoter parts of Central Asia. His travels yielded four books in quick succession, and a host of articles in a variety of academic journals.[16]

An austere, self-deprecating man with a dry sense of humour, Schomberg was probably never happier than in the company of his 'Hunza men'; they alone were permitted to share

Lieut Colonel R. C. F. Schomberg (centre) with fellow Seaforth Highlanders, c. 1919

Schomberg's 'Hunza men' c. 1935. Daulat Shah, his trusted headman, seated second from left

[RSAA Archives]

Camp, Soldduz, Urumiyeh Province
(c/o British Consulate,
Kermanshah): Sept. 11. 1936.

My dear Schomberg,

Your full & interesting epistle of June 24th reached me more than a month ago, and if I were not kept so busy by surveying & digging at ancient mounds, etc., I should have sent you my warm thanks for your welcome news sooner. It is good to know you well and looked after by your Hunza retainers in that rather trying region of Dravidia. I greatly admire your courage in going there for some time; for I can well imagine that neither climate nor people would be congenial to one who has travelled long in bracing mountain regions. Personally I have always felt a strong moral objection to spending one's energy in facing moist heat and all that it means for the human environment. That your Hunza people are keeping by you in such parts, too, shows their devotion to your person & their pluck, too. I trust the Indian Foreign Department will be able to find a more congenial place for making use of your services & your wide experience.

Letter from Sir Aurel Stein, 1936

Dusht Kalla
On the Caspian Sea
Septber 13th 1840

My dear Marianne

I thank God from my heart that I have been enabled to reach this in safety without the loss of either man woman or child – Heaven had mercy on the unfortunate Prisoners and granted us most favorable weather not a man or child or woman suffered from thirst hunger or fatigue not even a Camel or [illegible] lost – I have been most truly fortunate – The journey has been very exciting though rather [illegible] – What with bullying rascals [illegible] Knaves and humbugging fools there has been plenty to occupy my attention

Letter from Richmond Shakespear to his sister, Marianne Irvine, reporting his safe arrival at the Caspian 'without the loss of either man, woman or child . . .'

[RSAA Archives]

the rigours of his journeys, except on one occasion during the summer of 1946 when he was joined for a few weeks in Ladakh by a British compatriot. Mrs Marianne Williams, as the young bride of an officer in the Frontier Constabulary, recalls meeting Schomberg when he came to stay with them in the mid-1940s: she found him a considerate guest but a man with little small talk.[17]

Schomberg's typescript diaries cover his travels in Chinese Turkestan between 1926–1929 and 1930–1931. He also left the Society typescript drafts of four unpublished books: *Cold Deserts* (1937), 'an account of a journey in the deserts of a no-man's land that lies in Western Tibet beyond the Karakoram and Ladakh mountains'; *Baltistan Journey* (1943–1944); *Karakoram Finale* (1945); and *Tibetan Kashmir* (1946). In addition to Schomberg's handwritten diary for 1945, the collection also includes thirteen letters from Sir Aurel Stein (1862–1943).[18] These letters, reflecting the close friendship between the two men, afford fascinating glimpses of Stein's thoughts and preoccupations during the last seven years of his prodigiously active life.[19]

The Shakespear Papers

The papers of Sir Richmond Shakespear (1812–1861) and other members of his extended family are the pride and centrepiece of the archive.[20] They include personal letters, official documents (British, Russian and Khivan), notebooks, journals and diaries. Richmond Shakespear was born into a family with a long tradition of military and civil service in India and Afghanistan, and, later, in Assam and the Gulf. Shakespear's closest schoolboy friend was his cousin, William Makepeace Thackeray, the future novelist; from India they were sent together to school in England. Richmond's brother, George, was the model for Thackeray's Joseph Sedley in *Vanity Fair*.

Shakespear's career spans a formative period in the consolidation of British power in India, in British India's relations with Afghanistan, and in the related development of Anglo-Russian rivalry in Central Asia. In 1840, during his early career in the Bengal Artillery, he was given the task of persuading the Khan of Khiva to release 416 Russian prisoners, whom he then led on a hazardous journey to St Petersburg. This resulted in the reciprocal release by Russia of 600 Khivan captives (earning Shakespear a place 'in the calendar of [Uzbek] saints'), deprived the Russians of a

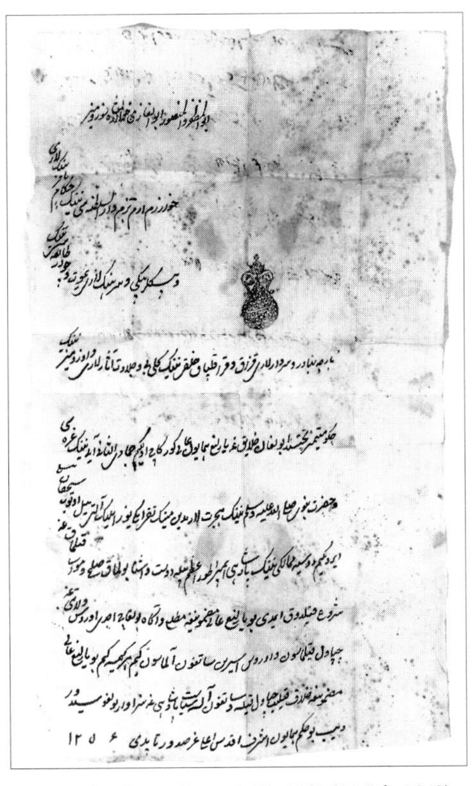

Decree dated Jumada 11 A.H. 1256 (31 July 1840) obtained by Richmond Shakespear from the Khan of Khiva, prohibiting Khivan subjects from buying Russian captives or raiding into Russian territory. Shakespear left Khiva on 15 August 1840, accompanied by 416 freed Russian prisoners, on a 500-mile march across the desert to Fort Nova Alexandroff on the eastern shore of the Caspian [RSAA Archives]

pretext for renewing their attempt to annex Khiva, and effectively delayed their conquest of the Khanate until 1873. In 1841, on the recommendation of Lord Palmerston, Shakespear, aged twenty-nine, was knighted by Queen Victoria. The following year, during the First Afghan War, he was involved in the relief of Jalalabad, and later, during the Second Sikh War, he took part in the battle of Chillianwala. He ended his career as Agent to the Governor-General for Central India, conducting important negotiations with the celebrated Rani of Bhopal, Sikander Begum, before his death at Indore in 1861.[21]

The collection also includes the unpublished autobiography of Richmond's younger son, Lieut Colonel John Shakespear (1861–1942); the diaries which he kept 1880–1896 while serving as Superintendent of the Lushai Hills on the Assam/Burma border; the unfinished manuscript of a book, together with an album of photographs, about the military expeditions (1889–1890) which led to the incorporation of the Lushai Hills into British India;[22] a manuscript history of Manipur, possibly compiled from local sources by a native clerk, and an album of photographs taken in Manipur, where Shakespear was Resident 1905–1914. Most, if not all, of these papers were presented by his widow in 1949 and 1955.

Captain John Shakespear (seated left) planning an expedition in the Assam borderlands, c. 1890 [*RSAA Archives*]

The archive also holds a typescript copy of the journal kept by a distant relative, Captain W. H. I. Shakespear (1878–1915), during his historic journey in 1914 from Kuwait, where he was serving as Political Agent, across Central Arabia to Sinai.[23]

The Stevens Bequest

In February 1904, on the eve of the Russo-Japanese War, two Russian warships, steaming out of the Korean port of Chemulpo, were attacked by a Japanese squadron. The crippled warships limped back into the harbour; the dead and wounded were carried ashore; the remaining crew were evacuated in friendly European vessels; the warships were then scuttled. At the European cemetery in Chemulpo a burial service was held for the Russian dead. Scenes of what became known as the 'Chemulpo incident' are captured in several faded images in an album of photographs bequeathed by Miss Florence Stevens (1903–1976). The album had belonged to her father, Thomas Stevens, who served in the Imperial Japanese Maritime Customs, Korea, during, and perhaps beyond, the first decade of the twentieth century. There are pictures of Chemulpo, with its Customs house, British Consulate and uncluttered landscape; of Seoul, with its pagoda-roofed city gates and busy streets; of Koreans in their distinctive national dress; and of Japanese, whose increasing presence in Korea from 1905 signified the country's new and involuntary status as a Japanese protectorate.[24]

Glass Slides

Money has been found to meet the cost of producing photographic prints from the Society's collection of more than 1,000 glass slides. With the important exception of the Bailey and Schomberg collections, most of these are the legacy of illustrated lectures given to the Society in the 1920s and 1930s. Speakers – and there is only space to mention fewer than half their number – included D. McCallum on the Nairn Route (1925), Captain Eccles on Muscat and Oman (1927), D. Bourke-Borrowes on Persia under the Pahlavis (1928), G. M. Lees on Southern Kurdistan (1928), W. E. D. Allen on Georgia (1929), M. Vyvyan on Qazwin to Trebizond (1931), H. St J. Philby on Mecca and Medina (1933), J. G. French on Afghanistan (1933), E. B. Howell on the North West Frontier (1934), J. B. Glubb on the Bedouin of Northern Arabia (1935), and W. H. Ingrams on a Journey in the Hadhramaut (1936). Prints of these slides have now been made.

Photographic Albums

For armchair travellers favouring a further, perhaps more sedate excursion through time and space, two options are recommended: a tour of the Holy Land through a sepia lens of 1875; or, at perhaps a slightly later date, following a voyage through the Suez Canal to Bombay, a tour of the metropolitan splendours of Victorian India! These two albums are of unknown provenance. There is a third, however, which deserves special mention, not only because of its intrinsic interest but because it bears the signature of the Society's founder, Alfred Cotterell Tupp.[25] This is *The Antiquities of Cambodia: A Series of Photographs Taken on the Spot* by the renowned Scottish photographer and East Asian traveller, John Thomson (1837–1921). He was the first photographer to visit Angkor Wat, and his elation at seeing what has become one of the most important sites of ancient architecture in the world, can be imagined. The book, Thomson's first, is illustrated with albumen prints, including two panoramas, pasted into the text, and was published in Edinburgh in 1867 by Edmonston and Douglas, the foremost publishers of illustrated books in Scotland at that time.

The Western Gallery, Angkor Wat

Terrace of the Elephants, Angkor Thom

John Thomson, 1866 [RSAA Archives]

The Royal Central Asian Society

Dinner Club

Index

Name	Table	No.
H.R.H. The Countess of Athlone, G.B.E.	A	11
Rt. Hon. The Earl of Athlone, K.G., P.C., G.C.B., G.C.M.G., G.C.V.O., D.S.O.	A	12
H. M. Andrews	G	30
Lt.-Col. F. C. C. Balfour, C.I.E. C.B.E.	D	66
H. R. Ballantyne	E	57
Col. E. F. W. Barker, C.B.E., D.S.O.	G	33
Major-General Sir William Beynon, K.C.I.E., C.B., D.S.O.	F	47
Miss Kathleen Beynon	E	56
The Rt. Hon. Lord Bingham, M.C.	A	1
Sir Edgar Bonham Carter, K.C.M.G.	E	50
Brig. H. E. R. Braine, C.B., C.M.G.	G	34
Mrs. Braine	G	29
Major H. M. Burton	E	55
Admiral the Earl of Cork and Orrery, G.C.B., G.C.V.O.	A	8
The Countess of Cork and Orrery	A	16
Colonel Sir Kinahan Cornwallis, K.C.M.G., C.B.E.	A	3
Captain H. F. Cox	F	39
J. C. Curry	F	41
Mrs. Curry	F	38
Colonel T. Denis Daly, M.C.	G	31
R. W. Dana, O.B.E.	D	67
Mrs. Dana	D	60
J. E. Dixon-Spain, O.B.E.	C	72
Miss Dixon-Spain	C	76
R. Faid-Ruete	E	51
Ian Fairbairn	C	73
Colonel L. H. K. Finch, D.S.O., O.B.E.	B	81
Mrs. Finch	B	90
Major R. Gale	B	88
Rt. Rev. Dr. Graham Brown, O.B.E.	F	40
J. R. Gregory	B	89
Mrs. Gregory	B	82
Major R. C. Hargreaves, M.V.O., M.C.	B	92
Col. A. P. Heneage, M.P.	E	50
S. Hillelson	E	52
Sir Ernest Hotson, K.C.S.I.	D	63
Alexander Howard	D	64
Captain E. L. Jerwood	F	44
Mrs. E. L. Jerwood	F	46
Colonel Sir Vernon Kell, K.B.E., C.B.	A	20
Admiral Sir Howard Kelly, G.B.E., K.C.B.	A	22
Lady Kelly	A	9
Group-Capt. R. T. Leather. A.F.C.	B	83
Dr. G. M. Lees, M.C., D.F.C.	E	58
Mrs. Lees	E	49
Rt. Hon. Lord Lloyd of Dolobran, G.C.S.I., G.C.I.E., D.S.O.	Chair	
The Lady Lloyd	A	14
E. D. McDermott	A	15
Brigadier N. M. McLeod, D.S.O., M.C.	G	28
Mrs. McLeod	G	35
J. G. Matthew, C.M.G., O.B.E.	F	37
Lt.-Col. H. E. Medlicott, D.S.O.	C	77
Miss V. Medlicott	C	79
Mrs. Patrick Ness	A	2
Colonel S. F. Newcombe, D.S.O.	E	48
Sir Edward Penton, K.B.E.	C	75
Richard Pilkington, M.P.	E	51
Major J. F. A. Postance	B	87
Sir John Pratt, K.B.E., C.M.G.	F	45
General Sir Felix Ready, G.B.E., K.C.B.	A	4
Sir Benjamin Robertson, K.C.S.I. K.C.M.G.	B	91
Lady Robertson	B	82
Major-General H. Rowan Robinson, C.B., C.M.G., D.S.O.	C	80
Mrs. Rowan Robinson	C	71
Colonel E. M. Routh	F	43
Rt. Hon. Sir Horace Rumbold, Bt., G.C.B., G.C.M.G., M.V.O.	A	17
Major F. F. Rynd	B	84
Major A. M. Sassoon, M.C.	C	78
Mrs. A. Sassoon	C	74
Sir Malcolm Seton, K.C.B.	D	59
Lady Seton	A	7
Sir Henry Sharp, C.S.I. C.I.E.	D	65
General Sir John Shea, G.C.B., K.C.M.G.	A	19
Miss Jane Shea	A	21
Major R. A. Slee	D	69
Miss Freya Stark	E	54
Mrs. F. E. Storrs	D	62
Lady Sykes	D	68
Miss Ella Sykes	D	66
Brig.-Gen. Sir Percy Sykes, K.C.M.G., C.B.	D	61
Colonel J. K. Tod, C.M.G.	A	23
Mrs. Tod	A	5
Mrs. Alec Tweedie	A	18
H. E. Sheikh Hafiz Wahba	A	10
General Sir Arthur Wauchope, G.C.B., G.C.M.G. C.I.E.	A	6
A. Kenneth Williams	E	53
Miss R. O. Wingate	F	42
Major W. S. Wingate-Gray, M.C.	G	36
Mrs. Wingate-Gray	G	27

Tuesday, January 10th, 1939

'. . . attended by some 29 ladies.'

from a low of mid-20s to an average of 50s to a high in the 70s. (Much as in 2001 in fact.) There was a suggestion that the dinners be alternated with luncheons, though nothing seems to have come of this. The 1930s saw as equally interesting a programme as the decade before. For example, 'American opinion of British policy in India and its repercussions in India'; 'Minorities in Iraq: Air operations against the Kurds'; 'Russia from a Businessman's Point of View'; 'Islam Today' (the Turkish and Egyptian Ambassadors and Mr Yusif Ali) and 'Islam and the War' (1940). During this period there were seven meetings on China and six on Palestine.

The Dinner Club was able to function throughout 1939 and the first half of 1940. In keeping with war-time economy it determined that the cost of meals should not exceed 4/- nor three courses. Draught beer was to be drunk instead of wine, and evening dress, which had previously been required, was optional. But the constant bombing throughout the autumn of 1940 and 1941 made it difficult to continue meetings. However, it was decided 'to carry on the objects for which the Club was established' and a few small luncheons were held. Their object was to allow the diplomatic representatives of Muslim countries to give their views informally about Islam and the War. In this way many useful conversations were held, and contacts established with the British government in a way which would not have been possible officially. This reflected Sir Harold Nicolson's comment about the Society in 1940: 'A marvellous safety valve through which steam can escape without doing any damage at all to the mechanism of State.' Attendance at these lunches was by invitation and no notices were sent out to members.

It was not until 1950 that the idea of resurrecting the Dinner Club was suggested and Colonel Newcombe, still nominally both its Chairman and Honorary Secretary, was approached. The Society's Secretary, Miss Wingate, wrote to Newcombe pointing out that thirty-six members had gone on paying their standing orders throughout the war. They could rightly expect a refund or have their Society subscriptions proportionately adjusted but either way 'in the Society's present financial position this would be rather a shock'. She suggested further that the interests of members had now turned somewhat to the Near East (the area best known to Newcombe, who had worked with T. E. Lawrence) and 'you did pick your Dinner Club pretty carefully before the war and none of them is likely to have turned into a bore in the meantime'.

Newcombe, who had by then retired as Honorary Secretary of the main Society, agreed to write to all past members but handed his Honorary Secretary post of the Club to Air Commodore A. C. Buss who, coincidentally, was also an Arabist. Thirty-nine of the former fifty-eight members still in contact agreed to continue their membership. The question of lady members again arose and Newcombe had to write to the two remaining saying: 'The Club will have to continue to be run in an economical way and, for the time being, as with similar clubs, will have to be for men only.'

The Dinner Club records for the period 1950–1960 are no longer extant but it seems the first resumed meeting was held in May 1950. By the 1960s, with Mr Colin Rees Jenkins as Secretary, the Club was functioning much as before except that there was one main speaker only at each meeting. Many of these were serving, or recently retired, senior diplomats both British and foreign, who could speak on their areas with fresh authority. The Club remained unavowed to the main Society and more than one Chairman was reprimanded by the Honorary Secretaries for letting its existence slip out. This arcanum seems strange given that notices about its meetings appeared occasionally on the Court Page of *The Times* and the *Daily Telegraph*. By 1968 membership had climbed to 156 and ladies were admitted as guests. By the mid-1980s, under Mr James Fulton, 21 international companies were admitted as Corporate Members and by 1995 with Lieut Colonel A. P. H. B. Fowle as the new (and current) Honorary Secretary, the permitted membership ceilings had been raised to 200 Ordinary and 70 Corporate Members.

Post-war meetings were held first at the RAF and RAC Clubs or the British Empire Society, but by 1970 had moved to the House of Lords where it was necessary for one of the Society's Peers to be present. They were held originally in the main dining room but after the House took to sitting in the evenings they were moved to the Cholmondeley Room, which remains the present venue. Subjects continued to reflect the current political concerns and a further selection are worth quoting to show this. In the 1960s, for example: 'Vietnam'; 'Interpretation of Recent Events in India' and 'The Naval Situation in S. E. Asia when we withdraw from the Far East'. In the 1970s and 1980s, 'Impressions of Soviet Central Asia'; 'Current Affairs in Japan' (HE Mr Maraichi Fugiyama, the Japanese Ambassador); 'Contemporary China' (Professor Wang Gung Wu); 'The Great Game revisited: Issues in the Sub-continent' and 'Observing Islam Today'. Finally, a selection from 1990–2000. 'Middle East Terrorism'; 'Central Asia: The End of the Cold War'; 'China: What is going on there?' and 'Succeeding Together: Britain and Asia in a Global Market Place'.

Though the *de jure* ruling which debarred women from full membership of the Club continued throughout the 1960s and 1970s there was a gradual increase in the number of women attending its dinners, both as guests and as members in their own right. In December 1994 the rules were revised to allow membership to be open, by invitation, to all members of the Society, regardless of sex or country of birth. The invitation was dependent on both Ordinary and Corporate Members being proposed and seconded and finally accepted by the committee, thus allowing women to become full members of this previously male enclave. Despite this relaxation it was not until February 1996 that this 'secret society' within the Society proper was given formal publicity to the entire membership.

The Royal Society for Asian Affairs is a charitable society and as such is not allowed to confer any direct personal financial advantage on its members. In order to meet this legal requirement the Dinner Club continues to be independent of the main Society, with a separate subscription and a separate membership. In December 2000 it numbered 130 Ordinary and 31 Corporate Members.

The Dinner Club remains indeed 'A special feature of the Society'. Apart from the recent avowal, little has changed in the pattern of its activities since its inception in 1921, except the costs. But the range of talks on topical political issues, still delivered on 'Chatham House rules', provides a uniquely candid and knowledgeable exposé not always possible in the open forum of the Society's main lectures.

XII

A ROLE IN EDUCATION

This Society has an enormous role and influence, particularly in education . . . it is the ability to spread that knowledge and educate others that is so important.

HRH The Princess Royal, Annual Dinner, 1993

The Founding Fathers of the Society saw one of its principal objectives as being educative. From the outset the rules stated an aim to be 'to advance the study of languages, literature, art, history, religious activities, usages, institutions, customs and manners of Central Asia and adjoining countries'. And 'to promote the study and investigation of questions and matters concerning those countries and to make more accessible to the general public a knowledge of all problems and conditions which affect them'. The Society has done this through the medium of its lectures, articles in its *Journal*, seminars, study groups and by creating a panel of speakers prepared to give talks to schools and institutions. As early as 1906 the retiring chairman, Sir Edwin Collen, was able to say: 'I believe the influence of this small society is growing, that it fulfils the aims and missions its founders had in view and that by degrees we may be able to break down the stupendous barrier of ignorance about Eastern problems which at present stands in all its solid indifference before us.'

In pursuit of its aim to advance the study of Asian languages and cultures the Society associated itself closely with moves to found a School of Oriental Studies (SOS) which later became the School of Oriental and African Studies (SOAS). This was on the initiative of General Edward Chapman, who had had a long and eventful career in India before his retirement in 1901. In a lecture to the Society in December 1903 on 'Our Commercial Policy in the East', Chapman said: 'I, for one, would hail with delight an announcement that our Council were prepared to initiate steps which may lead to the formation of a National Oriental School of Learning in London ... the Royal Asiatic Society would, I am certain, be ready to join us in an endeavour to create such a school.' Chapman prefaced these remarks with a quotation from a recent book by the influential *Times* correspondent, Mr Valentine

General Sir Edward Chapman

Chirol (Chairman of the Society in 1907–1908): 'That with our vast interests in all parts of the East, this country should still be [the] only one amongst the chief countries of Europe that does not possess any national institute for the study of Oriental languages ... is an almost unaccountable fact, which increases the difficulty of finding at a moment's notice suitable men even for the posts which are recognised to be the most urgently needed.' Chapman's idea was by no means new. It had first been voiced by Sir Richard Wellesley in 1798 when he was Governor General of India, and by the start of the twentieth century there were two colleges in London, and others at provincial universities, that did teach Oriental languages. But a need was felt to create one major establishment in London dedicated to this purpose.

In June 1904 the Royal Asiatic Society (RAS) replied favourably to Chapman's suggestion and a joint committee was set up with Sir Alfred Lyall, Colonel H. Picot, Sir Martin Conway, Sir Thomas Holdich, General Chapman and, later, Mr William Irvine, as the Society's representatives. In November of that year Professor T. W. Rhys Davids, Secretary of the RAS, lectured the Society on 'Oriental Studies in England and Abroad'. In November 1905, the Senate of London University agreed to a resolution from its Academic Council that 'A Committee be appointed to consider the re-organisation of Oriental Studies in the University and to suggest a scheme therefor'. In March 1906 Mr Irvine, who had become the Society's most active member on this matter, reported to Council on a recent meeting of that committee which he had attended. It was held under the auspices of the University of London and chaired by Lord Reay, a former Governor of Bombay and then President of both the RAS and the British Academy. The resulting proposal was that a joint deputation should be made to the Prime Minister, Sir Henry Campbell-Bannerman, and Council decided to write to all Members of Parliament who were members of the Society, to ask if they would join it. Action at this level was thought appropriate because one purpose of the proposed school was to train officials to undertake the government's imperial responsibilities more ably.

A joint delegation from those institutions interested in the creation of an Oriental Language School was received by the Prime Minister in December 1906. Members of the Society were included either by dint of having common membership with the RAS or, like the Society's Founder and Honorary Treasurer, Dr Cotterell Tupp, as members of the London University Committee in their own right. There is a terse and rather curious two-line entry in the Society's minute book for 4 December 1906: 'The Society received no notice of the Deputation on Oriental Studies which was received by the Prime Minister on December 3rd.' This suggests that the Society was not included under its own name and there is no mention of it being so in the official histories of SOAS[1] and the RAS[2]. While the leading part in subsequent developments was taken by the University of London it is likely that General Chapman's original initiative, and the Society's members on the joint committee, were major factors in turning talk into action.

In 1909 the government gave approval for the creation of such a school as part of London University. Because of the war and the delay in finding premises it was not opened until early 1917. The school's first Director was Sir Denison Ross who joined the Society in 1925, served on its Council and became a Vice President while still in that post. It can thus be seen that the Society had close links with SOS, which became SOAS in 1938, and these continue to this day. The 'Future of Asian Studies in the United Kingdom' was the subject of one of the Society's Special Study Groups in 1981 when, appropriately, it was chaired by Sir Cyril Philips, then recently retired as the Director of SOAS.[3] A

Sir Denison Ross

The first SOS building at Finsbury Circus

[Courtesy of SOAS]

representative from the School's academic staff is normally a member of the Society's Council.

The Society could not claim to have had any such similar role in the setting up in 1944 of an Arabic language school, the Middle East Centre for Arab Studies (MECAS), located firstly in Jerusalem and then at Shemlan in the Lebanon. The Centre, administered by the Foreign Office, was open to students from the Diplomatic Service, the British Council, the armed services, oil companies, banks and other commercial bodies.[4] But its concept was in keeping with the ideas of the Society and it is worth noting here that most of those involved in its foundation, in some way or another, and mentioned in the opening chapter of Sir James Craig's history of the school, were at that time members of the Society.[5] Among those were The Hon. Robin Maugham, Brigadier Sir Illtyd Clayton, Sir Kinahan Cornwallis, Sir Harold MacMichael, Brigadier J. B. Glubb, Mr E. A. Chapman-Andrews, Mr Albert Hourani and Miss Freya Stark. Also, importantly, Mr C. A. F. Dundas, who, based in Cairo, had from 1936 to 1942, been the British Council's first independent representative in the Middle and Near East, before being attached to the Foreign Office.[6] Bertram Thomas, who became its first Director, was a long-standing member, joining the Society in 1922. He served on the Council from 1931 to 1936 and then became a Vice President. In January 1945, six months after MECAS was founded, Sir Percy Sykes, one of the two Honorary Secretaries, wrote to Thomas expressing the Society's appreciation for maintaining such close links and for persuading so many of his students to join it. In 2000 some fifty-five members of the MECAS Association, its graduate 'Old Boys' body, were also members of the RSAA.

Hon. Robin Maugham

Robin Maugham's claims to have fostered the original concept of MECAS have, as Sir James Craig notes, to be viewed with some circumspection. In 1944 he tried to set up a counterpart establishment in London. In a long letter to the Society, dated 30 October 1944, he refers to his role in establishing MECAS and says there must be a corresponding Middle East Centre in London. He had discussed these ideas with Colonel Newcombe, Colonel Elphinstone, Major Altounyan, Brigadier Glubb and Mr Beavan of the British Council. The Centre, Maugham stressed, should be in the concept of a Club where officers returning from the Middle East could maintain contact and keep abreast of Arab affairs, young English students of Arab affairs and Arab students coming to London to study could meet and where arrangements could be made for Arabs to be invited to stay in British homes. It could also be a training centre for British Council officials. Maugham ends his letter by suggesting that all the associations in London, which are concerned in any way with Arab affairs, such as the Anglo-Egyptian and Anglo-Iraqi Societies, should house themselves under one roof, though in separate rooms. This conglomerate would become the Middle East Centre he had outlined.

Colonel Newcombe, joint Honorary Secretary, passed Maugham's letter to the Chairman, General Sir John Shea. The General, probably wishing to have little to do with the mercurial Maugham (who was the novelist Somerset Maugham's nephew), minuted somewhat drily: 'I am convinced that if there is any suggestion of forming one single central club that the approach to the other clubs be made by Maugham and not us.' Newcombe subsequently read the letter to Council who decided that the matter 'should be deferred', a favourite formula for getting rid of a troublesome item. Maugham eventually joined the Council in May 1948, resigning a year later 'as I am too much abroad but will re-join when settled in England', which in the event he never did.

However dismissive Council may have been of Maugham's report, when it came to offering evidence to the Scarbrough Committee, set up in early 1945 to study the question of the post-war teaching of Oriental, Slavonic, East European and African languages in Britain, it did draw on some of his suggestions. Three members represented the Society on the committee, Brigadier General Sir Osborne Manse, the Central Asian missionary Miss Mildred Cable and the Treasurer, Major Edward Ainger. The Earl of Scarbrough himself became both the President of the Society and Chairman of SOAS in the following decade. The Society's representatives emphasised that Oriental studies were not just a question of linguistics: 'It does not appear to us that the objects which your committee have in mind can be realised unless intimate sound contact between European and Oriental races can be achieved and existing race and class prejudices broken down... In order to provide greater facilities for these contacts between British and Foreign students we recommend that centres should be established in London... one for the Middle East, one for the Far East and one for India... Of equal importance will be the establishment of centres in each of the foreign countries where British students can freely meet their Oriental opposite numbers.'

In the early stages of the Second World War the Society received a letter from the Education Officer of the War Office asking it to provide lecturers to speak to soldiers and airmen based at establishments in the Home Counties. Soon after its end, the Society became concerned about the need to educate foreign students and for their welfare whilst in this country. It sent a memorandum to the British Council and to some government departments, suggesting that special officers be appointed in each university to look after the welfare of foreign students, and that places be kept open in British universities for Asiatic students, especially in the engineering field, after pre-courses in English. There was also a suggestion that Arabic should be taught at some public schools.

The Society, always with a mind to influence and educate young people, has had an interest in schools. In October 1922 Council proposed that the Society should 'give lectures to Public Schools and Working Men's Clubs'. Colonel C. B. Stokes, formerly of Skinner's Horse, a hero of Dunsterforce in Baku and a Military Attaché in Teheran, was appointed to make the necessary arrangements. The retired Bishop of Madras was asked to serve on the sub-committee formed for that purpose. Nothing much seems to have evolved from this unlikely coupling and a year later the minute book records that the idea had been postponed 'until it is seen whether schools would welcome this approach'. The first Headmaster of a public school to join the Society was Mr John Bell of St Paul's, London, in 1931.

In September 1949 the Chairman, Lieut General Sir Adrian Carton de Wiart, asked all members of Council to send their copies of the *Journal*, after use, to the Headmasters of their old schools for their libraries; this in the hope that schools would then become *Journal* subscribers. In the early 1980s there was a renewed attempt to penetrate the school system. Mr W. J. Watts was placed in charge of the education programme. He compiled a panel of some thirty speakers who were prepared to give lectures to schools, groups, businessmen, cultural organisations and colleges of further education. The Headmasters' Conference, selected public and state schools and institutions, the Royal Overseas League and the Royal Commonwealth Society were so informed.

In 1998 a new initiative was made to recruit schools as Affiliate Members and involve them in the Society's activities. It was interested especially in those in the London area. A fresh sub-committee under Mr Robert Binyon was formed and a new panel of speakers drawn up. At the time of writing the following schools have joined: Abingdon, City of London (Boys), Dauntsey's, Eton, Royal Grammar School High Wycombe and Westminster.

In October 1983 Dr Ina Russell replaced Mr Watts as the Society's education officer. In an article in the June 1985 edition of the *Journal* she outlined the Society's current activities in this field. She pointed out that if, as was often asserted, the twenty-first century would be that of the Third World then it was time that Asia, which included many of the developing countries, should be better understood. To make the idea behind the panel of speakers better known, the Society organised a seminar at SOAS to an invited audience that included participants from Bristol, Nottingham and Cambridge Universities, and Directors of Education and representatives of the multi-ethnic inspectorate of the Inner London Education Authority (ILEA). The theme, 'Britain's Farthest Neighbours', drew attention to the importance of Asia to the United Kingdom. Chaired by Professor Charles Beckingham, the speakers were Sir Michael Wilford, who spoke about the Far East, Mr St John Armitage on Arab countries of the Gulf and Dr Dennis Duncanson on the problems of education in South East Asia. Mr Peter Sandersley, of the Overseas Development Agency (ODA), an Affiliate Member of the Society, spoke on administering UK aid to the area.

A follow-up seminar was convened on 20 March 1986 at Millbank School in London, under the joint auspices of the Society, SOAS and the ILEA, the latter providing Mr Alyn Davies as Chairman. The three Society speakers stressed the importance of Asia in the modern world and the necessity for providing Asian studies as part of the curriculum at all stages of education in Britain. They explained ways in which RSAA resources could be utilised for this. Sir James Craig spoke on the importance of the Middle East, not only for British interests, but for the linguistic, religious and cultural achievements of its people. Sir Michael Wilford, in summarising the problems in the Far East, made the telling point that 'These are subjects which must be of interest because it is the youth who are going to have to live through them; we will all be dead!' Professor Charles Beckingham concluded his talk about the educational programme of the RSAA: 'I think that this ignorance about Asia, which so much worried the founders of our Society, is still a very serious factor.' A thirty-one page report on the proceedings entitled *The Challenge of Asia* was issued jointly by the Society and the ILEA.

The Society's educative role is still mainly exercised through the medium of its lectures and the articles carried in its *Journal*, with occasional study groups and seminars. It has found it more difficult to penetrate the education system as such, not through any lack of interest but because schools in particular are tightly bound up in their own activities, and they fail, perhaps, to comprehend fully the assets the Society can offer, which are thus under-exploited. Not only does it have its own panel of speakers, but it can find others outside the Society. Recently a London school wanted a speaker on the Middle East Peace Process. The Society was able to offer a Member of Council, a retired Ambassador, much of whose career had been spent dealing with the Arab–Israel conflict.[7]

It may be argued that information about Asia is available today from many sources, not least the Internet. But nothing can replace direct human contact between those who have had long experience of Asia and those who are keen to learn and question. The RSAA has a very considerable store of knowledge which it is keen to share with others. As Lord Jenkins, the Society's guest at its Annual Dinner in 1990 said: 'In modern jargon the Society has become a resource centre and anyone who seeks to learn about those parts of our globe can come to the Society and never go away empty handed.'

XIII

THE TOURS

by Marinel FitzSimons, MBE

When you have heard you must see and when you have seen you must judge then with your heart.

HE Phagna Inpeng Suryadha, Ambassador of Laos, quoting a Lao proverb to define the work of the Society, Annual Dinner, 1973

The year 1971 was the Society's seventieth anniversary, and to mark the occasion the Earl of Selkirk, then President, suggested a tour. This, enjoyable in itself, might also make the Society better known and attract new members. A two-weeks visit to Southern Anatolia was arranged, and in May of that year 36 members flew to Istanbul and on to Izmir, driving from there to Antalya and east along that beautiful coast to Ankara. On the group's return there were requests for another tour. No one at that time foresaw that they would become an almost annual event.

There have now been 28 tours, and 31 different countries visited, some more than once. The largest group was 40 members, the smallest 10. The original aim has been well achieved; over 600 members have travelled with the Society, some coming from Hong Kong, Australia, New Zealand, the USA and South America, as well as from Europe. New members have been recruited, lasting friendships made and, more importantly, the Society has been brought together as a family.

The choice of country was decided by Council, and there was always someone with knowledge of a given area, either there or among the membership, to advise on an itinerary. Only when every detail had been investigated would travel agents be asked for quotations. Thus costs were kept low, the tour tailor-made and time allowed for overseas members to apply. The itinerary for that first tour was planned by Mr Wilfred Seager, and its organisation was overseen by Air Chief Marshal Sir John Whitworth Jones, who went to great trouble over this and the following venture.

Although outside guest lecturers were invited on occasions, the excellent guides provided and the knowledge available within the group was usually sufficient. Ambassadors and British High Commissioners in the countries visited were frequently members of the Society and laid on receptions. Curators of museums, academics, local archaeologists and similar experts were always ready to meet us and give talks; British Council representatives were particularly helpful.

Accommodation varied enormously, and when the preliminary details of a tour were circulated a note was invariably included to the effect that 'those putting their creature comforts above the general interest should not apply'!

The age in the groups ranged from the early twenties to the mid-eighties, and there would be a mixture of interests: some were academics, some botanists or ornithologists, whilst others joined for nostalgic reasons or just had 'itchy feet'. They were happy groups. Our current President, Lord Denman, and our Chairman, Sir Donald Hawley, together with Lady Hawley, came on several occasions.

The early tours averaged two weeks: this was mandatory in China, whilst Burma permitted only one. But as distances increased three weeks became the norm. And although rest days were allowed for, they were not generally appreciated. Enthusiastic members would clamour for an extra excursion, saying they could rest when they got home.

Space allows for only glimpses into a few selected tours but these personal reminiscences should provide the reader with some idea of the pleasures, vicissitudes and excitements experienced.

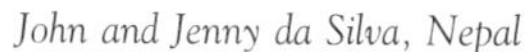

John and Jenny da Silva, Nepal

Dr Victor Funnell near Turfan, Sinkiang

Afghanistan 1972

The group visiting Afghanistan in 1972 was large so we divided into parties of twenty, each covering the same route reversely and using the Kabul Hotel as a base. Sir Gordon Whitteridge, a former ambassador to Afghanistan, led one group and Dr André Singer, a young anthropologist with experience of the country, the other. Mr Peers Carter, Ambassador at the time, enjoyed showing us over Curzon's embassy with its legendary garden and library. Word spread among young English volunteers who were working in and around Kabul that there was a strange English group in the Hotel. One by one they dropped in to investigate – and four became Junior Members.[1] Food throughout the tour, consisting of the traditional local dishes, was plentiful. However, one older member, dubious about culinary matters in Afghanistan, had taken forty hard-boiled eggs with her!

In Bamiyan our yurts, each holding two people, were pitched on a high plateau looking across to the two Buddhas set into the cliff on the far side of the valley. We climbed up inside the main Buddha, where frescoes were being restored by an Indian team, to be rewarded by a stupendous view of the valley with the snow-capped mountains of the Hindu Kush in the background.[2]

In Mazar-i-Sharif, reached after a kebab lunch eaten sitting on carpets in the bazaar at Tashkurgan, we were taken to see the shrine of Hazrat Ali, the Prophet's cousin and son-in-law. The sun was setting and our female members, by now well-versed, kept well to the perimeter. The road back to Kabul led us over the Salang Pass and through the Salang Tunnel. Little did we foresee its use some years later.

Memories of Afghanistan are happy for us: the peace and quiet of Babur's tomb and gardens, the wonderful displays in the Kabul museum, the drive over the Khyber Pass to Peshawar, the kindness and dignity of the people, the colourful clothes worn, especially in Mazar where men in splendid striped *chapans* galloped around on magnificent horses. In addition to the rugs, the blue pottery from Istalif and glass from Herat, brought back by many members, a small cutting from an oleander in Jalalabad flourished and blossomed for years on a Chelsea balcony.

China

We visited China three times, in 1974, 1975 and 1979. In February 1974 we were the first unofficial group to be allowed into the country. We owed this to our member Sir John Keswick, a former long-time resident in that country for whom the Chinese obviously had great affection. Together with Lady Keswick, he accompanied us on our first tour and Joe Ford, who started his career with the China Consular Service, came on the following two. We understood later that our visit was to give the Chinese the opportunity to decide whether more commercial groups might safely be allowed to enter. We must have behaved fairly well! It was an interesting time, still in Mao's day and in the midst of the Lin Piao–Confucius problem and a minor revolution.

From the Hong Kong border at Shumchun we had to carry our luggage across the bridge – there were no luxury trains then. On the Chinese side we were greeted by loudspeakers blaring out 'The East is Red'. We were ushered into a waiting room and given copies of *The Thoughts of Mao*, which one member thought was a copy of the New Testament until he looked inside. From the border to Guangzhou the countryside was lovely. There were no industrial cities then – just paddy fields, terrace cultivation and regiments of orderly ducks, a picture completed by the Hakka men and women in enormous lampshade hats.

The weather was cold but not bitterly so, and we had the Great Wall practically to ourselves, as we did the Ming Tombs. We saw these places again in the sunshine of September 1975, still deserted. But on our next visit, on a wet day in June 1979, there were hordes of other foreign tourists and this made some feel that our first visit, with its distinct touch of fear, had been more adventurous and more fun.

From Beijing, in 1974, we visited Changsha, en route for Mao's birthplace at Shao Shan. Unexpectedly our plane descended at a small airport in the middle of nowhere. We were given lunch and remained there for several hours. Only later did we learn that there had been riots and shooting in Changsha; we had arrived in the midst of a mini Cultural Revolution.

In Hanchow in 1975 our botanists in particular were in their seventh heaven. At the end of the tour they tactfully suggested it might be useful if the flowers at the Botanical Gardens were labelled with their Latin names and we believe this practice was subsequently adopted. In Sian in 1979 we were taken to a performance of *Swan Lake*. We asked if we might send the ballerina some flowers, a suggestion not well received. However, the next morning a bouquet was produced for us. It consisted of two artificial chrysanthemums and two artificial arum lilies!

The climax of our sojourn in Sian was a visit to the pit where the pottery figures and horses of the Emperor Ch'in Shih Huang Ti's army were being excavated. Looking down into what appeared to be a large construction site, we saw rows and rows of warriors and horses, some complete and some still being unearthed. These were images being uncovered after two thousand years, but the faces were so human and individual they seemed to be gazing up at us with the same wonder as we were down at them.

Flying to Lanchow and the Yellow River, the next one thousand miles to Urumchi were by rail with a two-night stop in Dunhuang, reached by alighting from the train at a halt in the middle of the desert. In Dunhuang, associated with the Society's eminent member, the late Sir Aurel Stein, we visited many of the Cave Temples in the small oasis, and stayed in an old Chinese inn.

Sunday was the day the local population went to the Kazakh horse races in the Tien Shan, the highlight of which was a form of *Buzkasi*, held in a huge valley surrounded by steep slopes. At the end of the game the competitors lined up to salute the spectators, some of whom accepted an invitation to try out the horses and were led sedately around. Suddenly our own Colonel George Bradbury rose up from his seat, tore down the hillside and mounted a horse. The Kazakhs soon saw that he and his mount were one and gave him his head. He galloped around the course imitating everything that had gone before, to the cheers of the spectators. We were all bursting with pride after we realised he was not going to break his neck. He said afterwards that he had not been on a horse since his polo days forty years before.

Iraq 1978

Although free to carry out our planned itinerary, we were certainly aware of a 'police state' atmosphere. Professor H. W. F. Saggs, from the Department of Semetic Languages, Cardiff University, was with us as Guest Lecturer. We flew to Basra and then continued by road to Al Qurna (alleged site of the Garden of Eden) and on to Al Kabaish on the Euphrates. Here we drifted along narrow waterways banked with reeds eight feet high, passing floating reed houses, waving children and half-submerged water buffaloes. We basked unashamedly in the glory of Wilfred Thesiger's name as a member of the Society. Everyone we met was delighted to have news of him.

We had hoped to visit the Rowanduz Gorge but, told the road was closed, were taken instead to the Dokan Dam built by Binnie and Partners. Geoffrey Binnie, a member of the Society, was unable to be with us but his wife, Elspeth, was. We were allowed to swim in the dam but photography was strictly forbidden, which prompted Elspeth to remark quietly 'they little know we have all the plans at home in a drawer'.

Outside Sulamania in Kurdistan, where a nightly curfew from 6 p.m. was in force, we had an unexpectedly pleasing encounter with the military. Taken into the mountains one afternoon, we had started back in good time and passed the 4 p.m. checkpoint when our bus broke down. It was soon obvious that despite our driver's efforts at repair we should not reach Sulamania by the 6 p.m. curfew, and our guide went off to seek advice from officialdom, leaving us locked up in the bus. We soon released ourselves. Luckily we were halted beside a *chaikhana*, which was soon denuded of Pepsi, orange, lemon fizz and the like. Professor Saggs agreed to give a talk on Babylon, which we were to visit subsequently. When darkness had fallen, our guide returned to find, to his astonishment, his charges perched on stools and upturned petrol cans, listening in fascination to the Professor. To our surprise jeeps then suddenly arrived and we set off with a military escort, guns at the ready, to spend the night on a high plateau in bungalows built for Turkish workers, as yet unoccupied.

North West Frontier 1981 and Chitral 1995

Twenty-nine members flew to Rawalpindi, where the Pakistan Embassy in London had arranged for two liaison officers to meet and escort us throughout the tour. They were good humoured, knowledgeable and a tremendous help.

Over the years we have been much impressed by the affection in which the British army is still held in India and Pakistan. And on this North West Frontier tour, wherever we went – in the bazaars or in the countryside or simply pausing at a wayside fruit or vegetable stall – there was usually someone whose brother, father or uncle had served in the British army, and who wanted to talk to us.

This memorable tour was planned with the help of Dr André Singer. We camped in the Kaghan valley beside the river from where we were able in the evening to watch the sheep, goats and cattle wending a zig-zag course down to the river to drink, bells ringing. A lovely sight and sound. Subsequently we made an alarming drive in jeeps to the 10,500 ft Lake Saif-ul-Muluk.

The flight to Gilgit from Rawalpindi was tense. After a delay caused by bad weather, the plane was about level with Nanga Parbat mountain when the pilot announced he was turning back due to cloud. 'No, no,' shouted our Colonel Tony Fowle, 'Go on.' The pilot was so startled he did go on! But as we neared our destination he announced dramatically, 'We are now approaching Gilgit, *Inshallah*. Goodbye.' One of our group had arranged a rendezvous with his old bearer who lived in the hills above Gilgit. As our plane touched down on the runway a little figure could be seen running across the field. It was the bearer, come to greet his old friend with enormous affection.

We visited the Mir's Palace in the Hunza valley, where we were confronted by photographs of Kings George V and VI and Lord Curzon, and the Raja of Punial at Shir Qila. The Raja was a regular listener to the BBC World News in Urdu and begged us to ensure the broadcasts continued.

This tour included a drive through the Khyber Pass to the Afghan border at Torkham. Two days were then spent in Swat, where the Wali entertained us to tea in his beautiful garden. He spoke warmly of his old friend Sir Olaf Caroe, one of many tributes to him during our visit. In Rawalpindi we were invited to a reception given by General Sawar Khan and his wife at the Artillery Officers' Mess. There were five generals present, all former pupils of Colonel Fowle.

There was a return to the area in 1995 to commemorate the centenary of the Siege of Chitral when we followed the route taken by the relieving forces led by Colonel Kelly and General Low.

It was in Gilgit that Kelly's epic march started and here we embarked in eighteen jeeps, two of which carried our cooks and tents. As we reached the Shandur Pass at over 12,000 ft we were able to appreciate the determination and courage of his men. Arriving at Mastuj Fort, which first had to be relieved by Kelly, we were welcomed by Colonel Khushwaqt-ul-Mulk, a son of Shuja-ul-Mulk, the twelve-year-old who had been installed as Mehtar.

Raja Jan Alam of Punial

Continuing to Chitral the various battles fought by Kelly's men along the route were studied. On arrival there we were welcomed by the Mehtar's uncle, Prince Asad-ur-Rahman, who introduced us to Fateh Ali Shah, whose grandfather and great grandfather had both been in the Fort at the time of the Siege. It was exactly one hundred years and six months since Robertson and his comrades had sat down to dinner in the Fort with Kelly and his officers. Hung inside were the horns of a Marco Polo sheep, the Society's emblem, under which our President was photographed.

The remainder of the tour followed in reverse direction the route taken by General Low's relief force, which had started at Nowshera. After a visit to Peshawar, a farewell dinner was held in Islamabad, when Colonel Khushwaqt-ul-Mulk presented a bronze *markhor* to our President and spoke feelingly of the peace and stability in Chitral that had followed the events of 1895.

Kashmir and Ladakh 1986

We visited Ladakh in 1986, after a week in Kashmir. There had been rumblings of trouble, and on our return to Srinagar from Ladakh to catch the plane to Delhi we were given an armed escort to the airport.

In Kashmir we enjoyed gliding gently in shikaras on the Dal and Nagin lakes, exploring the beauties of the Mogul and Shalimar Gardens, and visiting the old Residency where Sir Francis Younghusband ended his career in India. We acclimatised ourselves in Gulmarg at 8,000 ft, where two members located the old English church, unused for forty years but housing an old Christmas tree with decorations still intact.

We drove the 270 dramatic miles to Leh and after a night's stop at Kargil climbed over the Fatu-La Pass before curvetting down to the Indus valley. We reached our *serai* at Stok and slept peacefully in purpose-built yurts in a field surrounded by willow trees. We made visits to the *gompas* at Skey, Tiksi, Hemis and Atko, followed by an excursion down the Indus in inflatable rubber rafts.

During the tour a much-loved member, Major General Sir Maurice Dowse, was taken ill and moved to the hospital in Leh. This tragedy is being retold as it demonstrates again the close feeling between the two armies. The manager of the *serai* had asked the Divisional Commander if General Dowse could be moved to a military hospital. He immediately gave permission and personally supervised the move. Later, the Corps Commander, visiting Leh, called to see the General, who seemed to be rallying, and told him that when he was fit enough to travel arrangements would be made for a military aircraft to fly him to Chandigar with an orderly and all necessary equipment. The General asked about the cost: the answer was 'Nothing, we wear the same uniform'. Unfortunately he did not gain strength and died three days later. We learnt subsequently that the Indian army had given General Dowse a military funeral with full honours.

Kashgar 1990

The tour up the Karakoram Highway and over the Khunjerab Pass to Kashgar was a Mecca for the Society.

After a memorable journey from Islamabad to Gilgit, a detour to Hunza and a night at Gulmit, we embarked in Toyota Landcruisers for the drive to the border with China, marked at 15,072 ft by an obelisk. Our Uigher guide awaited us at Pir Ali, the Chinese immigration post, and took us to Tashkurgan. The next morning's drive provided splendid views of Mustagh Ata and Mt Kungar, and a herd of yaks obligingly arrived to greet us as we approached Lake Karakul. Our hotel, on arrival in Kashgar, had once been the Russian Consulate from where Nikolai Petrovsky had played the 'Great Game' with George Macartney.

A highlight of our stay there was the visit to the Sunday market, said to be attended by 100,000 people each week and where everything imaginable was sold – horses, camels, other livestock, clothing, furniture, timber, meat and vegetables. If you heard the cry 'Posh Posh' you jumped aside to avoid being mown down by galloping mule carts.

A memorable banquet was given for us in Chini Bagh, the home of Sir George and Lady Macartney and other British Consuls General for so long at the centre of that 'Great Game'. The house was in a sad state of decay, its rooms divided into dormitories and used as night stops for long distance lorry drivers, who had been turned out and the place cleaned up for our benefit. The room in which we ate gave on to a terrace overlooking the one-time garden created by Lady Macartney but now a heap of rubble preparatory to the building of a new modern hotel. The evening began with drinks on the terrace, and Hugh Leach, our bugler, sounded 'Officers Dress for Dinner'.

Next morning we made an early start for the long drive to Khotan where we spent three days of enjoyable activity, successfully searching for jade in the Jade River, sliding down the high sand dunes of the Taklamakan and watching the whole process of silk weaving. From here we travelled by air to Urumchi, before setting off by road for Turfan. Sightseeing included a visit to the cave paintings at Bezaklik and the workings of a *qanat*.

Siberia 1991

The Siberian tour started a week after Yeltsin's coup and on our arrival Moscow was in a state of euphoria. It was an interesting time to be there. We had with us our own Russian expert John Massey-Stewart.

Our guide was a sturdy young Russian with a pigtail reaching down to her waist, who showed us round the Kremlin. We were invited by Sir Roderick and Lady Braithwaite for drinks at the British Embassy and given the opportunity to see that imposing building as well as hearing the Ambassador's comments on the current situation. From Moscow we went by air to Tyumen for a night in Tobolsk. We heard the sound of singing coming from the church which we found packed and were given a warm welcome.

From Novosibirsk, our next stop, we flew to Gorno-Altaisk in a small aircraft that we practically filled, loading our luggage into it ourselves, filling the hold and then piling cases at the back of the plane and along the gangway. Arriving at the town, we had a long wait at the so-called hotel before being allowed to occupy the third floor where we found the sheets still damp. Who, we wondered darkly, had been evacuated for our accommodation? The consensus of opinion was that the hotel doubled as a brothel!

Another less than comfortable experience was an expedition to Lake Teletskoe, some 200 kilometres away in the mountains over terrible roads. This took six hours, but we managed to procure an ancient helicopter from Aeroflot for the return journey, at a cost of £1.13 per head.

Our next destination, Irkutsk, was preceded by another six-hour bus journey, to Novosibirsk, from where we were to catch a plane. Owing to the general economic situation there was very little fuel available and our bus had to stop at every likely petrol station en route, obtaining twenty litres here and there with the help of packets of Marlboro cigarettes. The flight itself took two hours and we arrived in pouring rain, cold, tired and hungry, to find no transport to take us into Irkutsk itself. However, more cigarettes produced a dilapidated coach in which we sat with umbrellas up, for the roof leaked copiously.

Next day we visited the Cathedral of the Holy Cross, which was packed with old and young, the House of the Decembrists, now a museum, and the *Angara* icebreaker, built on the Tyne in 1897 by Armstrong Whitworth and Co. and in use as a ferry until 1960, now also a museum. The sun shone for us in the afternoon and we appreciated the beauty of the city, well deserving its title 'the Paris of Siberia'.

Two days were spent beside Lake Baikal, the first in sunshine, the lake looking beautiful. The second day was cold, wet and windy. Nevertheless we embarked as planned on a full-day boat trip. The hotel staff, horrified, offered to lend us thick sweaters. We landed on an island to visit a research museum and enjoy a picnic lunch. It was bitterly cold but having built a huge bonfire, we toasted our slabs of bread and cheese over the flames, while the vodka flowed freely. On the return journey, a member was nearly decapitated as one of the lifeboats broke loose and flew across the deck, landing with a splash in the lake, sinking immediately.

'. . . we toasted our slabs of bread and cheese . . .'

From Irkutsk we travelled by night train to Ulan-Ude, capital of Buryatia, and from there by road to the border with Mongolia, making a detour to Novo-Selenginsk near the Selanga River where there is a memorial to four British missionaries who lived there in 1819.[3] Our bugler sounded the Last Post as we paid our respects, to the utter astonishment of villagers and hordes of children. We left Siberia at Naushki by night sleeper on the Trans-Mongolian Railway for two days in Mongolia, a journey enlivened by conversations with young Russian soldiers who had served in Afghanistan.

Uzbekistan 1994

The renowned sites in Samarkand and Bokhara were a wonderful reward for the effort of getting there, and complemented by a visit to the Fergana Valley. Two nights had been allotted to Urgench to allow for a day in Khiva, normally only visited for its architecture and termed a 'dead city' because of its dearth of inhabitants. But it turned out to be 'Veterans' Day', a public holiday, and Khiva was teeming with people wearing their most colourful clothes, the men proudly displaying their medals. Even weddings were taking place, the brides wearing long white dresses.

On the way back to Urgench a detour was made to the Oxus, where we walked across a pontoon bridge some 800 metres long to Burini, accompanied by friendly locals on their way home. We walked slowly back, enthralled with the changing lights on the water. Our pretty local guide, Svetlana, began to recite from Matthew Arnold's poem 'Sohrab and Rustam'; apparently they had all read at school the epic legend of how Rustam unwittingly kills his only son, Sohrab. But emotion proved too much and she dissolved into tears, so we had to finish the story for her.

These are but a few reminiscences from the many varied tours the Society made across Asia, listed in the Annex. There has been no space to enlarge upon our adventures. For example, how, when near Sharura in Yemen, travelling in trucks owned by wild-looking tribesmen, our party was ambushed by another tribe who had lost out on the battle for our trade; the delights, and physical challenge, of a tented trek across mountainous Bhutan; Korea where there were so few foreign visitors we were considered novelties, and our clothes were fingered by the crowds that surrounded us; or the pathos in Burma when, visiting Kalow, a favourite British Hill Station, we found a large Catholic church run by an Italian priest who had been there for forty years. He was delighted to see us. His congregation was down to two.

Most countries invoked individual nostalgia. In Sri Lanka two members, brothers, who had spent their childhood there were able to find their old home. And Cynthia Stephenson, who had worked in the country during the Second World War, was thrilled to find Lord Mountbatten's old Headquarters. Members unwittingly provided amusement. In Bangalore someone decided to miss the morning tour and write twenty postcards. Despite our having seen a green pillar box boldly marked VR just outside the hotel, she duly posted them in a long slit surrounded by shining brass in the polished mahogany at the Reception Desk. She had failed to read the notice 'Staff Christmas Gratuities'. It was only February. Members' birthdays were celebrated in the most unlikely places. None more so, perhaps, than on the train between Lanchow and Liuyuang in China, when the cook produced a magnificent meal topped by a birthday cake, all over an open fire in the tiny travelling galley. So many memories to savour.

China Tour, 1974

Nepal, 1980

Group at Karo La (17,000 ft), Centenary Tour, Tibet 2001 [Lady Fenn]

Miss Marinel FitzSimons led the Society's tours from 1971 to 1995; Mrs Helen McKeag in 1997 and Mr David Easton from 1998 to 2001. The following is his account of the centenary tour.

Tibet

To mark the Society's centenary in 2001 Council sought to combine two complementary objectives in choosing the tour destination. Tibet, in itself a first for the Society, was chosen and the theme of the journey would be to retrace, as far as possible, the route of Younghusband's mission to Lhasa in 1904. So it was that in late September 2001 a party of twenty-seven gathered in Calcutta, where a day's stopover had to suffice to view the faded splendour of the former seat of British rule in India, whence Younghusband's patron, Curzon, exercised power as Viceroy between 1899 and 1905. In Darjeeling, as well as enjoying a brief period of rest and acclimatisation in the comfort of the delightful Windamere Hotel, the group was able to imagine the scene of preparation for Younghusband's departure for Tibet in December 1903. The well-maintained Planter's Club remains as a monument to that era, as do a number of unkempt hotels!

Since Younghusband's route from India into Tibet via Sikkim had long been denied to travellers, it was intended that the tour party should enter the Tibetan Autonomous Region (TAR) of China across the land border from Nepal. However, the Chinese authorities closed this without notice just as the group was about to leave India for Nepal, necessitating a rapid adjustment of the itinerary. The only option was to take the direct Chinese airline flight from Kathmandu to Lhasa. This meant forgoing the rough but picturesque road journey between the Nepalese capital and Shigatse, via Shegar. A small consolation was sighting the summit of Everest clearly visible as the flight passed it. A secondary benefit was that the party gained two extra days in Tibet, allowing time for a side-trip to the sacred lake Nam Tso, some 120 miles north of Lhasa and at an altitude of 4,718 metres in an idyllic setting.

However, the main itinerary took the party from Lhasa to Shigatse, and then on to Gyantse and Tsetang. The sights in these four major centres and the beauty of the scenery in between were enchanting. In the context of Younghusband's expedition the most memorable sites were the fort at Gyantse and the Karo La Pass, where two of the main actions on the road to Lhasa took place. Seeing the terrain, and particularly the commanding position of the Gyantse *dzong* high on a steep rocky outcrop, it was not difficult to conjure up a picture of the fighting in both places, especially with the assistance of the accounts in Patrick French's biography of Younghusband.[4] While in Gyantse the group held an enjoyable discussion about the British invasion of 1904, attempting to analyse it in the context of its time.

Leaving Tibet, the final destination was Beijing, from where power over the destiny of Tibet has been exercised by the Chinese since 1950. That sobering thought did not detract from the group's appreciation of its great sites and bustling modernity.

TOURS ORGANISED BY THE SOCIETY 1971–2001

1971	Turkey – Southern Anatolia
1972	Afghanistan
1974	China
1975	Sri Lanka and South India (February)
1975	China (June)
1976	Iran
1977	Indonesia
1978	Iraq
1979	China
1980	Nepal
1981	North West Frontier, Pakistan
1983	Thailand and Burma
1984	Syria and Jordan
1985	Eastern Turkey
1986	Kashmir and Ladakh
1987	Korea and Taiwan
1988	Bhutan
1989	The Yemen
1990	Karakorum Highway and the Silk Road – Kashgar
1991	Siberia and Mongolia
1992	Sri Lanka and the Maldives
1994	Uzbekistan
1995	Northern Pakistan and Chitral
1997	Turkey – Alexander's Path
1998	Laos, Vietnam and Cambodia
1999	Iran
2000	Lebanon, Syria and Jordan
2001	Tibet

XIV

THE LAWRENCE OF ARABIA MEMORIAL MEDAL

The Lawrence of Arabia medal is just one indication of the strong place that Lawrence holds in the hearts of those who are interested in Central Asia.

General Sir Richard Gale, Chairman, welcoming
Professor Arnold Lawrence to the Annual Dinner, 1962

The idea that the Society should have a Gold Medal was first discussed at a Council meeting in October 1923. This followed a suggestion by the retiring Honorary Secretary, Lieut Colonel A. C. Yate, that it be awarded to the person who each year has given the greatest service to the British Empire in the countries covered by the Society. But, as was so often the case with novel conceptions, it was decided to postpone the issue for the present. It was not raised again until immediately after the death of T. E. Lawrence on 19 May 1935. The suggestion of a medal in his memory was made not so much by, but to the President, Field Marshal Viscount Allenby, Lawrence's war-time commander. He responded with enthusiasm and Lawrence's brother, the archaeologist Professor Arnold Lawrence, gave his support.

At the end of May a short article appeared in *The Times* together with a letter signed by three of Lawrence's war-time colleagues, Lord Lloyd, Sir Ronald Storrs and Colonel Stewart Newcombe. The letter asked the public for donations to reach a target of £500 'in order to institute a Gold Medal in his memory . . . Lawrence was a writer and a seeker as well as hero, and it is fitting that his memorial should encourage like, if lesser, achievement in an increasingly standardized and safety-first age.' A notice in the Society's *Journal* called upon members to contribute, pointing out that 'by instituting a Gold Medal in memory of Lawrence, members of the Society are given the means of showing their appreciation of contributions to the study and solution of the problems of Asia made by men who are working in the East'.

LAWRENCE OF ARABIA

TO THE EDITOR OF THE TIMES

Sir,—It has been decided by the Council of the Royal Central Asian Society that a gold medal shall be instituted by the society in memory of T. E. Lawrence, to be awarded from time to time for work of outstanding distinction in travel, research, or letters in the Near and Middle East.

The sum required is comparatively trifling: to wit, £500, the interest on which will provide the necessary sum. Subscriptions will be received by the secretary of the society.

Lawrence was a writer and a seeker as well as a hero, and it is fitting that his memorial should encourage like if lesser achievement in an increasingly standardized and safety-first age.

Yours, &c.,
LLOYD.
RONALD STORRS.
May 28. STEWART NEWCOMBE

The Society's previous connections with T. E. Lawrence and his world were binding. Of the names mentioned in *Seven Pillars of Wisdom* twenty-three were members. A few knew him before the First World War and the Arab Revolt, a good many more during it. Hogarth and Storrs launched him in his role; Parker, Garland, Bray and Vickery were early contacts in the field; and Joyce, Peake, Stirling, Winterton, Lloyd, Newcombe and Jaafar Pasha served through most of the fighting. Allenby, Clayton, Deedes, Cornwallis and Gertrude Bell were at base in Cairo or elsewhere; Barrow appears briefly and brusquely in Dera'a; Wingate in Khartoum; Churchill and Field Marshal Robertson in London. A few had joined the Society before the war, the great majority soon after it when others like Charlotte Shaw and Philby became his friends. Shortly after Lawrence's death his brothers Arnold and Montagu, and his mother Sarah, joined. All these members' connections with T. E. Lawrence and the part they played in the Arab Revolt, the campaigns in the Hejaz and Palestine and his post-war life, are too well known to bear repetition here.

A study of the *Journal* indexes reveals the wealth of material available in transcribed lectures, articles, obituaries, letters and book reviews. They were written by individuals who were involved in those historical events and who knew their subject. They reflect the diversity of views held so soon after the end of the war, views which may have become distorted by, or lost to, history and are thus of especial value to researchers.

There is no record as to Lawrence's own awareness of the Society. Certainly nothing supports Elizabeth Monroe's assertion in her book on Philby that Lawrence 'put in an appearance' at the Society's Annual Dinner on 11 July 1934 at which, she maintained, the Emir Abdullah of Trans-Jordan and Dora, Philby's wife, were present.[1] It is true that Abdullah was invited, but he left England four days before the dinner. In any case the Society's white-tie dinners were not the sort of event where one 'put in an appearance', least of all that Lawrence would do so. He was, at this time, at RAF Bridlington working on his air-sea-rescue speedboats.

Of those so associated with Lawrence some became the Society's Presidents: Allenby, Lloyd and Shea; some Chairmen: Holdich and Chetwode; and Newcombe, as previously mentioned, a leading Honorary Secretary. Yet others became members of Council. Thus it was not surprising that members, and indeed some non-members, readily contributed to the medal fund and when it closed in 1938 it had reached around £230. This included a donation of £110 contributed by all ranks of the Royal Air Force in recognition of Lawrence's service in its ranks.

The money was needed as capital to engage the services of a designer for the medal, for it to be cast by the Royal Mint and to provide sufficient interest to purchase copies from the Mint as they were required. The obvious choice of designer was the artist Eric Kennington, who was then in the process of carving the effigy of Lawrence that was later placed in St Martin's Church, Wareham, and whose portraits of leading characters who took part in the Arab Revolt later appeared in various editions of *Seven Pillars of Wisdom*. Kennington agreed to the commission 'on a minimum fee of £30 and a maximum of £50 if funds allowed' – which they did. He estimated that making the matrix would cost £40–£50: each silver medal £2 and a gold one £10. The front of the medal would bear Lawrence's image with the inscription 'Lawrence of Arabia', the verso a representation of the Society's crest – the horns of the *Ovis Poli* – and the Society's motto. When eventually cast it was described by Sir George Hall of the British Museum as a 'master medal'.

A sub-committee was needed to deal with these matters. Its initial members were those signatories of *The Times* letter, Lloyd, Storrs and Newcombe. There were early discussions

TEL. CHECKENDON 10.

Dec 3.

HOLLY COPSE
GORING HEATH · READING

Dear Sir Percy Sykes
I have heard from the Mint
a medal of the size agreed will cost.
— for 2 dies — between £40 & £50.

To strike one silver medal annually
with a good case to contain it, & the name
of the recipient round the rim will
cost about 25/—

For £30, I will design & model the
medal, & when it is approved by you will
see to the making of the dies.

If, as suggested, the £30 becomes £50
I shall be pleased to accept the
larger amount.

Yours sincerely
Eric H. Kennington
P.T.O.

Letter from Eric Kennington

Eric Kennington, 1936 [Family of the Artist]

(i) (fore)

(ii) (verso)

Fore and verso, Lawrence of Arabia Memorial Medal

as to whether it should in fact be a gold medal 'similar to that of the United Service Institute of India's MacGregor Medal, to mark special occasions and be awarded every three years, or a silver one to be awarded every year'.[2] The committee decided on the latter as it was soon clear that the hoped-for target of £500 would not be met.

The terms of the award were next formulated:

> In recognition of work, normally including hazard, of outstanding merit for the British Empire and of distinction in exploration, research or letters. Such service must have been rendered by members of the British Empire within the area covered by the activities of the Royal Central Asian Society. It is not intended to limit the objects for which the medal will be awarded, but Naval, Military and Air Force officers, explorers, writers, administrators, pioneers of trade routes, archaeologists and anthropologists may be specially mentioned; and the award will, generally speaking, be made to individuals who are in the field or who have only recently retired from it.

The reference to the British Empire was later omitted. An adjunct to the terms read:

> The medal is not awarded as an additional recognition of work done in the ordinary course of official or civilian employment, but for some unusual contribution, especially where this leads to a better understanding and friendship between British and an Eastern people, or when a primitive people have been helped to a better way of life.

The medal itself secured and the terms agreed upon, the sub-committee was enlarged to form a panel that would recommend to Council candidates they considered should receive it. This consisted of the Chairman, the Honorary Secretaries, the Treasurer, and three members of Council selected annually. In addition there were four permanent members who as late as 1950 were still Arnold Lawrence, Storrs and Newcombe – and Eric

Kennington, the designer of the medal. He, however, was a somewhat reluctant member, writing later to the Secretary: 'I would prefer to not vote, please. I am so ignorant of these people's achievements and the East.'

The first recipient in 1936 was Major J. B. Glubb (later Glubb Pasha) – 'For valuable services rendered while serving in command of the Levies in Iraq and the Desert Patrols of Trans-Jordan for some sixteen years. Through his remarkable influence over the Bedouin Arab he ended a state of disorder that had prevailed in the Trans-Jordanian deserts and paved the way to better relations between the rulers of those countries and King Ibn Saud.'

Glubb Pasha

The next recipient, in 1937, was the distinguished Tibetologist Sir Charles Bell who – 'has acquired greater knowledge of the Tibetan language, literature, manners and customs than any other Englishman. His friendship with the Thirteenth Dalai Lama was an outstanding event in British relations with Tibet. His valuable books cover every aspect of Tibetan life.'

Three more Arabists followed. In 1938 the medal was awarded to Major C. S. Jarvis, who had served in three desert areas, Libya, the western desert of Egypt and as a Governor of Sinai. In 1939 it was awarded jointly to Mr and Mrs W. H. Ingrams. As Political Resident in the Hadhramaut, the mid-southern part of Arabia, Harold Ingrams had, for the first time, pacified the tribes and his tenure of office was known as *Sulh Ingram*, 'Ingrams's peace'. Influencing the award was a long confidential letter, written in the small neat hand of the archaeologist Gertrude Caton-Thompson: 'It would be difficult to separate them, or to say which is doing the more valuable work ... I have seen her [Doreen, Harold's wife] in that sweltering heat, working in the office until far into the night and that after a long day which held no rest: this she sustains for months on end ... I was frequently told by the inhabitants that Mrs Ingrams' Arabic was even better than her husband's; and the respect and affection she has evidently gained both from men and women makes her a power in the land which the country may well be proud to possess.'

Harold and Doreen Ingrams with Hadhramis at Qabr Hud, 1939 [Courtesy of Leila Ingrams]

In 1940 the medal was awarded to Colonel F. G. Peake 'Pasha', also for services in Trans-Jordan, where he had established the Arab Legion. Peake had been Glubb's Commanding Officer and because of this it was felt necessary to leave a gap between the two awards and wait for Peake's retirement and return to England in 1939.

In 1938 Council decided to offer the Royal Air Force a replica of the medal both as a token of gratitude for the sum of money collected by all ranks and to commemorate Lawrence's time in the ranks of the service as Aircraftman Ross, later Shaw. The Air Ministry welcomed the idea. On 29 July 1939 Sir Percy Sykes, as senior Honorary Secretary, presented the medal at a parade of Cranwell cadets, taken by Lord Gort, Chief of the Imperial General Staff. In his speech Sir Percy said: 'The medal is instituted to keep alive the memory of that truly heroic officer, who described the conquest of the air as "the biggest thing to do in the world today"... May I express the hope that the medal may, in the not distant future, be awarded to a member of the Royal Air Force.' The medal continued to be displayed in the senior cadets' mess at Cranwell until the 1970s when it was moved to the Royal Air Force Museum storage depot at Stafford. In August 2000 an official of the museum said that it would be displayed at a proposed medal room in Hendon when a planned extension to the museum was built there.

There is insufficient space here to list in detail the achievements of all the medal winners. A survey of their endeavours would constitute a book in itself; indeed many have been written by or about them. They include anthropologists turned war-time tribe raisers, explorers, administrators, mountaineers, archaeologists, missionaries, soldiers, physicians, journalists, scholars, botanists and an etymologist. A roll is appended at the end of this chapter. Suffice it that here we should give more detail to the few who may be less well known.

During the Second World War the medal was awarded to some especially deserving and interesting recipients. In 1941 it was given to Captain C. E. Corry for his work in pacifying the tribesmen in the Muntafiq Liwa, the Iraq marshes, which cleared the way for Allied military operations in the area. Corry spent thirty years in Iraq, mostly in the police. The award followed closely upon the publication of his book *The Blood Feud* about his experiences in the Muntafiq.

In 1942 the recipient was Miss Mildred Cable, that remarkable lady who, in the 1920s, went out to work with the China Inland Mission with two equally remarkable sisters, the Misses Francesca and Evangeline French. During fifteen years they crossed the desert five times, often in primitive Chinese wooden carts, 'with Bible in hand, wearing Chinese clothes and speaking Turki'. In his Annual Dinner speech in 1934 Lord Lloyd had bracketed these achievements with Philby's crossing of the Empty Quarter. Between the three they gave ninety-eight years service 'to the business of the Kingdom of God'. In addition they acquired a great deal of scientific and other information, recorded in meticulous detail, that was useful to scientists and geographers. In his tribute to Miss

Mildred Cable (centre) and the French sisters

'... often in primitive Chinese wooden carts...'

Cable, after her death in 1952, the President, Sir John Shea, concluded: 'If you got to know her you would have found three things: a quiet sense of humour, an unmistakable aura of goodness and a faith such as can move mountains.' In 1944, after her return to England, she was welcomed as a Member of Council of the Society, which had been imaginative enough to give this award to a woman of peace at the height of war.

Miss Cable was followed in 1943 by, conversely, a man of war, Brigadier Orde Wingate, for his part in the Chindit campaign. Coincidentally, Wingate was a distant relative of Lawrence and on his death in March 1944 Field Marshal Wavell, writing his obituary in the Society's *Journal*, compared the two men: 'Both had high-powered minds which seemed unable to run in any but top gear however rough the going... In their theories of irregular warfare Lawrence was the amateur. Wingate had a professional background ... But Lawrence, as I knew him, was certainly more restful and had a sense of humour which I never found in Wingate ... Both were men of remarkable power and genius.'

In 1945 the medal was given to another extraordinary and little-known woman, Miss Ursula Graham Bower. Her recommendation came from Lieut General Slim, GOC of the 14th Army in Burma. In 1938 Miss Bower had gone to the Manipur area of North East Assam as an anthropologist, living with Nzemi Naga tribesmen, traditional head-hunters. Few Europeans had made contact previously and none won their confidence, which through sympathy and simple medical treatment she did. She secured a peace between the Nzemi and their blood enemies the Kuki. In November 1943 when the Japanese threat to Assam became real, using these tribesmen she organised a 'Watch and Ward' scheme which provided valuable intelligence to the military. In April 1944, when the Japanese had penetrated to within a day's march from her headquarters, despite being pressed by the army, she refused to move back. A supporting recommendation from Mr J. P. Mills, Adviser for Tribal Affairs, Assam, added: 'Living alone among head-hunters who were, at the time, at war with the British Government and to whom her scalp was particularly vulnerable, she successfully armed them in order to fight for the British against the Japanese at the extreme risk of their own lives.' The Commissioner of Kohima, in his own support, told how after he had despatched a number of shotguns to Miss Bower he got up one morning to find seven heads neatly laid out at his door 'to show what her tribesmen could do'.

In her letter of acceptance, written from the North Cachar Hills where, as Mrs Betts, she was now married to the local Political Officer, she wrote: 'Had it not been for the help and encouragement the Society gave me in 1938 [when she first became a member] I would never have gone to Assam in the first place.' This provides a good example of the way the Society has influenced many young people to pursue a career in Asia.

In the immediate post-war years Council became concerned about the difficulty of finding suitable candidates for the medal. In January 1946 it circulated a 'Private and Confidential' letter to various Commanders-in-Chief, Ambassadors and heads of institutes asking for suggestions. Assam was still in the news and in 1947 Council responded to recommendations from two successive Governors of that province that the medal should be given to Mr Charles Pawsey, who had been Deputy Commissioner of the Naga Hills during the last ten years. Similar to Miss Bower, but operating from a more secure base, he had been instrumental in persuading a primitive people to lay aside their blood feuds, adopt new methods of agriculture and, during the war, to adhere to the Allied cause, sharing with them the Siege of Kohima.

TELEPHONE ROYAL 1351.

YOUR REFERENCE

MINT REFERENCE 3398/1936

ROYAL MINT,
LONDON, E.C.3.

23rd May, 1945.

Dear Sir,

Thank you for your letter of the 17th May asking for the cost of Lawrence Memorial medals "struck in the proper way".

As this medal has never been a struck medal, I think it would be as well at this stage, to put on record the actual history of the production of the medal:- Plaster casts were supplied to the Mint by Mr. Kennington in February 1936, from these, relief nickel electrotypes (which are undamaged) were made. The relief of the medal was too high to give a satisfactory result by striking from steel dies in the usual way and and it was, therefore, agreed with Mr. Kennington that the first medal should be produced by direct reduction of the two sides in solid silver. The two sides were turned to size, and silver soldered together to form the medal, which was subsequently engraved on the rim "Founded by the Royal Central Asian Society of 1935". From this original medal, solid copper masters were grown in the electrotyping bath, for use as matrices in the production of the medals supplied to you between 1936 and 1943. These are solid silver electrotypes silver soldered together. It is these matrices which were destroyed by enemy action, and the medals supplied to you in 1943, were silver plated copper electrotypes, grown in gutta percha moulds obtained from a sample medal in our possession. To replace the destroyed copper matrices, we propose to use our sample medal, but before doing so we should like to compare it with your original.

Provided that our sample medal is perfect, the new copper matrices will produce silver medals exactly similar to those you have already had.

If it is not, we shall have to go back to the electrotypes. The cost of reproducing the destroyed matrices will not be charged for.

The present day cost of these silver medals will be £6.6.0. each plus the equivalent of purchase tax.

Yours faithfully,

P. H. Pettiford

for Superintendent.

Letter from the Royal Mint explaining the history of the Lawrence Medal

Meanwhile, the Royal Mint was having war problems of its own which had affected the production of the actual medal. Enemy action had damaged the matrices from which the medals were made. Because of this, during the war the Mint had produced a cheaper 'token medal' which was given to war-time recipients with a certificate saying that true medals would be substituted later. By 1945 the matrices had been repaired and the original medals could be made again.

The 1949 medal winner was surely one of the most deserving and truly fitted the terms of the award 'or when a primitive people have been helped to a better way of life'. He was Sir Henry Tristram Holland, who arrived in Baluchistan as a member of the Church Missionary Society's (CMS) medical mission in 1900. He had soon gained the respect and affection of Pathans, Baluch, Brahuis and Hindus alike, enabling him to make long treks into tribal territory where he might well have become a victim of the knife of a religious fanatic. Perhaps his best memorial is the CMS-built hospital in Quetta, which he helped restore after the earthquake in 1935, when he and his wife narrowly escaped death in the resulting rubble. An acquaintance recalled how 'alongside that modern hospital at Quetta was a caravanserai, in the middle of which you would see mules and donkeys tethered and a goat being milked, and families living and cooking their food in their own primitive way. These people had come thousands of miles from across the Oxus from Bokhara and Samarkand, because they had heard of his work.' He was equally known and loved in Upper Sind, where he ran an eye clinic at Shikarpur, and in other towns of the plains. At his prime Holland was famed as one of the foremost eye specialists in the world, sometimes performing as many as two thousand cataract operations on a single tour. In his time he would have given sight to some 100,000 people. On presenting the medal at the Society's annual dinner in October 1949 the President, Viscount Wavell, said: 'I can only say that the Lawrence of Arabia medal has never been better earned.'

Sir Henry Holland

The winner in 1950, Lieut Colonel Frederick Spencer Chapman, mountaineer and soldier, is perhaps better known through his books. *Lhasa the Holy City* describes his 1936–1937 expedition to Tibet and *The Jungle is Neutral* his wartime experiences behind Japanese lines. In his recommendation Viscount Wavell wrote: 'Colonel Chapman has not Lawrence's literary genius, nor his introspection. He has never received the publicity and fame that were his predecessor's lot. But for sheer courage and endurance, physical and mental, the two men stand together.'

Many of the more recent award winners are better known today than those we have quoted, none more so that the two great mountaineers Sir John Hunt and Sir Christian Bonington. Some have been mentioned at greater length elsewhere in this work. The majority saw service in Arab countries. For example, the explorer Sir Wilfred Thesiger, at the time of writing an Honorary Vice President of the Society; Mrs Violet Dickson who, with her husband Colonel H. R. P. Dickson, spent decades in Kuwait; Brigadier Stephen Longrigg, both a political and oil company representative in Iraq; Nevill Barbour, a journalist covering Arab affairs, who strongly supported the Palestinian cause; and Sir Charles Belgrave whose name is almost synonymous with Bahrain and who in his acceptance speech was able to quote some personal memories of Lawrence.

31, Madingley Rd.
Cambridge.

1. 3. 45

Dear Sir Percy,

Many thanks for your note and for getting Miss Wingate to send Gen. Shin's citation (enclosed). Obviously Miss Graham-Bowers is a very remarkable person, & should make herself felt in a larger sphere of activity.

I shall do my best to attend the Medal Committee, whenever it is held: last time I missed it as a result of being told to come at the wrong time. I should like too to tell you of an idea of mine about Persepolis & the Greeks.

I hope all goes well with you & yours.

Yours sincerely
Arnold Lawrence

Letter from Professor A. W. Lawrence

Kenya House
Boar's Hill
Oxford.
2nd. April 1955.

Dear Madam

Thank you very much for letting me know of the award of the Lawrence Medal. I am sure my brother would have been very pleased that it has been given for work and travel amongst the Arabs.

Yours sincerely
Montagu R. Lawrence

. . . and from Dr Montagu Lawrence

'Lawrence's two brothers . . . took a great interest in the Medal.' [RSAA Archives]

Colonel Sir Hugh Boustead

Sir Hugh Boustead was one of the Society's most colourful characters, and certainly the only one to have received a Royal Pardon for desertion. So determined was he to see active service on land, he jumped his Royal Navy ship off the Cape Station and then joined the South African Cavalry Brigade in an assumed name as a private soldier. He served subsequently on the Western Front where he was commissioned in the field and awarded the Military Cross, the first of many decorations. After early post-First World War service in Southern Russia and a crowded fifty years in Arab countries he left his heart in Arabia, literally: his ashes were scattered over the desert there. Sir Max Mallowan, husband of the novelist Agatha Christie, ran archaeological excavations in Iraq. Similarly, Professor Seton Lloyd, who, in his acceptance speech mentioned that whilst he had never met Lawrence himself, he had heard stories about him from Leonard Woolley, the archaeologist who supervised Lawrence at the Carchemish excavation between 1912 and 1914. Professor Serjeant was an Arabist and Islamic scholar of high standing and Elizabeth Monroe a writer on Arab affairs and Philby's biographer.

The award to the journalist Sandy Gall in 1986 is a fitting link to the Society's inexhaustible interest in Afghanistan. A century earlier service in that country would have provided many a medal winner. George Popov, who received the medal in 1995 is, like Ursula Bower, an example of an unsung hero. He spent fifty years in locust control work in Iran, the sub-continent, Arabia and Africa. He has been described as the least known but greatest scientific traveller of his time.

Lawrence's two brothers, Professor Arnold and Dr Montagu, while alive, took a great interest in the medal and would where possible be present at the award ceremonies, especially when they were connected with the Arab world.

The Lawrence Medal is a facet of the Society that has always attracted outside interest, especially from the younger generation. The words of that letter to *The Times* quoted at the start of the chapter – 'It is fitting that this memorial should encourage like, if lesser, achievement in an increasingly standardised and safety-first age' – are more pertinent than ever sixty-five years later. It would be a sad day if Council could no longer find candidates to satisfy the medal's original terms of reference, but as Sir William Dickson said, 'This Society will always recognise endeavour.' Sir Olaf Caroe, then one of the few surviving great pro-consuls of the former British Indian Empire and highly decorated by the government after thirty years service with the ICS, on receiving the medal himself in 1973 took a different perspective: 'An honour from one's peers is more valuable than any from the establishment.'

ROLL OF THOSE AWARDED THE LAWRENCE OF ARABIA MEMORIAL MEDAL

The summarised citations are as recorded in the Society's *Golden Book*.

1936 Major (later Lieut General Sir John) J. B. Glubb
For pacification work in the north Arabian desert
1937 Sir Charles Bell, KCIE, CMG
For his work in Tibet
1938 Major C. S. Jarvis, CMG, OBE
For development of the Sinai
1939 Mr & Mrs Harold and Doreen Ingrams (Jointly)
For ending the blood feuds of the Hadhramaut
1940 Colonel F. G. Peake Pasha, CMG
For services to Trans-Jordan
1941 Captain C. E. Corry
For work among the Marsh Arabs of Iraq
1942 Miss Mildred Cable
For exploration and work for the people of the Gobi desert
1943 Brigadier (later Major General) Orde C. Wingate, DSO
For the first Chindit expedition
1944 Miss Ursula Graham Bower (later Mrs Betts)
For anthropological work among the Nagas
1947 Mr (later Sir) Charles R. Pawsey
For services to Naga Hill tribes
1948 Sir Henry Holland, CIE, MB, ChB, FRCS, FICS
For medical work in Baluchistan and Afghanistan
1949 Lieut Colonel F. Spencer Chapman, DSO
For work in Japanese-held Malaya
1953 Brigadier (later Lord) Sir John Hunt, Kt, CBE, DSC
For the conquest of Everest
1954 Mr (later Sir) P. Wilfred Thesiger, DSO
For work and travel among the Arabs
1960 Mrs (later Dame) Violet Dickson, MBE
For work among the Bedouin women of Arabia and study of the flora and fauna of the desert
1961 Brigadier Stephen Longrigg, OBE, DLitt
For his work in Iraq and his books on political and economic development in the Middle East
1964 Mr Nevill Barbour
For his work as a journalist, broadcaster, writer and interpreter of Arab affairs
1965 Colonel Sir Hugh Boustead, KBE, CMG, DSO, MC
For his work as an administrator in Arabia
1966 Sir Charles Belgrave, KBE
For work in the Arab-speaking countries and in the Arabian Gulf and for many publications

1969 Sir Max Mallowan, CBE, MA, DLitt, FBE, FSA
For services to archaeology in areas covered by the Society

1970 Professor Seton Lloyd, CBE, MA, FSA
For services to archaeology in areas covered by the Society

1973 Sir Olaf Caroe, KCSI, KCIE, FRSL, DLitt
For work of outstanding merit for the British Empire and for contributions to research and literature

1974 Professor Robert Serjeant, MA, PhD
For services in the Yemen and South Arabia

1980 Miss Elizabeth Monroe, CMG, MA
For services to Arab studies

1985 Mr (later Sir) Christian J. S. Bonington, CBE
For the conquest of Everest

1986 Mr Sandy Gall, CBE
For his hazardous inquiry into the intervention by the Soviet Union in Afghanistan and the consequences for that country

1995 Mr George Popov, MBE
For his lifelong services as a locust control expert in Central Asia and Arabia

1998 Mr Hugh Leach, OBE
For exploration and research in Arab Countries and N.W. areas of the Sub-continent and leadership of Young People's expeditions

2001 Mr Colin Thubron
For his literary output, lectures and broadcasts, the product of forty years of travel in Asia through which he has enlarged knowledge of its peoples and cultures

XV

THE SIR PERCY SYKES MEMORIAL MEDAL AND OTHER SOCIETY AWARDS

We present this medal to the Society in the hope . . . that in its small way it may contribute to a better understanding and better fellowship between the peoples of this world.

Frank Sykes presenting the Sir Percy Sykes Memorial Medal to the Society, 24 March 1948

There can be few members who have given more to the Society than Brigadier General Sir Percy Molesworth Sykes, KCIE, CB, CMG. Or few who have absorbed more of the wisdom and history of Asia throughout a long and varied career there; twenty-one of his thirty active years were spent in Persia.

Commissioned in 1888 into the 16th Lancers based in India, he transferred forthwith to the 2nd Dragoon Guards (Queen's Bays) and subsequently to the Indian Political Service. He was sent on his first intelligence mission to Central Asia in 1892, aged only twenty-five, *inter alia* to report on the Transcaspian Railway. His second, the following year, entailed a six-month ride through Persia under cover of rejoining his regiment in India. This was the start of a love affair with that country which remained to the end of his life.

In 1894 Sykes was sent to Kerman to open the first British Consulate there. He was accompanied by his sister, Ella, who kept house for him. From this base he was sent on a variety of missions throughout South East Persia, which included the opening of a Consulate in Seistan ahead of the Russians. At the end of 1900, in his only major diversion from Asia, he became involved briefly in the Boer War in South Africa when he was wounded in the leg. During twelve months leave in England he published his first book, *Ten Thousand Miles in Persia*, and married Evelyn, daughter of Colonel Bruce Seton.

In early 1903, accompanied by his wife, he returned to his Consular post in Kerman. After two years he was transferred to Meshed as Consul General, both undertaking a 700-mile desert journey with their twenty-month-old first son, Frank, to get there. Lady Sykes has left a memorable account of this epic ride, their subsequent eight years in Meshed and various overland travels back to England on leave with a growing family. They left Meshed for good in November 1913. After two years in Europe, during which his two-volume work *A History of Persia* appeared in the spring of 1915, he was sent to Kashgar as temporary Consul General to cover the home leave of Sir George Macartney. He again took his sister Ella as housekeeper. In that year he was knighted.

Sir Percy Sykes and his sister Ella in the South Persian desert on their ride to Kerman, 1894 [Courtesy of Tristram Sykes]

British Consulate, Meshed [*RSAA Archives*]

In 1916 Sykes was sent back to Southern Persia in an attempt to retrieve a dangerous situation when law and order had collapsed and German agents were active in fomenting sedition. With the temporary rank of Brigadier General he raised a force of 8,000 locals, named the South Persia Rifles, to take the place of the unreliable gendarmerie. Recalled to London at the end of 1918, Sykes was retired at the early age of fifty-two and devoted the rest of his life to writing books and articles, mostly on Asian topics. At the start of the Second World War he was employed by the War Office to give lectures to recruits in order to stimulate their interest in the East.

Sykes's active life was one of considerable achievement. His years in Meshed covered the fall-out from the controversial Anglo-Russian Convention of 1907. With skill he fostered relations with the local government, thus hindering Russian attempts to use the area as a launch-pad into India. For this he received commendation from both Curzon and Lord Salisbury. For his mapping of little-known areas of south-east Persia he was awarded the Gold Medal of the Royal Geographical Society. Inevitably he had his critics, some of whom accused him of having no sense of humour and a naïve egotism. He died suddenly on 11 June 1945 aged seventy-eight the result of a heart attack while crossing Trafalgar Square on his way to the Athenaeum.

A current member, Colonel W. G. Neilson, recalls his uncle as 'a typically bluff Victorian, rotund, shortish and moustached. I remember how in the mid-1930s he took me out from school on my birthday. We went to the Royal Tournament at Olympia when he gave me signed copies of all three volumes of his *Story of Exploration*. Some years after his death Aunt Evelyn [Lady Sykes], who retained a sharp enthusiasm for keeping abreast of political events, persuaded me to join the Society.'[1]

Sykes himself joined the Society in 1907 and became its Honorary Secretary in 1932, continuing to hold that office until one month before his death. He was a prolific lecturer and contributor to the *Journal*; this was especially valuable during the Second World War when lecturers were hard to find. He gave his last talk only weeks before he died.

His sister, Miss Ella Sykes, who pre-deceased him, was one of the original members of the Society. She shared many of his Asian travels and was an authority on Persia in her own right.

Sir Percy was prodigious not only in his literary output, but also in his progeny: four sons and two daughters. One of the sons, Edward, followed in his father's Persian footsteps. A civilian, working as an accountant with various engineering firms in Iran, during the Second World War he was recruited by the Special Operations Executive. As 'cover' he served in a number of Vice Consular posts to prepare for what, at the time, appeared a German threat to that country via the Caucasus. He joined the Society in 1935. Frank, the eldest brother, joined in 1946. A cousin, Major Herbert Sykes, who had also travelled in Persia, joined in 1904.

One of Sir Percy's daughters, Elinor, married J. F. 'Sinbad' Sinclair, a senior executive of Burmah-Shell in India and himself a member of the Society. With her help Sinclair assiduously cultivated and employed Indians, making the company's eventual nationalisation a success. The other daughter, Rachel, married Sir Patrick Reilly, also a member, who rose to be ambassador in both Moscow and Paris.

With that background it is hardly surprising that upon Sir Percy's death the family decided to initiate a medal in his memory. Unlike the Lawrence Medal, where funds for its endowment were collected by public subscription, the Sykes family provided the necessary capital to set up a Trust Deed. The initial funds of £360 covered the artist's fees, manufacture of dies by the Royal Mint and the cost of the first two medals. From this sum £150 was invested, which it was vainly hoped might provide an income to cover both the cost and engraving of future medals.

The terms of reference for the medal were different from those of the Lawrence award, there being greater emphasis on research and letters, rather than exploration with risk, and nationality was not confined to British subjects:

> The Percy Molesworth Sykes Memorial Medal is open to persons of any nationality who have distinguished themselves in travel, archaeology, research or letters connected with Iran or other countries within the orbit of the Royal Central Asian Society. The medal may also be awarded for outstanding work in furthering cultural relations between the British Empire and any of those countries. The medal may be awarded annually should a suitable candidate be forthcoming. The award will be made by the Council of the Royal Central Asian Society.

Although not specifically written into the terms, the Sykes family had made clear their wish that in view of Sir Percy's first love being Iran, men and women connected with that country should be considered especially. However, they accepted that nominations lay entirely with Council.

Like the Lawrence Medal, the artist Eric Kennington was asked to design it. He again approached his task with enthusiasm, mentioning progress in letters to the Society's

(i) (fore)

(ii) (verso)

Fore and verso, Sir Percy Sykes Memorial Medal

Secretary. 'For the portrait I visited the Sykes family and Lady Sykes passed the head as like Sir Percy. She knew it would not be very like and was pleasantly surprised. She said "it's got the spirit more than the likeness and that's much more important" ... The Deputy Master of the Mint said he got more enjoyment from it than from all the Victory medals sent in to him.' The medal bears on one side the portrait of Sir Percy and on its verso a design of Marco Polo dictating his great work and the legend 'What thou seest write in a book'. The formal presentation of the medal to the Society was made by the Sykes family on 24 March 1948.

As with the Lawrence Medal a sub-committee was formed to nominate to Council their recommendations for the award. It included initially Edward Sykes, when he was in England, otherwise his brother Frank. The Editor of *The Times Literary Supplement* was also asked for his ideas about recipients.

The first nomination was made in 1947 to a Persian academic, Monsieur Mohammed Fakhri Dai Gilani, an historian long engaged in interpreting Western thought to his own countrymen. It was presented to him in Teheran by Edward Sykes, then working there.

A roll of awardees is appended and it may be noted that a fair percentage have been involved in activity in Iran, thus meeting the wish of the Sykes family. Sir Percy would have known personally several of the early recipients, especially Sir Reader Bullard, who was ambassador in Teheran during the war and who, rather unkindly, and perhaps not too seriously, dubbed Sykes's great book on Persia as 'dreadful'. Sykes would have felt a common bond with others, who, like himself, were travellers and authors.

Whenever possible members of the Sykes family would be present at the award-giving ceremonies, usually the Society's Annual Dinner. Even as late as 1987, when the award was made to Professor Beckingham by the Society's then Patron, the Prince of Wales, both Mr Edward Sykes and Mrs Elinor Sinclair were present. In 1992 when it was awarded to Mr Albert Hourani (his wife receiving it due to Hourani's recent premature death) three members of the extended family, Mrs Elinor Sinclair, Sir Patrick Reilly and Mr Richard Sykes, were all present, Edward having died the previous year. In 2001 when the beneficiary was Mr Mark Tully, Sir Percy's grandson, Mr Mark Sinclair attended. When a recipient was too ill to attend a public ceremony, or travel to London, the medal was given in private by the President or Chairman of the Society, or the local British ambassador.

Letter of thanks from Fakhri Dai Gilani: 'Your great gift of a medal will adorn my humble literary life with golden letters ...'

The Royal Society for Asian Affairs Special Award

In 1998 it was decided to augment the two standing medals with an additional award, though not a medal as such. This was to be known as the Royal Society for Asian Affairs Special Award:

> The award shall be made in recognition of exceptionally outstanding and unusual achievement in Asia, or any part of it or in connection with Asia. The achievement may be in any sphere, including service to humanity, contribution to science, the extension of knowledge, innovation, individual ingenuity and resource, personal effort and courage, endurance, fortitude or contribution to culture. The award is intended to supplement the categories of person who may be honoured by the Society by the award of the Sir Percy Sykes Memorial Medal or the Lawrence of Arabia Medal and should not exclude anyone who might also be considered for the award of one of these medals. The award shall be presented by the President of the Society.

The first recipient, in 1998, was an American, Mr Peter McMillan. In 1994 he had re-enacted the historic flight made from Britain to Australia in 1919 by Captain Ross Smith, who had been personal pilot to T. E. Lawrence during the Arab Revolt, and his brother Lieutenant Keith Smith. The flight was made in a replica of the Vickers Vimy FB 27A bomber aircraft which had been used for the original journey and along a similar route. It entailed many difficulties and hazards which McMillan had detailed to the Society in an illustrated lecture the previous year.

The second award was made to Dr Ina Russell in 1999 for long service to the Society both as a Member of Council and as an Honorary Secretary. She played a specific part in forwarding the Society's educational role.

The two medals, and the new award, are an important aspect of the Society; many outsiders have only heard of it through them. Further, they are a factor in recruitment. As we concluded in the previous chapter, it would be a sad day if Council could no longer find candidates to fulfil their terms of reference. Some may argue that the age of seminal exploration, geographic or academic, is over. This seems a negative approach; repeated fresh endeavours have proved otherwise, and the medals act as a spur for such continuance.

When the artist Eric Kennington was in the midst of designing the Sykes medal he wrote to the Secretary, 'Yes, we all fade out but the Royal Central Asian Society will go on and I hope its medals also.' May it be so.

ROLL OF THOSE AWARDED THE SIR PERCY SYKES MEMORIAL MEDAL

The summarised citations are as recorded in the Society's *Golden Book*.

1947 Monsieur Fakhri Dai Gilani
Persian Historian

1948 Professor K. A. Cresswell
Authority on Muslim architecture

1951 Miss (later Dame) Freya Stark
Traveller and Author

1954 Mr Tom Stobart
For his work in filming the conquest of Everest

1955 Mlle Ella Maillart
Traveller and Author

1956 Mr Douglas Carruthers
Naturalist, Explorer and Author

1958 Lieut General Sir Francis Tuker, KCIE, CB, DSO, OBE
Author, especially for his book 'Gorkha'

1960 Professor Ann Lambton, OBE, BA, PhD
Persian Historian

1962 Sir Reader Bullard, KCB, KCMG, CIE
Diplomat and Author

1963 Mr Hugh Richardson, CIE, OBE
For Services in India and Tibet and his 'History of Tibet'

1964 Dr Laurence Lockhart, LittD, PhD
Traveller, Scholar and Historian

1965 Professor C. von Furer-Haimendorf
Anthropologist, Traveller and Author

1966 Mr C. J. Edmonds, CMG, CBE
Diplomat and Author and for his work for the Kurdish people

1967 Lieut Colonel G. E. Wheeler, CIE, CBE
Director Central Asian Research Centre

1968 Miss Violet Conolly, OBE, DEconSc
For her work as a Russian specialist

1969 Mr S. C. Sutton, CBE
For his work as Director of the India Office Library

1970 Colonel C. H. Lewis, CMG, CBE
In recognition of his work on Transcaspia and adjacent regions

1971 Professor Guiseppe Tucci
For distinguished services to archaeology and study of Tibet and Buddhism

1972 Mr W. E. D. Allen, OBE, FSA
For his work on Caucasian and Turkish history

1973 Professor William Watson, MA, FBA, FSA
Keeper of the Percival David Foundation of Chinese Art. And for his contribution to the knowledge of East Asian Civilization

1974 Doctor Gunnar Jarring
For his contribution to the fields of learning and diplomacy and to the knowledge of Turkestan

1975 Sir Cyril Philips, MA Hon, DLitt, Hon, LLD, PhD
Director of the School of Oriental and African Studies. An academic who has furthered communications between Asian countries and this country

1977 Mr Basil Gray
Keeper of Oriental Antiquities at the British Museum

1980 Mr David Stronach, MA, FSA
In recognition of his services to archaeology

1983 Mr Tim Severin
In recognition of his work as author, traveller and historian

1985 Professor Mary Boyce
In recognition of her work in connection with Zoroastrianism

1987 Professor C. F. Beckingham
Emeritus Professor of Islamic Studies at the University of London. In recognition of his work in Islamic Studies

1988 The Lady Alexandra Metcalfe, CBE
In recognition of her work in Asia for the Save the Children Fund

1990 Sir Denis Wright, GCMG
In recognition of his knowledge of, and involvement in, Anglo-Persian relations and his advancement of understanding between the two countries over many years. And as an author

1992 Mr Albert Hourani
In recognition of his long and distinguished academic record and wide range of writings covering the history, culture and politics of the Arab and Islamic lands

1994 Professor Akbar S. Ahmed
In recognition of his notable contribution towards promoting knowledge and understanding of Asia and fostering cultural relations between Commonwealth and Asian countries

1999 Mr Peter Hopkirk
In recognition of his outstanding contribution to increasing man's knowledge of Central Asia through his extensive travels, scholarship and writings

2001 Sir Mark Tully, KBE
For increasing man's knowledge of the Indian sub-continent through his work as a journalist, broadcaster and writer, and for the empathy he has for the Indian people and the esteem in which he is held by them

ROLL OF THOSE AWARDED THE ROYAL SOCIETY FOR ASIAN AFFAIRS SPECIAL AWARD

1998 Mr Peter McMillan

For his ingenuity, resource and courage in re-enacting the original flight in 1919 from Britain to Australia by the Smith brothers in a replica Vickers Vimy FB 27A bomber

1999 Dr Ina Russell, OBE

For long and dedicated service to the Royal Society for Asian Affairs both as a Member of Council and as an Honorary Secretary

ANNEX OF OFFICE HOLDERS

Presidents of the Society

1918 The Most Hon. The Marquis Curzon of Kedleston, KG, GCSI, GCIE
1925 The Most Hon. The Earl Peel, GCSI, GBE
1930 Field Marshal Viscount Allenby, GCB, GCMG
1936 The Rt Hon. Lord Lloyd of Dolobran, GCSI, GCIE, DSO
1941 The Rt Hon. Lord Hailey, GCSI, GCMG, GCIE
1947 Field Marshal the Rt Hon. Lord Wavell, PC, GCB, GCIE, CMG, MC
1950 General Sir John Shea, GCB, KCMG, DSO
1955 The Rt Hon. The Earl of Scarbrough, KG, PC, GCSI, GCIE, GCVO, TD
1960 Marshal of The Royal Air Force Sir William Dickson, GCB, KBE, DSO, AFC
1966 The Rt Hon. The Earl of Selkirk, PC, GCMG, GBE, AFC
1977 The Lord Greenhill of Harrow, GCMG, OBE
1984 The Lord Denman, CBE, MC, TD

Chairman of Council

1901 General Sir Thomas Gordon, KCB, KCIE
1902 The Rt Hon. Sir Alfred Lyall, GCIE, KCB, ICS
1904 Colonel Sir Thomas Holdich, KCMG, KCIE
1906 General Sir Edwin Collen, GCIE, CB
1907 Mr (later Sir) Valentine Chirol
1908 The Rt Hon. The Earl of Ronaldshay, GCSI, GCIE
1914 The Rt Hon. Sir Mortimer Durand, GCMG, KCSI, KCIE
1917 Colonel Sir Henry Trotter, KCMG, CB
1919 The Rt Hon. Lord Carnock, GCB, GCMG, GCVO
1923 The Rt Hon. Sir Maurice de Bunsen, GCMG, GCVO
1924 The Rt Hon. Viscount Peel, GBE
1926 Sir Michael O'Dwyer, GCIE, KCSI
1927 Field Marshal Viscount Allenby, GCB, GCMG
1930 The Rt Hon. Lord Lloyd of Dolobran, PC, GCSI, GCIE, DSO
1934 The Rt Hon. Sir Horace Rumbold, Bt., GCB, GCMG, MVO
1937 Field Marshal Lord Chetwode, GCB, OM, GCSI, KCMG, DSO
1941 General Sir John Shea, GCB, KCMG, DSO

1947 Lieut General Sir Adrian Carton de Wiart, VC, KBE, CB, CMG, DSO
1950 Admiral Sir Howard Kelly, GBE, KCB, CMG, MVO
1952 Admiral Sir Cecil Harcourt, KCB, CBE
1957 Sir Hugh Dow, GCIE, KCSI
1959 Sir Philip Southwell, CBE, MC
1961 General Sir Richard Gale, GCB, KBE, DSO, MC
1964 Sir Gilbert Laithwaite, GCMG, KCB, GCIE, CSI
1967 Sir Esler Dening, GCMG, OBE
1971 Sir Norman Brain, KBE, CMG
1974 Sir Stanley Tomlinson, KCMG, LLD
1978 Sir Arthur de la Mare, KCMG, KCVO
1984 Sir Michael Wilford, GCMG
1994 Sir Donald Hawley, KCMG, MBE

Honorary Secretaries

1901 Major F. E. Younghusband, CIE
1902 Edward Penton, Jnr Esq. (from 1918, Sir Edward, KBE)
1919 Lieut Colonel A. C. Yate
1921 Lieut Colonel A. C. Yate
G. Stephenson, Esq.
1923 Lieut General Sir Raleigh Egerton, KCB, KCIE
G. Stephenson, Esq.
1926 Major General Sir William Beynon, KCIE, CB, DSO
G. Stephenson, Esq.
1927 Major General Sir William Beynon, KCIE, CB, DSO
H. C. Woods, Esq.
1928 Major General Sir William Beynon, KCIE, CB, DSO
Colonel H. Stevens
1931 Major General Sir William Beynon, KCIE, CB, DSO
Sir Harry Fox, KBE
1932 Brigadier General Sir Percy Sykes, KCIE, CB, CMG
E. M. Gull, Esq.
1933 Brigadier General Sir Percy Sykes, KCIE, CB, CMG
E. M. Gull, Esq.
Major E. Ainger
1939 Brigadier General Sir Percy Sykes, KCIE, CB, CMG
E. M. Gull, Esq.
1942 Brigadier General Sir Percy Sykes, KCIE, CB, CMG
Colonel S. F. Newcombe, DSO
1946 Colonel S. F. Newcombe, DSO
Lieut General H. G. Martin, CB, DSO
Sir John Pratt, KBE, CMG
1949 W. H. Ingrams, Esq., CMG, OBE
Lieut General H. G. Martin, CB, DSO
O. White, Esq., CMG

1952 W. H. Ingrams, Esq., CMG, OBE
Colonel H. W. Tobin, DSO, OBE
Group Captain H. St C. Smallwood, OBE
1956 Colonel H. W. Tobin, DSO, OBE
Group Captain H. St C. Smallwood, OBE
J. M. Cook, Esq.
1957 Group Captain H. St C. Smallwood, OBE
J. M. Cook, Esq.
Colonel G. M. Routh, CBE, DSO
1961 Group Captain H. St C. Smallwood, OBE
Colonel G. M. Routh, CBE, DSO
C. Rees Jenkins, Esq.
1962 Group Captain H. St C. Smallwood, OBE
C. Rees Jenkins, Esq.
1965 Group Captain H. St C. Smallwood, OBE
C. Rees Jenkins, Esq.
H. J. Evans, Esq., CMG, LLD.
1968 C. Rees Jenkins, Esq.
H. J. Evans, Esq., CMG, LLD
S. J. Fulton, Esq., CMG
1977 C. Rees Jenkins, Esq.
S. J. Fulton, Esq., CMG
D. J. Duncanson, Esq., OBE
1989 Lieut Colonel A. P. H. B. Fowle, MC
S. J. Fulton, Esq., CMG
D. J. Duncanson, Esq., OBE
1993 Lieut Colonel A. P. H. B. Fowle, MC
D. J. Duncanson, Esq., OBE
1994 Lieut Colonel A. P. H. B. Fowle, MC
D. J. Duncanson, Esq., OBE
Dr Ina Russell, OBE
1996 Lieut Colonel A. P. H. B. Fowle, MC
Dr Ina Russell, OBE
2001 Lieut Colonel A. P. H. B. Fowle, MC
Mrs Merilyn Hywel-Jones

Honorary Treasurers

1901 A. Cotterell Tupp, LLD, ICS Ret.
1914 Sir Evan James, KCIE
1919 Brigadier General A. C. Bailward
1920 Sir Edward Penton, KBE
1939 Major Edward Ainger
1975 P. C. Rees, Esq.
1982 J. F. N. Wedge, Esq.
1996 F. E. B. Witts, Esq.
1997 N. H. Green, Esq., OBE, FCIB

Honorary Librarians

1922 R. Michell, Esq.
1925 Mrs R. W. Frazer
1927 A. C. Wratislaw, Esq.
1928 Miss E. Sykes
1930 Lieut General Sir Raleigh Egerton, KCB, KCIE
1931 Colonel J. K. Tod, CMG
1945 Lieut Colonel F. M. Bailey, CIE
1960 F. de Halpert, Esq.
1967 J. Massey-Stewart, Esq.
1978 M. J. Pollock, Esq., MA, ALA

Editors of the *Journal*

1961 Mrs K. E. West (later Mrs K. E. Beckett)
1969 O. Stallybrass, Esq.
1970 A. Russell, Esq.
1972 P. Howard, Esq.
1975 Mrs P. Robertson
1982 E. Charlton, Esq., CBE
1982 Mrs K. E. Beckett (Stand-in until October 1984)
1984 R. A. Longmire, Esq.
1992 Mrs K. E. Beckett (Stand-in February–October)
1992 Dr V. C. Funnell
1995 J. G. T. Shipman, Esq.
1997 Ms S. Pares
2001 M. Sheringham, Esq.

Chairman of the Editorial Board

1961 Lieut Colonel G. E. Wheeler, CIE
1966 H. J. Evans, Esq., CMG, LLD
1968 E. H. Paxton, Esq.
1977 Dr D. J. Duncanson, OBE
1995 The Hon. Ivor Lucas, CMG

Secretaries

1901 Miss C. S. Hughes
1917 Miss L. B. Phillips
1921 Miss M. N. Kennedy
1944 Miss R. O. Wingate
1954 Mrs K. G. Putnam, MBE
1961 Miss M. K. Marsh
1966 Miss E. Kirby
1968 Miss M. FitzSimons, MBE

1995	Mrs H. C. McKeag
1997	D. J. Easton, Esq., MA, FRSA, FRGS
2001	N. J. M. Cameron, Esq.

Location of the Society's Offices in London

1901–1919	22 Albemarle Street	(Tenants of the Royal Asiatic Society)
1919–1929	74 Grosvenor Street	(Tenants of the Royal Asiatic Society)
1929–1938	77 Grosvenor Street	(Independent of the Royal Asiatic Society)
1938–1948	8 Clarges Street	
1948–1961	2 Hinde Street, Manchester Square	(Tenants of the Palestine Exploration Fund)
1961–1967	2nd Floor, 12 Orange Street, Haymarket	
1967–1985	42 Devonshire Street	
1985–	Canning House, 2 Belgrave Square	

NOTES

I GENESIS, BIRTH AND CONSOLIDATION 1901–1907

1 Jardine later presented the Society with the striking effigy of the Maharajah of Orchehaha which is displayed in the Society's offices.
2 Lynch, later a member of Parliament, was senior partner in the Lynch commercial empire which ran steam navigation services along the Tigris and Euphrates rivers and at Muhammarah (Khorramshahr) in the Persian Gulf.
3 *Tournament of Shadows*, Karle E. Meyer and Shareen Blair Brysac, Counterpoint, Washington, 1999, p. 295.
4 Titles include: *The Heart of a Continent*; *Wonders of the Himalaya*; *Everest the Challenge*; *The Reign of God*; and *Adventure of Faith*.
5 Titles include: *The Indian Civil Service and the Competitive System*; *Statistics of the North West Provinces of India*; *The International Monetary Conference in Paris and Bimetallism*; *Lectures and Papers on the Silver Question*; and *Early Proceedings of the Bimetallic League*.
6 The Society's interest in Egypt extended beyond Islam. In 1930 Professor K. A. Creswell was made an Honorary Member for his work on Muslim art and architecture in that country, later being awarded the Sir Percy Sykes Medal. And in 1948 Mrs R. Devonshire was elected an Honorary Member in recognition of her work on the antiquities of Egypt.
7 *Sir Alfred Lyall and the Understanding with Russia*, Sir H. Mortimer Durand, *Journal*, 1914, p. 20.
8 Oriental and India Office Collection, British Library (F/197/241).
9 Concluding remarks by Colonel Sir Thomas Holdich in *Life in Russian Turkestan and Germany's Menace to India*, Annette Meakin, *Journal*, 1919, p. 3.

II THE YEARS OF STRUGGLE 1908–1919

1 *Chinese Affairs*, Eugene Ch'en, *Proceedings of the Central Asian Society*, 1913.
2 *China*, J. O. P. Bland, *Journal*, 1919, p. 38.
3 The Society was represented by Sir Percy Sykes, Honorary Secretary, at the unveiling of a memorial tablet to Sir Mortimer Durand on 26 August 1937 at Penmayne House, Rock, Cornwall, where Sir Mortimer lived from 1915 until his death in 1924. Sykes was also Mortimer's biographer.
4 *Military Mission to N.W. Persia, 1918*, General Dunsterville, *Journal*, 1921, p. 79 and *Adventures of Dunsterforce*, London, 1920.
5 *The British Military Mission to Turkistan*, General Malleson, *Journal*, 1922, p. 96. Other members of the Society who served in this mission not mentioned here included Lieut Colonel E. A. F. Redl, Colonel C. B. Stokes and Colonel J. K. Tod. A proposed lecture to the Society by Stokes was vetoed by the Foreign Office.
6 *Caspian Naval Expedition, 1918–1919*, Captain David Norris, *Journal*, 1923, p. 216.
7 *In Russian Turkistan under the Bolsheviks*, Major F. M. Bailey, *Journal*, 1921, p. 49, and *Mission to Tashkent*, London, 1946. A more detailed account of Bailey's adventures is given in Chapter VI.
8 *Military Operations in Transcaspia*, Lieut Colonel D. E. Knollys, *Journal*, 1926, p. 89.

VI THE MEMBERSHIP

1 Both Mr Paul Ensor and Sir Roderick Sarell died in August 2001.
2 *Trespassers on the Roof of the World*, Peter Hopkirk, John Murray, 1982. *Setting the East Ablaze*, Peter Hopkirk, John Murray, 1982. *The Great Game*, Peter Hopkirk, John Murray, 1990. *On Secret Service East of Constantinople*, Peter Hopkirk, John Murray, 1994.
3 *Wars and Travels in Turkestan 1918–1920, Journal*, 1922, p. 4.
4 *The Spy who Disappeared: Diary of a Secret Mission to Russian Central Asia*, Reginald Teague-Jones alias Ronald Sinclair, Introduction and Epilogue by Peter Hopkirk, Gollancz, 1990. Teague-Jones's diary was discovered after his death in 1988 and was not intended for publication.
5 Re-published in 2001 by the Antique Collectors Club Ltd with fresh material by Kenneth Cox, Kenneth Storm Jnr and Ian Baker.
6 *My Hill So Strong*, Jean Kingdon Ward, Cape, 1952.
7 *The Chinese as a Dominant Race*, Owen Lattimore, *Journal*, 1928, p. 278.
8 *The Nomadic Tribes of Persia Today*, Dr Oliver Garrod, MBE, MB, *Journal*, 1946, p. 32.
9 *Proceedings of the Central Asian Society*, 1913, p. 3.
10 *The Douneside Story*, Ian Mitchell, The MacRobert Trusts, 1979.
11 *The Way of the Pathans*, London, 1962; *The Pathan Borderland*, The Hague, 1963 and *Pathans of the Latter Day*, 1996.

VII THE JUNIOR MEMBERSHIP

1 *Journal*, 1937, p. 300.
2 *Journal*, 1938, p. 260.
3 *Central Asian Youth Grows Up*, Lieut Colonel G. Fox Holmes, *Journal*, 1961, p. 221.
4 *Journal*, 1958, p. 115.
5 *An Arabian Trilogy*, Captain Hugh Leach, Captain Guy Hoad and Mr James Nash, 7 January 1970.
6 *From the Himalayas to the Hindu Raj*, Hugh Leach, *Journal*, 1993, p. 145.
7 *Racing Kelly across the Roof of the World*, Hugh Leach, *Journal*, 1996, p. 45. Six officers of Kelly's small force, including Kelly himself, became members of the Society.
8 *Mountains, Mules and Monks*, Adrian Steger, *Journal*, 1997, p. 3.
9 *Culford School Hindu Kush Expedition 1996*, J. W. Beatty, AFP Annual Report, 1996.
10 Mrs Isobel Shaw and Miss Susan Farrington, September 2000.
11 *To the Edge of Wakhan and Back, The Royal Russell School Expedition across the Hindu Kush. 1997*, Hugh Leach, AFP Annual Report, 1998 and *The Russellian*, 1997–1998.
12 Full details of the titles and speakers are given in notes on Junior Members' Meetings. *Journal*, 1997, p. 430. *Journal*, 1998, p. 366. *Journal*, 1999, p. 365. *Journal*, 2000, p. 374. *Journal*, 2001, p. 370.
13 *Kashmir: The Past Ten Years*, Alexander Evans, *Journal*, 1999, p. 21. *Prester John in Central Asia*, Johnny Wyld, *Journal*, 2000, p. 3. *Four Girls – 4,000 miles: By Horse and Camel Along the Silk Road*, Lucy Kelaart (Alexandra Tolstoy-Miloslavsky, Sophia Cunningham and Victoria Westmacott), *Journal*, 2001, p. 30.

VIII THE JOURNAL

1 Typical of such magazines were *The English Review, The Nineteenth Century, The Fortnightly Review, The Contemporary Review, Blackwoods, Blue Peter, Revue des Deux Mondes* and *Round Table*.
2 *Pan-Islamism*, Valentine Chirol, *Proceedings of the Central Asian Society*, 1906. *Storm Waves in the Mohamadan World*, Sir Valentine Chirol, *Journal*, 1922, p. 193.
3 *Pan-Islamism*, D. S. Margoliouth, *Proceedings of the Central Asian Society*, 1912. *Ideas and Ideals of Modern Islam*, D. S. Margoliouth, *Journal*, 1930, p. 55.
4 *Ferment in the World of Islam*, Sirdar Ikbal Ali Shah, *Journal*, 1927, p. 130. *The Changing Face of Islam*, Sirdar Ikbal Ali Shah, *Journal*, 1929, p. 181.
5 *Social Reactions in the Muslim World*, H. A. R. Gibb, *Journal*, 1934, p. 541.

6 *The Muslim in the Modern World*, Marmaduke Pickthall, *Journal*, 1936, p. 221.
7 *Pilgrimage to Mecca*, Lord Healey, *Journal*, 1924, p. 20.
8 *Observing Islam from Within and Without*, Hugh Leach, *Journal*, 1990, p. 3.
9 *Journal*, 1936, p. 369.
10 *Journal*, 1961, p. 6.
11 *Journal*, 1952, p. 95.
12 *Journal*, 1951, p. 215.

IX THE LIBRARY

1 Included were further books from Sir Percy Sykes; five from Lieut Colonel A. C. Yate, signed by their authors; Miss Gertrude Bell gave a copy of her own work *From Amurath to Amurath* and Sir Thomas Arnold of his on *The Caliphate*. Lord Curzon gave a collection including a copy of his own *Tales of Travel*.
2 Amongst these were: *Voyage D'Orenbourg à Boukhara*, Meyendorff, 1826; *Travels in Koordistan and Mesopotamia*, 2 vols, Fraser, 1840; *Residence among the Nestorians*, Perkins, 1843; *Les Hommes Illustrés de l'Orient*, 2 vols, Mazas, 1847; *Histoire des Koordes*, 2 vols, Zeinoft, 1860; *High Tartary, Yarkand and Kashgar*, Shah, 1871; *Report on a Mission to Yarkand*, 2 vols, Forsyth, 1873; *From Kulja to Tien Shan and Lop Nor*, Prejevalsky, 1879, and *Col. Grodekoff's Ride from Samarcand to Herat*, Marvin, 1880. Also destroyed was the only extant set of the Society's bound journals and its five-volume *Encyclopaedia of Islam*.
3 Amongst those who replaced books destroyed by enemy action were Sir Percy Sykes, who provided another set of the *Encyclopaedia of Islam*; Major General Sir William Beynon, who donated a set of *Journals* and books on India; Miss Gertrude Patterson, including a rare 1836 book on Syria; Mr H. E. Goad and Mr W. B. Lane. As recently as 1999 Mrs Mary Mackay replaced the rare volume by Prejevalsky. And subsequent to the destruction the library has put together two complete bound sets of *Journals*.
4 Other gifts during this period included a collection of Turkish books and parts of the *Turkish Encyclopaedia* from Mr Iain Gordon Campbell; books from the library of Sir Louis Dane presented by his daughter and books on China from the estate of Sir Eric Teichman.

X THE ARCHIVES

1 OIOC MSS.Eur.F.157-319, British Library: Bailey's typescript autobiography, p. 18.
2 See Bailey's *Mission to Tashkent*, Jonathan Cape, 1946.
3 *Tibet and the British Raj*, Alex McKay, Curzon, 1997, p. xxiii.
4 Elder brother of Sir Maurice Bowra, the renowned classical scholar and Warden of Wadham College, Oxford.
5 See Charles Drage's *Servant of the Dragon Throne: Being the Lives of Edward and Cecil Bowra*, Peter Dawnay, 1966.
6 Based on article, *Seen in Kashgaria*, John Shipman, *Journal*, 1998, pp. 54–59.
7 *La Vallée des Rubis*, Librairie Gallimard, 1955; English translation, *Mogok: The Valley of Rubies*, MacGibbon & Kee, 1960.
8 The late Lord Greenhill of Harrow was President of the Society 1977–1984.
9 *Pathan Borderland* (1910), was followed by *Realm of the Gods* (1915), *A Burmese Enchantment* (1916), *A Burmese Loneliness* (1918), *A Burmese Wonderland* (1922), and *A Burmese Arcady* (1923). His subsequent work included books on Ceylon (1927) and Malaya (1937).
10 I am indebted to Mr St John Armitage for contributing this note on the Lawrence sketch map.
11 Quoting letter from Carruthers to Professor A. W. Lawrence, 1935.
12 Lawrence's master copy – for several years in Hogarth's safe keeping – was sold by the Lawrence family to a private American collector in the 1970s and deposited in the Huntington Library, California. It was auctioned at Christies, New York, on 22 May 2001 for US Dollars 850,000.
13 See pp. 123–127 of *The Gilgit Game*, John Keay, John Murray, 1982.
14 Lady (Charlotte) MacGregor, who joined the Society in 1920, was his second wife; his first (Frances), who died in 1873, was the favourite sister of Sir Mortimer Durand, a future Chairman of the Society.

15 Major General Sir Charles MacGregor KCB, CSI, CIE, founded the United Service Institution of India (USI) in 1870. In 1888 it struck the MacGregor Memorial Medal in his memory. (See also Footnote 2 to Chapter XIV.)
16 *Peaks and Plains of Central Asia* (1933), *Between the Oxus and Indus* (1935), *Unknown Karakoram* (1936), and *Kafirs and Glaciers* (1938).
17 Schomberg declined an invitation to extend his visit, commenting 'guests are like fish, they stink after three days'!
18 Stein was greatly touched by Schomberg's tribute to him on the occasion of his eightieth birthday, published in the *Journal*, 1942, pp. 176–177.
19 The archive also includes five letters from Stein, written between 1930 and 1939 to Miss M. N. Kennedy, then Secretary of the Society. Oddly, there is no mention of Schomberg, nor of Stein's long-standing links with the Society, in either Jeanette Mirsky's biography of Stein (1977), or in Annabel Walker's (1995).
20 See also Dr Omar Shakespear Pound's detailed commentary on the Shakespear Papers in the *Journal*, Feb. 1991, pp. 121–124. Dr Pound's understanding that the collection was given to the Society by the Palestine Exploration Fund (PEF) cannot be corroborated, and probably arose from the fact that from 1947 to 1961 the Society shared premises with the PEF in Hinde Street, where the collection was held at that time. John Shakespear, and his cousin Colonel L. W. Shakespear (1860–1933) both joined the Society in 1920.
21 In her *Fifty Years with John Company*, John Murray, 1936, Ursula Low quotes extensively from Richmond Shakespear's letters written while he was in Afghanistan in 1839 and 1842, and in Khiva and Russia in 1840. Her family were related to the Shakespears, and in the foreword to her book she warmly acknowledges John Shakespear's help. There is a memorial tablet dedicated to Colonel Sir Richmond Campbell Shakespear, KCB, with a moving inscription, in St Anne's Church, Indore.
22 For a brief account of John Shakespear's exploits, see *Lushai Chrysalis*, Major A. G. McCall, Luzac & Co., 1949, pp. 54–64. Shakespear's own book, *The Lushei Kuki Clans*, Macmillan, 1912, reflects his intimate knowledge of, and affection for, the hill people of the Assam borderlands. His cousin L. W. Shakespear also served in, and wrote about, Assam.
23 Douglas Carruthers wrote an account of this remarkable but unpublished journey in the *Geographical Journal*, May 1922. The typescript bears a few pencilled annotations in his hand, which suggests that the document probably reached the Society through him.
24 I am indebted to Dr Jim Hoare, British Charge d'Affaires in Pyongyang, for identifying locations and landmarks, for distinguishing ethnic Koreans from Japanese, and for providing the historical background.
25 A. C. Tupp's signature is dated 1908. He delivered a lecture to the Society on *French Indo-China* in May 1906. The book may have been presented either before or after his death in 1914.

XI THE DINNER CLUB

1 Lady Evelyn Cobbold was the daughter of the 7th Earl of Dunmore, an original member of the Society. She converted to Islam in 1915, performing the pilgrimage in 1933, believed to have been the first English woman to have done so. She was helped in the Hejaz by another British Muslim member, Mr H. St J. B. Philby – 'Hajji Abdullah'. She published a book in 1933, the same year as her Dinner Club talk, *Pilgrimage to Mecca* (John Murray) which had a Foreword by another Muslim member, Sheikh Hafiz Wahba, the Saudi Arabian Minister in London. She sent a copy to the Society's Secretary, Miss Kennedy, inscribed 'In grateful recognition of all the help given'.

XII A ROLE IN EDUCATION

1 *Short History of SOAS* (SOAS Publication) and *School of Oriental and African Studies, University of London 1917–1967. An Introduction*, C. H. Philips.
2 *The Royal Asiatic Society. Its History and Treasures*, ed. Stuart Simmonds and Simon Digby, E. J. Brill, Leiden, 1979.
3 *The Future of Asian Studies in the United Kingdom*, M. E. Yapp, D. Duncanson, C. F. Beckingham and others, *Journal*, 1981, p. 173.

4 *The Middle East Centre for Arab Studies*, A. J. Wilton, *Journal*, 1965, p. 260.
5 *Shemlan. A History of the Middle East Centre for Arab Studies*, Sir James Craig, St Antony's/ Macmillan, 1998.
6 *The British Council: The First Fifty Years*, Frances Donaldson, Cape, 1984.
7 The Hon. Ivor Lucas, CMG.

XIII THE TOURS

1 Two of them, Robin Poulton and his wife, subsequently wrote their doctoral theses on the anthropology of Tajik villages in Northern Afghanistan. In October 2001 Dr Robin Poulton wrote a Review Article for the *Journal* entitled *The Kalashnikov in Afghnistan, Tajikistan and the other 'Stans'*, *Journal*, 2001, p. 295.
2 These two giant images of the Buddha were destroyed by the Taliban regime in Afghanistan in the spring of 2001.
3 Edward and Sarah Stallybrass, Robert Yuille and William Swann. The Society's member Professor Charles Bawden tells the story of this remarkable mission in *Shamans, Lamas and Evangelicals. The English Missionaries in Siberia*, Routledge & Kegan Paul, London, 1985.
4 *Younghusband: The Last Great Imperial Adventurer*, Patrick French, London, 1994.

XIV THE LAWRENCE OF ARABIA MEMORIAL MEDAL

1 *Philby of Arabia*, Elizabeth Monroe, Faber, 1973, p. 210.
2 The MacGregor Memorial Medal was instituted in 1888 by the United Service Institute of India (USI) for 'the best military reconnaissance of the year carried out by any officer or other rank belonging to the Indian Defence Establishment'. Several officers who became members of the Society were recipients. They included (ranks and decorations at the time of the award): Colonel M. S. Bell, VC, 1889; Captain Francis Younghusband, CIE, 1890; Captain A. W. S. Wingate, 1900; Major P. M. Sykes, 1910; Lieutenant A. T. Wilson, 1912; Captain F. M. Bailey, 1914; Captain E. W. C. Noel, CIE, DSO, 1918; Captain L. V. S. Blacker, 1920 and Colonel A. S. Lancaster, CIE, OBE, 1946, the only person to be awarded it twice, the first time in 1938. Major General Orde Wingate, DSO, was also a holder. (See Footnote 15, Chapter X.)

XV THE SIR PERCY SYKES MEMORIAL MEDAL AND OTHER SOCIETY AWARDS

1 I am grateful to Sir Denis Wright for sending me a copy of his paper *Sir Percy Sykes and Persia* published in *Central Asian Survey*, 1993, and to Colonel W. G. Neilson, Sir Percy's nephew, for the loan of a copy of Lady Sykes's personal memoirs, on both of which I drew for the short history of Sir Percy's life. I benefited also from conversations with the late Mrs Deborah Sykes, widow of Charles, Sir Percy's second son.

INDEX

Note: Titles, rank and decorations are given as at close of careers. Page numbers followed by 'P' refer to plates; 'n' indicates notes.

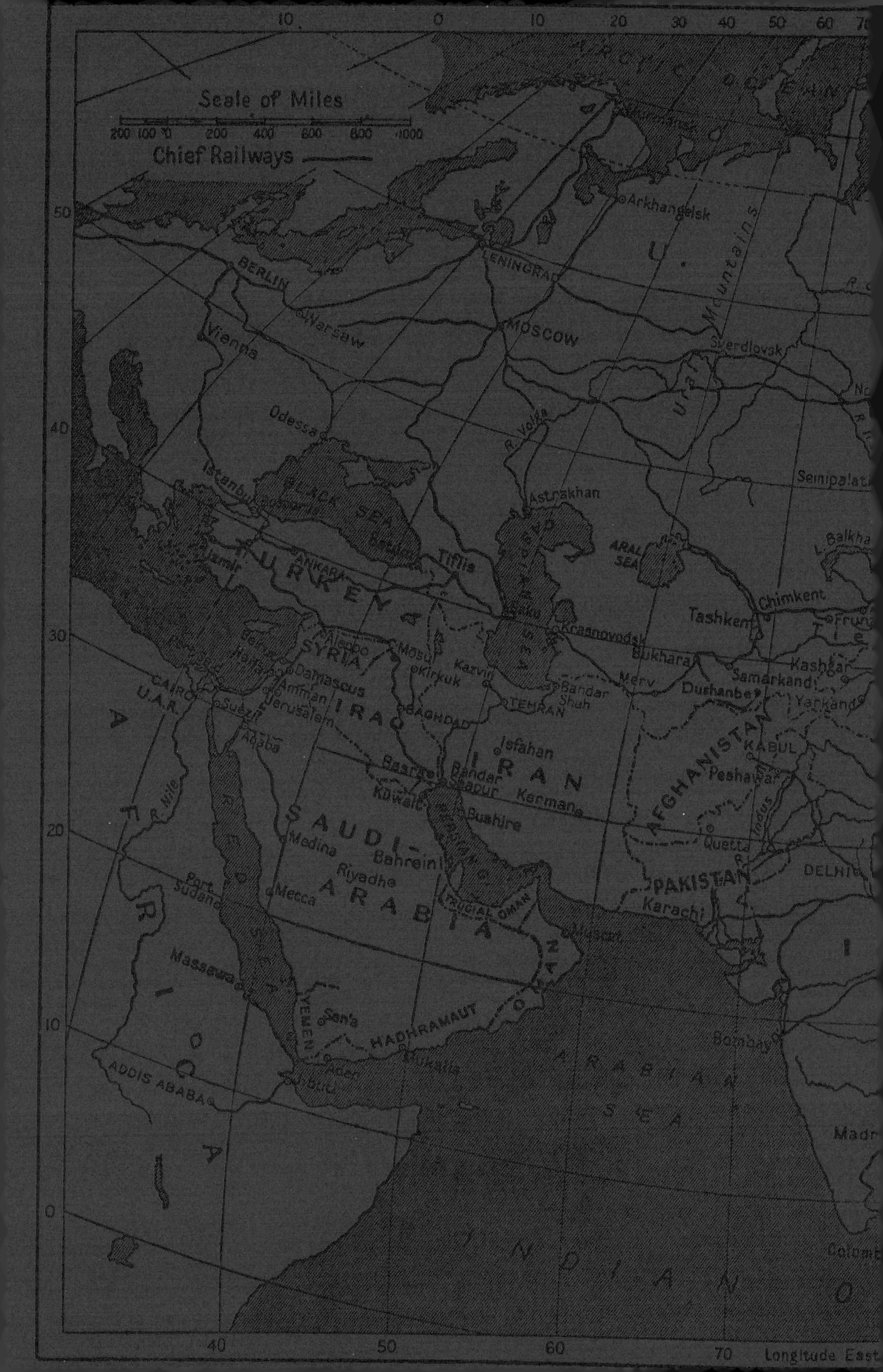
Scale of Miles
200 100 0 200 400 600 800 1000
Chief Railways
Arkhangelsk
LENINGRAD
BERLIN
Warsaw
MOSCOW
Vienna
Sverdlovsk
Ural Mountains
R. Volga
Odessa
Astrakhan
Istanbul
BLACK SEA
ANKARA
Tiflis
Izmir
TURKEY
ARAL SEA
Tashkent
Chimkent
Baku
Krasnovodsk
Aleppo
SYRIA
Mosul
Beirut
Haifa
Damascus
Kirkuk
Kazvin
Bukhara
Samarkand
Kashgar
CAIRO
U.A.R.
Suez
Amman
Jerusalem
IRAQ
BAGHDAD
TEHRAN
Bandar Shah
Merv
Dushanbe
Yarkand
Aqaba
Isfahan
IRAN
AFGHANISTAN
KABUL
Peshawar
Basra
Bandar Shapur
Kerman
Kuwait
SAUDI-ARABIA
Bushire
Medina
Bahrein
Riyadh
Mecca
Port Sudan
R. Nile
Quetta
PAKISTAN
DELHI
Karachi
TRUCIAL OMAN
Muscat
Massawa
YEMEN
San'a
HADHRAMAUT
Aden
ADDIS ABABA
AFRICA
ARABIAN SEA
Bombay
Longitude East